To: Sandy and Jay

from Gra...   ...des

Chris...

Reader's Digest

Secrets of the Seas

Marvels and Mysteries of Oceans and Islands

Reader's Digest

Secrets of the Seas

Marvels and Mysteries of Oceans and Islands

The Reader's Digest Association

Pleasantville, New York   Montreal, Canada   Sydney, Australia

INTERNATIONAL BOOK YEAR

Secrets of the Seas

Major Contributors

Part one
William J. Cromie

Part two
William H. Amos

Consultants

Part one: The Living Sea

Peter David, *National Institute of Oceanography of Great Britain*
Raymond de Lucia, *American Museum of Natural History*
Joel W. Hedgpeth, *Marine Science Center (Oregon)*
N. B. Marshall, *British Museum (Natural History)*
Olin Sewall Pettingill, Jr., *Cornell University*
C. Lavett Smith, *American Museum of Natural History*

Part two: Wonders of Island Life

Agatin T. Abbott, *University of Hawaii*
Stanley and Kay Breeden, *naturalists/authors (Australia)*
F. Raymond Fosberg, *Smithsonian Institution*
Thomas Gladwin, *University of Hawaii*
Richard Gould, *American Museum of Natural History*
Olin Sewall Pettingill, Jr., *Cornell University*
Garrett Smathers, *National Park Service; University of Washington*
Hobart Van Deusen, *American Museum of Natural History*

Science Editor: Durward L. Allen *Purdue University*

Contents

Part Two: WONDERS OF ISLAND LIFE

Part one

The Living Sea

The sea is the unique asset of our small world. As far as we know, ours is the only planet in the solar system with water on its surface. Although the sea covers seventy per cent of the earth, oceanographers have yet to chart most of its deepest chasms, and biologists are just beginning to understand the incredibly varied ways of its innumerable inhabitants. The sea is man's last frontier on Earth, the last great natural challenge to his ingenuity, courage, and insatiable curiosity

Life Along the Shore

Wherever land and sea meet—along rocky shores, sandy beaches, tidal marshes, mangrove thickets, and river estuaries—an astonishing variety of plants and animals thrives in a turbulent world swept by the tides

The sea has always held man in its spell. Fascinated by its vastness, power, and mystery, he inevitably turns to it in his reveries and meditations. Even when confined to the interior of a continent, hundreds of miles from the shore, he is drawn to the rivers and streams that lead, by whatever tortuous routes, to the sea.

Nearly three-quarters of the Earth is covered by the sea. Without the water that evaporates from it and falls as rain, there would be no life on land. Life arose in the sea, and the blood flowing through man's veins is, in a sense, little more than modified seawater. Perhaps this is why he has always looked to the sea for the key to his innermost self, for that intangible something Herman Melville once called "the ungraspable phantom of life."

Most people are content to experience the sea at its edge, where land and water meet in eternal conflict and compromise. Waves can smash with awesome force as frequently as ten times each minute against a rocky shore or break and tumble on a sandy beach in the incessant back-and-forth struggle that is common on exposed coasts.

The seashore is a narrow world—the widest beaches are seldom more than a few hundred feet across—but it extends for more than a million miles around all the Earth's islands and continents. The tide, with its slow, steady rhythm, marks the upper and lower boundaries of the in-between world of the seashore.

There is no typical seashore; each is unique, with its own community of plants and animals. Signs of life on the beach may be nearly invisible at first. Only the beach wrack—broken shells, tattered bits of seaweed, and occasional pieces of driftwood—and a few gulls skimming over the waves are obvious. But living things are everywhere—cemented to rocks, wedged in crevices, buried in sand and mud, nestled in the shelter of tide pools.

The plants and animals of the tidal zone live in one of the sea's harshest environments. Unlike inhabitants of the stable world of deep water, shore dwellers endure constant change. The waves pound and pull them incessantly. The daily comings and goings of the tide submerge them in water, then expose them to air. The passing seasons may bring periods of intense heat and bitter winter cold.

Yet all the basic requirements of life—light, water, oxygen, and minerals—are here in abundance. An astonishing variety of living things populates this world of ebb and flow.

Amid crashing surf, starfish cling to a rock on the coast of Washington's Olympic peninsula. Hundreds of tube feet acting as suction cups firmly anchor these starfish on rocks or prey. Possessing remarkable regenerative powers, a starfish can grow new arms to replace lost ones.

11

Breakers explode against the rugged headlands of California's Big Sur coast. Only the most tenacious plants and animals can survive on such exposed shorelines, where waves can slam into rocks with a force of several tons per square foot.

Ebb and Flow

As the apparent positions of the moon and sun change in the sky, their gravitational pulls create the shifting patterns of the tide. The moon, being much closer to Earth than the sun, exerts the stronger pull and produces two bulges in the seas at opposite sides of the globe. Because the Earth rotates, most coasts are "hit" by both of these bulges in a twenty-four hour period and so have two high tides daily.

The sun produces smaller bulges, which are usually masked by those of the moon. About twice a month, at full moon and new moon, the Earth, moon, and sun are in a straight line, and the gravitational tug of the sun is added to that of the moon. At such times, flood tides rise highest on the shore and ebb tides fall lowest. These are *spring tides*—referring not to the season of the year but to the "springing up" of the water. Also about twice monthly, the three bodies form a right angle, and the influence of the sun partially cancels out that of the moon. This is the time of *neap tides*, when the vertical distance between high and low tidemarks is smallest.

Geographic factors, such as the contours of shorelines and the depth of coastal waters, play a large part in determining tidal range. In the Gulf of Mexico and the Mediterranean Sea, and through much of the western Pacific, the difference between high and low tide seldom exceeds two feet. In the Bay of Fundy, between New Brunswick and Nova Scotia, spring flood tides may rise fifty feet above the low tidemark.

At the edge of the sea, the pulse of life beats to tidal rhythm. Shore creatures require a watery environment even when the tide is at its ebb. Some simply move out with the retreating waters, or take refuge in tidepools scattered among the rocks. Others that move slowly or not at all have developed ways of retaining moisture during the drought of the ebb tide. Mussels nearly shut their shells, keeping their own private bit of ocean inside. Limpets—snails with flattened, conical shells—form a watertight seal by clinging firmly to rocks. Sea anemones withdraw graceful crowns of feeding tentacles into soft, cylindrical bodies and secrete a gummy coating of mucus.

When the water rises again, the tempo of life quickens in the intertidal world. Mussels open their shells and filter water through their bodies, removing anything edible in the process. Limpets leave home bases to graze on miniature meadows of algae coating the rock surfaces. Anemones spread sting-laden tentacles to capture small animals drifting in the water.

Assault of the Waves

Just as living things have modified their behavior and anatomy to cope with alternate exposure and submergence by tides, so they have evolved defenses against waves. Under normal wind conditions, four or five waves crash on a shore every minute. Between waves, the backwash exerts a drag toward the sea.

Seaweeds hold their own against this pounding and pulling by gripping rocks with rootlike hold-

How Rocky Shore Organisms Survive in the Surf

On an exposed rocky shore, a plant or animal must resist being swept away from its home by the pull of the surf. Each of these six organisms, found in the intertidal zone of the rugged California coast, is equipped to hang on amidst the tons of swirling water that wash back and forth over it several times a minute, day in and day out.

Six-inch sea palms, like all algae, lack true roots but are anchored in place by many-branched holdfasts.

A starfish clings to firm surfaces with hundreds of hydraulically operated, elastic tube feet on its arms.

A sea urchin may shelter in a rock cavity hollowed out by the teeth and spines of generations of urchins.

Acorn barnacles secrete a powerful cement to permanently attach their six-sided limy shells to hard surfaces.

A mussel ropes itself to rocks with a tangle of tough byssal threads secreted by an organ near the foot.

The giant owl limpet, like a living suction cup, clamps its four-inch shell to the rock with a powerful foot.

fasts. Instead of resisting the waves, their flexible stipes (stems) and fronds (leaves) stream in and out with the rushing water. Mussels are anchored to rocks with tough threads, and oysters are cemented in place. Snails, abalones, limpets, and other mollusks hold on by the suction-cup action of a muscular foot. Starfishes cling to hard surfaces with hundreds of tube feet tipped with suction cups. Sea urchins wedge themselves into crevices with strong, needlelike spines. Sand dollars and razor clams burrow in sandy beaches.

Acorn barnacles confront the onslaught of the waves, sometimes withstanding forces that measure many tons per square foot. Their secret lies in the extraordinarily strong glue that cements them to rock surfaces, and in their sturdy, conical shells, which divert the flow of oncoming water.

An acorn barnacle, cemented securely to a rock, does not look much like its close relatives, crabs and shrimps. The family resemblance is more pronounced when the barnacle emerges from its egg capsule as a tiny, free-swimming larva. After several weeks of growth and metamorphosis into a clamlike bivalve stage, the young barnacle settles onto a solid surface, attaches itself with cement secreted by glands in its head, and develops the limy, six-plated shell of an adult.

When the tide recedes, a barnacle closes its shell and seals in enough water to survive. When the tide advances again, the barnacle opens its shell and rhythmically kicks its long, feathery legs, trapping food particles on fine bristles. Each time it pulls its legs back in, comblike mouth parts scrape off the food.

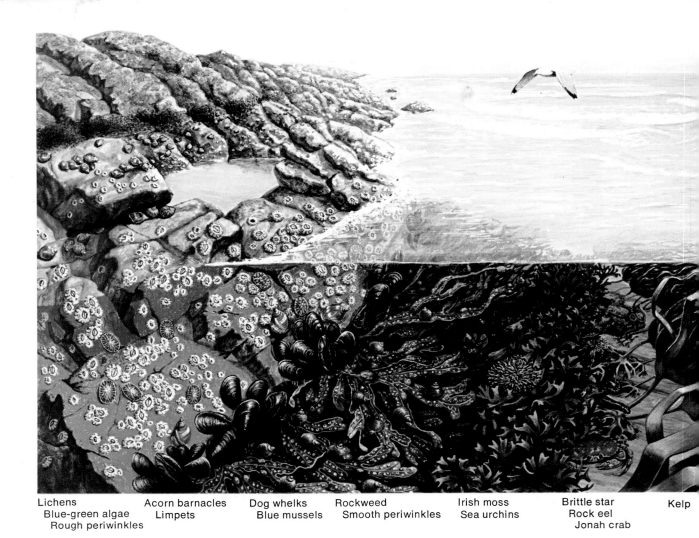

Lichens   Acorn barnacles   Dog whelks   Rockweed   Irish moss   Brittle star   Kelp
  Blue-green algae   Limpets   Blue mussels   Smooth periwinkles   Sea urchins   Rock eel
  Rough periwinkles   Jonah crab

Boundary Lines on a Rocky Shore

Acorn barnacles flourish on rocky shores exposed to the full force of waves. Their limy shells may be packed together so tightly that they form a white band midway between the low and high tidemarks. Here, rushing water washes in ample food and scours off debris that could interfere with the attachment of larvae.

Not all animals and plants of the shore could survive where barnacles live. Each species can tolerate only so much exposure to waves and air, and tends to gather where its particular requirements are met. Zonation of life occurs in many habitats, but nowhere is it more apparent than on rocky coasts. Unlike sand and mud, rocks provide a stable, unshifting surface with few hiding places. As the tide ebbs, the different bands of life are gradually exposed to view, one by one.

With minor variations, the sequence of zones on temperate rocky coasts is much the same the world over. There is an upper zone dampened only by the highest tides and the splash of the surf; a middle zone where the tide ebbs and flows continuously; and a lower zone where there is little exposure to air.

The upper zone is usually blotched with gray or yellow lichens. Just below the lichens is a dark band of blue-green algae. Probably the most ancient plants on Earth, blue-green algae have rimmed the edge of the sea for three billion years or more.

In this upper zone also grows sea hair, a green alga with slender, hollow fronds. Most seaweeds dry out and die after a few hours of exposure to the sun, but sea hair can survive on splash from the waves. In winter it grows lower on the intertidal rocks than during the rest of the year. The individual plants do not actually migrate toward the water, but their waterborne reproductive cells develop only where the sea provides a warming blanket. Most of the parent plants, higher up, die from exposure to cold air.

Zones of Life on a North Atlantic Rocky Shore

Life on a North Atlantic rocky shore lies in definite zones, for many permanent residents differ in their tolerance to exposure. The less time a zone is under water, the sparser its population. The uppermost zone, wet only by splashing surf and very high tides, is nearly barren. Dominant plants are algae and lichens; animals, periwinkle snails and rock lice.

The middle zone is characterized by barnacles and various rockweeds. Most midzone dwellers need periodic immersion to breathe, feed, and replenish moisture, but can stand hours of exposure to air and sun. When the tide ebbs, some animals take refuge in rock pools, which can be death traps as oxygen levels sink and salinity rises.

Life in the lower zone, exposed only at the lowest tides, resembles that of offshore waters. Kelp and Irish moss blanket the rock, providing hiding places or hunting grounds for animal inhabitants. Fish move in and out with the tides.

Lumpfish	Herring gull	Blackfish	Blood star
Northern starfish	Sea peaches	Sea cucumber	Sea anemone
Red beard sponge		Bread crumb sponge	

At the bottom of the upper zone, rough periwinkles browse on the slippery algal coating or hide in crevices. These tiny snails are gradually making the transition from sea to land. Instead of taking oxygen from the water and casting their eggs and sperm into the sea as most marine animals do, rough periwinkles breathe air through lunglike gills and hatch their young within the protection of their shells.

Rock lice are other upper-zone creatures on their way to becoming land animals. These inch-long scavengers breathe air and will drown if held underwater. No longer dependent upon the sea for reproduction, rock louse females protect their young from drying out by carrying them in abdominal pouches.

As the tide ebbs, it reveals the zone between high and low water, where organisms are alternately covered and uncovered by the vacillating waters. On a shore with moderately heavy surf, the most conspicuous feature of the middle zone is a white ribbon of acorn barnacles. In some places, more than 3000 may be crammed into a square foot. Among the barnacles, and also living below them, are mussels. Both are prey of voracious dog whelks. These brightly colored snails force open barnacle and mussel shells with a powerful foot. Or they use their radula, a tongue-like organ equipped with horny teeth, to drill holes through the shell and rasp out the soft parts inside. Cannibals, they eat their own eggs as well as the eggs of other snails. And even while still inside egg capsules, some young devour their siblings.

Scattered among barnacles and mussels of the middle zone are cone-shaped limpets. Each limpet scrapes out a shallow, circular depression that conforms exactly to the shape of its shell. When covered by the tide, it creeps as far as three feet away and scrapes algae off rocks with its radula. When the tide begins to ebb, the little snail finds its way back to its own rock scar—no mean feat considering that it lacks eyes, ears, and a nose.

Once or twice daily, seashore animals are alternately exposed and submerged by the tides

The characteristic plants of the middle zone are brown rockweeds with branching, ribbonlike fronds. On exposed shores, stunted rockweeds less than a foot long grow just below the white band of barnacles. But in sheltered bays and inlets, rockweeds six feet long may completely cover the intertidal rocks. Atlantic coast varieties bear small, gas-filled bladders that buoy up the plants when they are submerged.

As the tide goes out, these rubbery seaweeds collapse into a sodden, jumbled mat—an ideal place for marine animals to escape the drying wind and sun. Smooth periwinkles with olive-green, yellow, or orange shells hide among the rockweeds. Unlike rough periwinkles of the upper zone, these smooth periwinkles cannot breathe oxygen directly from the air and must stay wet when the tide ebbs. Entirely dependent on the rockweeds, these snails eat tissue scraped from the plants and lay their eggs on the fronds.

The lowest zone of a rocky coast is uncovered only by the ebbing spring tides. Here, where exposure to air is minimal, there is a marked increase in the number and variety of living things. Rockweeds give way to low cushiony bands of reddish Irish moss, dripping ribbons of dulse, and dense tangles of large, straplike kelp. Frequently Irish moss grows on heavy, bulging horse mussels, and brittle stars and young starfishes find shelter among the clustered shells.

In some areas there is hardly a stem of Irish moss that is not encrusted with a "sea mat," or bryozoan colony, resembling a piece of brittle lace. Under a hand lens, rows of minute limy cups appear, each holding a tentacled tenant. On a single stem of Irish moss, there may be thousands

Low tide on the Pacific coast exposes a variety of rocky-shore organisms. Oval limpets hug sandstone stained by iron deposits. Sea anemones wave their tentacles amid delicate branches of coralline algae and clumps of green seaweed.

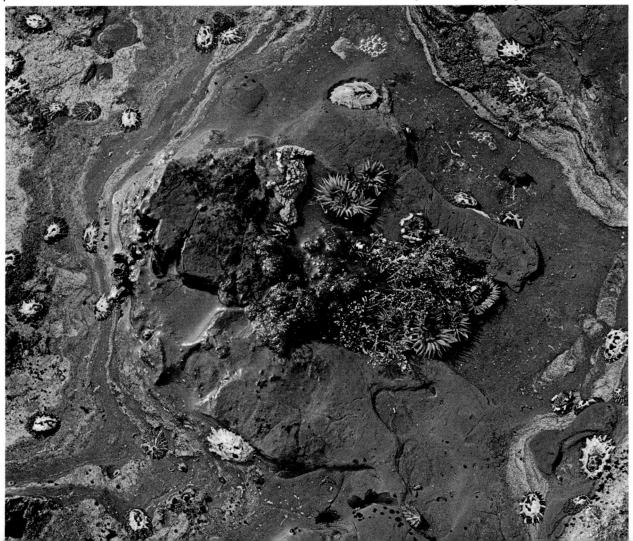

of such individuals, each using its tentacles to snare microscopic plants and animals.

Many kelp fronds bear what look like delicate clusters of flowers. Each cluster is a colony of hydroids—tiny tubular animals wearing crowns of threadlike tentacles. Despite the hydroids' fragile look, their gossamer tentacles are armed with poisonous stinging structures. When a small creature blunders near, it is impaled on tiny darts and injected with a paralyzing venom. The tentacles then push the prey into a mouth at the center of the "flower."

In addition to fixed animals, larger, more mobile creatures live in the lower zone. Sea urchins move slowly on tube feet among the holdfasts, feeding on bits of dead animals and on algae coating the rocks. Spider crabs, camouflaged by scraps of seaweed on their shells, creep along on slender, jointed legs. In the Irish moss, flat-shelled Jonah crabs hide from watchful gulls and wait for nightfall to feed. When the tide is in, rock eels, rock bass, big-eyed gobies, and other fishes swim among the swaying kelp fronds.

Below the low tidemark, the influences of tides and waves diminish. Shore life blends imperceptibly into ocean life.

Zonation on a rocky shore provides a vivid picture of plant and animal adaptation. Life originated in the shallow seas, but over millions of years, the competition for food, shelter, and living space in the lower zone forced many creatures to adapt to conditions higher up on shore. Here life was somewhat less competitive, but there was a new danger: exposure to the air. More and more species joined the first pioneers, and competitive pressures again mounted. As living things pushed farther and farther landward, gills gave way to primitive lungs, body coverings grew watertight to retard evaporation, and legs were modified for movement on land. Many organisms became less and less reliant on the sea and eventually severed all attachment to it.

Two quarter-inch sea spiders cling with hooked legs to a branching hydroid colony attached to intertidal rocks.

Pugnacious garibaldis patrol a California kelp forest. The eight-inch fish defend their territories against all comers.

A tiny tidepool harbors a purple starfish and three sea anemones, one covered with pebbles that may camouflage it or protect it against the surf. If menaced by a starfish, an anemone can retract its tentacles and form a tight mound.

Life of the Tidepools

Ebbing tides leave behind miniature seas on rock-rimmed coasts. Tidepools protect marine plants and animals from exposure to air, but they also present problems in survival. As their waters heat up, oxygen is driven off and animals may suffocate. Also, heavy rains can decrease salinity, or evaporation can increase it to dangerous levels. If a tidepool becomes too fresh, starfishes, anemones, crabs, and other animals may absorb too much water, bloat, and die. If the tidepool becomes too briny, they can lose fluid and shrivel.

Waving tentacles that vaguely resemble rabbit ears, a sea hare lays strings of millions of eggs in a tidepool. One sea hare laid 478 million eggs in four months. Sea hares often reproduce once, then die.

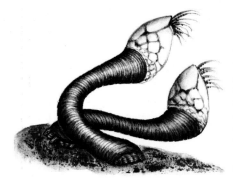

Goose barnacles cling tenaciously to rocks along the shore, the limestone-covered parts of their bodies supported by tough stalks. At low tide, barnacles close their plates and thus avoid drying out. When again submerged, they open their plates and extend feathery "legs" to trap microscopic food particles in the water.

Tubeworms in their stony homes stir the waters of a protected Oregon tidepool with cilia on their feathery gills and strain plankton from the water. On the slightest provocation, the colorful gills snap back into the tubes.

An empty whelk shell provides a home for a hermit crab and a place of attachment for sea anemones. The anemones may help protect the crab with their stinging tentacles; the crab, in turn, leaves scraps that the anemones can eat.

Water cascades from one pool to another over blue mussels and white goose barnacles, often found together on rocky Pacific shores. Sea urchins lie submerged in the upper pool, and pink acorn barnacles encrust mussels at the left.

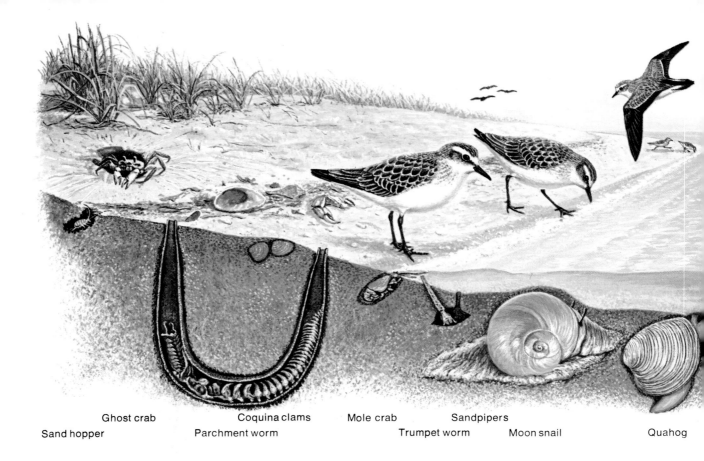

Ghost crab   Coquina clams   Mole crab   Sandpipers

Sand hopper   Parchment worm   Trumpet worm   Moon snail   Quahog

Life on Sandy Shores

The zonation of life, so sharply etched on a rocky shore, is blurred and indefinite on a sandy beach. The sand offers no firm foothold for organisms such as kelp and barnacles. Beach dwellers tend to be mobile, free to move in and out with each turn of the tide, or even with each wave. Yet zonation is apparent even here.

On the upper beach, beyond reach of the highest tides, live land insects and marine creatures, such as ghost crabs and sand hoppers, that may be in the evolutionary process of leaving the sea. On the intertidal beach, burrowing animals such as clams and mole crabs live in the sand. On the lower, or subtidal, beach are animals that cannot stand much exposure to air—burrowing sea cucumbers, sand dollars, anemones, shrimps, swimming crabs, eels, and other fishes.

The best-known inhabitant of the relatively barren upper beach from New Jersey to Texas is the swift, sand-colored ghost crab. Its legs are useless for swimming; when it dashes into the surf to avoid an enemy, it runs along the bottom. The crab normally enters the water only to wet its gills. It still must get oxygen from water in the manner of a fish, and always carries a bit of the sea in a chamber surrounding its gills.

Ghost crabs live in the sea only as larvae. The females drop their eggs in the water, and the tiny larvae that hatch from the eggs spend a few weeks drifting wherever tides and currents carry them. When ready to take up life ashore, they must make a successful landing on a suitable beach, or soon perish.

As they grow older, young ghost crabs burrow farther and farther up the beach. Home is a shaft in the sand with a room at the end and sometimes an additional escape shaft leading to the surface. At night, the crabs emerge to feed on tidbits in the beach wrack; during the early morning hours, they repair their burrows; about midday, they close the entrances and retire until feeding time. On cold northern beaches, ghost crabs move up in autumn to the dry area beyond the tides. There they dig deeper than usual, stock their burrows with food, and close their entrances until the warmth of spring returns.

With few exceptions, burrowing is the common way of life on intertidal beaches, and inhabitants spend most of their lives hidden from view beneath the sand. Only a few barely noticeable signs betray their presence.

A V-shaped trail may lead to half-buried, spine-covered heart urchins. Heart urchins plow along

How Animals Survive in the Sand of an Atlantic Beach

Life abounds on a seemingly barren mid-Atlantic sandy shore. The surface may become deadly hot, but the underlying sand remains cool and damp, with little temperature change. There is a gradual transition from the permanently submerged subtidal life to the nearly terrestrial animals of the dry zone. Above the high tide line, ghost crabs and sand hoppers retreat in their burrows by day, emerging at night to hunt. Closer to the water, trumpet worms in cone-shaped tubes sift through the sand, while mole crabs and coquina clams, which follow the tide up and down the beach, strain food from the surf. Predators such as moon snails dig into the sand to seize hidden mollusks.

Channeled whelk
Lady crab
Sea cucumber
Flounder
Sand dollars

eating scraps of organic material mixed with the sand grains. Their sharp spines usually point backward to make the going easier but can straighten up quickly and inflict a painful wound in a collector's hand or bare foot.

A ribbonlike track may lead to a sand dollar or burrowing starfish. Sand dollars are extremely flat, waferlike sea urchins that move by walking on their short spines. Sand dollars ingest sand grains coated with plant matter and tiny edible particles mixed with the sand. Burrowing starfishes, on the other hand, eat small snails and crustaceans, swallowing them whole, then regurgitating the shells. Unlike their rocky-shore relatives, these starfishes have no suction cups on the tube feet of their rays. They cannot cling to rocks, but they are excellent burrowers. When placed on the sand, they quickly sink out of sight.

A moving hill of sand may hide a moon snail searching for clams. The snail shoves aside sand with its large foot, its passage eased by a smoothly rounded shell. When it finds a clam, the moon snail curls its foot around the prey, drills a neat, circular hole in the shell with its radula, and rasps out the flesh inside. Moon snails eat more than a third of their weight in clams each week.

The pace of life on intertidal beaches is keyed

A ghost crab stands poised for flight, ready to disappear down the burrow it has dug near the high tidemark. A mature crab can scuttle along at a speed of up to five feet per second, fast enough to elude most predators.

to rhythms of the sea, and activity increases tremendously as the tide comes in. Parchment worms in U-shaped tubes begin moving their fanlike "paddles" back and forth, creating a current of water from which they filter out one-celled plants. Clams push up their tubelike siphons and draw in seawater, extracting oxygen and trapping tiny organisms on the sticky mucus of their gill filaments. Whelks cruise on the bottom and locate clams through currents set up by their siphons. Blue crabs seize clams and mole crabs in powerful pincers. Small fishes search out a variety of crustaceans, worms, and feebly swimming larval creatures. Large fishes devour small ones. Skates and rays, seeking clams and snails, plow the bottom.

Some of the more mobile sand dwellers follow the tide back and forth. Hordes of mole crabs suddenly bubble up from the quiet sand and are carried up the beach as a wave sweeps over them. When the force of the rushing water slackens, they swiftly burrow backward in the sand and feed only as the water flows back to the sea. Fine bristles on two long feeding antennae strain microscopic organisms from the backwash. Their oval, molelike bodies and flattened, pawlike limbs make these crabs well suited for rapid digging.

Colorful, one-inch coquina clams also follow the tide. As the water comes in, hundreds, sometimes even thousands, of them rise out of the sand at one time and allow waves to wash them up the beach. Before the backwash can carry them away, they use their feet and wedge-shaped shells to dig into the sand. Then they thrust up their siphons and begin feeding. As the tide goes out, the clams move farther down the shore, always staying within the wash of the surf.

With the ebb tide, activity slackens on the intertidal beach. Razor clams and soft-shelled clams cease feeding, and large predators move offshore. Heart urchins and sand dollars continue their never-ending task of sorting bits of food out of wet sand. A few birds wheel in the air or run up and down the beach, thrusting their bills expectantly into the sand. But most burrowers on the exposed beach have stopped feeding and await the return of the flood.

Thousands of grunion wriggle up southern California beaches to spawn during the highest tides every spring. At right, a half-buried female deposits her eggs beneath the sand, while a male wraps himself around her and releases his milt.

The reproductive cycles of some seashore animals are adjusted to tidal rhythms

Many seashore animals synchronize not only their feeding activities but also their reproductive cycles with the patterns of the tides.

On California beaches during high tides of spring and summer, grunion, silvery fish five to eight inches long, engage in a spawning ritual precisely keyed to tidal rhythms. From March to August on the second, third, and fourth nights after a full moon, grunion begin arriving just as the tide starts to ebb. First a few scouts swim in with the waves and are washed out again. Gradually more and more fish arrive, until thousands may be thrashing about in the surf.

A grunion spawning run may go on for an hour, but the mating time of individuals is astonishingly brief. Females, each accompanied by one or more males, ride the incoming waves as far up the beach as they can, then bore into the sand with their tails. Each female deposits a thousand eggs or more about two inches below the surface. Males curl around the females, cover the eggs with milt, and immediately slip back into the water. The females free themselves and follow the males on the wash of the next wave. The entire process may take only thirty seconds.

This extraordinary performance ensures that the fertilized eggs will be hidden from predators in the moist sand and kept warm for about ten days. The lower tides that follow do not reach the eggs; when the next series of spring tides uncovers them, the embryos are fully developed, ready to leave the protection of the egg. Minutes after the waves pick up the eggs, the baby grunion hatch and drift out to deeper water.

The critically timed spawning of the grunion is a strikingly effective adaptation to conditions on tidal shores. If they spawned during lower tides, or even an hour earlier on the same tides, their eggs would be washed away and probably destroyed. If they spawned during the high tides of the dark moon, when the water rises higher than it does during the full moon, the eggs would have to wait a month to be uncovered again. No one knows how the grunion developed this uncanny timing ability. Somehow, over millions of years, the pulse of the tides has become part of them.

On the east coast of North America, there is another annual spawning congregation as impressive as that of the grunion. Certainly it is far older, for the creatures involved are the only remaining members of a group that has existed for half a billion years. These are horseshoe crabs—not crabs at all, but distant relatives of scorpions and spiders, shaped like a large horse's hoof to which a long, daggerlike tail has been added.

On nights of the spring tides in May and June, the horseshoe crabs crawl ashore in huge numbers, males clinging to larger females. The females scoop out nests, and each lays several thousand eggs. Males release their sperm, and waves carry it to the eggs. As the ebbing tide covers the eggs with sand, the parents return to the sea.

Within a few days, the small, greenish eggs expand to several times their original size. In about two weeks, those not dug up and devoured by crabs, sandpipers, plovers, and other predators are ready to hatch. The next spring tide uncovers the eggs, and the abrasive action of wave-stirred sand tears them open, freeing the young. They scramble into the surf and head for deeper water.

Spawning horseshoe crabs congregate on Atlantic beaches from New England to Mexico during May and June. Each female, dragging a smaller male, plows several shallow nests in the sand and deposits as many as 20,000 eggs.

Labels on illustration: Plover, Eelgrass, Fiddler crab, Mud snail, Flounder, Hydroids, Sea slug, Bent-nosed clam, Goby, Goby, Scale worm, Ghost shrimp, Clam, Lugworm, Innkeeper worm, Pea crab

The Mud Flat World

In the protected, virtually level environment of a mud flat, life zones are not sharply distinguished. Most inhabitants are burrowers and scavengers, feeding on organic detritus and often sharing the burrows of other species such as the innkeeper worm. The difficulty of obtaining sufficient oxygen in the mud limits the number of species, but population densities are very high. Ghost shrimps, snails, and worms dominate this west coast flat.

Life in the Mud

Mud flats rim gently sloping shores of bays and river mouths, wherever there is protection from the assault of the waves. Mud flats contain rich deposits of plant and animal material—remains of dead mud dwellers, debris from adjacent grassy tidal marshes, and organic matter carried in from the sea by the tides. Some people find the pungent odor of the flats unpleasant, but it is the smell of life—an indicator of vast reserves of food available to mud dwellers. Sand is often mixed with mud in varying amounts, and it is in such localities that the largest populations of animals live. Fine mud particles hold nutrients, and the leavening of larger sand particles produces a firm bottom, ideal for burrowing.

As on sandy shores, most animals live beneath the surface, burrowing down to avoid exposure to air and to predators that come from land, sea, and air. A mud flat, however, is not as porous as a sandy beach, and the dense, closely packed silt inhibits the circulation of water carrying vital dissolved oxygen. Thus burrowing animals that breathe through their skins, such as some sea urchins and starfishes, seldom inhabit mud flats. Only those animals with special adaptations for obtaining oxygen can survive.

The adult soft-shelled clam, a common inhabitant of mud flats on both coasts of North America, lives permanently imbedded in mud. To obtain oxygen and tiny food particles, it pumps water in and out of its body through a fleshy siphon extending to the surface. When the tide goes out, the buried soft-shelled clam can switch over to anaerobic, or oxygenless, respiration—a metabolic process akin to fermentation, used by many bacteria and by some animals to supplement their oxygen intake. In a laboratory, soft-shelled clams have survived for as long as eight days without oxygen.

Lugworms abound on many mud flats, sometimes reaching concentrations as high as 82,000 per acre. These rough-skinned creatures, normally about six inches long and an inch thick, live in U-shaped burrows and continually pump a current of water over their large, bushy gills. They feed in the same way as earthworms: by swallowing large quantities of mud and digesting whatever organic matter is present. Wastes from this diet form piles around one opening of each burrow.

One of the most curious inhabitants of California mud flats is the fat, foot-long innkeeper worm. This flesh-colored, sausage-shaped creature lives in a U-shaped burrow through which it continually pumps water in much the same way as a lugworm. Instead of eating mud, however, the innkeeper spins a slimy mucus net that catches tiny food particles brought in with the current. When enough of these particles have accumulated, the innkeeper eats the net and begins to spin another.

The innkeeper is so named because its burrow is nearly always occupied by a variety of guests. A two-inch red scale worm lives only in the innkeeper's burrow; it stays in almost constant contact with its host, nibbling on rejected food and sometimes on the net itself. A pair of pea crabs may also occupy the burrow and fight with the scale worm over larger bits of food. Gobies frequently shelter in the innkeeper's burrow, too. But rather than fighting with the crabs, these little fishes have actually been observed bringing the crabs pieces of food that were too big to swallow.

Other mud flat burrowers that take in boarders are the ghost shrimps. A single ghost-shrimp burrow may shelter nine different kinds of creatures, including small clams, pea crabs, worms, several tiny shrimplike animals, and gobies. Each burrow consists of a nearly vertical shaft with a number of tunnels leading laterally off it. Tunnels branch and rebranch, widening at junctions to provide room for their owner to turn around.

To excavate its tunnels, a ghost shrimp digs out mud with its first two pairs of legs, storing the accumulated particles in a receptacle formed by fleshy appendages around its mouth. When this receptacle is full, the shrimp goes to the burrow entrance and pushes the load of mud outside.

The Eelgrass Community

From the Arctic to the tropics on the coasts of North America, Europe, and Asia, marine meadows of eelgrass frequently grow on the seaward sides of mud flats. Eelgrass thrives in protected waters from the low-tide zone out to a depth of about twenty feet; its long, branching roots anchor in sandy and muddy bottoms that will not support seaweed holdfasts.

Eelgrass is not a true grass at all, but is related to the pondweeds. Its popular name was probably inspired by its thin, ribbonlike leaves, a quarter-inch wide and often a yard long, which resemble blades of grass. Eelgrass invaded the sea from land, and it is one of the relatively few flowering plants that have adapted to salt water. The flowers—small, inconspicuous, and short-lived—bloom in late spring and summer. The pollen grains are transferred from plant to plant by currents, and the seeds are eaten by many birds.

Eelgrass provides shelter for a variety of an-

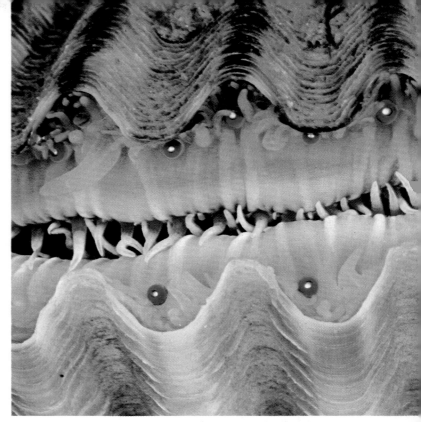

Two rows of bright blue eyes peer from between the fluted shells of a bottom-dwelling scallop. Tentacles fringing the fleshy mantle, sensitive to chemicals in the water and to touch, also alert the scallop to prey and predators.

imals. On the east coast of the United States, large numbers of scallops live in eelgrass beds. These clamlike creatures swim about by quickly clapping together their valves, causing a jet of water to shoot out and propel them forward. They can also move backward by squirting water through openings on either side of the hinge. When disturbed, jackknife clams can also swim through the eelgrass beds by shooting water from their siphons or from between their valves. Many different snails and worms creep on the bottom among the stalks and roots of these underwater jungles. Small snails fall prey to larger ones, and their empty shells often are occupied by hermit crabs. Eels, flounders, and other fishes come in from deeper water to hunt. On both coasts of the United States, eelgrass beds support large flocks of wintering brant, small geese that nest in the Arctic.

A microcommunity lives on the surfaces of the eelgrass leaves. Older and longer blades may be completely covered by tiny organisms such as hydroids, tubeworms, and tufts of red algae. These in turn may be coated with other plants and bits of organic matter. A variety of animals grazes on this abundant food supply.

Too often considered wastelands, salt marshes are among the richest wildlife communities on Earth

A black-necked stilt skims over the murky waters of a salt marsh. Stilts searching for insects and small fishes wade in breast-deep waters on their spindly legs. They nest in the marshes, heaping up sticks on dry hummocks.

From the intertidal area to dry land, along the shoreward edge of mud flats and their twisting maze of tidal creeks, grow meadows of cordgrasses. Like eelgrass, cordgrasses are flowering plants that invaded the sea from land.

Two kinds of cordgrasses dominate the extensive tidal marshlands of the Atlantic and Gulf coasts of the United States and the smaller marsh areas of southern California. The short, fine cordgrass grows no taller than two feet and forms a lush carpet on flats shoreward of the taller, coarser cordgrass, which may reach a height of ten feet. Where tall cordgrass grows thickly, almost no light penetrates to the mud. Tidal currents sweep away dead leaves, leaving a clear, dark floor under this dwarf forest. Because they are farther back from shore, the stands of shorter cordgrass are not swept by currents. There dead plants mat the floor, forming an ideal moist shelter.

Cordgrasses provide food and shelter for a distinct community. Black snails crawl up the leaves to feed on algae coating them. Purple marsh crabs come out of their burrows at low tide to nibble on marsh grass. Clamworms as big as small snakes feed on dead razor clams. Ribbed mussels lie buried to their midsections in mud.

The marsh snail shelters under tall cordgrass at low tide but avoids the rising water by climbing the stalks. It has a lung and breathes air. If a particularly high tide submerges the snail, it can survive without breathing for about an hour—the time it takes for the tide to ebb. Interestingly enough, the marsh snail anticipates the flood tide and climbs the grass *before* the water reaches it. Apparently it possesses some kind of internal clock that sounds an alarm every twelve hours.

One of the most conspicuous animals of the salt marsh is the fiddler crab. At low tide, large groups of these inch-wide crustaceans flit across the mud beneath the tall cordgrass in search of edible morsels in the mud. The fiddler crab is named for the brightly colored outsized claw that develops on one of its front legs. Only the male grows this claw, which he uses in disputes with other males and to attract a female at breeding time. When a female is near, the male extends his claw full length and then whips it back toward

his body. The gesture is repeated until the female either departs or retires with him to his burrow.

The fiddler crab seems nearly independent of the water. Under its shell, just above the legs, the fiddler has a primitive lung cavity. As long as this stays moist, the fiddler can breath oxygen from the air, sometimes surviving for several weeks without immersing itself in water.

Beneath the tall cordgrass the fiddler excavates a deep burrow, bringing mud out in neatly formed pellets and piling them up at the entrance. As the tide approaches, the crab constructs a tightly fitting door of mud pellets, and in the burrow's air-filled chamber awaits the departure of the water. When the tide ebbs, the fiddler again emerges and resumes the fighting, feeding, and wooing activities that occupy much of its time.

By constantly "turning over" the bottom, fiddler crabs—and other burrowing animals as well —replenish the depleted surface mud with nutrient particles from below, thus performing a vital function in the ecology of the marsh.

At high tide, predators from offshore—squid and fishes—hunt in the cordgrasses. At low tide, visitors from land invade the marsh: swarms of insects and spiders, a large variety of birds, diamond-backed turtles, raccoons, swamp rabbits,

Waddling across the marsh, a diamond-backed turtle heads for the water—and a meal of snails and other small invertebrates. The reptile itself is a prized dinner; turtle-meat fanciers have nearly killed off the species.

white-footed mice, otters, mink, and even deer.

Birds are everywhere in the marsh. Long-billed marsh wrens, red-winged blackbirds, seaside sparrows, and long-legged, henlike clapper rails nest in tall cordgrass. Secretive sharp-tailed sparrows prefer short cordgrass. Marsh hawks sail overhead looking for small rodents. Many other birds on migration journeys rest and feed in marshes.

A bed of cordgrass or eelgrass is often the first stage in the slow transformation of shallow, open water into a wet meadow and, eventually, into dry land. These rooted plants prevent waves and currents from carrying away sediment washed in by rivers. Gradually, the area fills up with sand and silt, which becomes mud as it is enriched with decaying plants and bodies of dead animals. Small muddy islands start appearing; the cordgrasses trap more and more sediment. Soon the grassy islands begin growing together.

As land builds up, it is flooded at high tide for shorter and shorter periods. Short cordgrass replaces tall cordgrass, only to be replaced in turn by rushes. Land plants become established, and terrestrial animals begin colonizing the area. As marshland becomes dry land, the different kinds of plants and animals appear in a definite order, or succession.

Fiddler crabs scuttle beneath tall cordgrasses at low tide. When high water floods the marsh, these one-inch crabs seal themselves inside airtight burrows. Males wave their enlarged claws in mating or territorial displays.

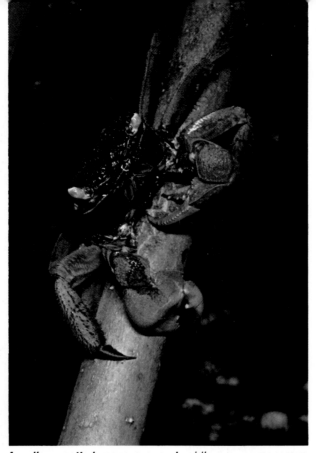

A yellow-spotted mangrove crab sidles up a mangrove prop root. During its larval stages, the crab lives in the water among the tangled mangrove roots; as an adult it scurries among the branches, feeding on green leaves.

Mangrove trees build new land as soil and debris collect among their prop roots

On the coast of southern Florida and along thousands of miles of other tropical coasts, there is a similar type of land-building and succession, but here mangrove trees are the pioneer plants. Red mangrove trees drop seedlings that have already germinated and sprouted roots. Some of these anchor in the muddy waters beneath the parent; others drift out with the tide.

Mangrove seeds grow into strong young trees buttressed by arching prop roots that penetrate deep into the bottom mud. As more and more seedlings take root on a shoal, their prop roots form an impenetrable tangle in which silt, sand, decaying vegetation, shells, coral fragments, and other debris come to rest. Soon the prop roots become encrusted with reddish-purple coon oysters, so named because they are a favored food of raccoons. The floating larvae of barnacles and mussels also settle on the prop roots, grow into adults, and compete for space with the oysters. Snails feed on algae coating the mangrove roots,

Stately wood ibises nest in a colony atop red mangroves on Pelican Island, Louisiana. Wood ibises (actually the only American storks) feed on small fishes caught in their bills as they wade through the muddy waters of mangrove swamps.

mussels, and oysters. Crown conch snails pry open oysters with their powerful feet and devour the succulent meat. Mangrove crabs spend their larval stages in the water, then take up residence in the mangrove branches and gnaw on leaves.

Many animals common to mud flats and salt marshes, such as fiddler crabs, hermit crabs, marsh crabs, marsh snails, and ghost shrimp, live among mangrove roots. And other animals that could not survive on mud flats, such as sea squirts, starfishes, and brittle stars, also live here.

Foraging for these creatures are a variety of predators, including clapper rails, killifishes, diamond-backed turtles, water moccasins, and, occasionally, a crocodile. In the upper branches, pelicans, herons, egrets, wood ibises, roseate spoonbills, and other birds roost or nest.

Like eelgrass and marsh grasses, red mangroves colonize a mud flat and are the first stage in a succession of plant communities that transform intertidal areas into dry land. Soil collects around their prop roots in such large quantities that the trees eventually die from lack of oxygen. Black mangroves, however, thrive in this built-up region, for their roots contain cavities that hold air. But finally the black mangroves, too, are replaced— first by white mangroves and then by other trees that take root as more soil accumulates.

A hungry raccoon crouches beneath arching prop roots at the edge of a mangrove swamp, its nimble fingers searching along the shallow bottom for fishes and small crustaceans. Raccoons frequently visit Florida mangrove flats.

An American crocodile suns itself beneath red mangroves in Everglades National Park, Florida. Crocodiles seize unwary birds and mammals and hold them underwater to drown. They also hunt underwater, crushing and gulping down fishes.

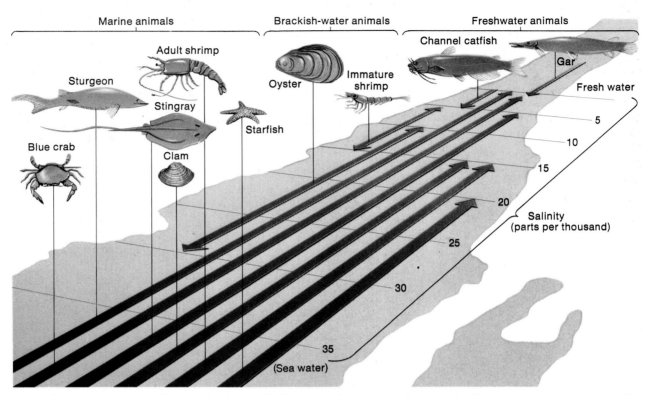

Marine animals   Brackish-water animals   Freshwater animals

Adult shrimp

Sturgeon

Stingray

Starfish

Oyster

Immature shrimp

Channel catfish

Gar

Fresh water

Blue crab

Clam

5

10

15

20

Salinity (parts per thousand)

25

30

35

(Sea water)

In an estuary, some animals live only in the brackish waters where river and sea meet; others come downstream from the river or swim up from the sea. Most are restricted to a specific salinity; a surge of fresh or salt water can cause disaster.

Gateways to the Sea

Mud flats with their accompanying marshes and mangrove stands are commonly found in estuaries —the regions where rivers and streams empty into the sea. Here fresh water flowing from the land mixes with salt water.

Living conditions in estuaries can be hazardous. As a river spreads out in an estuary, it slows down, and the fine silt that it brings from land settles to the bottom in a smothering blanket. Water temperatures may rise and fall drastically from season to season and even from day to day. But by far the greatest danger to estuarine life is the abruptly changing salinity, or salt content, of the water. Salinity may fluctuate more or less regularly twice daily as tides move back and forth through the river mouth, and it may also fluctuate erratically with shifting weather conditions as rain makes the water less salty or drought makes it more salty.

Plants and animals that live in water—whether salt or fresh—must maintain a certain concentration of dissolved salts in their body tissues. If an organism gets into water with a lower concentration of salt than that in its body fluids, water

flows into its tissues and it may bloat. If it gets into water with a higher concentration of salt, water flows out of its tissues and it may shrivel. Many water dwellers have limited tolerances for such salinity changes, and they perish if these tolerances are exceeded.

As the brackish waters of an estuary give way farther upstream to the progressively fresher waters of a river, one group of plants and animals is slowly replaced by a different one. This gradual change is a kind of zonation, but it is based on a tolerance for varying degrees of salinity rather than on an ability to withstand exposure to air. Starfishes and sea urchins, for example, need the full salt concentration of the sea; they can live only at the mouths of estuaries where there are thirty to thirty-five parts of salt for every thousand parts of water. Razor clams can live in water with as little as twenty-five parts of salt per thousand; oyster drills can live in water with only nine parts of salt per thousand. Thus these creatures can venture farther from the sea. Some marine worms, oysters, and crabs survive in water with less than five parts of salt per thousand and are found where the water is almost fresh.

Fresh and salt water mingle in the estuary at the mouth of the Salinas River, which empties into the Pacific Ocean at Monterey Bay, California. Some small animals, such as certain copepods, live only in brackish estuarine waters.

Despite the constant stress of changing salinity, life abounds in estuaries. Indeed, estuaries support many of man's principal food animals: oysters, crabs, scallops, shrimps. Estuaries also serve as nurseries for a variety of commercial and game fishes: flounder, fluke, bluefish, striped bass, tarpon, and several herrings. In fact, about 85 per cent of the fishes and shellfishes sold in markets of the world come from coastal waters, and many of these creatures spend all or part of their lives in estuaries.

Unfortunately, estuaries now reflect man's failure to conserve the Earth's most valuable natural assets. From rivers too often regarded as convenient natural sewers, estuaries receive large volumes of pesticides, industrial chemicals, sewage, silt, garbage, and trash—plus a more subtle but equally dangerous pollutant, heat, discharged from power plants and factories.

Many harbors have become so polluted that fish and shellfish cannot be safely taken from them. In 1970, the Massachusetts Division of Natural Resources said that an oil spill of several tons could be expected in Boston Harbor about once every three weeks. Recent oil spills in San Francisco

Bay and Long Island Sound have gravely endangered what life still remains in these once beautiful waters. Southeast of New York, dumping of sewage sludge and dredging spoils has created a twenty-square-mile "dead sea," where even worms cannot survive on the bottom. Parts of the oyster grounds in Mobile Bay, Alabama, have been closed by state health officials because of water pollution.

Many countries have hardly an estuary or salt marsh that is not polluted. Some of the damage already done may be irreversible, but much can be undone, and all of it should be checked. Great Britain has made good progress in cleaning several of its rivers; fish are surviving in the Thames estuary even in London, and in the summer of 1970, a dolphin got all the way to Richmond (several miles upstream from London) before biologists turned it around and headed it back to sea.

Wherever the gateways to the sea are choked by pollutants, the task of cleaning them is urgent —not only to preserve abundant sources of food but to protect the natural beauty of the shores. And who can say that man can live in the absence of either?

The Bountiful Coastal Seas

The shallow waters covering the submerged margins
of the continents harbor the greatest — and most
varied — concentration of living things on our planet

Almost four-fifths of all the plants and animals on Earth live in the shallow coastal seas fringing the continents. Countless minute plants drift in the waters, staining them green. Billions of tiny animals graze these floating "pastures" and in turn are eaten by huge schools of prowling fish. Seabirds skim above the waves, scooping up prey with their bills. On the sea floor, forests of undulating seaweed cling to rocks; a host of bizarre creatures filter the water for bits of food; a steady rain of dead and dying organisms fertilizes the bottom ooze.

Only awesome numbers can describe the density of coastal-sea populations. A thimbleful of water contains thousands of planktonic organisms — drifting plants and animals that form the first links in the ocean's chain of life. An estimated 10,000 cod live above each acre of ocean floor on the Grand Banks off Nova Scotia and Newfoundland. On some parts of the sea floor near Great Britain, 250 million brittle stars crowd into each square mile.

The coastal seas — collectively, about equal in

A complex community of bottom dwellers thrives just below the high tidemark on a wharf piling. Mussels, tentacled sea anemones, and sponges feed on plankton brought by the current; several spiny sea urchins graze on a slimy coating of algae; a starfish pries open a mussel with its muscular arms.

area to Asia — make up less than one-tenth of the ocean's expanse, but they yield almost nine-tenths of the world's annual harvest of fish and shellfish. Compared to these fertile seas, the open ocean is a barren desert.

Most coastal waters lie over continental shelves, extensions of land once believed to be nearly as flat and featureless as their name implies. Detailed studies have revealed, however, that they are wrinkled with gentle hills and carved with deep gorges. The shelves' gradual descent from shore — only five feet in every mile — would go almost unnoticed on land.

The continental shelves average about forty-five miles wide, but range from less than a mile wide off stretches of the western coasts of North and South America to over 900 miles off the arctic coast of Siberia. At the outer edges, the sea is around 450 feet deep. Here, the slightly pitched bottom suddenly becomes a steep slope or, in some places, a sheer wall plunging thousands of feet to the deep ocean floor. A mighty precipice 500 miles long lies in the Gulf of Mexico off the Florida coast; in one place there is an almost perpendicular drop of over a mile. Near Santiago, Chile, the narrow continental shelf ends in a steep incline that drops without interruption to a depth of 20,000 feet. These continental slopes, as they are called, form the true boundaries of the continents.

During the Ice Ages, the seas were much lower

Continental shelves—sediments that edge the great land masses— are from one to 900 miles wide and range from gentle inclines to cliffs

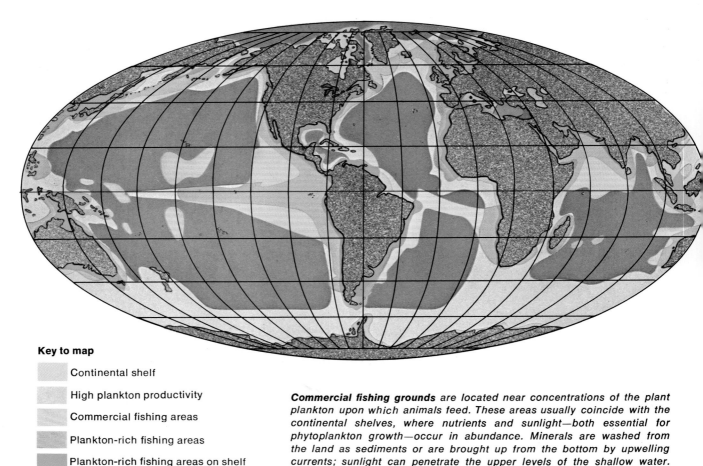

Key to map

Continental shelf

High plankton productivity

Commercial fishing areas

Plankton-rich fishing areas

Plankton-rich fishing areas on shelf

Commercial fishing grounds are located near concentrations of the plant plankton upon which animals feed. These areas usually coincide with the continental shelves, where nutrients and sunlight—both essential for phytoplankton growth—occur in abundance. Minerals are washed from the land as sediments or are brought up from the bottom by upwelling currents; sunlight can penetrate the upper levels of the shallow water.

than they are today because glaciers locked up vast amounts of water. Large areas of the continental shelves were exposed. Bones dredged up from what is now the ocean floor reveal that musk oxen, giant moose, horses, tapirs, and huge ground sloths once ranged far beyond present coastlines. Brick-size mammoth and mastodon teeth have been discovered off the east coast of the United States, far from where they could have been carried by currents and tides. Fire-heated shells— probable remnants of an ancient oyster dinner— were found by a research submarine cruising 140 feet under the waters of Chesapeake Bay. There is little doubt that ancient land animals and prehistoric men once roamed where fishes and whales now swim.

As the glaciers pushed their way south, they

planed down the land in one of the greatest earth-moving operations of all time. In some places the glaciers—like bulldozers spreading landfill—extended the shelves. The rubble pushed ahead formed the peninsula of Cape Cod and offshore islands such as Martha's Vineyard, Nantucket, and Long Island.

Rivers meandered across the exposed shelves and cut deep channels that still exist. Marine geologists think that turbidity currents—torrents of silt-laden water cascading down underwater slopes —have extended and deepened some of these ancient river beds into spectacular canyons. The Hudson Canyon, a continuation of the Hudson River beyond its mouth at New York City, is one of the best examples. This canyon has been traced more than 100 miles away from land and 12,000 feet down the continental slope to the floor of the abyss. The V-shaped notch formed at the edge of the shelf is 3600 feet deep and 5½ miles wide from rim to rim. Yet this Grand Canyon of the ocean is not the largest undersea gorge. The Ameghino Canyon off Argentina claims that title, but it is possible that canyons still deeper await discovery.

The rivers of the world carry nearly 750 million tons of sediment into coastal waters every year. Millions of tons are deposited as silt on the shelves, and millions more are dissolved in seawater. The minerals present in this sediment read like the list of ingredients on a bag of lawn fertilizer: phosphates, nitrates, calcium, silica. All are essential for life in the sea. Just as plants on land cannot exist without minerals in the soil, so marine plants require the same minerals in the water surrounding them.

Nutrients are also brought into coastal seas by currents called upwellings. Winds and the Earth's rotation cause surface currents to flow away from the land. This water is replaced by vertical currents that bring up accumulated minerals and organic materials. Surface temperature changes also cause these currents. Thus the coastal seas are fertilized with nutrients from both the land and the ocean floor.

Life on the Continental Shelves

Nowhere else in the ocean are sunlight and nutrients—the basic elements of life—brought together in such profusion as over the continental shelves. Surface waters farther out have ample sunlight but lack a plentiful supply of vital nutrients; the waters of the abyss may be rich in nutrients but receive no sunlight. In the shallow coastal waters marine plants, upon which all animal life in the sea depends, have everything they need for growth.

Like the familiar plants of gardens, grasslands, and forests, plants of the sea convert inedible minerals into food through photosynthesis. They absorb water, carbon dioxide, and various minerals and use the energy of sunlight absorbed by their green pigment, chlorophyll, to create the various sugars, starches, fats, and proteins of their living tissue.

During photosynthesis, plants give off more oxygen than they need, and thus supply oxygen for sea animals as well. In fact, scientists estimate that marine plants produce 70 per cent of the oxygen necesary to support all animals now living on this planet.

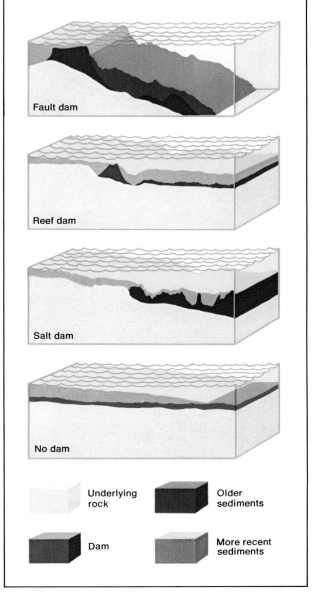

Four Kinds of Continental Shelf

*Most continental shelves are composed of recently deposited sediments covering deeper layers of sediment turned to rock. Where a dam exists, the sea bottom tends to be extremely rugged, especially on the seaward side. Beyond a **fault dam**—a wedge of rock thrust up from the floor by volcanic or earthquake activity—the dropoff is dramatically steep. A fault dam rims the U.S. west coast shelf. A **reef dam** may consist of ancient algae or coral growths or even living coral, as around the Florida Keys. The upward movement of an offshore salt bed forms a **salt dam**: one holds the western Gulf coast shelf. If **no dam** or barrier holds back sediments, as along much of the Atlantic coast, the shelf slopes almost imperceptibly downward.*

Fault dam

Reef dam

Salt dam

No dam

Underlying rock

Older sediments

Dam

More recent sediments

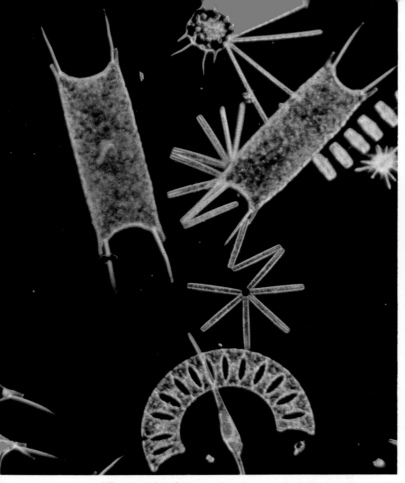

Microscopic diatoms, the "grasses of the sea," are the most important and numerous of the marine plants. One gallon of seawater may contain millions. Each species secretes a silica shell of unique form and design.

The jewel-like silica shell of a diatom is magnified 600 times in this photomicrograph. Thousands of species of the single-cell greenish-yellow algae, all basically similar in structure, exist in nature and form the indispensable first links in many ocean food chains. Enclosed in miniature silica "pillboxes" and kept afloat by droplets of oil, diatoms use the energy of sunlight to convert carbon dioxide and nutrients dissolved in seawater into living plant tissue. These minute drifters flourish in colder northern waters. During a spring plankton bloom they may occur in such abundance as to actually stain the waters a dark greenish-brown.

Diatom Division

Diatoms reproduce by dividing in two. First the cell nucleus divides, and the rest of the cell material separates into two masses, each containing a nucleus. Then each mass of cell material forms a cover to fit its half of the box. Now two diatoms exist where there was one. Since new box covers form within the old box, one of the new boxes will be smaller than the old box (the other will be the same size). In this way, the average size of a group of such diatoms will be smaller. But the process cannot go on forever. At some point, after a number of divisions, the very small diatoms will discard their shells and secrete new ones, two or three times larger.

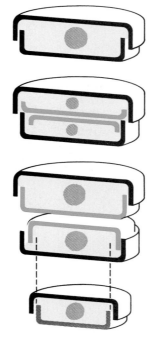

Grasses of the Sea

Along rocky coasts, the leafy growth that people associate with the word "plants" is abundant in the form of seaweed, but seaweeds support only a very small percentage of marine animals. The great majority of sea plants are minute one-celled organisms that drift with the currents. The most abundant of these are the diatoms, which are often called the grasses of the sea.

A single quart of seawater may contain hundreds of thousands of diatoms. Under a microscope, they look like exquisite, transparent jewel boxes, each containing a tiny blob of brownish-green living matter. The "boxes" actually are external skeletons of silica, a mineral that diatoms extract from seawater and secrete around themselves. Each skeleton has two parts that fit together neatly like the top and bottom of a pillbox. These may be round, rectangular, spindle-shaped, or oval; often they are drawn out in lacy lattices and spiny designs of astonishing beauty.

Striations, pits, and perforations on the surfaces of diatom skeletons form intricate patterns peculiar to each of the estimated 9200 species. The designs strengthen the plants and slow their sinking by increasing friction with the water. Many species also contain oil globules that help keep them afloat.

Each single-celled diatom carries out the same activities as any shrub or tree on land: It manufactures food, it grows, it reproduces. A diatom usually reproduces by simply dividing in half. One part of the living blob goes with the "lid" of the box, the other with the bottom. Then each daughter cell secretes the missing half of the skeleton. In some species, the dividing cells do not separate but remain attached to each other, gradually forming long, sparkling chains.

Diatoms flourish best in colder waters, especially around Antarctica and in the northern Pacific. Voyagers in polar seas often see floe after floe of pack ice stained brown by billions of these minute plants. When diatoms die, they sink to the bottom. Their skeletons pave twelve million square miles of ocean floor.

The Curious Dinoflagellates

In warm waters, diatoms are frequently outnumbered by dinoflagellates, single-celled organisms possessing characteristics of both plants and animals. Like diatoms, some dinoflagellates use the sun's energy to make food from water, carbon dioxide, and minerals. Others do not photosynthesize but capture food with their tiny whiplike appendages, or flagella. Many dinoflagellates are encased in cellulose, the same material that gives bulk to land-dwelling plants. Droplets of oil often provide buoyancy.

During the day, dinoflagellates usually swim toward the surface. A small red "eyespot" senses light, and one of their two flagella propels them toward it. The other flagellum, lying curled in a groove around the cell wall, controls their pitch and roll. Some species migrate 150 feet vertically in a twenty-four–hour period—nearly two million times their own length. To match this feat proportionally, a grown man would have to swim more than 2000 miles in a day. Although dinoflagellates can control their up-and-down movements to some extent, they are swept along horizontally wherever ocean currents carry them.

Many dinoflagellates are luminescent. The same complicated chemical reaction that makes fireflies flash produces light within the bodies of dinoflagellates. These marine "fireflies" bear such names as

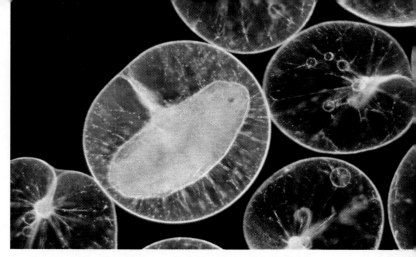

Luminescent dinoflagellates called Noctiluca (*night light*) *feed on smaller planktonic animals. The bean-shaped pod within the largest* Noctiluca *shown—about half an inch across—is a recently eaten copepod.*

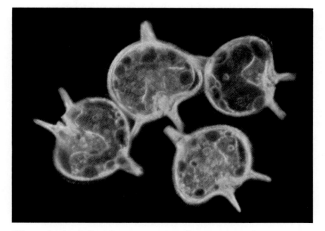

Characterized by three prominent spines and orange-red *pigment, this versatile species of dinoflagellate can eat food, as animals do, or produce it, as plants do, depending on whether prey or light is more abundant.*

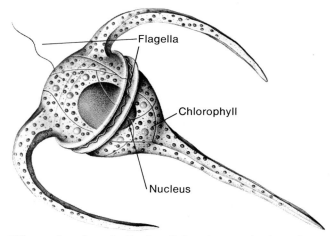

Flagella

Chlorophyll

Nucleus

This anchor-shaped dinoflagellate photosynthesizes its own food. It is armored with cellulose plates and buoyed by its three horns, which grow longer in tropical seas, where warmer waters offer less resistance to sinking.

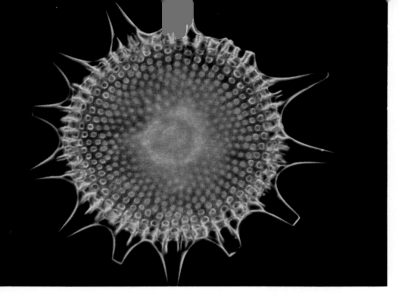

Gypsies of the Sea

Permanent wanderers, these members of the animal plankton—scarcely larger than the diatoms and dinoflagellates—spend their lives drifting with the ocean currents. They form an important link in the food chain between diatoms and the larger flesh-eating animals of the sea. Radiolarians (left), which secrete silica skeletons in fanciful geometric forms, trap their prey on sticky strands of protoplasm. The skeletons of dead radiolarians carpet large areas of the ocean floor. A copepod female (right) retains her eggs until they hatch. The minute copepods are the most plentiful of the zooplankton—and may also be the most numerous animals on Earth. A Tomopteris (far right), one of the planktonic worms, can swallow a young herring almost its own size.

Noctiluca (night light) and *Pyrocystis* (flaming cyst). Billions drifting near the surface at night can turn the water an eerie blue-green. In Phosphorescent Bay, Puerto Rico, these living sparks sometimes glow brightly enough to read by. In the north, on a summer night, a splashing oar may stimulate the dinoflagellates' telltale flashes of light.

Dinoflagellates sometimes bring disaster to shelf communities. When temperatures are high, nutrients abundant, and skies clear, certain species undergo population explosions, which stain the waters green, yellow, brown, or red. They use up more oxygen than they produce. Then the bloom ends and the dinoflagellates—and most other living things—suffocate.

Some dinoflagellates also secrete poisons that kill fishes and other marine organisms. In waters off the Atlantic and Gulf coasts of the United States, one such species less than a thousandth of an inch across periodically occurs in concentrations of ninety million per quart of water. Just one outbreak of this so-called Red Tide can kill thousands of tons of fish.

Diatoms and dinoflagellates are the two most important synthesizers of food in the ocean, but they are not the only floating plants. Bright green *Halosphaera* cells, less than 1/25 inch in diameter, occur in all seas from the tropics to the polar regions. Coccolithophores, microscopic plants covered by plates of lime, sometimes turn parts of the North Sea white and may even outnumber diatoms at certain times of year.

The composition of the plant plankton changes from place to place, from season to season, and during a single season. As one kind of plant is heavily grazed by animals, another species replaces it. Fluctuations in temperature or in the amount and kind of nutrients available also affect the populations of drifting plants.

Eventual Drop-Outs

Some planktonic animals spend only their early lives adrift. These fish fry, and larvae of most bottom dwellers, often bear no resemblance to the adults they are destined to become. In a harsh nursery where the rule is "eat or be eaten," the odds are that only one egg in every 100,000 in the plankton will survive to adulthood. A sea snail larva (left) swims about, using two hairy winglike lobes—which disappear before adulthood—as oars. Hollow cavities help keep a larval sea urchin (right) afloat. Sea urchins drift in the plankton after hatching; then suddenly, upon becoming tiny adults, they plummet to the bottom. Sea bass eggs (far right) float in the plankton. The fish embryo curls around the yolk sac, which contains a globule of oil to buoy the egg.

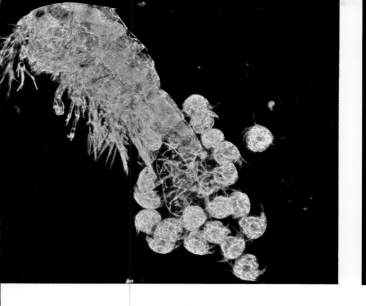

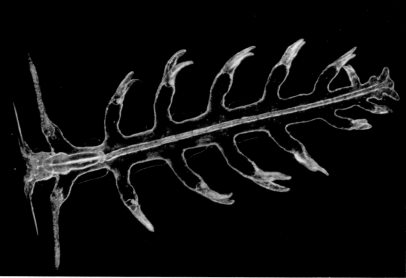

Grazers of the Sea Pastures

The "pastures" of diatoms, dinoflagellates, and other plants are grazed by zooplankton, hordes of drifting animals. The most abundant of these are copepods. Seldom bigger than grains of rice, they are even more numerous and omnipresent in the sea than are insects on land. Concentrations of up to 3000 individuals per cubic foot are not unusual in fertile coastal waters.

Copepods are lifelong members of the zooplankton, but many fishes and invertebrates—including sponges, clams, snails, starfishes, crabs, and barnacles—are planktonic drifters only during their egg and larval stages. These temporary zooplankton no more resemble their parents than caterpillars resemble butterflies. A larval sailfish, for example, has relatively small fins, immense eyes, a rounded snout, and bristles extending backward from its head—in short, it looks nothing like the streamlined adult, with its long bill and sail.

Perpetual Breeders

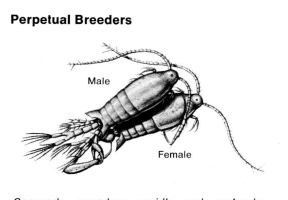

Male

Female

Copepods reproduce rapidly and profusely. Males fertilize eggs by transferring their sperm to the female with a specially formed claw. Females then carry the fertilized eggs for several days until they hatch. One to two weeks later, the new generation is already able to reproduce.

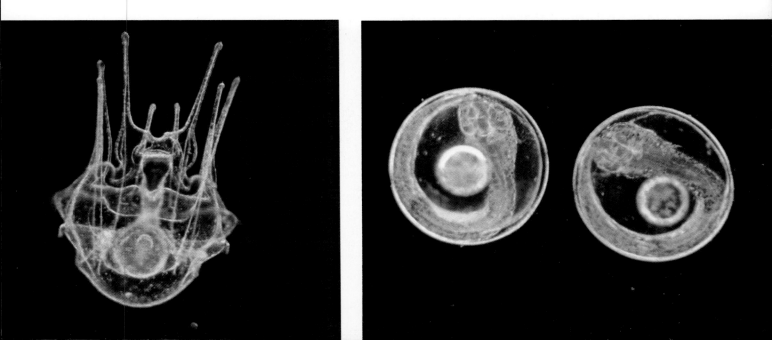

The Cycle of Life on the Continental Shelf

Billions of microscopic plants create the food on which all marine animals depend. These one-celled plants grow most profusely in shallow coastal seas over the continental shelves, where nutrients are more abundant than anywhere else in the ocean. Millions of tons of fertilizing minerals (red arrow) are carried from the land by rivers. Upwelling ocean currents (green arrow) bring additional organic material and minerals up from deep water. The rich sea pastures of tiny plants are grazed by small animals, which are food for baleen whales and such fishes as anchovies and herring. In turn, swiftly swimming predators such as squid, tuna, and sharks eat the fish. Dead and dying plants and animals and the scraps from numerous meals feed bottom-dwelling scavengers and predators (blue arrow). Finally, bacteria in the bottom ooze break down the wastes into the basic nutrients needed by the microscopic plants, and the cycle begins again.

From tiny, one-celled plants to giant sharks and voracious killer whales, every marine organism is a part of the food chain

The fate of every animal in the ocean is to eat and be eaten. Not even the killer whales, which go unchallenged during their lifetimes, are exceptions to this rule. When they die, their bodies are broken down by decay organisms, and the nutrients released are recirculated along the ocean's endless interlocking food chains.

Diatoms, dinoflagellates, and other marine plants form the first links in all ocean food chains. There would be no life in the sea without the plants, which through photosynthesis convert inorganic substances into food.

Copepods, the chief consumers of diatoms, are the second links in many food chains. By vibrating their antennae, they set up currents that sweep diatoms into their bristly mouth parts. Enormous numbers of diatoms are consumed by these diminutive crustaceans in just one season; a single copepod can eat 120,000 diatoms in a day, and the worldwide copepod population is estimated to be larger than that of all other multicellular animals combined.

Copepods themselves are eaten in huge quantities by herring, among the most numerous fishes in the sea—and the third links in many ocean food chains. Herring have gill rakers, structures that strain food from water passing over their gills. Each time a herring swallows a copepod, it is indirectly eating thousands of diatoms.

The herring itself may be eaten, perhaps by a porpoise. And the porpoise then may be caught by a killer whale.

Clearly, something is lost at each link in a food chain; the porpoise does not convert every bit of the herring into flesh. In fact, the porpoise "burns up" most of the herring's food value just in the process of staying alive—swimming, feeding, breathing, and so on. From diatom to copepod, copepod to herring, herring to porpoise, porpoise to killer whale—at each step in the food chain, 80 to 90 per cent of the food value passed on from the previous link is converted into energy and dissipated by the activities of the living.

This situation in which food is passed along to progressively larger animals may be compared to a pyramid. The base of the ocean's pyramid of life is the enormous mass of drifting plants, which use solar energy to convert raw materials into living tissue. On the next level are the most abundant animals in the sea, the copepods and other minute creatures that feed on the plants. They convert some of the plants into flesh, which is eaten by the next level's animals, ranging in size from herring to blue whales. At each successive level, the animals tend to be larger but fewer in number, and the total mass of animal life decreases. At the peak of the pyramid is a relatively small number of dominant carnivores: killer whales; giant squid; and large fishes, such as white sharks, that are rarely hunted by other animals.

The Bottom Dwellers

The shallow sea floor of the continental shelf supports an animal community different from that of the waters above. A continual rain of food slowly falls from the sunlit surface waters to the dim seabed. This detritus—the bodies of planktonic organisms, large dead and dying animals, and debris swept from land—is the base of the sea-floor food pyramid, and a host of animals feeds on it. Some live permanently attached to the bottom; others burrow, crawl, hop, or slither across the silt and sand.

Fixed feeders such as sponges, mussels, and sea squirts feed directly from the sea, by filtering food particles from the enormous amounts of water that they pump through their bodies. Other creatures burrow through the bottom, eating embedded food particles. Bristle worms, the most important burrowers, literally eat their way through the ooze inches below the surface.

Leathery, sausage-shaped sea cucumbers gather food from the bottom with sticky tentacles around their mouths. Spiny sea urchins creep slowly over rocky shallows chewing off algae and detritus with their teeth. Snails crawl across the sea floor, feeding on detritus or on living matter.

More mobile bottom dwellers prey on the filter feeders, burrowers, and plant eaters. The eighteen-inch clamworm eats young clams and mussels. Carnivorous snails attack mussels and clams or even their own kind; rasping a hole through their victims' shells, they suck out the flesh. Skates and rays, flattened relatives of sharks, cruise along the bottom and with teeth like nutcrackers crush the shells of crabs, snails, and other invertebrates.

Starfishes move slowly on rows of tube feet that line the bottom of their arms. Each cylindrical foot has muscular walls and a sucker on the end.

Eating the Plankton

Plankton eaters—from minute copepods to baleen whales—feed in remarkably varied ways. Some strain their meals from seawater or trap it on sticky strands; some swallow plankton as they swim; others actively hunt prey.

Sponge

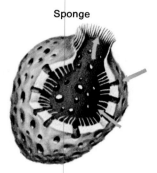

Tiny whips within a sponge's body cavity create a current of water that enters minute pores. Collar cells filter out and digest food particles.

Sea cucumber

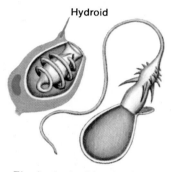

Mucus-bearing tentacles that ring a bottom-dwelling sea cucumber's mouth trap dead and decaying plankton. Other tentacles scrape off the food.

Sea squirt

Hairlike cilia drive a current of water into a sea squirt's gill basket, where food particles are trapped. The water spurts out an exit siphon.

Fanworm

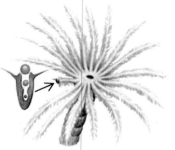

The sticky, feathery gills of a fanworm protrude from its tube burrow to snare plankton. Mucus channels carry the food to the animal's mouth.

Hydroid

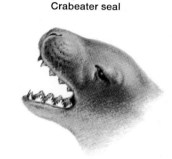

The barbed whip of a hydroid stinging capsule springs out to paralyze prey. When not in use (left), the whip lies coiled within the capsule cavity.

Crabeater seal

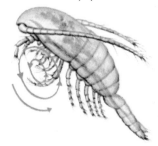

A crabeater seal gulps mouthfuls of water, filtering out shrimplike krill as it expels the water through tiny spaces between its teeth.

Herring

Water entering a herring's mouth pours over the stiff gill-rakers. These sieves strain out the plankton on which these schooling fish feed.

Seahorse

The sharp-eyed seahorse, actually a fish, sucks water in through a trapdoor in its snout, sweeping plankton one at a time down the gullet.

Copepod

Fanlike appendages around a copepod's mouth swirl water through a sieve. Screened-out plankton are pushed into the mouth from time to time.

Continental shelf bottoms harbor a rich variety of animals: fixed feeders, creepers and crawlers, and mobile hunters that glide through the water

When a tube foot touches something solid, its muscle fibers contract, the sucker adheres, and the starfish is drawn toward the point of attachment. When a starfish chances on a clam, oyster, or slow-moving scallop, it wraps its arms around the victim and exerts a steady pull with its tube feet. When the valves separate slightly, the starfish inserts its stomach through the small opening and dissolves the soft body inside with powerful digestive juices.

Brittle stars, close relatives of starfishes, slither across the bottom with snakelike movements of their five long arms. Some dig in the bottom with tube feet and eat decaying material. Others lie bottomside up and extract food from the water. These brittle stars can pass food to their mouths by "bouncing" it from one tube foot to another.

Many fishes spend their lives on or near the bottom of the continental shelf. Large schooling fishes, such as hake, cod, haddock, pollock, and ocean perch, are caught commercially in coastal waters throughout most of the Northern Hemisphere. They feed on one another as well as on their own young, on other fishes, and on inverte-

A starfish envelops a mussel, prying at its shell with five arms lined with sucker-tipped tube feet. When the shell opens, the starfish inserts its stomach to devour the mussel. The whelks and sea urchins await leftovers.

Jonah crabs mate shortly after the female molts. While her new shell hardens, the presence of the male crab safeguards the female. She carries the eggs until they hatch; the larvae temporarily join the plankton.

brates such as crabs, mollusks, and starfishes.

Flatfishes—flounders, halibuts, turbots, and soles—are beautifully adapted for life on the bottom. A newly hatched flatfish swims upright like other fishes and has an eye on each side of its head. But in the first months of life, it begins leaning over to one side. Gradually the eye on the down side of the fish moves across or through the head until both eyes are on the upper side. Most flatfishes turn their left side toward the bottom. This eyeless underside becomes white. The upper side remains pigmented and can change color to match the pattern of the bottom.

The Tiny Decomposers

A diver observing the concentration of life on the floor of a shallow coastal sea would not see one of the most important links in any food chain —the link connecting bottom and surface dwellers, the living and the dead. Countless bacteria work in the bottom sediments decomposing dead carcasses and leftovers from the bottom and surface. Without these microscopic scavengers, nutrients plants need would remain locked in the remains of dead organisms. Bacteria disintegrate animal and plant tissues into basic components— carbon dioxide, phosphates, nitrates, and other nutrients. Upwelling currents eventually carry these vital compounds back to surface waters, where they can be used by plant plankton.

The bottom community of the continental shelves is one of the most complex in the ocean, and all the links in its tangled food chains have not yet been traced.

A sea anemone is attacked by a sea slug that appears immune to the tentacle's stinging capsules. The curling of the anemone tentacles may be a defense mechanism, although a beleaguered anemone usually retracts into its tube.

Gliding over the bottom, this eagle ray of the Great Barrier Reef pounces on crustaceans and clams and crushes their shells with its powerful flat tooth plates. Rays, most abundant in the tropics, may grow to a fin span of seven feet.

Bizarre Bottom Fishes

Bottom-dwelling fishes feed voraciously on invertebrates and each other. Modifications such as camouflaged and flattened bodies, retractable fishing lures, and sense organs developed from fins enable these species to live and hunt successfully on the ocean floor.

A blackbacked flounder lies camouflaged, waiting to seize its prey—usually small invertebrates. Flounders change color and pattern to blend with the sea floor.

A squirrel hake probes the sea floor for food with fins that have become sensory organs. The hake uses its mouth like a steam shovel to dig small animals out of the mud.

An awkward swimmer, the comical batfish of the Galápagos Islands waddles across the bottom on its pectoral and ventral fins. It entices small fish with a retractable lure and "fishing pole"—an unusual modification of the dorsal fin.

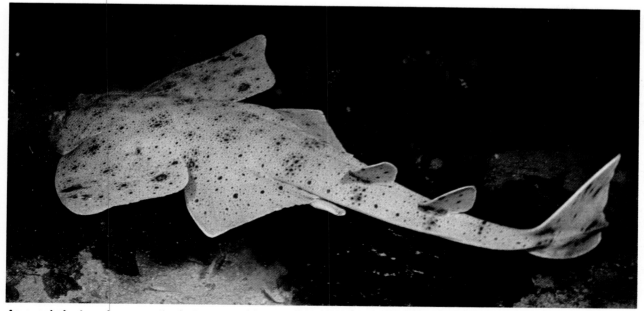

An angel shark cruises near the bottom searching for flatfishes and crustaceans. Named by pious medieval observers who mistook the broad pectoral and pelvic fins for wings, the squat, bottom-dwelling angels are the flattest sharks.

Vital nutrients, lifted from the depths by upwelling currents, enrich upper waters and renew the marine cycle of life

The seasons in shallow, temperate seas are well defined. In spring, sunlight pours into water rich in nutrients stirred up from the bottom by winter storms. A phytoplankton bloom results, followed by zooplankton growth. By summer, most nutrients are used up in the warm surface layer, and colder, well-fertilized waters do not rise. Plants and animals die. Mixing resumes in the fall, and there is a brief bloom of life. In winter, weak sunlight discourages plant growth, but with spring's arrival, a new cycle of life begins.

On some parts of the continental shelves, nutrient-rich waters rise to the surface throughout the year. These areas of continuous upwelling are the richest in the sea and produce almost half the world's supply of fish.

Upwelling occurs when offshore winds and strong currents carry water away from the land, or when two currents diverge. Mineral-laden waters from the depths rise to fill the gap. Such fertile areas of upwelling exist off the west coasts of Africa and South America and off California and southern Arabia.

In the coastal waters of Peru, westward-blowing trade winds and the cold Humboldt Current from the south combine to produce an upwelling that gives rise to the world's largest fishery. More tuna are caught here than anywhere else. The largest black marlin ever recorded—a 1560-pound giant—was taken within sight of the Andes Mountains.

It is the silvery anchovies, however, that make the Peruvian coastal waters unique. Millions of tons of these small fish are netted every year. Large shimmering patches of foam mark the

Seasons in the Coastal Seas

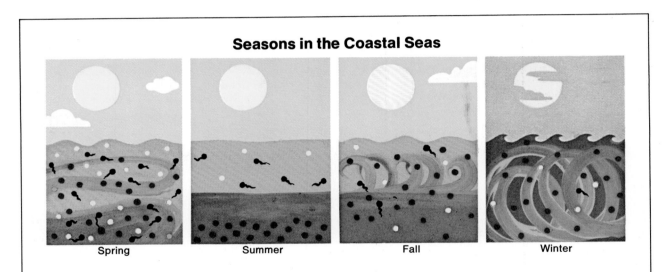

Spring   Summer   Fall   Winter

Spring is the season of lush growth in the sea. The sun rises higher each day and nutrients (red dots), carried to the sunlit top layers of coastal waters by winter storms, are abundant. Planktonic plants (yellow dots) flourish and the tiny animals (black dots) that eat these plants multiply rapidly. In summer, sunlight is ample, but warm upper waters do not mix with cooler nutrient-rich deeper waters. Plant and animal populations diminish drastically. In the fall, as upper waters cool, the circulation of nutrients from bottom to surface resumes. Plants—and animals—thrive briefly under the weak autumnal sun. Winter storms stir the coastal seas deeply, bringing huge amounts of nutrients to the surface to lie unused until the strengthening sunlight of spring again causes the rebirth of life in the sea.

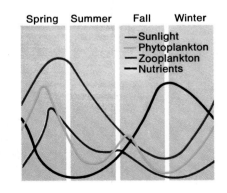

Spring   Summer   Fall   Winter

—Sunlight
—Phytoplankton
—Zooplankton
—Nutrients

Peruvian guanays, unlike other cormorants that search for fish underwater, sight their prey from the air and hunt in vast flocks for anchovies, their favorite fish. A large bird colony may consume over thirty million anchovies every day.

places where immense schools of anchovies graze on phytoplankton, especially diatoms. Most anchovies are not directly consumed by humans; they are ground into fish meal for cattle, swine, and poultry.

Huge flocks of birds vie with fishermen for anchovies. Long-necked cormorants dive into glittering schools, gulping fish until they can eat no more. Flocks of flying boobies plunge into the water as a single mass. Gannets drop like rocks, disappear, and emerge with fish. Brown pelicans bob on the surface and thrust long bills into the sea. Mounds of guano—nitrogen-rich bird dung—cover the cliffs and islands of the Peruvian coast, where the birds roost and nest. Valuable as fertilizer, the guano has brought more wealth to Peru than all the gold and silver wrested by the Incas from their mountain mines.

El Niño

The trade winds from the southeast, which help push the waters of the Humboldt Current past Peru, usually slacken during the southern summer. About every seventh year, these winds diminish so much that the Humboldt Current is displaced. Warm, nutrient-poor equatorial waters travel southward along the Peruvian coast, and little upwelling occurs. The warm current is known as El Niño, "The Child," because it arrives during the Christmas season.

El Niño brings no joy. It chokes off supplies of nutrients, and planktonic plants die by the billions. Some anchovies swim to cooler, richer waters, but many also die. Numerous seabirds, especially young fledglings, starve as their food supply dwindles. Guano production decreases, and there is a shortage of fertilizer.

El Niño is a dramatic example—and warning—of what happens when the first link in the food chain is weakened. In 1965, cormorants nesting on the shores and islands off Peru numbered twenty million. El Niño came that year. Four years later the cormorant population was only about six million, and the guano harvest had plummeted from 170,000 tons to a scant 35,000. Fishermen blame El Niño for the decline. But guano harvesters blame the fishermen; so many anchovies are caught, they say, that the birds are starving. Anchovy catches jumped drastically in the 1950s and 1960s, and the drop in the number of birds may indeed be due to excessive fishing.

Conservationists fear that if the birds die off, the anchovies may disappear as well. In the truly interdependent communities along these shores, fish rely on birds as much as birds on fish. Nitrogen- and mineral-rich guano fertilizes the water when El Niño chokes off nutrients from the deep. If the supply of guano is drastically depleted, the fishing grounds may not recover the next time El Niño returns.

A dredging barge scrapes oysters from the bottom off the New England coast. Fishermen spread oyster shells on the seabed so that two-week-old spat can attach. The young are protected from predators such as crabs and oyster drills; mature oysters are harvested about four years later. Oysters are also farmed in Chesapeake Bay and on the Gulf coast.

Sea farming and improved fishing techniques increase annual seafood harvests, but the possible yields are limited

The plight of the Peruvian fishery demonstrates that man cannot continue to take more and more out of coastal seas without eventually endangering their productivity. Improved fishing techniques alone will not guarantee larger future catches. Only by intensively cultivating coastal waters can man greatly increase the annual seafood harvest. Instead of searching miles of water and dragging nets and hooks below the surface, he can rear fish and shellfish in coastal waters just as he rears cattle and crops on land.

Aquaculture—the application of farming techniques to raising animals and plants in fresh, brackish, or salt water—embraces everything from merely transplanting animals from one unattended "pasture" to another to raising them in enclosures where they are fed automatically by machine, given hormones to increase the number of their offspring, and bred selectively.

Biologists John H. Ryther and John E. Bardach surveyed aquaculture's world potential for the National Council on Marine Resources and Engineering Development of the U.S. government. They determined that more high-grade animal protein can be produced in an acre of coastal water than on an acre of fertile land. An advanced pig farm produces twenty-five tons of live pigs per acre yearly, while an oyster farm produces fifty tons of oysters (shells excluded) and a trout farm about forty tons of trout. Mussels raised on rafts in Spain annually yield as much as 120 tons of nourishing, tasty meat per acre.

According to Ryther and Bardach, a body of coastal water the size of Long Island Sound could produce each year an amount of mussel meat equal to three times the total current fish catch of the world. And sewage might be used to fertilize such a sea farm in Long Island Sound. By the year 2000, New York City will have to dispose of a billion gallons of raw sewage every day. Ryther and Bardach propose treating this effluent to release inorganic nutrients, then diluting these with twenty-four billion gallons of water. This solution could fertilize a twelve-mile by three-mile by ten-foot-deep aquafarm, promoting the growth of 1000 tons of diatoms and other one-celled plants a day. These in turn would provide food for shrimp, oysters, or mussels, which could be harvested at the rate of 100 tons a day.

The Japanese lead the world in aquaculture. In Japan, shrimp farming is a highly profitable business. Adult shrimp spawn in laboratories, and

Green turtle hatchlings *are reared in pens on Grand Cayman Island in the Caribbean. Later they will be placed in fenced-off coastal areas to fatten for market on turtle grass.*

Fingerling steelhead trout, *yolk sacs still attached, cluster in a Pacific coast hatchery. Selective breeding of trout and salmon produces meatier and hardier species of fish.*

their offspring live in controlled environments until they reach market size. The very young are fed diatoms and flagellates. As they grow, they receive brine shrimp, then a diet of ground up scrap fish, unmarketable shrimp, mussels, and clams. These Japanese methods have been exported to the United States, and shrimp farms have been established in Florida waters under the tutelage of experienced Japanese aquaculturists.

Japanese sea farms also produce fishes, such as yellowtails, puffers, filefishes, porgies, and sea eels. The puffer production goes mainly to restaurants in big cities. Yellowtails, on the other hand, are basic staple in the Japanese diet. Young yellowtails gathered from the sea mature in nylon net bags attached to bamboo frames floating in bays. The fish are fed anchovies, sand eels, horse mackerel, and manufactured food.

Japanese yellowtail farms produce as much as 126 tons per acre per year, or 62 pounds of fish per square yard. This figure sounds incredible, but market-size, two-pound fish are removed and juveniles added continuously. Ryther and Bardach regard the success of yellowtail farming as proof that millions of fish can be raised on sea farms in coastal waters.

In the United States, trout and salmon are hatchery-reared from eggs to the migration stage. Turned loose to fend for themselves in the open ocean, they reach market size without expense or labor. Eventually they return to the hatchery and are selectively bred.

Dr. Lauren Donaldson, a scientist at the University of Washington, has raised salmon that grow faster and larger, produce bigger eggs, and are more resistant to disease and temperature changes than other salmon. Some of his salmon have a survival rate in the open sea as high as thirty times the natural one.

Aquaculture and improved fishing techniques can probably further increase the annual seafood harvests, but there are limits to how much can be taken from the sea. John Ryther believes that the annual harvest cannot much exceed 100 million tons. Several other scientists are more optimistic and believe the harvest could reach 550 million tons—or about ten times the amount of seafood caught annually in the late 1960s—if fishermen would pursue marine species not presently being exploited.

The sea can no longer be considered a copious horn of plenty with enough food to solve any world shortage. Sardines are gone from the California coast; mackerel populations have declined in the North Atlantic; several species of whales are nearly extinct. It will take greater intelligence than man has yet shown, and that most difficult effort, international cooperation, to increase seafood yields without irreparably damaging the ocean's fragile food chains.

The Coral Reef Community

*Inch by inch, year by year, a coral reef grows as millions
of tiny animals deposit their limestone skeletons. This living
labyrinth, while massive, is astonishingly vulnerable*

Nowhere on Earth does life exhibit a greater diversity of color and shape than in the coral reefs. They are the cities of the underwater world— crowded, bustling communities populated by creatures belonging to nearly every major group in the animal kingdom.

Reef dwellers have evolved a spectacular variety of adaptations and associations while competing —and sometimes cooperating—in the struggle to find food, to protect themselves from predators, and to reproduce their kind. Female crabs dwell in cloistered coral chambers, safe from predators but imprisoned for life. Fanworms, undersea relatives of the familiar earthworm, filter food from the water with gorgeous, feather-like tentacles that withdraw into leathery tubes the instant a shadow passes overhead. Fishes with teeth fused into strong beaks pulverize coral rock as they graze on algae encrusting the reef. Four-foot, quarter-ton clams take nourishment from microscopic plants growing inside their own bodies.

Everywhere in the coral reef world there are dazzling colors: in the myriads of scuttling, creeping, burrowing worms, mollusks, and crustaceans; in the flower-like anemones and the five-armed starfishes; in the darting, boldly patterned fishes; in the multiform corals themselves. Some animals are made conspicuous by their brilliant coloration, which may scare away potential predators or help attract a mate. Other creatures are so perfectly camouflaged that they are indistinguishable from their surroundings.

The reef itself is the work of living things. Coral animals change minerals dissolved in seawater into the limestone of the reef. Other animals, such as clams and tubeworms, contribute the hard parts of their skeletons to the reef. Lime-secreting plants, the coralline algae, repair the windward edge of the reef by cementing loose pieces of coral rock into near-solid ramparts. Powdered remains of one-celled organisms settle in and fill the tiniest openings.

Formed over many centuries, coral reefs expand an inch or two each year, and in volume dwarf man's mightiest structures. The largest of all, the Great Barrier Reef, extends for nearly 1300 miles along the northeastern coast of Australia. It could supply enough limestone to build some eight million replicas of Egypt's largest pyramid.

Unlike a static construction of man, a coral reef is a dynamic creation. Some organisms are constantly building it up, while others are tearing it down. The result is a labyrinth of ledges, crannies, grottoes, crevices, and tunnels.

A school of grunts hovers before a treelike colony of sea whips. Named for the sound they make by grinding their teeth together, grunts are common inhabitants of Caribbean reefs. They cluster by day in isolated reefs, but spread out at night to feed individually in nearby seaweed beds.

An immense breakwater, the Great Barrier Reef stretches 1300 miles along the northeastern coast of Australia. Fifty-acre Heron Island, at the center of this aerial view, is one of hundreds of islands dotting the reef.

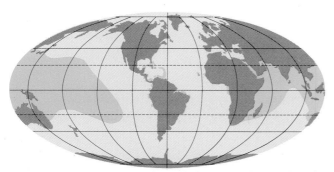

Reef-building corals flourish only in warm, clear, relatively shallow water. Shaded regions on the map indicate coral reef areas. There are three types of coral reefs: fringing reefs, which extend directly out from the shore; barrier reefs, parallel to the shore but separated from land by deep water; and coral atolls of the open sea, narrow circular reefs enclosing lagoons.

Building a Coral Reef

Probably you have handled pieces of dried, bleached coral skeleton. If you looked closely, you might have noticed that the surfaces were riddled with tiny, cup-shaped pits. These pits were the homes of the individual coral animals, or polyps. Relatives of sea anemones and jellyfishes, these stony corals are the chief architects of reefs.

A coral colony may consist of thousands of polyps, all arising from a single individual. The colony begins life when a free-swimming, near-microscopic coral larva attaches to a solid support—often the remains of its own ancestors. Once anchored, the larva grows, changes shape, and secretes a limestone cup around itself. New polyps then bud from the sides of this first individual. These in turn grow and produce buds of their own, each attached to its parent by a veil of living tissue that may be brown, lavender, yellow, green, crimson, or pink. The colony grows upward and outward, gradually assuming a shape characteristic of its species. Names given to a few of the hundreds of species of stony corals suggest their diversity of shape: staghorn, elkhorn, brain, finger, flower, star, cactus.

A coral polyp's vase-shaped body is topped by a ring of feeding tentacles. The soft body tissues are housed in the protective limestone cup. When it is not feeding or is disturbed, the animal draws its tentacles into the cup. Most stony corals feed at night, and daytime visitors seldom see the expanded polyps.

Coral animals do not dwell alone in their stony apartments. Dinoflagellates also live within their body tissues. The exact nature of the relationship between the polyps and their plant tenants is unknown, but it appears to be beneficial to both.

Coral animals offer their plant guests a sheltered environment rich in carbon dioxide. This gas, given off as a waste product by coral, is one of the raw materials necessary for photosynthesis. In using the carbon dioxide, the plants act as a built-in disposal system, and they may also help out in the secretion of limestone. Whatever is involved in this plant-animal partnership, it is certain that stony corals form reefs only when they harbor dinoflagellates in abundance.

A single coral colony does not constitute a coral reef. A reef is a complex of many colonies and many different kinds of coral, most growing on the limestone laid down by past generations. The Great Barrier Reef contains over 350 species and millions of active colonies.

Not all corals are reef builders. Some stony corals live as solitary individuals, each in a separate limestone cup. Other corals, known as soft corals, lack the limestone skeletons of their stony relatives. When solitary and soft corals die, they contribute very little material to the reef.

The principal coral reefs of the world exist within a 3600-mile-wide band extending about thirty degrees north and south of the Equator, or roughly from the latitude of northern Florida to that of southern Brazil. Reef-building corals only grow in warm, clear water less than 150 feet deep, where there is enough light for their plant partners to carry on photosynthesis. They do not grow along the west coasts of continents where cold currents and upwellings chill the sea. Their growth is also inhibited by silt, which blocks the light and has a suffocating effect. Hence corals are not found, for example, where the sediment-laden Mississippi empties into the Gulf of Mexico.

The Coral Animal

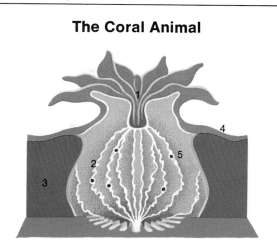

Tentacles around the mouth (1) of a coral polyp capture food, which is digested by filaments (2) lining the central cavity. The soft polyp secretes limestone partitions and a stony cup (3), which protect it. A thin tissue layer (4) links neighboring polyps. Reproductive organs (5) produce both eggs and sperm. Fertilized eggs hatch into larvae, swim about briefly, then settle on a hard surface. The single polyp then produces a new colony by budding or fission.

In budding, new polyps form from cells of the live tissue connecting mature polyps. The new polyps immediately begin secreting their own stony cups.

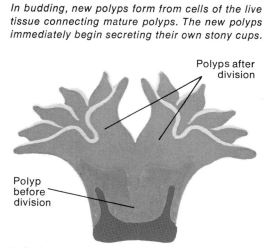

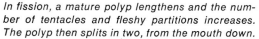

In fission, a mature polyp lengthens and the number of tentacles and fleshy partitions increases. The polyp then splits in two, from the mouth down.

The Colorful, Carnivorous Corals

The limy skeletons of stony coral colonies make up the bulk of most coral reefs. The carnivorous, tentacled polyps of a living colony are linked to one another by a mantle of flesh that covers the skeleton, and each feeds all the others. As the polyps divide, or as new polyps bud from the old, the colony grows upward and outward as much as an inch or two each year. The soft corals, most of them stiffened by crystals or by horny, flexible skeletons, contribute little to the reef's structure. Unlike reef-building stony corals, soft corals can live far from the Equator in the cool waters of temperate and polar seas.

A mushroom coral is a single giant polyp housed in a stony skeleton up to seven inches long. This specimen withdrew its tentacles into the central mouth.

The inch-long tubular polyps of cup coral emerge at night to feed. They form small colonies in shaded areas of reefs.

The thousands of tiny polyps fringing this sea fan's branches are expanded and feeding in a strong current. When the current slackens, the polyps will contract.

Finger coral may sometimes spread for acres in shallow water where sunlight is intense and currents are strong. Polyps are extended and feeding on some of the "fingers" shown here, but are contracted and inactive on others.

Bubble

Tree

Brain

Staghorn

Elkhorn

Lettuce

Seiners and Sifters

Many reef animals, including the corals, move very slowly or are entirely immobile during their adult lives. Instead of chasing after prey, they sift through the sand or catch food the currents bring near them.

The tentacles of coral polyps, like those of jellyfishes, are studded with batteries of poison-injecting nematocysts. Any small creature unlucky enough to brush against a tentacle is quickly paralyzed, and passed through the mouth into the polyp's digestive cavity.

Some corals have short tentacles lined with minute, hairlike structures, called cilia, that help bring food to the mouth. Beating rhythmically, cilia set up water currents strong enough to waft small prey inward along the tentacles. When the polyp is not feeding, the ciliary beat reverses direction, sweeping away silt and other debris.

Similar to corals in both body plan and feeding habits are the sea anemones, close relatives of the corals. Anemones are found in all the world's oceans from the tropics to the poles, and from the tidal zone to the abyssal depths. But these flowerlike animals reach their fullest development on coral reefs. Cold-water anemones usually measure only a few inches across, while some reef species exceed three feet in diameter.

An anemone looks like a single coral polyp; its hollow, cylindrical body is topped by one or more rings of stinging tentacles surrounding a central mouth. Depending on the size of the anemone, its prey may be microscopic zooplankton or small fishes and crabs.

A sea anemone usually remains fixed to a hard surface by a muscular, mucus-secreting plate, but if a location ceases to suit its needs, the animal can move around. Some anemones creep snail fashion, at a top speed of about four inches an hour, by rippling contractions of their base plates. A few turn themselves over and "tiptoe" on the ends of their tentacles, or lie on their sides and inch along the bottom like measuring worms.

More mobile than anemones, sausage-shaped sea cucumbers crawl along the floor of the reef on tube feet resembling those of their starfish relatives. Some cucumbers plow through bottom sand feeding on detritus; others use their tentacles to net plankton. Any small organism touched by a cucumber's sticky tentacles is trapped as surely as a fly on flypaper. From time to time each tentacle is pushed into the mouth and the accumulation of victims is consumed.

Several sea cucumbers are equipped with an extraordinary defense mechanism. When one is disturbed, it contracts its body violently, and expels a tangled mass of internal organs from its rear opening. This act of self-evisceration does not permanently harm the sea cucumber; it possesses remarkable powers of regeneration and replaces

A bronze-spot sea cucumber crept too close to a damselfish nest on the sandy floor of the Great Barrier Reef. The sea cucumber was repeatedly sideswiped by the damselfish, a six-inch vegetarian intent on defending the eggs. In a fright reaction, the sea cucumber ejected a mass of white threads, like strands of spaghetti. They become extremely sticky on contact with salt water, and are distasteful to fishes. These threads are strong enough to entangle and immobilize smaller crustaceans.

the lost organs within a few weeks.

One of the reef's most beautiful plankton gatherers is the delicate feather star. Forming a lacy bowl with its branching, cilia-lined arms, it wafts tiny prey into a central mouth. A feather star anchors itself to a coral branch or other support with a cluster of clinging appendages, or cirri. Although it tends to remain stationary for long periods, it can creep along on its cirri or swim by slowly flapping its arms.

The feather star's ancestors carpeted great stretches of ocean floor 300 million years ago, and from them and other ancient relatives all modern echinoderms, or spiny-skinned animals, are descended. The echinoderms include starfishes, sea urchins, and sea cucumbers, and they are characterized by tube feet and symmetrical bodies divided into five parts or multiples thereof.

The little female gall crab is among the most curious plankton eaters of the reef. After passing through several free-swimming larval stages, she settles down on a coral branch. By some means not fully understood, she alters the coral's growth so that a limestone chamber, or gall, forms around her. Currents set in motion by her gills bring oxygen and plankton through pores in the gall. At breeding time the pores also admit a tiny male gall crab—which otherwise leads a free, but more hazardous life on the reef's surface. The pair mate and their offspring drift out through the pores.

A white feather star, perched on a cluster of red sea whips, fans out twenty arms to catch what the current brings. Each arm has a groove lined with whips that pass microscopic food particles into the central mouth.

A Female Gall Crab Imprisons Herself for Life in a Coral Cell

A young female gall crab settles on a coral branch (left) and in some way stimulates the coral to grow into a protective shell. The coral walls eventually meet above the crab, forming a hollow chamber, or gall (center). Water bearing oxygen and food circulates through small openings. The tiny male crab swims in these openings for mating. New branches sprout from the gall (right) as coral growth continues.

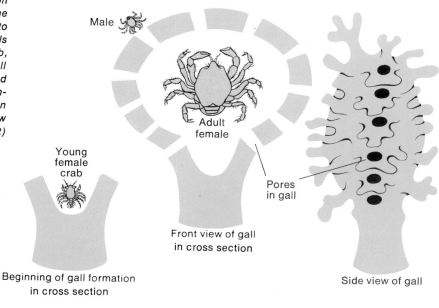

Male

Adult female

Pores in gall

Young female crab

Beginning of gall formation in cross section

Front view of gall in cross section

Side view of gall

Stalking small fishes and other reef animals is a host of hunters without backbones — shrimps, slugs, and snails

Not all reef invertebrates passively filter plankton from the water; many are skilled and active hunters. The skeleton shrimp, a gaunt, transparent animal less than an inch long, prowls the coral in search of prey. Its two pairs of hooked, grasping appendages are poised like the forelegs of a praying mantis, ready to snatch at any small creature that ventures too close.

The "gunman" of the reefs is the two-inch pistol shrimp. One of its claws is greatly enlarged and modified so that when the "thumb" is snapped sharply against the "palm," a loud bang results.

The shrimp, lying in ambush in a coral crevice, has only its sensitive antennae exposed. At the approach of a small fish, the shrimp rushes forward, aims its pistol at the victim, and pulls the trigger. The shock wave momentarily stuns the fish. Before it can recover, the victim is captured.

Reef snails and slugs are far more colorful and active than their placid dry-land and freshwater relatives. Cowries, much prized by collectors for their exquisitely patterned shells, feed on a wide variety of animals including coral polyps; the striped helmet snail devours spiny sea urchins; the trumpet snail preys upon clams and starfishes.

The most dangerous of the predatory marine snails are the cone shells. Instead of the file-like feeding apparatus of most snails, a cone shell has a proboscis armed with minute hollow darts that inject potent venom. When a fish or worm comes within striking range, the cone shell swiftly pushes its proboscis against the victim and releases a

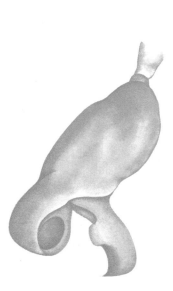

Claws at the ready, a pistol shrimp waits for prey beneath the tentacles of a sea anemone. One of the two fingers on its large right claw is equipped with a peg that fits into a socket on the other finger. When powerful muscles snap the fingers together, the shock waves produced by the sudden expulsion of water from the socket can stun a small fish long enough for the shrimp to grab it.

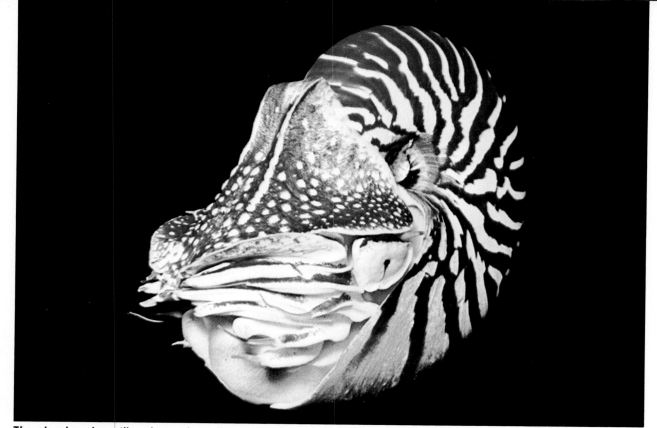

The chambered nautilus descends to the ocean floor or ascends to shallow reefs by adjusting the amounts of gas in its more than thirty chambers. Distant relative of the octopus, it snares its prey with many small tentacles.

Undulating its body, a brightly colored sea slug glides through the reef waters. This species, one of the more mobile, has the exposed gill tufts (right) and sensory tentacles (left) typical of sea slugs.

Poisoning a cousin for a meal, one species of cone snail stings another. Other cone snails paralyze passing fishes or worms with their venom-filled harpoons, which are modifications of the raspy snail "tongue," or radula.

dart. Once paralyzed, the prey is slowly engulfed by the proboscis and consumed.

Should an unwary shell collector wading on the Great Barrier Reef pick up a cone shell, he would be likely to feel a sharp, jabbing pain in his palm, followed by numbness, tingling, and spreading paralysis. Coma could ensue, and possibly death from cardiac arrest within four or five hours. Cone shells are the only snails fatal to man.

Nudibranchs, or sea slugs, are among the most beautiful of the coral reef's invertebrates. *Nudibranch* means "naked gill" and refers to the feathery respiratory organs projecting from the creatures' backs. Although nudibranchs are not closely related to land slugs, both are essentially snails that have lost their shells.

Nudibranchs range in length from an inch to a foot and sport the most garish color combinations imaginable: striped, spotted, or solid patterns of deep blue, azure, electric pink, crimson, bright orange, or yellow, often with gills and head tentacles of contrasting colors. Usually a nudibranch glides along on a flat, muscular foot, but it can swim short distances.

Nudibranchs eat animals no other predators seem to want: sponges filled with needle-like spicules and anemones armed with stinging nematocysts. As a nudibranch feeds on an anemone, the nematocysts that it swallows are somehow "defused" and fail to discharge. But this neat trick of

adaptation does not end here. As the still-intact nematocysts pass through the slug's intestine, they penetrate the intestine wall, migrate through the body, and finally come to rest in the skin of the slug's back. There they accumulate and protect the slug against predators—just as they had previously protected their original owner.

The Eight-Armed Predators

The reef's largest and most formidable invertebrate predator is the octopus. Across the widest span of its eight rubbery arms, an octopus may measure from two inches to more than thirty feet, but the species found in coral reefs seldom exceed two feet. The octopus possesses eyes as highly developed as our own, and the most sophisticated brain of all the invertebrates.

The octopus is a master of disguise. With dazzling rapidity, it changes its color from chocolate brown to milky white to brilliant green or bright red as it glides across the shifting background of the reef. In shallow water, the waves of color moving across its body duplicate the stippled pattern of sunlight in the ripples overhead. Fright, anger, and excitement elicit vivid blushes.

The sinister reputation of the octopus is really undeserved. A timid and retiring creature, it responds to the approach of a swimmer by retreating. Sufficiently provoked, however, the octopus delivers a nasty, venomous bite from a parrot-like beak. Luckily, such occurrences are rare.

The octopus feeds on fish and crustaceans, especially crabs. Its sinuous, sucker-covered arms as well as its high intelligence make it a superb hunter. With catlike stealth, it slowly moves near its prey. Then, in a flash, it pounces. After injecting the victim with a numbing venom it closes its powerful beak, and the shellfish is crushed.

The octopus hunts at night and retires to its den—either a natural crevice in the reef or a scooped-out hollow beneath a rock—during the day. Outside the entrance to the den is a pile of empty crab shells; the entrance itself is usually no wider than an octopus's arm, since the animal has an extraordinary ability to squeeze through small openings.

The nemesis of the octopus is the savage moray eel. Although the moray's usual diet consists of crabs, shrimps, and fishes, it also preys upon the octopus, if only because both sometimes seek out the same hole to hide in during the day. But the octopus is not entirely defenseless: it may confound its attacker with a cloud of ink and then scurry to safety.

Largest and brainiest reef invertebrate, the sharp-eyed octopus—here coiled in its burrow after a shellfish dinner—appears ferocious, with its staring eyes and sucker-covered arms. Actually, it is timid and unaggressive.

The octopus is a mollusk, although it lacks the shell of its distant ancestors. (Some species have a vestigial internal shell, as do the squids.) Inside the flabby, saclike body of the octopus are its internal organs. A slightly narrowed "neck" joins the body to the head. The powerful, parrotlike beak is on the underside of the head and cannot be seen from above. Springing from the head are eight muscular arms, joined at their bases by a web. Octopuses normally crawl along the bottom on their arms, but they can also swim by jetting water from their siphons or by flapping their webs.

Reef Builders and Reef Destroyers

Many creatures live and die on the coral reef without changing it in any apparent way. Feather stars cling to it, crabs scuttle across it, octopuses lurk in its crevices, and all leave few marks. But there are creatures that profoundly affect the reef's structure. Some strengthen it by cementing loose pieces of coral together, some contribute shells and hard parts when they die. Others scrape away at the reef's surface, bore holes in it, or eat the living coral polyps, stinging tentacles and all.

Sponges are simple animals found on all coral reefs; they can be either reef builders or reef destroyers. Little more than pore-riddled masses of gelatinous material, sponges are sometimes interlaced with particles of limestone or silica. They constantly pump a current of water through their bodies by means of "whip-bearing cells" lining their interiors. The flow of water brings in oxygen and food (bacteria, plankton, and bits of decaying organic matter) and carries away waste products.

Even a small sponge passes a surprisingly large amount of water through its body in the course of a day. A sponge of the genus *Leuconia*, about four inches tall and half an inch in diameter, pumps more than five gallons every twenty-four hours. A large reef sponge may pump several hundred gallons in the same period.

Sponges thrive in the clear, silt-free waters of

A two-foot-wide giant clam *displays its mottled dark-blue mantle as it filters plankton from the water. When the shadow of a predator passes over the light-sensitive mantle, the clam's massive fluted shell closes with tremendous force.*

coral reefs, and often grow as big as washtubs. Their presence is usually constructive, for many species hold together fragments of coral, much as plants on a hillside hold the soil in place. However, one family of sponges, the boring sponges, are reef destroyers. They tunnel their way into the coral, hollowing out galleries that weaken the limestone. This boring process is not fully understood, but entails the sponge's removal of tiny limestone chips—a remarkable accomplishment for so lowly an animal.

There are also boring species in the reef's clam population. Some clams rasp away the limestone with the edges of their serrated shells; others dissolve it with acid secretions. When they die, they leave their shells imbedded in the reef, partially compensating for the damage they did while alive.

The giant clam of the Indo-Pacific coral reefs is a supplier of building material. The biggest clam in the world, it produces fluted shells up to four feet wide, weighing as much as 500 pounds. Aside from sheer bulk, the giant clam's most distinctive feature is the "farming" it does to supplement its diet of plankton. Swarms of one-celled plants live in its body tissues, just as they do in coral polyps. These plants absorb some of the clam's wastes and provide it with oxygen and food substances through photosynthesis. In addition, surplus plants are periodically "harvested" as food by the immense bivalve.

Two families of fanworms, relatives of the common earthworm, also help build the reef by constructing protective tubes for their soft bodies. Serpulid worms use limestone taken from seawater; sabellid worms secrete mucus to cement together grains of sand.

Both kinds of worms possess gorgeous crowns of delicate feeding and respiratory tentacles. These tentacles have light-sensitive organs so that the mere shadow of a passing fish causes the whole array to close up—like an umbrella turned inside out—and swiftly disappear into the tube. Sometimes the fanworms are not fast enough, however, for their crowns have been found in the stomachs of reef fishes.

Worms can also weaken the coral structure in a variety of ways. There are species that feed on the reef's cementing coat of coralline algae, or on the coral itself, or on the dinoflagellates living in the coral polyps. Other species, like the sixteen-inch palolo worm, bore into the coral. This worm passes the day deep within the reef and emerges at night to forage for small invertebrates. The palolo worm burrows through the reefs of the South Pacific; a related species does similar damage to the reefs in the Caribbean.

Reef-Burrowing Palolo Worms Multiply After Dividing

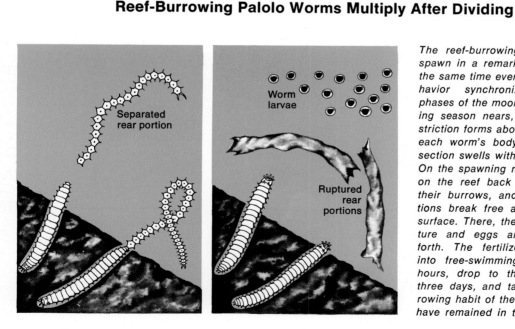

Separated rear portion

Worm larvae

Ruptured rear portions

The reef-burrowing palolo worms spawn in a remarkable manner at the same time every year, their behavior synchronized with the phases of the moon. As the spawning season nears, a ringlike constriction forms about midway down each worm's body, and the hind section swells with eggs or sperm. On the spawning night, the worms on the reef back partway out of their burrows, and the hind sections break free and float to the surface. There, the thin walls rupture and eggs and sperm pour forth. The fertilized eggs hatch into free-swimming larvae within hours, drop to the bottom after three days, and take up the burrowing habit of their parents—who have remained in their tunnels.

A crown-of-thorns starfish (above) on the Great Barrier Reef slowly eats its way across a coral head, leaving a wake of dead skeletons. A triton snail (below) is not deterred by the bristling spines as it attacks a foot-wide crown-of-thorns. Removal of the triton by shell collectors may be a factor in the starfish population explosion.

The balance of life on some Indo-Pacific reefs is threatened by a coral-devouring starfish

Damage caused by boring sponges, clams, and worms does not pose a great threat to the world's reefs. Any healthy coral community maintains a dynamic balance between destructive and constructive forces. In the 1960s, however, a much more dangerous reef wrecker, a starfish, appeared in alarming numbers on Pacific reefs.

Named for the red, needle-sharp spines that cover its sixteen-armed body, the crown-of-thorns eats coral polyps. Clinging to a coral mass with dozens of tube feet, the starfish extrudes its stomach through its mouth and floods the living coral tissue with strong digestive juices. When the crown-of-thorns moves on, it leaves behind a patch of bare white coral skeleton.

Before 1960, the crown-of-thorns was something of a rarity, but by 1965 it became apparent that the species was undergoing a population explosion. Where divers had previously seen only one of the prickly stars in an hour, a hundred could be counted in ten minutes. By 1969, the crown-of-thorns had laid bare 140 square miles of Australian reefs. It was also appearing in large numbers on many Pacific reefs where it had not been seen before.

Marine biologists have been unable to isolate the cause of this population increase. Some point to human tampering with the reef's natural balance: pesticide poisoning of planktonic creatures that eat the eggs and larvae of the crown-of-thorns, or the indiscriminate collecting of the giant triton, a large snail that preys on the adult starfish. Others suggest that the population increase might occur regularly at intervals of hundreds of years.

To stop the destruction, groups of divers have collected the thorny marauders or killed them with injections of formaldehyde. Some scientists advocate breeding large armies of tritons or other predators to turn back the onslaught. Many other biologists, however, fear that a measure such as this might further upset the balance of reef life.

Until more is known about the life history of the crown-of-thorns starfish and the ecology of coral reefs, man's attempts to check this menace will probably not be successful. But reefs have survived natural disasters in the past, and most likely nature itself will correct the imbalance.

A formidable predator, the barracuda, which may reach five or six feet in length, has been known to attack man. To feed, it rips through a school of fish, slashing and tearing with its sharp teeth, then swims back to eat the pieces.

Coral Reef Fishes

Adapt or perish is the first rule of life everywhere. In the severely competitive setting of the coral community, fishes have evolved a fantastic array of adaptations to ensure their survival.

The four-foot moray eels have muscular, snakelike bodies with no side fins. Adapted for life in the reef's holes and crevices, moray eels are found nowhere else. Using their sharp, grasping teeth and keen sense of smell, they probe deep into the nooks and crannies for octopuses, fishes, crabs, and shrimps.

Morays do not make unprovoked attacks on swimmers, but a diver who reaches into a moray den may be bitten. Contrary to popular belief, moray bites are not poisonous, but they easily become infected.

When morays retire for the day, the barracudas come out to hunt. In many ways, a barracuda's tactics are the opposite of an eel's. It patrols sunlit, open waters, relying on its sharp eyesight and great speed. When a school of fish comes within striking range, the barracuda passes through it in a single rush, slashing and tearing with knifelike teeth. Then the barracuda returns at leisure to feed on the fragments. Barracudas reach six feet in length and have jaws capable of severing a human arm or leg in a single snap.

Two parrotfish slumber in a coral crevice, snug in silvery mucus cocoons secreted each night by glands in their skin. The mucus cover, which may protect the fish from enemies, is open-ended to allow water to pass over the gills while the fish rest. Parrotfish are named for the powerful beaks they use to crunch living coral, a dietary staple.

As a defense against the tearing, stabbing teeth of predators, some reef fishes have evolved suits of protective armor, often at the expense of mobility. The trunkfish lives within a bony box almost like the shell of a turtle. Propelled only by the paddling of its small fins, it is a slow and awkward swimmer. The closely related filefish is plated with small, prickly scales that give its skin the texture of sandpaper.

A rough, leathery skin also protects the triggerfish, which carries a unique defensive weapon: a three-spined dorsal fin that can be locked into an upright position. At the approach of danger, the fish darts headfirst into a coral crevice and wedges itself in tightly by erecting this fin. No amount of tugging can dislodge it.

Several kinds of surgeonfishes carry a pair of switchblades on either side of their body near the tail. Each is a razor-sharp spine. When threatened, a surgeonfish gives a warning sweep of its tail. If the intruder persists, the surgeonfish waves its tail violently from side to side. Once the danger has passed, it returns to placidly grazing on algae.

Some fishes avoid being eaten simply by being unpalatable. The soapfish responds to attack by exuding a sudsy froth of mucus that may be poisonous. Certain species of parrotfish spend the night in loose-fitting "cocoons" of stringy mucus secreted by their skin. Quite a few reef fishes are poisonous to man, so it seems likely that some are poisonous to other fishes as well.

A number of reef-dwelling fishes rely on tricks of behavior to elude predators. Brightly colored, four-inch damselfishes never venture far from tangles of coral branches, and they quickly seek shelter at the first sign of trouble. When the pearly razorfish, which feeds on small mollusks of the reef floor, senses danger, it simply dives headfirst into the sand and buries itself. The yellowhead jawfish excavates a twelve-inch burrow in the sand and lines it with pebbles. Hovering tail-down just outside this home, it feeds on plankton. Should a large creature approach, the jawfish backs into the safety of its fortress.

When threatened, the spiny puffer pumps water into itself until it looks like a thorn-covered ball. Faced with the impossibility of swallowing something like this, the attacker retreats. When taken out of water, the puffer gives the same performance, using air to inflate itself.

Camouflage is vital to reef dwellers. They mimic coral and plants, or change color to blend with the background

Color plays a vital role in the lives of fishes that live in the coral reef's shallow, well-lighted waters. Camouflage—color that conceals—serves as a device both for offense and for defense, hiding predator as well as prey.

A barracuda hovering motionless near the surface is made less conspicuous by a type of camouflage known as obliterative shading. Seen from above, the barracuda's gray-green, slightly dappled back matches the tone and texture of the water; from below, its silvery belly blends equally well with the brightly lighted surface water. Virtually all fishes that spend much time in open water have this dark-above, light-below shading.

Brightly colored reef fishes, on the other hand, would seem to advertise their presence. But strong colors, which may stand out glaringly in open water, can break up a fish's outline and make it almost invisible against the dazzling, multicolored background of a coral reef. Butter hamlets sport liveries of blue, pink, yellow, and orange, yet do not appear conspicuous against a multicolored backdrop of corals.

Another type of camouflage common among reef fishes is disruptive shading: contrasting bars, stripes, and blotches that obscure prominent body features. Butterfly fishes, damselfishes, gobies, and blennies hide large, staring eyes with black patches or bands, and wear "false eyes" on their bodies or tails that are simply dark spots ringed with contrasting colors. When a predator lunges for what appears to be the head, it often comes up with just a bit of the tail or a mouthful of water as the intended victim speeds away.

Shape as well as color can contribute to a fish's camouflage. The incredibly elongated trumpetfishes and pipefishes spend much of their time poised head-down among stands of soft corals,

The golden long-nosed butterfly fish seems to be staring with its conspicuous black eyespot—on its tail. This false eye confuses would-be predators, who often get only a mouthful of water or a bit of a tail as the six-inch butterfly fish darts quickly away. The fish's real eyes are near the front, camouflaged by the first colored band.

Like a weed-covered rock, *a ten-inch-long stonefish lies half-buried in sand, awaiting an unwary fish. Sluggish by nature, the stonefish is defended by thirteen dorsal spines carrying the most potent venom found in fishes.*

How Fishes Change Their Colors

Fishes change color when pigments in chromatophore cells in the skin expand or contract. The section of fish skin shown here has black and red chromatophores, plus cells having a white or iridescent appearance. Both red and black pigments are contracted in figure 1; red is contracted, black expanded in figure 2, and the reverse in figure 3. Both colors are expanded in figure 4. Various combinations give a wide color range; the exact shade depends on how much pigment is dispersed or contracted. Chromatophores can produce both solid colors or mottled patterns, so the fish can blend with a variegated background. Reflexes trigger the color changes.

gently swaying in unison with the waving stalks of coral.

The stonefish of the Indo-Pacific reefs is a master of disguise. Lying half buried in the sand, it looks exactly like a pitted, irregularly shaped rock, complete with encrustations of algae. When a smaller fish approaches, however, the "rock" suddenly develops a capacious mouth, and the startled victim is abruptly swallowed. Humans deceived by the stonefish's camouflage may fare little better: concealed along the fish's back are thirteen spines, whose venom can cause excrutiating pain and sometimes death.

Some fishes camouflage themselves by changing color. Cells in their outer skin, called chromatophores, contain black, brown, or gray pigment. Other cells have yellow, red, or orange substances called carotenoids (the same substances that give carrots their characteristic color). The skin also contains crystals of guanin, a reflective substance that catches the light and emits a silvery or iridescent sheen.

The pigments in the chromatophores are controlled by a finely branched network of nerves and can be expanded or contracted to expose more or less color to view. As the pigments are spread out or drawn in, hues and markings flow across the fish's body. In some species, such changes require many minutes; in others, only seconds. Tropical groupers can flash through a whole repertoire of spotted, striped, and blotched patterns in an instant. The Nassau grouper is particularly adept at changing its color scheme to match its surroundings.

Several reef fishes wear bright colors by day and take on duller colors at night—possibly to make themselves less conspicuous to predators. The Spanish grunt's silver and yellow become dull and blotched; the porkfish's large yellow dorsal fin turns black.

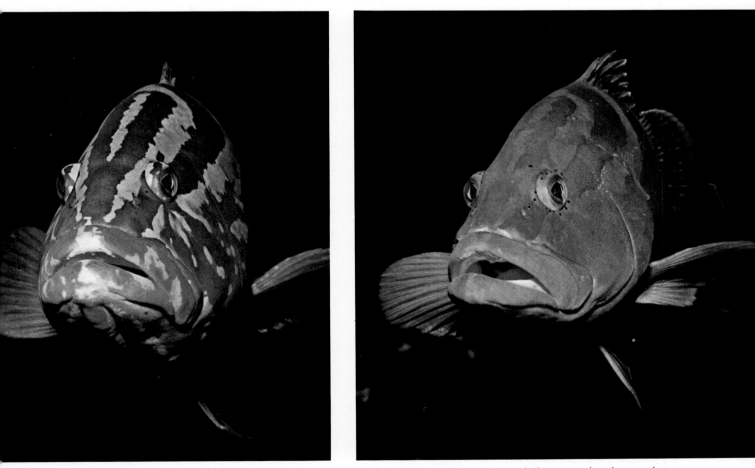

The quick-change artist of West Indian reefs, a Nassau grouper can produce eight color variations, ranging from uniformly light to mod combination of bands and blotches to austere dark. The banded pattern (left) may signify alarm.

The peacock flounder, an active hunter, matches the white sandy bottom of a Caribbean coral reef by lightening its dark rings and general coloration.

Camouflage: The Key to Survival

Camouflage is a life-or-death matter for many members of the coral reef community, enabling them to elude predators or dupe wary prey. Both deceptive shapes and disguising shading can be effective; misleading behavior may also help. Some fishes have a permanent coloration that masks them against the coral reef. Groupers change colors, adjusting to their backgrounds. Certain crabs masquerade by attaching bits of shells or seaweed to themselves. Gobies and blennies have false eyespots to fool predators; stripes hide their real eyes. Long, thin trumpetfishes sway in the current, posing as coral stalks as they await the appearance of crabs or other prey.

Cardinal fish, barely two inches long and nearly defenseless, try to evade predators by hiding amidst branches of a colony of staghorn coral. Their normal daytime hue of red fades to silver, and they virtually disappear among the light-gray staghorn coral branches. Vertical black bands help to break up their outlines.

A scorpion fish mimics the algae-encrusted rocks of a South Pacific reef. (Two spine-fringed fins are visible near the center; one eye near the pale-pink sponge at the left.) Almost perfectly camouflaged, the scorpion fish lies on the bottom snapping up smaller fishes and crustaceans that swim by. Venomous spines, though less poisonous than those of the related stonefish, can inflict painful wounds.

Barely visible against a coral reef's encrusted bottom, a lizard fish gulps down a cardinal fish tail-first. The green-and-yellow–striped onlookers are wrasses.

Hovering head-down, shrimpfishes find safety among the needle-sharp spines of a giant sea urchin. Black stripes on their side simulate the urchin's spines.

Flaunting candy-stripe patterns and strikingly bold colors, the lionfish defies aggressors. Like other members of the scorpionfish family, this eight-inch specimen is armed *with sharp—and highly venomous—dorsal spines. Lion-fishes cruise along the bottom of reefs, using their non-stinging pectoral fins to sweep fishes into their mouths.*

Gaudy colors attract a mate or warn off a rival, signal cleaner-fish or discourage predators

Scientists are cautious about assigning reasons for the brilliant hues and patterns of reef dwellers. Presumably, each color scheme has survival value, or the highly selective processes of evolution would not have produced it. However, the precise nature of this survival value is not always easy to determine.

No one seeing a stonefish can doubt the effectiveness of its extraordinary camouflage. But who can judge the extent to which predators are "fooled" by a trumpetfish's imitation of a stalk of soft coral? And a more fundamental question can be posed: If concealing coloration carries such a high degree of survival value, why are there so many coral reef fishes with color schemes that,

far from concealing them, actually seem to advertise their presence? Some intriguing answers have already been supplied by scientists, and undoubtedly more will be forthcoming as the intricate reef world becomes better understood.

Fishes with prominent defensive weapons often use conspicuous color as a warning to predators to keep their distance. On the lionfish's back is a row of brightly striped venomous spines. An animal that comes too close is likely to be severely stung and will be much less likely to come as close in the future. Similarly, the color of a surgeonfish's scalpels sometimes contrasts sharply with the rest of its body.

Bright colors frequently announce unpalatable flesh. The triggerfishes, whose flesh is poisonous or at least highly distasteful to other species, are among the most boldly colored reef fishes.

Fish learn to avoid poisonous spines and flesh the hard way; they do not inherit such behavior. Silversides are a favorite food of gray snappers on Caribbean reefs. In a laboratory study, silver-

Brightly striped South Pacific stinging catfish may be conspicuous, but they are well equipped for defense—highly venomous spines protect them from reef predators.

Conspicuous black and white lancet blades contrast with a surgeonfish's somber, speckled gray body. If threatened, it thrashes its lancet-armed tail and rips at the enemy.

sides were colored red and injected with an unpleasantly flavored chemical. At first the gray snappers preyed on the red fish, but soon began avoiding them altogether. The snappers quickly learned to associate red silversides with bad taste, and remembered this association for a relatively long time.

Conspicuous coloration sometimes serves as a sort of safe-conduct pass. The four-inch cleaner-wrasse eats parasites and dead tissue that it finds on other fishes, including predators that normally snap up small fish. The wrasse's vivid blue-and-black stripes and its dancing movements signal other fishes that it is a friend rather than a meal. Even voracious predators such as moray eels patiently submit to the picking and scraping of cleaner wrasses.

Fishes wishing to be cleaned may communicate with color. The Atlantic surgeonfish, nearing the station of a bluehead wrasse, changes from purple-brown to olive, which evidently tells the wrasse that it has come to be cleaned and will not use its sharp blades to tear the wrasse.

Some fishes mimic the conspicuous coloration of other species. The saber-toothed blenny imitates not only the color but the invitational dance of one kind of cleaner wrasse. If an unsuspecting fish approaches for a grooming, it gets instead of the expected cleaning a series of painful bites that chop away pieces of skin and fin. One quite edible filefish is carefully avoided by predators because its bright colors duplicate those of the poisonous four-saddle puffer.

Colors of Territory and Mating

Many reef fishes stake out territories and vigorously defend these feeding or breeding areas against members of the same species. Such fishes are frequently marked with distinctive color patterns that, in effect, serve as "no trespassing" signs. While territorial defense may cause occasional bloodshed between individuals of the same species, it benefits the species as a whole by keeping its members spaced out and hence not in the struggle to find their food.

Many fishes assume special courtship colors to attract mates. As is common among birds, the male is often more colorful than the female. At mating time, the male redtail parrotfish has a gorgeous green and blue body and orange-red fins; the female is a uniform pale red with a touch of bright yellow on her tail fin. Male gobies, which attract females to their lairs by elaborate courtship dances, are brilliantly colored during the breeding season.

In territorial fishes, bright patterns that ordinarily keep individuals well separated may undergo changes at mating time. Some species lose their aggression-provoking colors during courtship and regain them afterward. Others permanently abandon their gaudy livery and territorial behavior on reaching sexual maturity. The blue angelfish and the beau gregory, however, do not change their colors at mating time; males and females are paired off permanently and jointly defend territories.

Vivid rainbow colors make a harlequin tusk wrasse immediately recognizable by members of its species, and possibly caution them against territorial infringement. This wrasse feeds on shrimps and small fishes in Australian waters.

This pink-tailed triggerfish of the Great Barrier Reef, like other triggerfishes, can lock together its erect dorsal fin spines, thus wedging itself in a crevice. The gaily colored tail may signal that triggerfish flesh tastes bad.

Conspicuous—and puzzling—marks on the white-spotted triggerfish may help species members to recognize each other, warn rivals off a home fish's territory, or advise predators that a spiny triggerfish would be a prickly mouthful.

*A **squirrelfish** permits a cleaner-wrasse to scour its body. Normally the nocturnal squirrelfish feeds on smaller fishes, but the prancing ritual of the approaching inch-long juvenile wrasse inhibits attack.*

The Cleaners of the Coral Reef

*At a **reef-cleaning station**, a cleaner-wrasse (center) ministers to a school of goatfish. One goatfish (above the wrasse's tail), ready to be cleaned, signals by extending fins and barbels. The barbels are sense organs.*

Gatherings of various species of fishes at certain locations on a reef once puzzled scientists. Now it is known that the fishes are waiting to be cleaned. Some small fishes and shrimps specialize in nibbling parasites and dead tissue from larger fishes. The territories of these cleaners become established as "cleaning stations," to which clients return at regular intervals.

Bold coloring and a ritual dance identify cleaners to prospective clients and safeguard them from attack. (Many client fishes normally feed on smaller fishes and crustaceans.) Clients have their own ritual postures and motions—some even change color—to signal their readiness to be cleaned or to end the process.

Both sides benefit from the relationship. Cleaners are guaranteed an ample food supply, and clients are kept healthy.

A coral cod opens its gill covers for a cleaner-wrasse. These fearless little wrasses will also enter their clients' mouths to search for parasites and dead tissue. When the trout has had enough, it will signal the wrasse by movements.

Menacing jaws harmlessly agape, a giant moray eel welcomes the attention of a one-inch cleaner-shrimp. The shrimp waves its conspicuous antennae to attract clients, then climbs aboard to remove parasites and loose tissue.

Brightly patterned clownfishes habitually shelter from predators among the tentacles of sea anemones. The relationship appears to be mutually beneficial, for clownfishes keep their hosts free of debris and sometimes nip off diseased tentacles.

A snapping shrimp emerges from the burrow it shares with gobies, which flank the entrance. The shrimp digs the burrow and keeps it clean of debris; its tenants do not appear to contribute to the household arrangements.

Living Together

One of the most fascinating aspects of the coral community is the vast number of partnerships that exist—in some instances between animals, in others between animals and plants. Scientists use the term *symbiosis* (meaning "living together") to describe the associations, and use other, more specific terms for the various types of symbiotic relationships.

Commensalism is a partnership that may benefit one or both organisms but is not essential to the welfare of either. *Mutualism* is a relationship in which two organisms are so truly interdependent that neither can live successfully without the other. Finally, *parasitism* is an association in which one partner benefits at the expense of the other organism.

Often a particular symbiotic relationship does not fall into any of these categories. There is no clear-cut dividing line, for example, between commensalism and mutualism. In a great many cases, scientists simply do not know enough about the details of a partnership to give it a label.

Is the relationship between the coral polyps and the one-celled plants that live in their tissues an instance of mutualism or of commensalism? In nature they are always found together, which would point to mutualism. In the laboratory, however, coral polyps can be made to release the plants; the corals will continue to grow, and the plants take up life as free-swimming dinoflagellates. This suggests commensalism. Such distinctions, of course, are largely academic, and the fact remains that in the reef world many creatures live together in strange and unusual ways.

Frequently, one creature takes up residence in the living body of another. The pearlfish, for example, spends its entire adult life in the lower digestive tract of a sea cucumber, only emerging from the anal opening at night to feed. Remarkably, the fish's comings and goings do not provoke the sea cucumber to eject its internal organs, even though this reaction is easily triggered by what seem to be lesser irritations. Some observers believe that the pearlfish gets board as well as room, supplementing its diet by eating the cucumber's easily regenerated internal organs. Some pearlfishes use clams, oysters, starfishes, and other animals as homes. Another fish, the two-inch conchfish, lives in the mantle cavity of the queen conch snail.

Sometimes two different kinds of animals share the same burrow. In Indo-Pacific reefs, small gobies station themselves at the entrance to the sandy burrows of snapping shrimp. When an enemy appears, the fish dart inside. The shrimp

A slender pearlfish, its spine and internal organs showing dark through a transparent body, wriggles tailfirst into the anal opening of its host, a sea cucumber. Their relationship is completely one-sided: The pearlfish has a refuge, and occasionally a meal, when it eats the sea cucumber's easily regenerated internal organs, but the sea cucumber derives no known benefit.

Interdependent Creatures
of the Coral Reef

Reef dwellers all depend on the coral, and on each other. This assemblage includes species from Caribbean and Indo-Pacific reefs crowded together more than they would actually be on a reef. Innumerable coral polyps slowly build up the reef, aided by discarded shells and coralline algae. Meanwhile, predatory clams and starfishes rasp away the limestone and destroy the polyps. The delicate, deadly tentacles of corals and sea anemones sway in the current. Starfishes, snails, and worms crawl over the reef; more mobile mollusks and fishes flit in and out of narrow crevices. Alive with color, coral reefs are enchanted underwater gardens of the tropical seas.

1. Sea whip
2. Flamingo tongue
3. Basket star
4. Sea cucumber
5. Brain coral
6. Fanworm
7. Sergeant major
8. Encrusting sponge
9. Sea slug
10. Sea anemone
11. Cowry
12. Tube sponge
13. Giant clam
14. Coral shrimp
15. Starfish
16. Boxer crab
17. Sea fan
18. Damselfish
19. Staghorn coral
20. Parrotfish

In the coral reef world, where animals often depend on each other for food and protection, many strange partnerships are formed

may benefit by the warning; but the gobies also eat young snapping shrimp.

A number of creatures use the shells of dead animals for protection. Lacking the hard outer covering of their relatives, hermit crabs move into the shells of dead snails. As the crabs grow, they periodically "trade in" their old shells for larger ones.

Some hermit crabs gain added protection by placing sea anemones on their acquired shells. The anemones profit from the association by feeding on scraps from the crabs' meals. When the crabs move to larger shells, they carefully transfer their anemones to the new homes. Anemones also protect boxer crabs, which brandish the stinging creatures in their claws.

Many other reef animals live under the protection of other organisms. Clownfishes shelter among the venomous tentacles of sea anemones. These fishes secrete mucus that inhibits the discharge of the anemones' stinging nematocysts, thus enabling them to live in direct contact with the tentacles. Possibly the anemones benefit from the presence of their tenants, which have been observed cleaning debris from the anemones and nipping off diseased tentacles. There is no doubt about the advantage for the fishes. Conspicuously marked with bands of red-brown and pale blue, clownfishes are quickly snapped up by predators when removed from the anemone and released elsewhere.

Long, needle-like spines of sea urchins often serve as a protective thicket for a dozen or more thin shrimpfish. The fish hover in a vertical, head-down position, with their longitudinal stripes looking very much like urchin spines. One species of cardinalfish also seeks the sanctuary of spines when threatened and repays the protector by cleaning its body.

These examples constitute only a minute sampling of hundreds of such associations known to exist in coral reefs. Indeed, the coral reef community can be regarded as a huge, complex symbiotic system in which thousands of plants and animals live together, bound by an intricate web of interdependencies.

The Open Ocean

The open ocean remains a region of mystery, awe-inspiring in its sheer vastness. Scientists are slowly learning about its varied forms of life, but much remains to be discovered, and many myths linger on

Beyond the shallow coastal seas lies the pathless immensity of the open ocean: over 300 million cubic miles of salt water covering nearly three-quarters of the Earth's surface. Averaging more than two miles deep, the open ocean provides several hundred times the living space of all the continents and islands. On land, most life is concentrated in a relatively thin film between the treetops and the first dozen feet or so of the soil. In the ocean, life can be found from the sunlit surface waters to the bottom of the deepest trench, almost seven miles down.

The open ocean is mankind's last frontier. Its dark, near-freezing depths, where pressures mount to tons per square inch, are as inhospitable to human life as the dry "seas" of the moon. Even the relatively accessible surface of the open ocean has had its forbidding and mysterious regions.

Perhaps the most famous of these is the Sargasso Sea, lying in the mid-Atlantic between Florida and the Azores. Christopher Columbus is credited with being the first to sail through this mid-ocean sea and describe its floating weeds. His

The voracious hammerhead shark, up to fifteen feet long, feeds on bony fishes, rays, and other sharks—and has been known to attack humans. The wide spacing of its nostrils and eyes (they are located at the tips of the weird, flattened head) help it to pinpoint prey from a distance.

crew became alarmed when they sighted the plants, believing that their ship was near shore and might run aground.

Over the centuries exaggerated tales of the Sargasso Sea were accepted as fact. Early writers pictured the sea as a vast, impenetrable tangle of seaweeds. According to popular accounts, any ship venturing there would be trapped forever in an eerie graveyard of rotting ships and unspeakable monsters.

In 1855, Matthew Fontaine Maury, America's first oceanographer, described the Sargasso Sea: "Covering an area equal in extent to the Mississippi Valley, it is so thickly matted over with gulf weeds . . . that the speed of vessels passing through it is often much retarded." In 1897 a British magazine warned: "It seems doubtful whether a sailing vessel would be able to cut her way into the thick network of weeds even with a strong wind behind her." Even as recently as 1952, a French physician who crossed the Atlantic in a life raft carefully avoided the Sargasso Sea.

Thus the legend persists, although for many years ships have regularly navigated the Sargasso Sea. They sight plenty of weed—but rarely in patches larger than a doormat. Scientists estimate that there are seven million tons of the weed floating in the mid-Atlantic, but the plants are spread across nearly two million square miles of the ocean's surface. Far from trapping a ship, the Sargasso weed would not even slow a dinghy.

A transparent comb jelly paddles through the water with eight rows of cilia. Comb jellies, close relatives of jellyfishes and sea anemones, gather in great swarms and devour fish fry and other planktonic animals.

Near-perfect transparency helps many inhabitants of the open ocean elude their enemies

The sparsity of floating weeds in the Sargasso Sea emphasizes the true nature of the open ocean. Most of it is a biological desert incapable of supporting the dense populations of coastal seas.

The sunlit surface waters of the open ocean do not receive minerals washed from the land and so contain relatively low concentrations of nutrients essential for plant growth. The deeper waters, where there is too little light for plant growth, are rich in these nutrients but do not readily mix with the surface layers.

Thus plant production is much lower in the open ocean than in coastal waters fertilized by minerals washed down from land or brought up from the deep by upwelling. Plant production in the mid-South Pacific is about half of that off the California coast and only one-sixth of that off parts of Saudi Arabia and western Africa.

Despite its low fertility, the open ocean provides a more stable and less demanding environment than, for example, the seashore. Sudden or severe fluctuations in temperature or salinity do not occur. And even violent storms have little effect a few yards beneath the surface.

But inhabitants of the clear, well-lighted surface waters face a threat to survival that does not confront most seashore creatures: a total lack of hiding places. The animals of the open ocean cannot dart into a rock cranny or burrow into a sandy bottom. There are no sheltering kelp meadows, no coral citadels. Yet the open-ocean inhabitants are hardly defenseless. Several of the larger drifters, such as jellyfishes and their relatives, bear nematocysts—stinging capsules that ward off potential enemies. Other forms rely on superior speed to elude predators; flying fishes and squids even take to the air. Some fishes find safety by banding together in large schools.

But the odds against survival in the open ocean are tremendous. Many species produce prodigious numbers of eggs to compensate for the high mortality rate. A female ocean sunfish may discharge as many as thirty million eggs in a single breeding season; if just one or two of the hatchlings reproduce, the maintenance of the population is assured.

With no hiding places, camouflage plays an important role in open-ocean survival. The larger

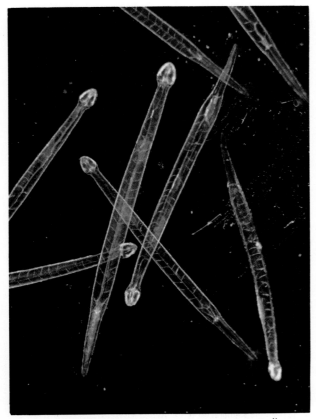

Barely visible, gluttonous arrowworms are not easily seen by the small crustaceans and young fish they prey on. Like some other plankton, most arrowworms sink to deep water by day and swim up to the surface at night.

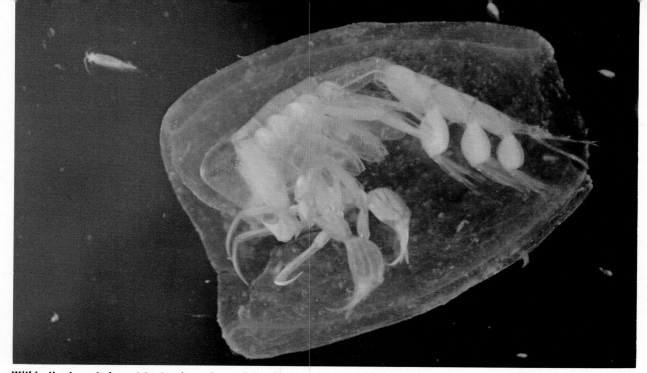

Within the barrel-shaped body of a salp, a shrimplike crustacean with huge claws lives and broods its young. It shaped its floating home by eating the salp's internal organs, and now propels it through the water by swimming.

creatures—from sea slugs and snails to the biggest sharks and whales—have blue or green backs and silver or white undersides. Many planktonic creatures—copepods, comb jellies, and larval fishes—achieve an astonishing degree of invisibility by being nearly transparent. Arrowworms are so clear and colorless that they were not discovered until 1768, although they occur in surface water throughout the world and grow to four inches.

An arrowworm often hangs motionless and unseen in the water waiting for a copepod or young fish to come within striking distance. Eyes that see in all directions, hairs that respond to vibrations in the water, and a primitive brain all help the arrowworm sense the presence of prey. Once a meal is detected, the creature shoots forward with startling speed and grabs the victim with the hard, pincerlike bristles around its mouth.

Transparent as arrowworms and almost as abundant, comb jellies are also carnivorous. They propel their gelatinous bodies by rhythmically beating cilia arranged in eight longitudinal rows. By day the comb jellies are all but invisible, except for a glassy iridescence when the cilia reflect the sunlight; at night they shine with flashes of blue-green luminescence. Most comb jellies catch their food with long, trailing tentacles bearing "lasso" cells, whose sticky coating traps prey.

Like comb jellies and arrowworms, the delicate salps are nearly as insubstantial and transparent as the water they inhabit. Relatives of the bottom-dwelling sea squirts, salps move freely through surface waters, feeding on plankton. The most common varieties are shaped like kegs open at both ends. Muscular "barrel hoops" rhythmically expand and contract, pumping water in the front opening and out the back, and propel the animals through the sea.

Frequently a salp will have a passenger in its barrel-shaped body—the remarkable large-eyed, transparent, shrimplike animal called *Phronima*. By eating the internal organs of a salp, the crustacean obtains an excellent mobile home in which to live and brood its young.

The individual salps range in length from half an inch to about six inches. But colonies of salp-like animals, known as pyrosomes, have been reported to reach a length of forty-five feet. Worldwide in distribution but most common in tropical and subtropical seas, these pinkish-red, brilliantly luminescent animals appear to be solitary creatures. But each pyrosome is really composed of hundreds or even thousands of tiny individuals, all joined together to form a hollow cylinder. Each individual faces the exterior surface of the cylinder and sucks in water and small planktonic food. The water is discharged into the center of the cylinder and flows through it and out the back, moving the colony through the sea with a sort of gentle jet propulsion.

Camouflaged by its mottled coloration, a young sargassum triggerfish shelters among the tangled weeds. A prickly dorsal spine snaps erect, as here, to deter predators.

Slender, toothless pipefish resemble the branches of the weeds among which they live. Unable to open their jaws, pipefish suck tiny prey into their tubelike mouths.

Creatures of the Sargasso Sea

The once forbidding, still mysterious Sargasso Sea, an expanse of seaweed floating in the mid-Atlantic, offers a unique refuge for animals in the open ocean. Some, such as the sargassum pipefish, sea slug, and crab, mimic the mottled seaweed. Dolphinfish and jacks come here to breed; eels make the long journey from North American and European rivers for the same purpose. Flying fishes lay their eggs in long strings anchored to the sargassum. Feeding on the sargassum, and on the invertebrates and smaller fishes that live among the weeds, are larger animals such as porcupine fishes, dolphinfish, and sargassum fish.

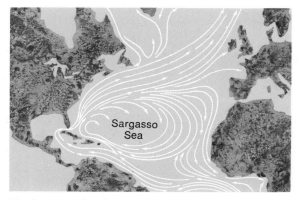

The Sargasso Sea is an oval expanse of warm, seaweed-strewn water trapped by the major ocean currents that flow clockwise around the northern Atlantic Ocean.

A grotesque sargassum fish, whose bumpy skin mimics the weed's fronds and floats, jiggles a fleshy lure over its mouth to attract prey. The fish can actually crawl over the sargassum on specially adapted, armlike pectoral fins.

A half-inch-wide sargassum crab clings to a bit of weed beside beaded strings of sea slug eggs. Partially hidden behind the branch just to the right of the eggs is the well-camouflaged body of the adult sea slug that laid them.

Delicate drifters of the open ocean, jellyfishes are armed with poisonous tentacles

The many-mouthed jellyfish draws in planktonic prey through thousands of tiny, cilia-lined openings on its hanging lobes—lips with canals leading to a central stomach. The fringed, domelike bell may be up to a foot wide.

All plants and animals living near the surface of the open ocean must somehow avoid sinking into the abyss. To carry on photosynthesis, plants must stay within a few hundred feet of the surface. Many animals, in turn, must remain near the drifting unicellular plants that form the first link in the ocean's food chain.

A few seashore animals manage to find a place of attachment even in the open ocean. Barnacles fasten to driftwood, ships' hulls, large fishes, turtles, and whales. Whales, indeed, are veritable living ocean liners, whose passengers include barnacles, algae, remoras, copepods, and some eighteen different kinds of "whale lice."

Floating clumps of weed in the Sargasso Sea furnish island anchorage for a unique community of animals. Shrimps, crabs, tubeworms, sea squirts, nudibranchs, barnacles, sargassum fishes, and the only marine insect survive in the weed.

These hitchhikers are exceptions, however. Most open-ocean organisms, with nothing to cling to, must depend on built-in adaptations to stay afloat. Many planktonic plants and animals possess needlelike spines, fine hairs, or wing-shaped structures that add little weight but produce drag and increase resistance to sinking. Just being small is an advantage. The smaller an organism, the greater the ratio of its friction-producing surface area to its body volume, and the more slowly it sinks.

But adaptations that increase friction can only slow sinking; they cannot prevent it. Even the tiniest plants and animals must somehow counteract gravity in order to stay in the sunlit surface waters. Diatoms contain oil globules that reduce their weight. Microscopic radiolarians buoy themselves up with bubblelike chambers full of water and carbon dioxide. Dinoflagellates "tread water" by lashing their whiplike flagella. Copepods kick their legs and antennae back and forth as fast as 600 times a second.

A creature perfectly adapted to a drifting life should weigh only as much as the water it displaces so that it neither rises nor sinks. Jellyfishes, with tissues that are 95 per cent water, approach this ideal.

A jellyfish's umbrella-shaped bell is a thin, double-walled sac filled primarily with a gelatinous substance. In the center of the bell is a digestive cavity, and hanging from it like a tattered curtain is the creature's funnel-like mouth. Simple sense organs responding to light or gravity help to orient the animal in an upright position. Rhythmic contractions of the bell give the jellyfish a slight upward push to keep it from sinking.

Trailing beneath the bell, tentacles studded with nematocysts paralyze small animals that contact them. Tiny adhesive pads hold the victims until the nematocysts have delivered their poisonous darts. The paralyzed prey is then hoisted into the jellyfish's mouth and digested.

One of the most widely distributed jellyfishes, the moon jelly, has a six- to eighteen-inch transparent bell made conspicuous by hairlike tentacles fringing the edge and four oval reproductive organs on the underside. The moon jelly preys on copepods and other tiny animal plankton, but the sting of its short tentacles is innocuous to humans. In addition to tentacles, it has sticky bands of mucus on the surface of its bell. The mucus, together with any food that has become stuck to it, is constantly moved by the beating of cilia toward the edge of the bell. There accumulating blobs of food are licked off by tonguelike extensions of the central mouth.

Considerably more dangerous, to man as well as to other animals, are the lion's mane jellyfishes. In the frigid Arctic Ocean, one gargantuan species attains a bell diameter of eight feet and has tentacles that extend downward for 100 feet or more—making it the largest planktonic animal in any ocean. The lion's mane jellyfishes inhabiting temperate latitudes of both the Atlantic and Pacific reach bell diameters of from one to three feet and may trail tangles of tentacles seventy-five feet long. Their sting can kill a foot-long fish and raise angry red welts on human swimmers.

For sheer virulence, however, no jellyfishes can equal the sea wasps of the tropical Pacific and Indian oceans. These creatures have dome-shaped bells that may grow to heights of ten inches or more, but are usually considerably smaller. From the bottom of the bell hang clusters of relatively short tentacles, the sting of which can kill a man. Marine toxicologist Bruce Halstead has called one species of sea wasp the most deadly organism alive.

Brilliantly luminescent and beautifully tinted with delicate shades of rose, lavender, and ivory, *Pelagia noctiluca* is more completely adapted to life in the open ocean than most other jellyfishes. After budding from the body of an adult, most young jellyfishes settle on the ocean floor, gradually grow into saucer-shaped larvae, and then float to the surface. *Pelagia noctiluca*, however, discharges its larvae directly into the open sea, where they mature without going through a bottom-dwelling stage.

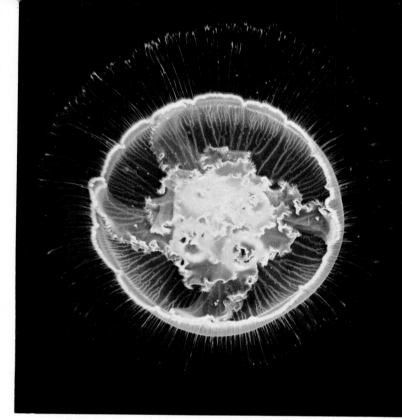

A moon jellyfish, its four circular reproductive organs visible here, swims by rhythmic contractions of its shallow bell. Moon jelly larvae settle on seaweed or on rocks, develop first into fixed polyps, then into mobile adults.

Among the deadliest of sea creatures, tropical sea wasps are jellyfishes with stinging tentacles so poisonous that they can kill almost on contact. Human swimmers and divers fall victim, as well as fishes that the sea wasps eat.

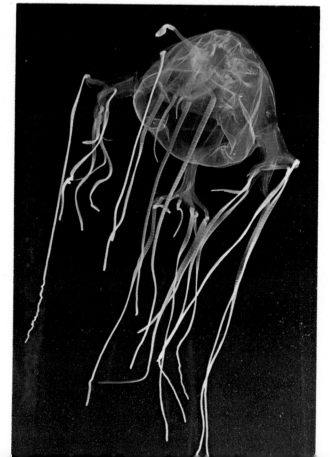

Watery Sailors on the Surface of the Ocean

Four types of polyps, specializing in flotation, digestion, prey-catching, or reproduction, combine forces in a Portuguese man-of-war colony, which may include 1000 individuals. From the gas-filled float, up to a foot long, trail tentacles armed with stinging capsules. The fish Nomeus, apparently immune to the venom, shelters among the tentacles.

Colonial Sailors

By clustering in colonies, some animals increase their ability to survive. Often highly specialized, each individual contributes to the overall needs of the colony and benefits from association with the others.

Among the most successful of these colonial animals, in terms of varieties and numbers, are the siphonophores, close relatives of jellyfishes. A siphonophore colony behaves much like a single animal, yet it may consist of 1000 or more varied individuals. None could live independently of the colony.

For convenience, some biologists call the different types of individuals "persons." Some "persons" specialize in capturing food, others in digestion. Still others are responsible for locomotion, flotation, defense, or reproduction. This division of labor represents an evolutionary step toward higher organisms constructed of completely specialized, completely interdependent organs such as stomachs and muscles.

Common in all oceans, most siphonophores drift passively beneath the surface, propelled by

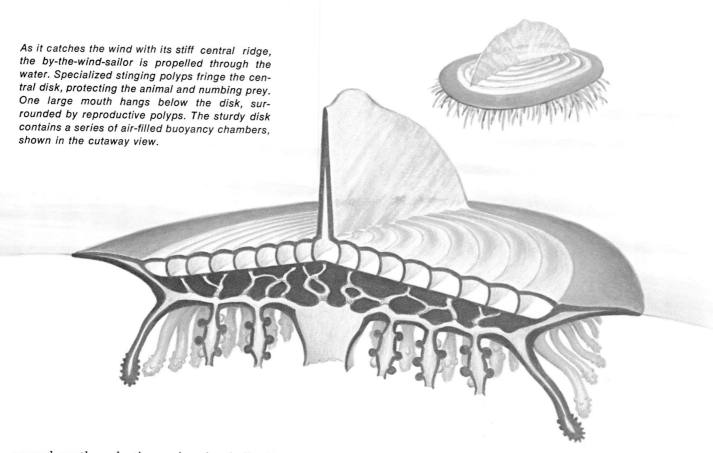

As it catches the wind with its stiff central ridge, the by-the-wind-sailor is propelled through the water. Specialized stinging polyps fringe the central disk, protecting the animal and numbing prey. One large mouth hangs below the disk, surrounded by reproductive polyps. The sturdy disk contains a series of air-filled buoyancy chambers, shown in the cutaway view.

several gently pulsating swimming bells. But one of them, the Portuguese man-of-war, has a gas-filled float that reaches above the surface and catches the wind. Sometimes men-of-war gather in huge flotillas, stretching for miles across the open sea.

The Portuguese man-of-war's balloonlike float, tinted pink, purple, and blue and crested with a narrow, frilled sail, may measure nearly a foot in length. Gas-secreting "persons" at its base inflate the float. Every few minutes, the man-of-war momentarily "capsizes" itself to moisten the delicate float membrane. Beneath the float, stinging tentacles trail through the water for thirty feet or more. The venom they eject, chemically similar to that of the cobra, can kill fishes the size of full-grown mackerel. As the tentacles contract, the prey is hoisted up to the many mouths of the feeding "persons," digested, and distributed to the entire colony.

For humans, any contact with the stinging tentacles—even dried, disintegrated ones mixed with beach sand—causes a painful, nettlelike rash. A swimmer encountering a living man-of-war can receive disabling or fatal injuries. Man-of-war stings have been blamed for a number of human deaths, but some may not have been caused by the venom itself. A swimmer entangled in the tentacles could react with panic or shock and die by drowning.

Curiously, one animal is a constant companion of this deadly sailor. The man-of-war fish spends most of its life swimming with apparent impunity among the toxic tentacles. A deep blue with vertical black stripes, it blends in well with the siphonophore's tentacles.

Just how a finger-length man-of-war fish manages to stay alive in its lethal stronghold is not clearly understood. It nibbles the man-of-war's tentacles, and possibly this diet partially immunizes it to the venom. In laboratory experiments the fish has survived venom injections ten times as potent as those that kill fishes of similar size. On the other hand, men-of-war have been caught in the act of devouring their little companions. Perhaps the man-of-war fish survives by avoiding all but the most minor contacts with the tentacles of its host.

The Versatile Mollusks

The mollusks—soft-bodied animals characterized by a protective shell and a large fleshy foot—have spread out in several directions from the shallow seas of their ancestors. Some have migrated to dry land or fresh water; a few kinds have taken up a free-floating life in the open ocean.

The pteropods—modified snails—have developed winglike extensions of the foot and have drastically lightened, or altogether eliminated, the shell. Popularly called sea butterflies, these dainty creatures flutter along through the water. Cilia on their "wing" surfaces drive diatoms and other small organisms toward their mouths.

Abundant in the open ocean, pteropods often form dense shoals that attract hungry herring, cod, and haddock. In parts of the South Atlantic they are present in such enormous numbers that the frail, cone-shaped shells of dead pteropods cover large areas of the bottom.

Unlike its pteropod relatives, the purple sea snail has retained a relatively large shell, but compensates for this burden by secreting a raft of mucus-covered bubbles to which it clings upside down. This upside-down life has led to a reversal of the typical open-water color pattern: what would normally be the snail's upper surface is white, and what would be its lower surface is a deep purple-blue. Found in all warm seas, the purple sea snail eats planktonic animals such as copepods, jellyfishes, and by-the-wind-sailors.

The shell-less nudibranchs, or sea slugs, have contributed *Glaucus* to the open-ocean community. Its relatives creep over the bottom in tidepools and coral reefs, but *Glaucus* glides upside down on the underside of the ocean's surface film. Since it spends much time upside down, the slug has evolved an inverted color scheme similar to that of the purple sea snail. *Glaucus* also feeds on by-the-wind-sailors and, like some of its coral reef relatives, uses its victim's stinging nematocysts for its own defense. After devouring a by-the-wind-sailor's tentacles and feeding polyps, *Glaucus* may leave behind a clutch of its own eggs on the derelict float.

A deep blue tufted sea slug nibbles the feeding polyps of a floating siphonophore related to the dreaded Portuguese man-of-war. Somehow immune to the poisonous capsules of its watery victim, the slug incorporates them in its own tissues for defense. The planktonic slug floats upside down, clinging to the surface film.

The squid is the undisputed monarch of the sea's mollusks and of all the ocean's invertebrates. Like its close relative the octopus, the squid has humanlike eyes, a powerful parrot-like beak, and high intelligence. The heavy shell of its snail ancestors has been reduced to a thin, leaf-shaped internal "shell" adding little weight but providing rigidity. The cumbersome ancestral foot has evolved into a streamlined "head" and ten sinuous, sucker-laden arms.

By forcibly expelling water through a narrow siphon beneath the head, the squid jet-propels itself faster than the fastest fish over short distances. Usually the squid darts backward. But it can reverse direction by shifting the position of its siphon, as it does when it shuttles back and forth in a school of fish. For more leisurely movement or for hovering, the squid slowly flaps two triangular fins near the rear of its body.

Because of its superb swimming ability, the squid must be ranked with the vertebrate masters of the sea: fishes and whales.

The Skillful Squids

The sharp-eyed and quick-witted squids are among the most agile animals in the ocean. Using jet propulsion, they squirt water from a siphon to speed through the sea, sometimes with such force that they rocket out of the water into the air. Some squids emit inky or phosphorescent "smoke screens"; others rely on speed for defense. After mating (above), females deposit clusters of membrane-enclosed eggs on the ocean floor. In nearly developed embryos (below), the eyes, round black ink sacs, and still unabsorbed pear-shaped yellow yolks are visible.

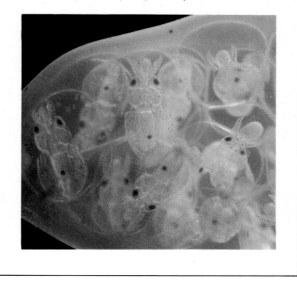

A purple sea snail clings upside down to a frothy raft of mucus bubbles. It can squirt out a camouflaging purple fluid that may anesthetize its planktonic prey.

Adaptations for an Aquatic Life

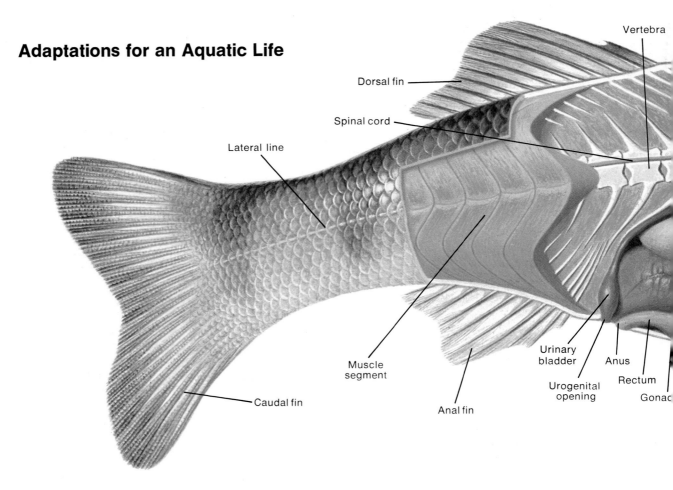

Dorsal fin

Spinal cord

Lateral line

Vertebra

Muscle segment

Caudal fin

Anal fin

Urinary bladder

Urogenital opening

Anus

Rectum

Gonad

Masters of the Sea

Of all the animals on Earth, none is more beautifully adapted for moving through the water than a fish. The structure and streamlining of a fish are the culmination of 400 million years of constant adjustment, selection, and refinement. What has emerged is a marvel of dynamic beauty and supple grace. Man is slow and awkward on land compared to fishes in water.

More than 95 per cent of the 25,000 species of fishes have hard, bony skeletons. These bony fishes are the most versatile feeders and the fastest swimmers in the sea. Sharks and rays—fishes with skeletons of cartilage—are big and fast, but they do not exhibit the variety of forms, habits, and adaptations found among their bony cousins.

To swim, a fish sends waves of muscular contractions down its body from head to tail, pushing its curving sides backward against the water. A sweep of the tail ends each wave and gives an added push.

The fins of a bony fish are used primarily for orientation and balance. The dorsal fin on the back and the anal fin on the belly are keels that keep the fish from wobbling. The caudal, or tail, fin smooths the swimming; a fish with an injured tail fin "staggers" erratically. The pectoral fins, located just behind the gill openings, are for backing up, braking, and turning sharply. The pelvic fins, set below and sometimes behind the pectorals, are also for braking, and prevent the fish from nosing up when it thrusts out the pectoral fins.

Some fishes use their fins for other purposes. Ocean sunfishes, with their ponderous, rigid bodies, cannot swim conventionally, and propel themselves forward by sculling with their dorsal and anal fins. Remoras attach themselves to larger fishes with a dorsal fin on top of the head modified as a suction cup. In angler fishes, the dorsal fin has become a living fishing pole, often complete with wiggling bait.

Fins make possible the spectacular aerial excursions of flying fishes. Among "two-winged" species, the greatly enlarged pectoral fins can stretch out rigidly to form gliding planes. In the "four-winged" species, the pelvics are similarly

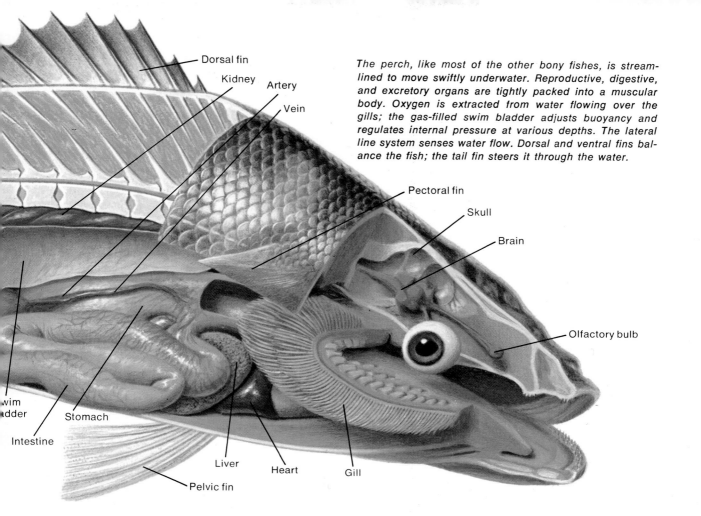

Dorsal fin
Kidney
Artery
Vein
Pectoral fin
Skull
Brain
Olfactory bulb
wim
dder
Stomach
Intestine
Liver
Heart
Gill
Pelvic fin

The perch, like most of the other bony fishes, is streamlined to move swiftly underwater. Reproductive, digestive, and excretory organs are tightly packed into a muscular body. Oxygen is extracted from water flowing over the gills; the gas-filled swim bladder adjusts buoyancy and regulates internal pressure at various depths. The lateral line system senses water flow. Dorsal and ventral fins balance the fish; the tail fin steers it through the water.

modified. In both types, the lower part of the tail fin vibrates rapidly to get the fish airborne. Once in the air, a flying fish can soar for 150 feet or more, at speeds of up to forty miles an hour.

Most bony fishes that feed in the open ocean have mouths at the front of their bodies, usually with lower jaws that jut out farther than the uppers, so that they can grab a meal from any position. Some fishes, such as the John Dory, have protrusible jaws that shoot forward as the mouth opens. When the prey is seized, the jaws quickly retract.

The upper jaws of marlin and sailfishes are drawn out into rounded bills for clubbing other fishes. Swordfish have broad, flat bills. Flailing left and right, they swim into schools of mackerel, menhaden, small fish, and squid. Then these toothless marauders swallow their beaten victims whole. They will attack almost anything, often without apparent purpose. Numerous broken-off swords have been found in the planking of wooden ships: sometimes they penetrated both the inner and outer timbers of sturdy oak. In 1967 a nine-foot swordfish attacked the re-

search submarine *Alvin* at a depth of about 1900 feet off the Georgia coast. The entire length of the sword, thirty-eight inches, penetrated the outer fiberglass hull of the vessel, which was forced to surface. The crew extracted the trapped fish and ate it for dinner.

Swordfish also apparently attack whales. Broken-off swords have been found in the sides and backs of blue whales and fin whales captured in the Antarctic Ocean, around the Aleutian Islands, and off Newfoundland.

Fishes preying on animals of "pan" size or larger possess sharp, slender teeth for grabbing and holding their meal. Barracudas have both long "canines" for seizing victims and smaller, daggerlike teeth that slice up victims as cleanly as a fishmonger's knife. Lancet fishes, which may reach six feet in length, have curved teeth the size of a man's finger. Stout teeth, one-eighth to one-fourth inch long, arm the jaws of bluefish. Schools of bluefish often attack schools of herring or other small fish, leaving behind nothing but a trail of bone and flesh fragments. These killers have no known natural enemies.

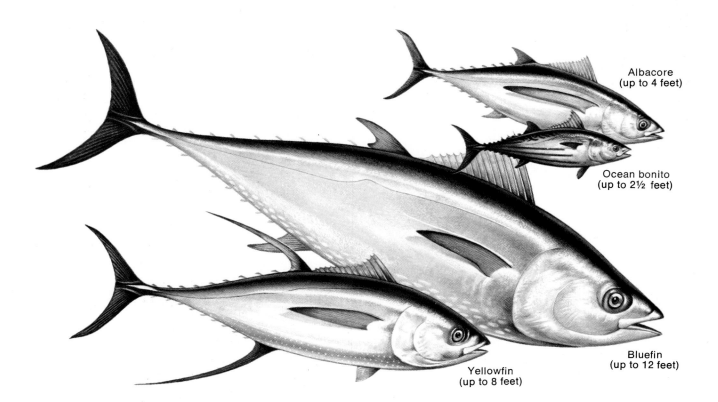

Albacore
(up to 4 feet)

Ocean bonito
(up to 2½ feet)

Bluefin
(up to 12 feet)

Yellowfin
(up to 8 feet)

A marlin bursts from the water in a frantic attempt to shake loose a fisherman's hook. These formidable fishes, armed with lethal spikes, reportedly swim forty miles an hour.

Far-ranging tunas, among the swiftest of ocean fishes, are found in all tropical and temperate seas. Bonito and commercially important albacore are not much larger than mackerel—about twenty-five pounds. Yellowfins, another major food fish, average 125 pounds, but some grow as large as 500 pounds. Giants of the tunas— and the largest bony fishes—are bluefins. 200- to 500-pound fish are common; the record is a 1000 pounder.

Two ways of life

No bony fishes range more widely through the open ocean than do tunas. Being heavier than the water they displace, tunas and their smaller relatives—mackerel, bonitos, and albacore—must swim constantly to remain afloat. If they stop, they drift tailfirst toward the bottom. To get enough oxygen-rich water flowing across their gills, they must swim fast. Their deeply forked, bone-hard, sickle-shaped tails drive them through the sea with vigorous side-to-side strokes.

No fishes can outswim tunas. Everything about their appearance indicates speed: the beautifully streamlined and satiny smooth body; the gill covers tightly fitted against the sides; the fins lying retracted in special grooves where they offer minimum resistance. Yellowfin tuna have been clocked at forty-five miles an hour, the wahoo (a tuna relative) at forty-eight miles an hour—the ocean's speed record. At the sight,

A pair of perch cleans parasites off the skin of an ocean sunfish, which signals them to begin by tilting itself backward. A full-grown sunfish may reach a length of ten feet and weigh over a ton, although this is unusual. A slow swimmer, lacking pelvic fins, the sunfish floats sluggishly at the surface and feeds mainly on jellyfishes.

smell, or sound of food, tunas accelerate quickly and reach top speed in less than a second. Their appetites are boundless and their diet versatile: herring, mackerel, anchovies, sardines, flying fishes, and squid are all gulped down as a tuna speeds through the water.

Tunas maintain body temperatures as much as eighteen degrees Fahrenheit warmer than the surrounding water. This adaptation speeds up metabolism and thereby contributes to the tunas' speed and strength—their rates of digestion are high, their nerve impulses travel faster through their bodies, and their massive swimming muscles contract and relax about three times as rapidly as those of other fishes.

Contrasting sharply with the swift tuna, the ocean sunfish passes much of its adult life lying on its side at the surface, apparently basking in the sun. Lacking a true tail, the languid sunfish swims so slowly that it might almost be considered a planktonic drifter despite its enormous size. Several specimens exceeding ten feet in length and over a ton in weight have been caught.

Feeding primarily on jellyfishes and other drifters, which it consumes with a loud slurp, the ocean sunfish seems to have few predators. A two- to three-inch layer of tough gristle just beneath the skin protects the fish from many enemies, but parasites take their toll. Virtually every specimen examined has been riddled inside and out with a variety of parasites. Remoras even live inside the gill chambers of the ocean sunfish.

Recent investigations suggest that this creature may not deserve its reputation for laziness. The stomach contents of dissected sunfish sometimes include animals found only in deep waters, indicating activity far below the surface. Some scientists who have studied the fish contend that individuals at the surface are diseased, and that far from enjoying the sun, they are actually dying.

A white shark opens its terrifying jaws armed with razor-sharp, serrated teeth. Capable of swallowing creatures half its size, this shark may reach a length of twenty-one feet and weigh as much as three and a half tons. The aggressive white shark ranges worldwide, hunting a variety of marine animals such as seals, sea lions, other sharks, sea turtles, and porpoises. It also preys upon people frequently enough to be called a mankiller.

Thresher shark

Hunters of the Open Ocean

Sleek streamlined sharks, their mouths set with razor-edged teeth, arouse an atavistic dread in man. Flesh-eating sharks can be considered potential killers when provoked or in a feeding frenzy. However, the rare and primitive frilled shark and the small-mouthed thresher are not believed to be dangerous under normal conditions. The great white shark, the largest flesh-eating fish, is a known man-eater; blue and white-tipped sharks are also suspect.

The Sharks and Rays

Despite 2000 years of accumulated lore and observation, sharks are among the least understood marine animals. Like snakes and octopuses, they arouse irrational emotions in humans. But dispassionately viewed, sharks must be ranked among the most beautifully designed, superbly functional animals in the sea.

Several characteristics distinguish sharks from other fishes. They have no true bones; their skeletons are made of cartilage, a flexible, gristly substance. They have five to seven gill openings on each side, instead of just the one bony fishes have. Their tough skin is covered not with scales, but with tiny toothlike projections called denticles. Most sharks bear their young alive; few bony fishes do.

Because they lack true bones, sharks have left few fossils, but in the 1800s the remains of an ancient shark that lived some 350 million years ago were discovered near Cleveland, Ohio. Judging from this and other evidence, sharks have changed little in the last sixty-five million years. Their simple and efficient body plan and several special adaptations account for their durability.

Reproduction is one of these adaptations. Male

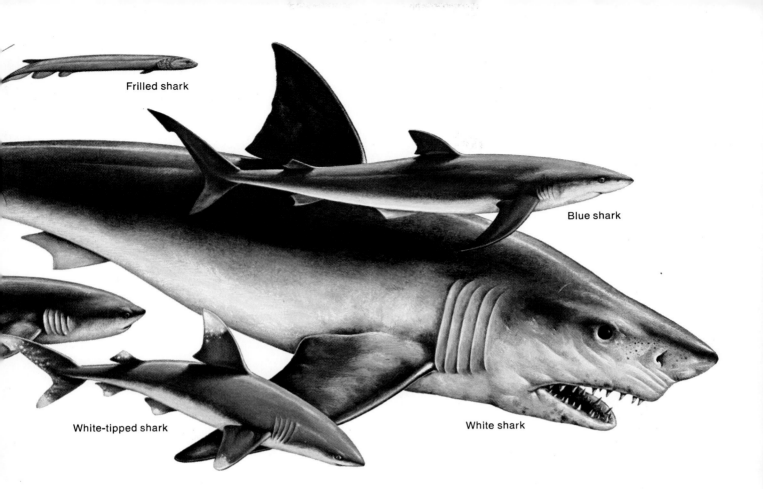

Frilled shark

Blue shark

White-tipped shark

White shark

and female sharks mate directly—unlike most bony fishes, which discharge sperm and eggs into the water. Direct mating is an effective mode of reproduction in the open sea, for the eggs are almost certain to be fertilized. In most sharks, the fertilized eggs hatch in the female's body, and the young remain for a time in the mother's reproductive tract, where they are nourished by a milky fluid.

A few species of sharks reproduce almost as most mammals do. These sharks have a placental connection with the young in the reproductive tract, and an "umbilical cord" that supplies the embryos with nourishment from the mother's blood. The blue shark, the hammerhead shark, and the smooth dogfish reproduce this way. Only a few species, such as the whale shark, the cat shark, and possibly the Greenland shark, lay eggs in the water. A leathery capsule sometimes known as a "mermaid's purse" envelops their eggs.

Compared with bony fishes, which may produce thousands of offspring each breeding season, sharks bear few young. A blue shark, for example, gives birth to about thirty young, which are born about two feet long with a full set of teeth, ready to fend for themselves. Sharks will eat anything,

including their own young, but during pupping season the males leave the schools and females cease to feed, subsisting on oil in their livers.

Shark teeth vary so much in shape and size that a species can be identified by one or two teeth left embedded in a wooden boat or by tooth marks left on a victim. The teeth are in rows, one behind the other. Sometimes the teeth in the first two rows are set at angles to each other, like the teeth of a crosscut saw. When a tooth is lost, another one moves up to take its place from the five or more rows of replacement teeth. New rows of teeth are always developing in a deep groove along the inner margin of the jaw. In some species an entire row moves up to replace a worn row.

Although their jaws are underslung, sharks need not turn sideways or roll over to bite. Most sharks can slide both jaws forward to seize a meal. If the prey is too large to be swallowed whole, a shark clamps its teeth into the victim, shakes its head with quick jerks, and tears out a large chunk of the animal's flesh.

Most sharks prefer fish, but they will eat almost anything, including squid, seals, birds, sea turtles, smaller sharks, dead or injured whales, garbage, and, on occasion, humans. The stomachs of cap-

Peaceful giants of the open ocean, manta rays and whale sharks cruise near the surface, feeding on plankton and small fishes

A fourteen-foot manta ray flaps gracefully through the water. Several remoras cling tightly to its fins and body. Fleshy protuberances next to the ray's mouth suggest horns, hence the manta's nickname of "devilfish." The horns are actually fins that funnel small fishes and plankton into the manta's mouth as it swims along.

A docile whale shark cruises slowly near the surface, its chin festooned with clinging remoras. Whale sharks, found in all tropical seas and sometimes straying into temperate latitudes, may reach a length of forty feet or more. Despite their formidable size, whale sharks feed on plankton, which they sieve through gill rakers.

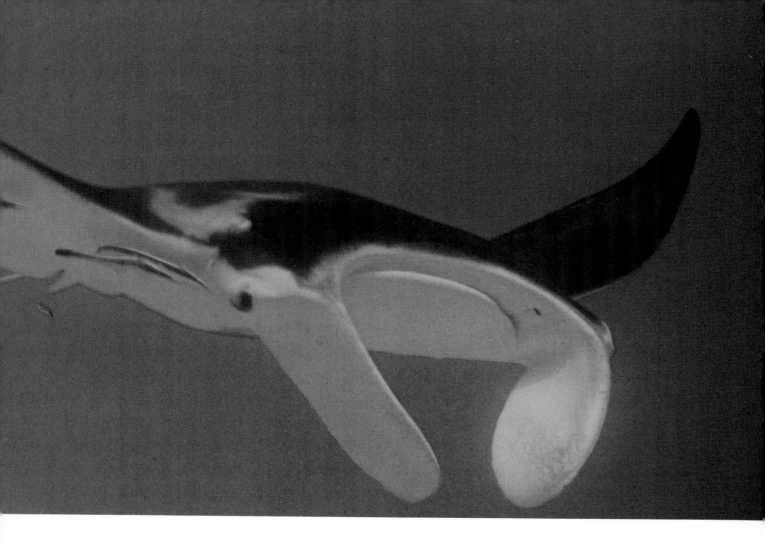

tured sharks have contained the head and forelegs of a crocodile; a whole reindeer, minus the antlers; coal; unopened canned goods; grass; broken clocks; empty beer cans; and parts of cows, pigs, sheep, and dogs.

Incongruously, the largest sharks—whale sharks and basking sharks—are docile plankton feeders. Whale sharks reach lengths of up to forty-five feet and weigh fifteen tons; basking sharks are only slightly smaller. Both species cruise slowly at the surface filtering food from the sea with hairy mats, or gill rakers, which lie inside their long gill openings. Neither of these sharks has the formidable teeth of the flesh eaters, but they have attacked boats when provoked.

Flatten a shark from top to bottom, broaden its pectoral fins until they extend like wings from head to tail, move the gill openings beneath the body, and the result is a ray. This branch of the shark group includes skates, stingrays, sawfishes, and electric rays. Most rays live on shallow bottoms, but several kinds, including the largest

rays of all, live in the open ocean. These are the manta rays, or devilfishes.

Full-grown manta rays may have "wingspans" of eighteen feet or more and weigh as much as one and a half tons. Mariners once believed that mantas seized ships by their anchor chains and towed them to an unknown and fearful doom. It was also believed that mantas wrapped unlucky swimmers in their "wings" and then devoured them. Such tales are, of course, quite groundless, but a giant manta ray that has been harpooned or otherwise provoked can reduce a good-size fishing boat to splinters.

If left to their own affairs, however, the devilfishes are among the most placid creatures in the sea. Like the largest sharks—and, indeed, like the largest whales—the manta rays feed only on small fishes and plankton, which they channel into their underslung mouths with two fleshy extensions of their pectoral fins. Perhaps this way of life ensures that there will always be enough food for the giants of the open ocean.

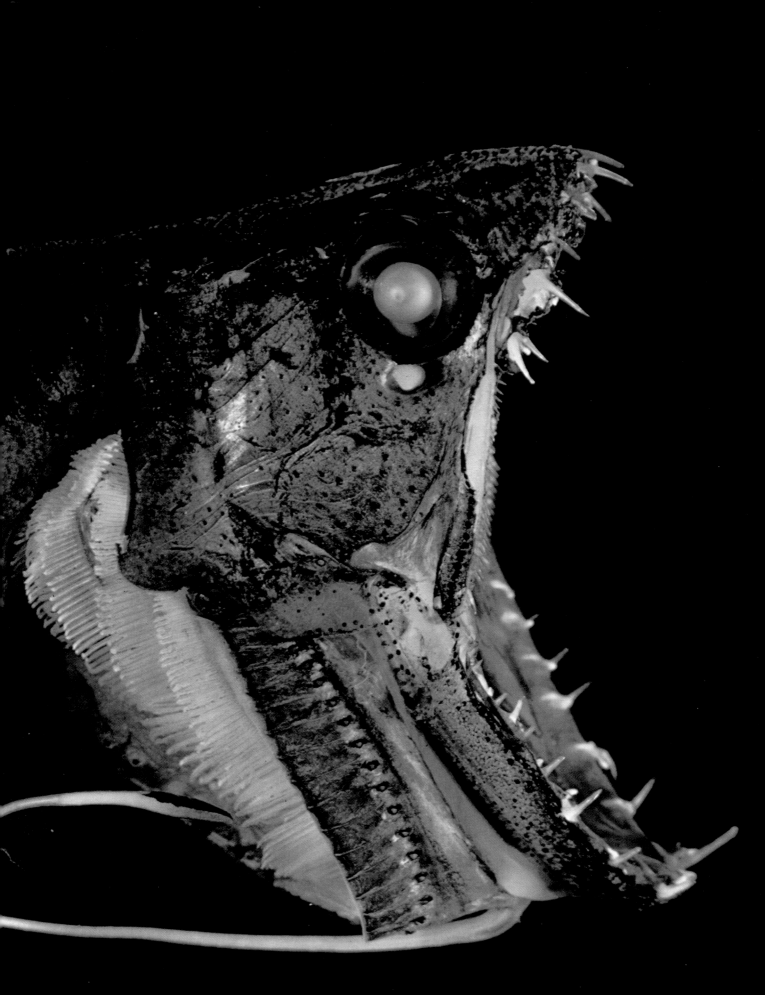

Life in the Depths

No part of the sea is more alien to man than the abyssal deep.
It is a chill, dark, incredibly forbidding world sparsely inhabited by some
of the strangest creatures to be found anywhere on our planet

All night long the dripping cable wound back onto the huge reel aboard the Royal Danish Research Vessel *Galathea*. For many hours, the ship had been cruising over one of the deepest ocean trenches in the world, a long chasm in the sea floor running parallel to the east coast of the Philippine Islands. Scientists aboard awaited the reappearance of the sturdy trawl that had been secured to miles of heavy wire and lowered into the abyss 32,565 feet below. Would the trawl bring back evidence that living creatures could survive in eternal darkness and immense pressure?

At last the ship's searchlights picked up the outline of the trawl's voluminous triangular bag. Anton Bruun, leader of the *Galathea* expedition, later described the tension and excitement of that moment: "During the work of taking in the trawl . . . we prepared for the disappointment of seeing a bag without any bottom animals in it . . . . 'There's clay on the frame!' somebody cried. 'It's been on the bottom!' . . . Everybody on board who could leave his job gathered round . . . . We hardly noticed the red prawns . . . or black

fishes; we all knew these to be pelagic animals, caught on the way up. . . . But there, on a rather large stone, were some small whitish growths— sea anemones! Even if no more animals had been found, this would still be the outstanding haul of the expedition! It was proof that higher animals can live deeper than 10,000 meters [more than 30,000 feet]. Is it surprising that all were overjoyed? And that pleasure became excitement when out of the grayish clay with gravel and stones we picked altogether twenty-five sea anemones, about seventy-five sea cucumbers, five bivalves, one amphipod, and one bristle worm?"

Such commonplace creatures have seldom created more of a stir. Their recovery from the bottom of the Philippine Trench on July 22, 1951, pushed the known limit of life another 8000 feet into the ocean depths.

Eight and a half years later, animals were found at even greater depths. Swiss engineer Jacques Piccard and U.S. Navy Lieutenant Don Walsh took the bathyscaphe *Trieste* to the bottom of the Challenger Deep, 200 miles east of the Mariana Islands. At 35,800 feet, their searchlight picked out a flatfish on the bottom. Apparently undisturbed by the *Trieste*'s arrival, the foot-long fish rested quietly for a minute or so and then swam off slowly into the darkness. The explorers also saw a little red shrimp. Like the fish, it resembled shallow-water relatives. Here was proof that animals can live in the greatest depths.

The star eater, a fish of the twilight zone, has a powerful "spotlight" below each eye and rows of light organs running along its jaws and down its sides. A luminous chin barbel may serve to attract prey. Luminescence is typical of fishes inhabiting the twilight zone.

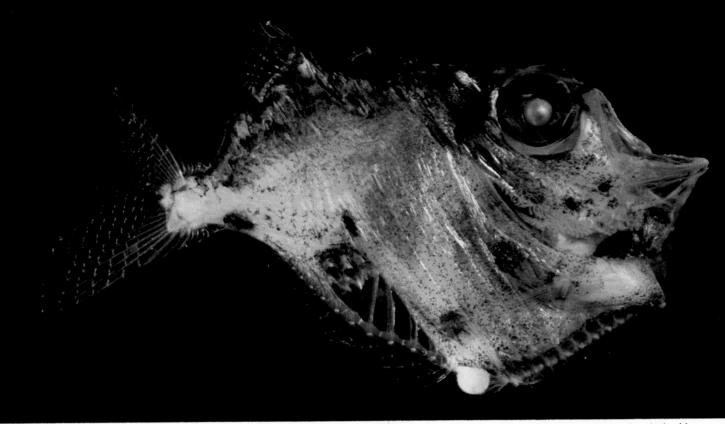

Two-inch hatchet fishes live in the dimly lighted zone between 300 and 1500 feet. When seen from above, the dark skin of their backs may camouflage them; from below, the light organs studding their sides may have the same effect.

Light fades rapidly with increasing depth — below the twilight zone, the sea is a world of darkness

Early nineteenth-century scientists would have been astonished by the findings of the *Galathea* and the *Trieste*. As late as 1843, the distinguished British naturalist Edward Forbes concluded that no animal could survive below about 1800 feet. His theory was quite plausible, for conditions in the abyss appear inhospitable to life.

Sunlight fades away rapidly with increasing depth, so that animals living in deep water must find food and seek mates in darkness. More important, even in the clearest water there is not enough light for photosynthesis below 400 feet. The sun's warmth, too, is quickly absorbed by surface waters, and temperatures in the abyss remain uniformly frigid throughout the year.

In addition to darkness and cold, there is tremendous pressure. For every thirty-three feet a creature descends, the pressure exerted on each square inch of its body increases almost fifteen pounds. At 3300 feet, therefore, the pressure is 1500 pounds per square inch — a hundred times greater than at the surface. At 35,000 feet, it is almost 7½ tons per square inch.

As forbidding as these conditions may seem, they are at least stable. During the course of billions of years, life has spread slowly throughout the oceans, from the sunlit surface waters to the deepest trenches.

Curiously, the enormous pressure — which early scientists believed would crush any animal to pulp — required few special adaptations. Certain sea urchins, starfishes, worms, and other organisms live both in very shallow water and at depths of 10,000 feet or more. These creatures are little affected by pressure because their tissues are permeated with fluids at the same pressure as the surrounding water. Body fluids push outward just as hard as seawater pushes inward, and the two forces offset each other.

Nor has the chilling cold restricted the spread of life into the depths. Nearly all deep-sea animals are cold-blooded and have body temperatures close to the low temperature of the water. As a result, they probably grow more slowly and reproduce later and less frequently than warm-water species. Because of this reduced tempo of life, the animals require less food, and food in the depths is scarce.

The lack of light has had far more evolutionary impact than the high pressures or low temperatures. As depth increases and light diminishes, the inhabitants of the sea change dramatically.

In well-lit waters near the surface, fishes bear light-colored bellies and green or blue backs. From about 500 feet down to about 1500 feet—in the twilight zone of the sea—there is still enough light for countershading to help camouflage an animal. At these depths, finger-size lantern fishes, carrying batteries of luminescent organs, are grayish, light brown, or silvery; many kinds have silvery-white undersides and pink-tinged sides. Hatchet fishes, named for their shape, frequently have silvery or beautifully iridescent bodies with brownish backs.

But not all the creatures of the twilight zone are countershaded. Living there, and in the darker zone below, are animals with a variety of colors. Black stomiatoid fishes gleam with an iridescent sheen. Fishes called gulpers and swallowers, which prowl below 6000 feet, are velvety black or deep brown. Whalefishes, resembling their namesake in shape but only a few inches long, bear jaws and fins of bright orange or red. Blood-red shrimp snap up crimson arrowworms and scarlet copepods. Squids, so quick to change color near the surface, wear a permanent livery of deep red, purple, or brown, sometimes studded with luminous organs.

Why are some creatures camouflaged by countershading or dark bodies while others seem to flaunt their presence with bright colors? The answer involves the way light is absorbed as it passes through water.

Sunlight is a mixture of different colors, each with a characteristic wavelength and energy level. On a bathysphere descent near Bermuda, marine biologist William Beebe observed that red light waves, the least energetic, penetrated only about twenty feet. By the time the bathysphere had descended to fifty feet, a large scarlet shrimp that he carried with him appeared black. The shrimp could reflect only red light, so it appeared black below the depth penetrated by red light waves.

Even in the clear water off Bermuda, orange light disappeared at about 150 feet, yellow at 300 feet, and green at 350 feet. At 800 feet, nearly all wavelengths were absorbed, and Beebe saw only "the deepest blue-black imaginable."

A scarlet opossum shrimp, so called because the females carry egg pouches between their legs, can emit a luminous cloud that confuses predators. This species migrates vertically each day between 3000 and 12,000 feet.

Absorption of light waves by water makes this marine fish —an opah—change color with increasing depth. Red, the longest visible wavelength, is absorbed first. This diagram shows light absorption in clear ocean water; the more particles, the less deep light waves can penetrate. Light penetration also varies with the brightness and angle of the sun.

Living Light

Although sunlight penetrates only a few hundred feet below the surface, many deep-sea creatures produce their own light. This bioluminescence—"living light"—is especially common in animals found from about 1000 to 8000 feet below the surface.

Some organisms, including certain crustaceans, squids, and fishes, have their own light-producing cells. Other deep dwellers harbor colonies of luminescent bacteria, always in the same locations on a particular host species. This arrangement aids both parties: The bacteria furnish illumination for the host, and the host provides food and shelter for the bacteria. Some hosts switch on the bacteria by pumping oxygenated blood to them, and extinguish them by reducing the blood flow.

Bioluminescence occurs when a substance known as luciferin (from the Latin word meaning "light-bearing") combines with oxygen in the presence of an enzyme called luciferase. During a sequence of chemical changes, energy is released in the form of light. Electric light bulbs produce considerably more heat than light, but bioluminescence can be virtually 100 per cent efficient, generating light and practically no heat.

Most bioluminescence in marine organisms is blue-green, although red, yellow, and other colors have been reported. The lights may be located almost anywhere on the body. A number of deep-sea fishes carry rows of lights on their bellies and sides. Some wear lights on their heads or on fleshy growths—barbels—suspended from their chins. Squids have luminous spots on their arms and circling their eyes.

Such brightly illuminated creatures moving along in the dark would seem conspicuous targets for predators. However, bioluminescence in the twilight zone may take the place of countershading in surface waters. If the intensity of a fish's belly lights matches the intensity of sunlight filtering into the twilight zone, the fish will create neither silhouette nor shadow when seen from below.

Bioluminescence also helps attract potential

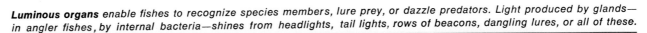

Luminous organs enable fishes to recognize species members, lure prey, or dazzle predators. Light produced by glands— in angler fishes, by internal bacteria—shines from headlights, tail lights, rows of beacons, dangling lures, or all of these.

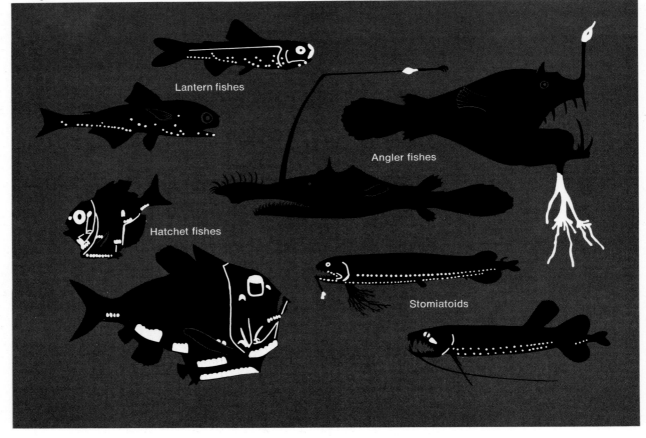

Lantern fishes

Angler fishes

Hatchet fishes

Stomiatoids

prey, as anyone who has ever fished at night with a lamp can understand. Angler fishes and stomiatoids actually "fish" with luminous lures that may entice animals whose normal prey is luminescent.

At breeding time, the pattern and color of an animal's lights could serve to identify it as male or female. Male lantern fishes, for example, bear powerful lights atop their tails; females carry only small lamps on the underside of their tails. Just as female fireflies flash signals to males during the mating season, deep-sea creatures may announce their readiness to mate by flashing lights.

Closely related animals sometimes have different sizes and arrangements of luminous spots. One species of lantern fish has three rows along its belly; another has only two. Such differences may help the animals recognize others of their species as they form schools or find mates. Dr. Beebe could easily differentiate between species of lantern fishes by their pattern of lights. "In absolute darkness," he said, "I could tell how many of each species were represented in a new catch, solely from their luminous hieroglyphics."

Bioluminescence may help animals to see prey. Dr. Beebe watched copepods caught in a sheet of light from the belly of a lantern fish. The fish suddenly twisted around and began to gulp them down. Lights near the eyes of one type of stomiatoid fish illuminate whatever it looks at. Such creatures have been seen to "catch" schools of krill in these eyebeams and snap them up with a sudden rapid movement. Krill, too, possess lights around their eyes that may enable them to locate still smaller food in the dark.

Bioluminescence can also be used defensively. In the gloom of the depths, the ink cloud with which some squids confound their enemies would be ineffective. At least one deep-sea species expels a cloud of brilliant, luminous fluid. The cloud confuses any would-be attacker long enough for the squid to dart to safety. Some deep-sea shrimps employ a similar tactic by releasing a substance that bursts into a miniature Milky Way of luminous particles.

A long-fanged viperfish tempts little shrimps and fishes with a beacon of light; 350 photophores on the roof of its mouth illuminate a deadly trap. Viperfishes also have rows of luminous organs along their lower jaws and bellies.

The upward-staring telescopic eyes of Scopelarchus *face in the same direction. This arrangement provides depth perception, an advantage in judging the position of potential prey. (Most fishes have a separate field of vision on each side.)*

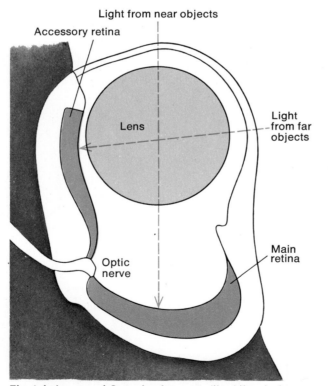

Light from near objects

Accessory retina

Lens

Light from far objects

Main retina

Optic nerve

The tubular eye of Scopelarchus *acts like bifocal glasses. The accessory retina, at the side, detects distant objects; the chief retina registers nearby objects. Neither retina has a focusing lens that provides clear images.*

Some inhabitants of the depths are blind. Others have the most sensitive eyes in the animal world

Fishes of the twilight zone possess highly sensitive eyes—perhaps the most sensitive in all the animal kingdom. British biologist N. B. Marshall examined the brains and eyes of species of fish living as deep as 3000 feet. He concluded that despite the virtual absence of light, these fishes "can probably see their kind, their food, and their enemies. The eyes are surely too cunningly fashioned to be mere registers of phosphorescent light." Instead, they seem sensitive enough to utilize whatever faint sunlight penetrates to the lower portions of the twilight zone.

Although most vertebrate eyes are roughly spherical, those of many deep-sea fishes are tubular and contain two retinas, or light-sensitive fields. One is for images of distant objects, the other for images of closer objects. Fishes with tubular eyes have unusually good depth perception. They can judge accurately the distances to potential prey—a decided advantage in an environment where food is scarce.

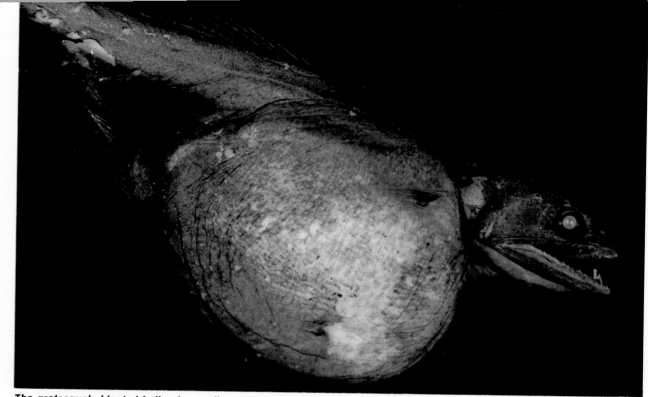

The grotesquely bloated belly of a swallower fish contains a recent victim, seized by sharp teeth and gulped down whole. This voracious predator, no more than six inches long, distends its jaws to ingest fishes larger than itself.

Eventually there comes a level, says biologist G. L. Walls, "at which the eye seems to 'quit' and becomes smaller." This seems to be somewhere between 3000 and 5000 feet. Angler fishes have well-developed eyes during the first period of their life, which they spend in well-lit surface waters. But as the females grow, sink below 6000 feet, and take up life as adults, their eyes stop growing and may even degenerate.

Some inhabitants of the abyss—both fishes and invertebrates—have tiny, weak eyes or are altogether blind. These creatures must rely on touch, taste, and smell. Most of the weak-eyed fishes have highly developed lateral line systems, which detect vibrations and movements in the water.

Food in the Depths

Food is scarce in the sunless depths, for there are no green plants. Scraps, waste products, and dead organisms drift down slowly from surface waters. Some of this meager rain is consumed during its fall. But enough food eventually reaches the bottom to support a community of animals attached to, burrowing through, or creeping along the ocean floor. In turn, these detritus feeders are food for larger, more active animals.

Not all deep-sea food chains are based upon this rain of particles. Countless invertebrates and small fishes make daily vertical journeys, rising at night to feed nearer the surface and descending again into deeper water before daylight. Larger animals follow and prey on the small migrants. Such movements extend to great depths, so there is also a "bucket brigade" transfer of food from rich surface waters down to the barren abyss.

Garbage from ships and decaying vegetation swept down from the land supplement the meager deep-sea menu. Wherever the *Galathea* trawl came up with tree branches, coconut shells, or other debris from rivers and swamps, the catch of deep-sea animals was exceptionally good. In general, however, a meal is hard to come by in deep water, and deep-sea animals have evolved some bizarre adaptations for getting whatever is available.

Many fishes of the depths are little more than tooth-filled mouths attached to expandable stomachs and long, thin tails. The gulpers, common at depths below 5000 feet, have trap-door jaws and elastic, baglike stomachs that can expand to several times their normal size to accommodate prey even bigger than the gulpers themselves. One six-inch gulper had a nine-inch fish coiled inside.

Gulpers grow up to six feet long, but their whip-like tails account for most of this length. The tips of the tails are often luminescent, and may lure animals within reach of the gulpers' mouths.

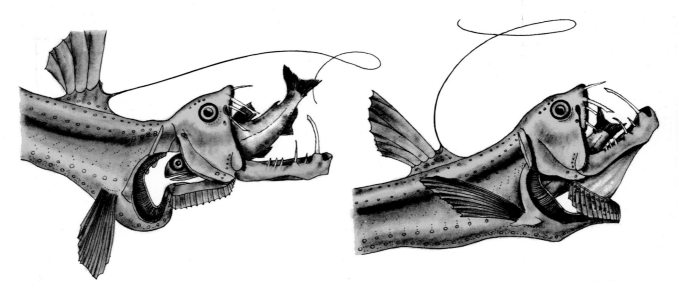

A stomiatoid fish is adapted for swallowing large prey. The skull swings up and the lower jaw protrudes, enlarging the throat opening, while muscles pull heart and gills aside. Movable teeth in the throat push the victim into the stomach.

Bizarre midget hunters of the depths, angler fishes entice their prey with luminous lures

Stomiatoids are another group of deep-sea fishes that can engulf surprisingly large prey. Usually six or seven inches long, they have fanglike curved teeth, large heads, and elongated bodies that taper into small tails. They are abundant in the twilight zone down to about 2000 feet.

A typical stomiatoid has a barbel dangling below its chin or throat. Depending on the species, this barbel ranges from a short "whisker" to a sinuous whip ten times the length of the body. There is a 1½-inch species with a barbel about fifteen inches long, and an 8½-inch species with a barbel nearly a yard long. Barbels vary in form as well as in length. Some are merely single strands, others branch and rebranch like leafless twigs, and still others resemble bunches of grapes or exotic flowers. Many are luminescent.

Scientists are still debating the function of these elaborate whiskers. Perhaps the stomiatoids use their barbels to probe for food in the bottom ooze, or perhaps they use the organs to lure other fishes to their tooth-studded mouths. The barbels may be species-recognition devices, enabling stomiatoids to identify mates in their dimly-lit environment.

There is no doubt that the bony appendages of the black, scaleless, deep-sea angler fishes found at about 6500 feet attract prey. Most species have a luminescent lure at the tip of a "fishing rod," which is a modified spine of the dorsal fin.

To an angler fish's prey—possibly a lantern fish or another angler fish—the lighted lure dangling on the pole might very well look like a luminous worm or shrimp. As the prey moves closer to investigate, the angler brings the lure back nearer its mouth. The lower jaw suddenly drops open, and the gill covers expand to create a cavity large enough to accommodate a dinner the size of the diner itself. This rapid action creates a powerful suction that sweeps the victim into the angler's mouth. The jaws snap shut, impaling the prey on long, curved teeth. The prey is swallowed whole and pushed into the angler's expandable stomach by teeth in the throat.

Over millions of years, anglers have evolved into some of the most successfully specialized fishes. Through a series of adaptations, the first spine of the dorsal fin separated from the others, moved forward, and lengthened into a fishing pole that lies flat in a groove on top of the head. Some species have short, stubby poles; others have long, slender ones. Muscles swing the pole forward, back toward the mouth, or out of the way when jaws and teeth come into play.

Perhaps the most unusual angler of all was brought to the surface from a depth of 12,000 feet off the western coast of Central America. This jet-black, broad-headed, eighteen-inch species dredged up by the *Galathea* has achieved the ulti-

A female angler fish attracts prey with a movable luminous lure—a modified spine—atop her head. Lacking pelvic fins, angler fishes swim slowly through the depths by beating their tails and steering with the stubby pectoral fins.

mate in the placement of its luminescent lure: It dangles from the roof of the mouth behind curved teeth.

Certain deep-dwelling anglers possess adaptations for reproduction as astonishing as those for feeding. In the dark, sparsely populated depths, these fishes may have difficulty finding a mate. Therefore, when a male meets a female, he sinks his teeth into her and hangs on—sometimes for the rest of his life. If he belongs to the species whose males are lifelong parasites, the skin around his mouth and jaws fuses with the female's body; only a small opening for breathing remains on either side of his mouth. His eyes degenerate, as

do most of his internal organs. His circulatory system becomes connected with hers, and from then on he is nourished by her blood. In effect, the male becomes an external appendage producing sperm to fertilize the female's eggs.

Although the female probably releases her eggs in the deep sea, they quickly float upward and hatch in surface waters, where the newborn find plenty of copepods and other small plankton to eat. As they grow, females begin to develop fishing poles and males acquire gripping teeth on their snouts and chins. When the anglers change from larvae to adults, they descend to deep water and take up their strange way of life.

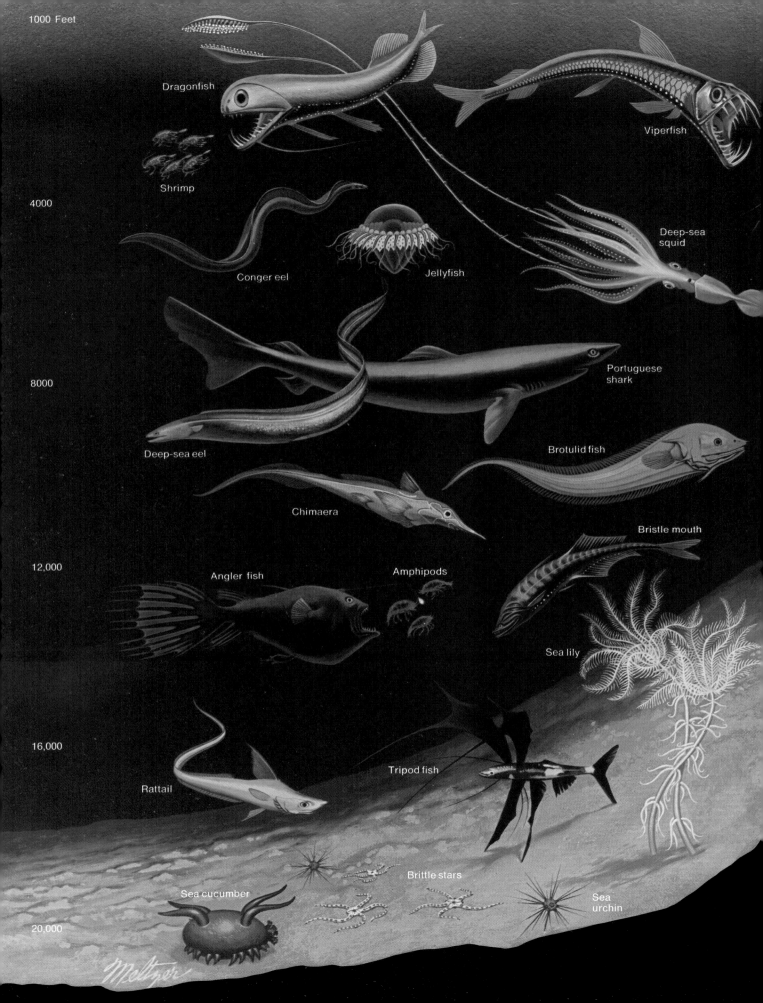

1000 Feet

Dragonfish

Viperfish

Shrimp

4000

Conger eel

Jellyfish

Deep-sea squid

8000

Portuguese shark

Deep-sea eel

Brotulid fish

Chimaera

Bristle mouth

12,000

Angler fish

Amphipods

Sea lily

16,000

Rattail

Tripod fish

Brittle stars

Sea cucumber

Sea urchin

20,000

Meltzer

Spirula

Halibut

Hatchet fish

Euphausid
shrimp

Greenland
shark

Tulip
sponges

Sea
pens

Barrel
sponges

Blind lobster

Sea
spider

Sea
anemones

Sea
cucumber

Lantern fish

Sea
urchin

Angler fish

Octopus

Blind
lobster

Gulper

Amphipods

Strange Inhabitants of the Midnight World at the Bottom of the Sea

Faced with a lack of light and a shortage of food, animals of the deep sea
have evolved a variety of solutions to
their problems. Inhabitants of the twilight zone—fishes, shrimps, and jellyfishes—are often luminescent; many migrate to the surface at night to feed. Dark
waters above the ocean floor are home to
bizarre fishes, swallowers, gulpers, and

anglers—existing on meals that are few
and far between. The main residents of
the deep-sea bottom are echinoderms,
such as brittle stars, and crustaceans,
some of which have totally lost their
ability to see. Oceanographers have
discovered that animals manage to live
even in the very deepest part of the
sea, seven miles below the surface,

Flapping its muscular fins, a four-foot-long giant squid flies through the sea 3500 feet below the surface. (Squids usually

A pink rockfish and a long-legged crab search for food on the ocean floor 3000 feet down off the southern California coast. At this depth, food is scarce; consequently, animals tend to be few in number. Rockfish hatch their eggs internally; the young emerge ready to swim.

A giant of the deep, this sea pen flourishing at 16,000 feet is three feet tall. (Top size for a shallow-water species is about twelve inches.) Sea pens are closely related to corals.

expel water to propel themselves like jets.) Some giant squids may be more than fifty feet long, mostly tentacles.

Living in the abyss are some invertebrate giants—huge shrimps, hydroids, sea urchins, and squids up to fifty feet long

Most deep-sea fishes are small, but the invertebrates are frequently giants compared to their shallow-water relatives. On the floor of the abyss live sea urchins with bodies a foot wide; most shallow-water species are only a few inches across. Hydroids, usually just a fraction of an inch high, reach the prodigious height of eight feet in the deeps off Japan. Sea pens, ordinarily knee-high, also grow to eight feet in deep water. And isopods —crustaceans related to the pill bugs on land— attain lengths of eight inches in the depths.

Shrimps, too, grow unusually large in the deep sea. Some scarlet and brilliantly luminescent species are nearly a foot long. Some have antennae twice as long as their bodies. Biologists believe that shrimps use these flexible, whiplike structures as fishing lines to catch small prey.

No deep-sea creature is more spectacular than the giant squid, the largest of all living invertebrates. Its eight muscular arms, sometimes as thick as a man's thigh and studded with thousands of suckers, may reach twelve feet. Extending from this writhing mass are two thin tentacles, sometimes more than forty feet long. The flattened ends of these tentacles bear a hundred or more suckers with serrated rims. The arms and tentacles carry prey to the squid's great beak, capable of tearing the toughest flesh into small bits.

The largest squid ever found was washed up on a New Zealand beach in 1888. It measured fifty-seven feet, with two stretched-out tentacles accounting for forty-nine feet. This specimen was of the genus *Architeuthis*, which includes several species of giants. Although none has ever been weighed precisely, reliable estimates run up to nearly a ton.

Little is know about giant squids. They live in all the world's seas, but spend most of their time at depths of 600 feet or more. Scientists do not even know what the creatures prey on; educated guesses have ranged from small, inactive invertebrates to huge sperm whales. Unquestionably, squids do battle whales in what must be the most titanic struggles since the days of dinosaurs. Whales have been found with scars from the tooth-rimmed suckers of squids. The whales are probably always the aggressors, for the remains of giant squids turn up in the stomachs of whales, and never the other way around.

Giant squids use the same method of swimming as their smaller, faster relatives—by shooting water out of a tube under the head in a sort of jerky jet propulsion. Giant squids have reportedly overtaken ships traveling at twelve knots (about fourteen miles per hour), yet their anatomy suggests they are actually weak swimmers, unable to pursue and capture active prey. Flamboyant accounts of these monsters grabbing wooden ships as large as 150 tons and dragging them under are probably not true. Still, the actual nature of these powerful and dangerous invertebrates may never be fully known.

Crew members survey the ocean through the Nemo's *thick plastic hull, which provides unobstructed views of the marine life around them. The* Nemo *observatory can be lowered as deep as 1000 feet for twelve hours.*

Aquanauts Explore "Inner" Space

Since 1934, when William Beebe and Otis Barton made the first bathysphere descent, one-half mile into the sea off Bermuda, man's knowledge of the depths—and of the fascinating array of life found there—has increased enormously. Modern technology led to the development of deeper-diving bathyscaphes. The *Trieste* descended 35,800 feet in the Marianas Trench off Guam, in 1960, a record still unequaled. Scientists now explore the sea in scaled-down submarines with thick Plexiglas portholes. These minisubs range freely over the ocean floor as dangling bathyspheres could not, sometimes plucking up specimens for further study with mechanical arms.

Flying her colors proudly, the French bathyscaphe Archimède is towed to a diving site. The Archimède explored the 450-mile-long, 27,000-feet-deep Puerto Rico Trench during the first bathyscaphe dives in the Atlantic.

An egg-shaped yellow submarine (above) prepares for a spiraling descent to the floor of the San Diego Trough. Shorter than a large automobile, the eighteen-foot Deepstar 4000 is jammed with equipment and crew members, as this fisheye view (right) of the cabin shows.

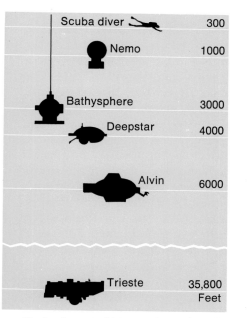

Scuba diver	300
Nemo	1000
Bathysphere	3000
Deepstar	4000
Alvin	6000
Trieste	35,800 Feet

Technology enables man to explore the sea at depths ranging from the free-swimming scuba diver's 300 feet to the record-setting 35,800 feet of the Trieste.

The depths shelter animals known as "living fossils," the last survivors of ancient lines long extinct elsewhere

Scientists have long been intrigued with the possibility that the ocean depths conceal creatures long thought extinct. Animals and plants evolve in response to changes in their surroundings. Since conditions in the abyss are believed to have been nearly stable for hundreds of millions of years, it is reasonable to suppose that some creatures survive there with the same form and habits that they had in the remote past.

The idea that the depths harbor "living fossils" won many adherents after 1864, when Norwegian oceanographers dredged up a sea lily from 1800 feet. Sea lilies, close relatives of feather stars, are colorful, multi-armed "blossoms." Similar primitive, living sea lilies had never before been seen, although their fossil remains had been chiseled from rocks 120 million years old.

Shortly after the 1864 discovery, two more living fossils were dredged up from the deep sea. A large scarlet sea urchin, previously known only as a fossil in the 100-million-year-old chalk cliffs of Dover, England, was found in the North Atlantic in 1870. Then a curious three-inch mollusk with short, thick arms and a jar-shaped body was netted by the *Challenger* expedition of 1872–76. Called *Spirula* for its internal spiral shell, it swims head downward. The shell is divided into chambers filled with gas. Belemnites, mollusks with similar internal-chambered shells, were common in the sea 100 million years ago, but they had disappeared by fifty million years ago—all except the ancestors of *Spirula*.

When the ancestors of *Spirula* roamed the seas, large numbers of mollusks that were neither squid nor octopus but a little of both flourished. Some had arms joined by broad webs and roundish bodies equipped with paddle-shaped fins. All vanished from the fossil record some 100 million years ago, but in 1903 one velvety black animal was discovered in the deep sea. Its ancestors apparently survived by retreating into the cold, dark depths from 3000 to 9000 feet.

This archaic animal is evidently a poor swimmer, for its muscles are soft and pulpy. It probably drifts or moves along feebly in the eternal darkness, head down, arms hanging limply, the

Living fossils, the bizarre Spirula *and vampire* squid *survived after their shallow-water relatives perished.*

webs forming a sort of loose bag around the mouth. Its name—the vampire squid—befits its bizarre appearance.

The vampire squid was first thought to be an octopus, but then its two additional arms were discovered. Apparently used only as feelers, these long, suckerless arms can be coiled into special pockets on the web. Ten appendages are characteristic of squids, but these "feelers" are so different from the strong, prey-grabbing tentacles of other squids that biologists have placed the vampire in a category all its own.

Vampire squids have been found off the coasts of India, Indonesia, New Zealand, and South Africa. Apparently they spend their entire lives in the deep; one was netted 9850 feet down in an undersea canyon north of New Zealand. They have good eyesight and are studded with luminous organs, including two particularly large ones that can be covered with flaps of skin. Their food is probably small, relatively inactive animals detected by their feelers.

A male vampire squid fertilizes a female by inserting a packet of sperm into her with one of his arms, in much the same way as more familiar

Untouched by evolution, the tassel-finned coelacanth looks just like its 300-million-year-old ancestors preserved as fossils. Unlike other living fossils, taken from the depths, coelacanths were found in fairly shallow Indian Ocean waters.

squids and octopuses. Spawning and hatching take place 6500 to 8500 feet down. The young at first have only eight arms. But by the time they are two-thirds of an inch long, the two extra arms have developed, along with the web and light organs. The largest vampire squid ever captured was an 8½-inch female; no males larger than 5 inches have been found.

The most exciting living fossil was discovered in 1938. Fishermen working in the Indian Ocean, off South Africa, brought up a strange metallic-blue fish almost six feet long. It had large, thick scales covering its body and strong, meaty fins that it probably used to move along the bottom. The creature was a coelacanth, the descendant of an ancient line of fishes thought to be extinct for seventy million years. Coelacanths are not strictly deep-sea dwellers. The first one was discovered at a depth of about 240 feet, but the few other specimens subsequently captured have come from depths between 600 and 1200 feet.

Another living fossil emerged from the dark, muddy clay 12,000 feet down in the Pacific off Costa Rica in 1952. Oceanographers aboard the *Galathea* made the catch: ten living specimens of a limpetlike animal believed extinct for 350 million years. Similar to the limpets of rocky shores, it has a fragile, pale yellow, conical shell 1½ inches long and half an inch high. The creature probably moves along the sea bottom on its large pink and blue foot, possibly aided by structures also used for breathing. A pair of short, fleshy tentacles behind the mouth may gather food from the mud.

This primitive animal, named *Neopilina*, is believed to be a link between worms and mollusks. Its body is segmented, as is that of a marine bristle worm. But at the same time, its shell, body structure, and rasping tongue show that it is also related to mollusks. In other words, both worms and mollusks are probably descended from a common ancestor much like *Neopilina*.

Past experience has demonstrated that living fossils, even in the changeless world of the abyss, are the exception rather than the rule. But oceanographers, now probing the depths with greater intensity than ever before, will no doubt discover more of these startling creatures. The possibility of finding them will always quicken pulses and raise hopes whenever a trawl returns from the mysterious ocean depths.

Ocean
Odysseys

Many sea creatures, from tiny protozoans to giant whales,
respond to an instinctive urge to migrate. Their journeys may
cover only a few hundred feet, or span entire oceans

Each afternoon around sunset, one of the grand biological rhythms of the marine world begins anew. With the waning light, myriads of sea creatures start to move upward. By midnight, much of the planktonic and free-swimming life of the ocean is concentrated near the surface. As night ends and the sky begins to lighten, the travelers reverse and descend once again into the depths.

From the shallows to the abyss, members of nearly every major group of sea animals participate in these vertical migrations. Legions of protozoans, copepods, arrowworms, and jellyfishes; swarms of snails, shrimps, and krill; schools of squids, lanternfishes, and other deep-sea dwellers move up in the evening and down in the morning.

Feeble swimmers make surprisingly rapid and lengthy journeys. Copepods no larger than grains of rice climb from 350-foot depths to the surface at rates of 50 to 200 feet an hour. Minute larval barnacles move upward at 50 to 75 feet an hour. Such daily round trips may take eight hours or more and require tremendous amounts of energy. In the process, plankton animals some-times endure pressure changes of several atmospheres and temperature fluctuations equivalent to traveling in surface waters from Iceland to the Equator and back.

What impels these creatures to make such arduous migrations? As far as scientists can determine, their behavior is a reaction to light. Each species moves up and down following a certain intensity of light as the sun sets and rises. Even bright moonlight drives plankton animals to lower levels at night, and they stay farther from the surface on sunny days than on cloudy ones.

Assuming that waning or increasing light causes plankton migrations, the question remains: What are the advantages of these movements? One answer is that tiny vegetarians such as copepods have developed a behavior pattern that both provides them with food and protects them from predators. Under cover of darkness, they swim up to the surface and feed on the abundant plant life there; in the daytime, they sink into the shadowy depths where their enemies have more difficulty locating them. Bigger, carnivorous shrimps, copepods, and worms could be migrating up and down merely to catch the vegetarians. Perhaps these predators in turn attract the more active shrimps, fishes, and mollusks.

This plausible explanation, however, does not fully account for the luminescent organs, which advertise the presence of many vertical migrants. Around Antarctica, for example, large numbers of

After laying a clutch of eggs on a South Carolina island, a female loggerhead turtle swims out to mate with a male waiting offshore. Like other marine turtles, these lumbering reptiles, each weighing several hundred pounds, migrate between sheltered breeding sites and feeding areas.

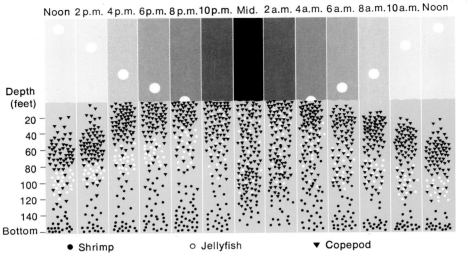

Noon 2 p.m. 4 p.m. 6 p.m. 8 p.m. 10 p.m. Mid. 2 a.m. 4 a.m. 6 a.m. 8 a.m. 10 a.m. Noon

Depth
(feet)
20
40
60
80
100
120
140
Bottom

● Shrimp   ○ Jellyfish   ▼ Copepod

The Ups and Downs of Plankton Life

Most animal plankton make daily vertical migrations: to the surface at night to feed on phytoplankton, down a few hundred feet during the day. The three migrants shown here—copepod, jellyfish, shrimp—move at different times, but all move up and down each day. Vertical migration is most pronounced in summer, when sunlight is strongest. Migratory behavior may help plankton avoid predators or take advantage of currents to drift into new feeding grounds.

The deep scattering layers, sources of misleading sonar readings, are probably composed of great masses of plankton or small fishes

luminescent krill glow an eerie green. Obviously darkness provides no protection for these creatures, and apparently conspicuousness is not a serious drawback or they would long since have become extinct.

Sir Alister Hardy, an eminent British marine biologist, argues that vertical migration may give weak swimmers the added mobility needed to reach fresh feeding grounds or return to rich pastures. Surface waters usually move faster than deeper waters, and often in different directions. A copepod making a night climb of only 100 feet may find itself a mile or two away from where it was the day before, surrounded by a new food supply. On the other hand, krill in the Antarctic Ocean climb 650 feet during the evening into cold, northward-flowing waters. At dawn, they descend into a warmer current flowing southward. This migration pattern keeps them in rich pastures of their diatom food.

Phantom Bottoms

While the vertical migrators intrigue biologists, they have played havoc with the instruments and charts of navigators and mapmakers. During and after World War II, ship captains using echo-sounding equipment (electronic devices that bounce sound waves off the ocean bottom to measure depth) reported shallows where the water

was supposed to be deep. Over the years, nautical charts came to display hundreds of shoals designated *ED*—"existence doubtful." Evidently something in the mid-depths scattered the sound waves and reflected a portion of them back before they reached the true bottom, thereby misleading navigators.

Whatever these shoals were, they seemed to be linked in some way to the vertical migrations of animals. A study made off the California coast in 1942 revealed that these deep scattering layers, or DSLs as they came to be called, rose toward the surface at sundown. Then, at the first light, they descended to depths of 700 feet or more. Further investigation showed that DSLs stretching continuously for hundreds of miles were present throughout the Atlantic, Pacific, and Indian oceans.

Biologists could only assume that DSLs were caused by echo-sounding signals bouncing off the bodies of countless marine animals. But what animals? The bands on the echograms were more clearly defined than those that planktonic organisms might be expected to produce. For a time, commercial fishermen were excited by the possibility of huge, hitherto-unknown schools of fish. Large fishes, however, make dark, individual marks on echograms, and the DSLs were showing up as continuous traces.

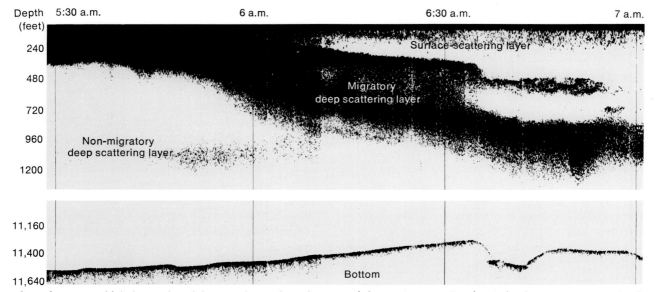

Depth (feet) — 5:30 a.m. — 6 a.m. — 6:30 a.m. — 7 a.m.

240 — Surface scattering layer

480 — Migratory deep scattering layer

720

960 — Non-migratory deep scattering layer

1200

11,160

11,400

11,640 — Bottom

An echogram, which is produced by an electronic echo sounder, clearly reveals the presence of deep scattering layers (DSLs). A migratory deep scattering layer is visible as a black smudge that moves away from the surface between 5:30 a.m. and 7 a.m. A DSL that is much fainter and does not appear to migrate is also apparent at a depth of about 1000 feet. The sea floor appears as a thin, undulating line at the bottom of the echogram. The cause of the deep scattering layers is still uncertain, but densely packed plankton and fishes may be responsible.

Nets and remote-control cameras lowered into the layers produced no conclusive results; the mysterious sound scatterers, apparently frightened away by the camera lights, were agile enough to avoid the nets.

Finally, researchers descended in bathyscaphes to investigate. During day trips off the California coast, Eric G. Barham of the U.S. Navy Electronics Laboratory found great numbers of hakes at depths between 600 and 1000 feet, and dense concentrations of siphonophores hovering motionless between 850 and 1500 feet, their long tentacles stretched out in every direction like "a living net." Between 1200 and 1500 feet, Dr. Barham saw so many shrimp that he could not count them. Two hundred feet below the shrimp he spotted schools of luminous three-inch lanternfish, and between 2150 and 2300 feet he observed thousands more of these fish.

The locations of these animal concentrations generally correspond to depths at which DSLs are found off California—at about 1000 feet, 1400 feet, and 1700 feet. Although much is still to be learned about their composition and movements, clearly some of the DSLs are caused by sound waves reflected from the hard, shell-like coverings of shrimps and other crustaceans, from the gaseous floats of siphonophores, and from the swim bladders of fishes.

Millions of schooling lanternfishes take part in daily vertical migrations. At night, they rise to the surface, following their copepod food. During the day, they swim as deep as 3500 feet, casting a glow with batteries of luminous organs. Their gas-filled swim bladders may deflect sound waves and produce deep scattering layers.

Responding to changes in the environment, many ocean dwellers make seasonal journeys to feeding or breeding grounds

The vertical migrations of planktonic organisms are caused by automatic responses to changes in light intensity. A tiny copepod, for example, does not "choose" to swim upward at sunset; its nervous system simply reacts to the decreased light level, initiating muscle movements that carry the creature toward the surface.

In the same way, the more extensive migrations undertaken by many marine animals are triggered by environmental changes—changes in water temperature, in daylength, in the abundance of food—

and by internal chemical changes, such as the secretion of hormones. Animals setting out on migratory journeys do not think forward through time and across space to definite goals; they merely respond to an instinctive urge to be off. Along the way, they follow signs in the sea and sky that have guided generation after generation of their ancestors over hundreds or thousands of miles to the same destinations.

Like the great animal migrations on land, the long-distance journeys of marine creatures are usually seasonal movements to places where food is more abundant or where conditions are more suitable for the birth and growth of young. Large sea animals, such as whales and tunas, cross entire oceans in their wanderings; salmon travel between the open ocean and rivers and streams; eels swim from inland brooks and lakes to the depths of the Sargasso Sea. Sharks, marlin, and

A cavalcade of spiny lobsters marches along the sea floor near Florida, each clutching the tail of the one ahead or flicking it with antennae to maintain contact. The queuing formation is protective, for each vulnerable abdomen is covered by the next lobster. Lobsters seem to migrate after depleting the local food supplies.

sea turtles travel singly or in small groups, while herring, squids, and mackerel migrate in immense schools, which may help protect them.

Many coastal crustaceans—particularly crabs, lobsters, and shrimps—move into deeper waters to spawn. Their offspring are planktonic for a while, then settle to the bottom, crawl to shallow water where food is plentiful, and grow to maturity. Each fall off Bimini in the Bahamas, thousands of spiny lobsters migrate from shallow reefs to deeper offshore waters. During this annual journey, the lobsters assume a "marching order" when they cross relatively open areas. Lining up in single file, each individual hooks one pair of its front legs around the tail of the animal in front. Males and females join together to form chains more than fifty lobsters long, which move over the sea floor as fast as a man can swim. Why they do this is not fully understood, but it may be a defensive maneuver to protect their vulnerable abdomens from hungry predators.

Many ocean animals take advantage of prevailing currents in their breeding migrations. The typical pattern is for the strong, experienced adults to travel against the current to reach the spawning grounds; the weak, unprotected young then drift with the current on the return trip to adult feeding areas. The plaice—a bottom-dwelling flatfish found in many parts of the North Sea—exhibits this behavior pattern. The large population of plaice that lives in the sandy shallows off the Netherlands migrates southwestward against the current to spawning grounds at the northern end of the English Channel. Millions assembled here each year between January and April produce billions of floating eggs. These hatch while drifting northeastward with the current back to the feeding grounds.

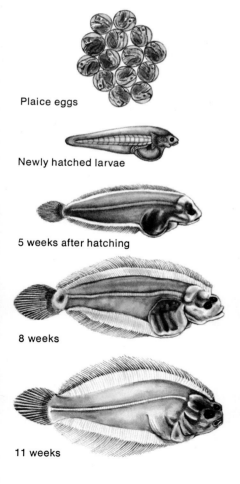

As a plaice grows, its skull twists so that its left eye is brought to the right side, which becomes the fish's back.

Plaice eggs

Newly hatched larvae

5 weeks after hatching

8 weeks

11 weeks

A wary plaice lies camouflaged on the bottom. Adult plaice undulate slowly against the current, in typical flatfish fashion, to spawn in the lower North Sea, then return north to Holland. Plaice fry drift north after hatching.

Migrating Seals and Sea Lions

Protected by hairy coats and thick layers of blubber, seals and sea lions range the world's oceans, thriving in polar seas or cold currents of temperate seas. Each year they return to the islands or shores where they were born, to give birth and mate. In some species, embryo development is delayed so the single pup will be born about a year later—when its mother is back on land. Fur seals and sea lions paddle with powerful forelimbs; seals such as the harp, crabeater, and leopard scull with their hind flippers. All dive underwater to seize animal prey such as fishes, squids, and crustaceans.

A harem of fur seals—a bull may have fifty mates—and newborn pups cluster on St. George Island off the Alaskan coast. Migrating as far south as San Diego each winter, gregarious fur seals return in June to form huge breeding colonies.

A crabeater seal and a leopard seal share an Antarctic iceberg. The crabeater (left) feeds on tiny krill; the leopard seal on larger prey such as fishes and penguins. In winter both migrate as far north as Australia and New Zealand.

Harp seals do not come ashore even to breed; pups are born on drifting ice floes in the North Atlantic. When just a few weeks old, this suckling pup will be weaned, and will become gray.

A California sea lion nurses her nearly full-grown pup from the previous year, while her newborn pup tries to suckle. California sea lions allow juveniles to nurse; some other species wean their youngsters before giving birth.

A herd of California sea lions on San Miguel Island off Santa Barbara stampedes to safety at the first sign of danger. After the spring breeding season, bulls migrate north to waters off Oregon, Washington, and British Columbia.

Salmon undertake long and often remarkably strenuous journeys from sea to fresh water. Then the exhausted fishes spawn and die

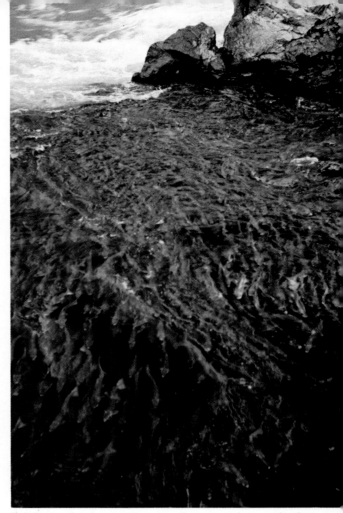

Hundreds of salmon, *after spending several years in the ocean, fight their way into the river they once descended.*

A number of different fishes migrate from the sea into fresh water to spawn. Striped bass and shad live close to shore and travel only relatively short distances up rivers to lay their eggs. Salmon, however, make truly remarkable journeys, sometimes traveling as far as 3000 miles between their feeding grounds in oceans and spawning sites in rivers, streams, and lakes far inland.

The most spectacular spawning migrations of salmon are those made by five Pacific species: sockeye, silver or coho, king or chinook, pink, and chum. These fishes mature in the frigid, food-rich waters of the Gulf of Alaska. At the age of two to four years, they leave these feeding areas and return to freshwater breeding grounds ranging from northern Korea to Siberia, and from central California to Alaska.

The journey is long and arduous. Once they enter fresh water, salmon cease to feed and are sustained wholly by the fat and muscle tissues of their bodies. They often swim for weeks against swift currents and through turbulent rapids, leaping and swimming up waterfalls, climbing fish ladders, dodging bears' claws and fishermen's nets.

Covering up to fifty miles a day, salmon reach points as far inland as 2000 miles up Alaska's Yukon River and 1000 miles up the Columbia River system in the northwestern United States. Nothing but death can stop these beautiful, streamlined fishes from reaching their destinations—and death awaits them at the end of their journey. Only rarely does a Pacific salmon survive long enough after spawning to return to the sea.

After the Return

The gaunt, emaciated salmon arriving at the spawning grounds bear little resemblance to the fat, sleek fishes that left the ocean a few weeks earlier. Their bodies are cut and bruised, their fins ragged and torn, their eyes and gills infested with fungus and other parasites. Weakly, the female digs a shallow trench in the bottom gravel and deposits her eggs; the male fertilizes them with milt, and the female covers them with gravel.

Then the adults usually die. Their bodies litter the stream and lake bottoms and line the banks, sometimes piling up in windrows several feet high. Scavengers come from miles around to take advantage of the feast.

The fertilized eggs buried in gravel hatch in three to twelve weeks. The hatchlings stay in the nest for about three weeks longer, nourished by yolk sacs that remain attached to their bodies after they leave the eggs. Then the young dig their way to the surface and take up life as free-swimming fry. After a period ranging from less than a month to two years, depending on the species, they start their journey to the sea. This migration, which begins in the spring, is apparently triggered at least in part by the lengthening day. The increasing amount of daylight stimulates the salmon's hormone production, bringing about a general increase in bodily activity.

Young salmon travel primarily in twilight and darkness, spending the bright hours hidden from predators in the sand or gravel bottom or among the rocks. The fishes feed and grow along the way,

Returning to spawn *in the very streambed where they hatched, female Pacific salmon scoop nests in the bottom and lay their eggs. The hook-jawed males jealously guard their mates by driving off interlopers, then cover the eggs with milt.*

undergoing physiological changes necessary for the years they are in salt water.

The strong currents that their parents battled to reach their spawning grounds now favor the young, guiding them swiftly and surely toward the ocean. Those hatched far upstream, however, must pass through large lakes where there are no river currents. Here they probably rely on such guideposts as the position of the sun or the polarization of light from the sky. Ultimately, young salmon reach the sea and proceed to feeding grounds where they will live until they, too, are spurred by instinct to return to their ancestral spawning streams.

The Atlantic salmon—actually an ocean-going species of trout—makes similar migrations up rivers and streams in continental Europe, Great Britain, the northeastern United States, and eastern Canada. Unlike Pacific species, a few Atlantic salmon reach the sea again, and return to spawn a second, third, and, rarely, a fourth time.

Male Pacific salmon die *soon after spawning; females survive—perhaps to guard their nests—a few days more.*

Guided mainly by taste and smell, salmon unerringly find their way back to the very streams and lakes in which they hatched

To chart the salmon's migrations, techniques have been developed for keeping track of the movements of individuals. Young salmon captured alive either during their seaward migration or before their release from hatcheries are marked by clipping away portions of their fins. This does not harm a fish, and provides positive identification of its origin. Over many years, millions of salmon have been given "home addresses" in this way and then released.

A marked salmon, recaptured at sea, is tagged with a numbered disk and then released. If it is captured once more—perhaps two or three years later in its spawning grounds—scientists can consult their records and determine where the salmon has been. A remarkable fact emerged from these tagging programs: An adult salmon, migrating from the sea to fresh water, does not travel merely to the river system where it originated. It seeks out the very stream where it hatched several years earlier.

The first conclusive evidence of this extraordinary homing ability was gathered in the early 1940s. Some young Atlantic salmon were captured from the northeast Margaree River in Nova Scotia in 1938. They were marked by removal of a small fatty fin from their backs, then returned to the river. In June 1940, one marked fish was caught in the Atlantic, 550 miles from the site of its first capture. Tagged and released again, it was caught ninety-six days later—back in the northeast Margaree River. In 1943, two tagged Pacific salmon returned to their spawning creek in Vancouver Island, British Columbia, after years at sea.

Over the years, the recapture of many tagged salmon confirmed absolutely that they return home to their birthplace with almost unerring accuracy. They seem driven by one of the strongest instincts in nature.

Homeward-bound salmon challenge any obstacle—here the Siletz River falls in Oregon—in their drive to return and spawn. After repeatedly attempting to leap man-made barriers such as dams, salmon often exhaust themselves and die.

Sometimes this drive to get home requires heroic exertion. A one-year-old silver salmon was released from the Prairie Creek Hatchery in Humboldt County, California. A year later, it returned from the ocean, swam up Redwood and Prairie creeks, flopped across a nearly dry streambed, made its way through a culvert under a highway, traversed a storm sewer, got through another culvert, and went up eighty feet to a flume. It then wriggled through a four-inch vertical pipe with a right-angle bend, knocked a screen cover off the mouth of the pipe, leaped over a nearly impassable wire net, and plopped wearily into its old rearing tank. Astonished hatchery workers christened the fish "Indomitable."

Salmon Navigation

How does a salmon find its way home? As the fish travels hundreds of miles up a complex system of rivers and streams, how is it able to choose repeatedly and accurately between one branch or another at a fork?

The salmon is guided largely by its highly developed sense of smell. It literally sniffs its way home, singling out from all others the distinctive scent of the stream in which it was hatched. Since fishes live in a world of limited visibility, they rely on the chemical senses—taste and smell—to a much greater extent than do most land animals. Their anatomy reflects this: The olfactory lobes of the brains of most fishes are enormous compared to those of other vertebrates. In laboratory experiments, minnows have demonstrated a sense of smell 500 times as acute as that of man.

In the middle 1950s, Warren Wisby and Arthur Hasler, at the University of Wisconsin, devised an experiment that proved conclusively that the sense of smell can guide a salmon to its spawning stream. About 300 returning silver salmon were taken from two branches of Issaquah Creek in the state of Washington. The salmon in each branch were divided into two groups; the nostrils of one group were plugged with cotton, while those of the other group were not. All the fish were released downstream at the junction of the two branches and allowed to resume their journey. Nearly all salmon with unplugged nostrils swam into the branch where they were captured, but less than a quarter of the fish that could not smell found the branch.

Apparently salmon "memorize" the characteristic odor of their home stream—its distinctive blend of vegetation, soil particles, minerals, and animals. This "memory" is not inherited. Rather,

it is learned at a very early age, perhaps during the first week of life. If salmon eggs are transferred to another stream or to hatchery tanks, the adult fishes return to the place of hatching and not to the place where the eggs were laid.

More perplexing than how salmon locate their home streams is how they find their way from far out at sea to the rivers that lead to their home streams. In the open ocean, a home-stream odor must be diluted far beyond the ability of even the salmon's keen sense of smell to detect. There salmon must get their bearings at least partially from the position of the sun. But salmon do not rely solely on the sun for orientation; some of them travel at night.

Perhaps fishes, like many birds, have developed a way of navigating by the stars. Sensitivity to changing water temperature may also play a role. Each water mass has a characteristic temperature; hence a fish could sense its drift from one mass into another, and alter its heading accordingly. Perhaps salmon use a combination of these clues to hold a course, compensate for drift, and find their way home.

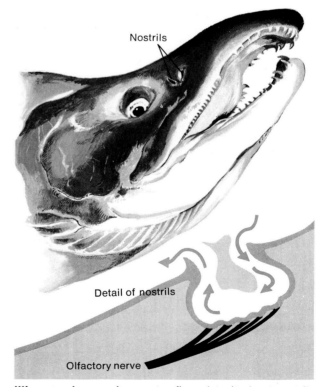

When a salmon swims, water flows into its front nostrils past olfactory receptors, which are linked by nerves to the brain, and out the rear nostrils. Without its sense of smell, a salmon could not find its home stream.

The eel life cycle reverses the salmon pattern. Eels spawn in the Sargasso Sea, mature in northern freshwater streams and ponds

Fishes such as salmon that migrate into fresh water to spawn are called *anadromous*, or "running up." A smaller number of species are *catadromous*, or "running down." The best known catadromous fishes are the freshwater eels, which mature in streams and lakes on both sides of the Atlantic, swim into the sea, reproduce, and die.

For many centuries, the breeding habits of freshwater eels remained one of the great unsolved mysteries of nature. Both Pliny the Elder and Aristotle insisted that eels arose from mud by spontaneous generation. It was not until 1777 that anyone saw a female freshwater eel with fully developed sex glands, and not until 1824 was a comparably mature male found.

In 1896, the Italian naturalists Giovanni Battista Grassi and Salvatore Calandruccio uncovered the first real clue to the origin of the eels. In an aquarium they had several specimens of a small fish known as *Leptocephalus brevirostris* ("short-snouted puny head"). Except for two tiny black eyes, the fish were transparent as glass and had the flat, elongated shape of a willow leaf. Grassi and Calandruccio observed that as the fish grew they became rounder, lost their transparency, and eventually transformed into elvers, or baby eels. *Leptocephalus* was only the larva of the common eel. Since the leaflike young were found only in salt water, the naturalists theorized that baby eels hatched somewhere at sea. This supposition tallied with the yearly disappearance of adult eels into the ocean. But the breeding season and location remained mysteries.

The brilliant biological detective work of Danish oceanographer Johannes Schmidt solved part of the mystery. In 1904, while studying the breeding habits of North Atlantic cod, Schmidt discovered eel larvae between Iceland and Great Britain. Intrigued, he recruited hundreds of fishermen, who towed deep nets in many parts of the Atlantic and kept the hauls for examination by Schmidt.

By analyzing the hauls from the nets, Schmidt traced the distribution of different-size eel larvae throughout the Atlantic. As his data accumulated, an unmistakable pattern appeared on his charts: Eel larvae taken nearer and nearer the Sargasso

Sea were smaller and smaller; those caught in the depths of the Sargasso Sea itself were the very smallest. Here were the eels' breeding grounds.

North American eels hatch in an area to the west of, but overlapping, the birthplace of their European relatives. Spawning takes place in spring, at a depth of about 1500 feet. By summer, the larvae rise to the surface into the currents of the Gulf Stream. The North American eel requires about a year to transform from a *Leptocephalus* to an elver—exactly the time required for the Gulf Stream to carry it to North American shores. The European eel, on the other hand, remains a larva for 2½ to 3 years—again, exactly the time required for currents to carry it to the mouths of European rivers.

The Gulf Stream sweeps both kinds of eels along together, but at some point in their migration they part company. One enters North American rivers while the other continues to Europe. The mechanics of this separation are unknown. Possibly the separation is not complete.

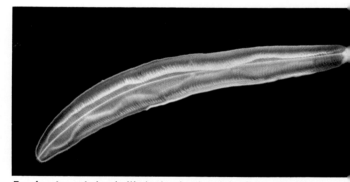

Freshwater eels *begin life in the depths of the Sargasso Sea as leaf-shaped* Leptocephali *(above). By the time they reach the mouths of North American and European rivers, they have become transparent, three-inch elvers (below).*

Nevertheless, swarms of young eels do reach their destinations on both sides of the Atlantic. Males settle in the brackish water of estuaries, but the females swim far upstream to headwaters and lakes. Some even slither through dew-dampened grass to ponds with no links to the sea.

Once established in fresh water, eels remain for five to fifteen years. They hide by day and hunt at night, feeding on anything from carrion to small water birds. Females grow to four or five feet, but males rarely to more than two feet.

As they mature, eels undergo changes in preparation for their return journey to the sea. Some are external changes: The bronze-green or yellow skin is replaced by glistening silver, a color that makes the eels more difficult to see in the open ocean. The eyes grow until they nearly cover the sides of the head, presumably in preparation for the passage through the dimly lighted ocean depths. Internal changes enable the eels to withstand life in salt water. Stores of body fat accumulate to sustain them on their trip to the Sargasso Sea, when they apparently do not eat.

In autumn, mature females leave streams, lakes, and ponds and join males in estuaries. Together they set out for the Sargasso Sea on a trip that may take them across 4000 miles of ocean. None will return. Like Pacific salmon, eels die after spawning.

Many questions about the eels remain unanswered. How do the adults find their way to the breeding grounds? An instinctive urge to swim against the current may play a part, yet females must swim *with* the current to reach the males in estuaries. Do the eels use visual guideposts in the sea or sky? What triggers the urge to migrate?

A host of superstitions surrounding these curious fishes has been dispelled—no one continues to believe that eels arise spontaneously from mud or from dew or from horsehairs dropped into water, or that their parents are a species of beetle, as was suggested as recently as 1866. But the life history of freshwater eels still remains, to a large extent, a mystery.

Marathon Migrations from the Sargasso Sea to Coastal Waters

After hatching in the Sargasso Sea, eels are carried by currents to coastal areas on either side of the Atlantic. The dotted lines show the distribution of American eel larvae; solid lines, European larvae. No larvae smaller than the size given on a line have been found beyond that line. The outermost lines show the greatest distances from the Sargasso Sea that larvae are found. Larvae change into elvers, and elvers become adults.

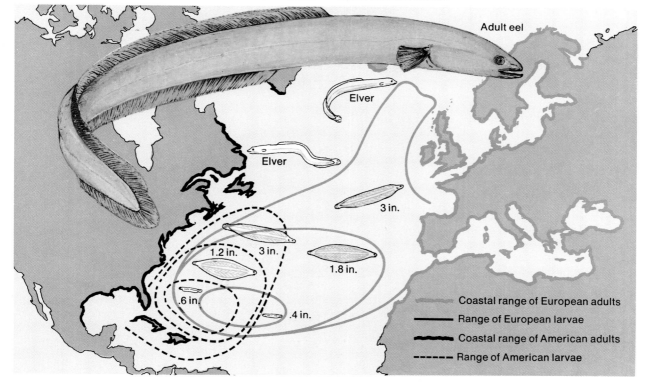

Adult eel

Elver

Elver

3 in.

1.2 in.   3 in.

1.8 in.

.6 in.

.4 in.

Coastal range of European adults
Range of European larvae
Coastal range of American adults
Range of American larvae

How Scientists Study Animal Migration

To study the thousands of fishes, reptiles, birds, and mammals that migrate each year, scientists have developed numerous devices that enable them to find out how far—and sometimes how fast—a particular migrant travels. The ultimate "tag"—a radio transmitter—lets scientists track the entire route of a migrant.

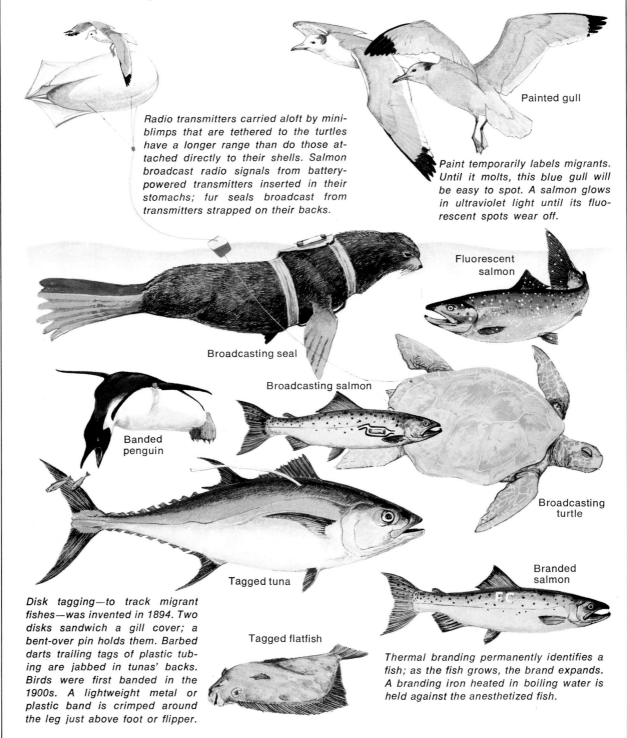

Radio transmitters carried aloft by miniblimps that are tethered to the turtles have a longer range than do those attached directly to their shells. Salmon broadcast radio signals from battery-powered transmitters inserted in their stomachs; fur seals broadcast from transmitters strapped on their backs.

Painted gull

Paint temporarily labels migrants. Until it molts, this blue gull will be easy to spot. A salmon glows in ultraviolet light until its fluorescent spots wear off.

Fluorescent salmon

Broadcasting seal

Broadcasting salmon

Banded penguin

Broadcasting turtle

Branded salmon

Tagged tuna

Disk tagging—to track migrant fishes—was invented in 1894. Two disks sandwich a gill cover; a bent-over pin holds them. Barbed darts trailing tags of plastic tubing are jabbed in tunas' backs. Birds were first banded in the 1900s. A lightweight metal or plastic band is crimped around the leg just above foot or flipper.

Tagged flatfish

Thermal branding permanently identifies a fish; as the fish grows, the brand expands. A branding iron heated in boiling water is held against the anesthetized fish.

Tunas and Their Relatives

The great journeys of swift-swimming tunas and their relatives, marlin and sailfishes, point up our ignorance about how marine animals navigate across the trackless stretches of the sea. Tunas regularly cross both the Atlantic and Pacific oceans. Biologists do not know for certain what natural signposts the tunas follow, but it is suspected that they navigate by the sun. These strong, streamlined fishes are truly oceanic travelers, for they never enter fresh water.

In May and June, large tuna schools move north between Florida and the Bahamas. In the fall, tuna schools are seen off New York, New England, and Newfoundland. These schools were once believed to be a single stock of fish that spawned in southern waters in early spring, then migrated north in summer and fall. But it now appears that two separate stocks of these fishes roam off the east coast of North America.

In 1954, Frank J. Mather III of the Woods Hole Oceanographic Institution on Cape Cod, Massachusetts, started a program in which sport and commercial fishermen attached metal identification tags to bluefins and other tunas. Of the first 7000 tagged, more than 1700 were recaught. Plotting the dates and locations of the recaptures, Mather made the first maps of Atlantic tuna migrations. Surprisingly, none of the 670 bluefins tagged off the Bahamas was recaptured off the northeastern United States. It was therefore concluded that another spawning ground exists in the northern Gulf Stream, supplying the stock for the schools found along the New York, New England, and Newfoundland coasts.

Mather's project also uncovered several remarkable long-distance journeys. Six bluefins tagged near Florida were later recaptured near Norway—5000 to 6300 miles away. One giant tuna made the voyage in the incredible time of fifty days. More than thirty smaller tunas traveled from the coast between Maryland and Cape Cod to the Bay of Biscay off France. But these are probably not regular migration patterns followed by large numbers of fishes each year.

The number of tunas crossing the Atlantic may increase with the strength of westerly winds blowing from North America to Europe. Strong westerlies mean a strong North Atlantic Current (the eastern part of the Gulf Stream that reaches European shores). At such times, a large number of fishes may swim to Europe, or be carried there inadvertently. No tunas tagged off Norway or the Bay of Biscay have been recaptured off the United

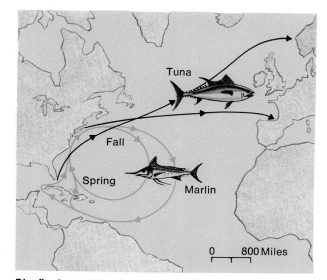

Bluefin tuna and white marlin both make long-distance journeys. Marlin migrate clockwise around the western Atlantic and Caribbean; tuna from North American schools stray as far as Norway and France, but do not return.

States. Apparently they do not return, but instead join European schools regularly migrating between Norway and Spain.

Bluefins cross the Pacific in both directions. It is believed that young fish are born in equatorial waters in the central Pacific, then join adult schools moving north in the warm currents off Japan. Later they come south to California coastal waters, where they feed for two or three years. As they grow older, they head back to the mid-ocean feeding grounds and to the coast of Japan.

Tagging has also revealed two regular migration patterns among marlin. White marlin spend the summer between Cape Hatteras and Cape Cod, then head out to sea in late summer and early fall. They swing clockwise down toward the West Indies and South America. Some skirt the coast of Venezuela and follow currents around the western tip of Cuba, through the Florida Straits, and up the east coast again. Others turn north before reaching Haiti and Puerto Rico and move up past the Bahamas. Striped marlin regularly leave southern California waters in September and October and reach areas of Baja California and the Mexican mainland in November and December. One striped marlin made the longest migration yet recorded for its species, swimming in six months from Catalina Island, California, to a point 975 miles north of the Marquesas—a distance of 2000 miles.

Gray Heermann's gulls and white-and-gray Western gulls wait out a Pacific storm on Monterey peninsula. Nearly all Heermann's gulls breed on tiny Isla Raza in the Gulf of California, then fly to British Columbia in midsummer.

Birds That Migrate Over the Oceans

Tirelessly beating their wings and often fasting until they reach their goal, some birds fly as far as 12,000 miles over the ocean between their winter and summer homes at speeds of up to sixty miles an hour. Migration is triggered by changes in temperature or daylength or by inexorable internal biological clocks. Even flightless penguins migrate, swimming and waddling across ice-strewn Antarctic waters, to and from their rookeries.

From nesting grounds in northern Europe, Eurasian golden plovers fly south to spend their winters around the Mediterranean.

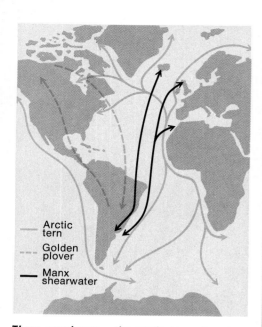

Three wanderers—the arctic tern, American golden plover, and Manx shearwater—migrate thousands of miles each year. The farther north the arctic tern (right) nests, the farther south it migrates. Terns nesting at the Arctic Circle fly to the opposite pole for the Antarctic summer; terns nesting in New England fly only over the Caribbean to South America.

Marauding skuas devour an unguarded egg. South polar skuas nest near the Adélie penguins, whose eggs and chicks they eat. During the Antarctic winter, some skuas migrate to the North Pacific, eating carrion and food stolen from other seabirds.

Churning the waters violently, air-breathing green turtles struggle to stay at the surface while mating near shore.

Flailing her front flippers, a female green turtle digs a flask-shaped nesting chamber with her hind legs.

Brazilian green turtles migrate over 1000 miles to tiny, isolated Ascension Island, lay their eggs, and mate just offshore

Marine turtles are among the great ocean travelers. Like tunas, these animals are superbly adapted to life in the ocean. With front limbs modified into oarlike flippers, they scull across hundreds of miles of open water. Awkward on land, they are as graceful in water as birds in air.

The smallest sea turtle, the Atlantic ridley, reaches a shell length of 2 feet; the biggest, the leatherback, reaches a shell length of 7½ feet, a flipper span of 12 feet, and a weight of 1500 pounds. Between these two are the green turtle, the loggerhead, and the hawksbill.

The green turtle is the best known, largely due to the work of Dr. Archie Carr, a zoologist at the University of Florida. In 1955, Dr. Carr and his associates began an intensive study of green turtles in the Atlantic Ocean, with special emphasis on their breeding and migrating behavior.

Green turtles feed in warm, shallow, continental waters where there are extensive beds of turtle and manatee grass. They breed, however, on remote islands and shorelines that are often separated from their feeding grounds by vast stretches of open ocean. One green-turtle group grazes on manatee grass along the Brazilian coast and migrates all the way to Ascension Island, a six-by-seven-mile island midway between Africa and South America.

Around December, a number of the turtles leave Brazil and head for Ascension Island, 1400 miles away. All the turtles do not migrate every year. Dr. Carr's tagging studies show that some breed at two-year intervals; others wait three years.

Upon reaching Ascension, the females come ashore four or more times, at twelve-day intervals. Each time they dig nests in the sand and deposit about a hundred golf-ball–size eggs. Between trips to the beach, the females mate with the males who remain just beyond the surf, and receive sperm that fertilizes the eggs they will lay two or three years hence. No lush pastures of marine grass exist off Ascension, so when the urge to reproduce is satisfied, the turtles set out again for Brazil.

Some two months later, the eggs hatch in the sun-warmed sand, and the baby turtles dig their way to the surface. No bigger than silver dollars, they invariably head for open water, even when the nest is out of sight of the sea. Apparently they are guided by the quality of the light over the ocean. Once the baby turtles have disappeared into the surf, they presumably eat plankton and drift with the current until reaching suitable coastal feeding grounds.

Adult turtles return to the same breeding sites year after year, and Dr. Carr believes that it is likely that they return to the very beaches where they were hatched, just as salmon and eels return to their native streams. Proof of this is lacking, however—primarily because a practical means of permanently marking or tagging the two-inch-

About 100 eggs are laid *each time the female turtle waddles ashore. She makes at least four such expeditions.*

Erupting simultaneously *from the nest after sixty days of incubation a clutch of young green turtles scurries seaward.*

long turtle hatchlings has not yet been devised.

The breeding migrations of the Brazilian green turtles pose an intriguing and exceedingly difficult question: Why do they travel all the way to Ascension Island when there appear to be suitable breeding sites much closer to their feeding grounds? Dr. Carr suggests that the theory of continental drift may provide an answer. Millions of years ago, when the ancestors of the Brazilian green turtles were evolving their migrating patterns, Africa and South America may have been much closer than they are now; some turtles may have fed off South American shores and bred on African beaches. As the continents drifted apart, successive generations of turtles had to swim farther and farther. Eventually they used Ascension Island for stopovers, and later for the sites where they mated and laid eggs.

Even if the Brazilian turtles' migration patterns can be explained by the theory of continental drift, how do these animals navigate across 1400 miles of open sea and find an island only seven miles long and six miles wide? The question remains unanswered.

Theories abound regarding the homing abilities of not only the green turtles of Ascension Island but also those of other green turtles and any ocean animal that must find its way to distant destinations over long stretches of open ocean. The senses of taste and smell may play a part. Hearing, too, may contribute; turtles cannot make echo-producing sounds of their own, as can bats, but noises made by other animals—such as the loud snappings of schools of shrimp—may

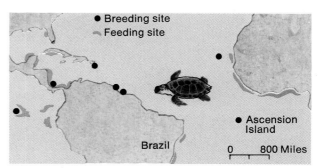

Green turtles migrate *from coastal feeding grounds to the same remote beaches where they hatched. Nesting areas were once more numerous. If the turtles at a site die out, those nesting elsewhere will not take over the site.*

serve as guideposts. Perhaps some animals are sensitive to the Earth's magnetic field, or to the Coriolis force—the force created by the Earth's rotation that deflects moving bodies to the right or left when they are moving north or south. Possibly some animal navigators possess an "inertial sense"—they might detect and record all changes in their speed and direction throughout a journey. To return to a breeding site, they would only have to "remember" all the twists and turns they took since leaving it, then follow them in reverse.

Dr. Carr believes that the green turtles and some other marine animals navigate by the sun—that they possess biological equivalents of the sextants, compasses, clocks, and maps with which human navigators determine their location and chart their course.

The Backboned Conquerors

Written in the rocks of the Earth is one of the greatest adventure stories of all time: the rise to supremacy of the animals with backbones. Their astonishing history begins in the sea some 500 million years ago

Life on Earth began in shallow coastal seas more than three billion years ago. The earliest living things, probably one-celled organisms of some sort, grew by absorbing chemicals from the sea and reproduced by dividing in half. With the passing of millennia, the tiny floating cells became differentiated into plants and animals. All organisms evolved from these simple predecessors.

By 600 million years ago, the seas were populated with representatives of nearly all the major groups of organisms that dwell there today. Only vertebrates—among them fishes, turtles, birds, seals, and whales—had not yet appeared. Although vertebrates are latecomers to the marine community—and, indeed, to the Earth itself—they have attained a mastery of their environment unmatched by animals without backbones.

Vertebrates tend to be large animals. Their size both increases the variety of organisms that they can feed on and reduces the number that can prey on them. They are strong enough to move about freely and to travel widely in search of food. Their highly developed senses provide a steady stream of information about the surrounding world; their complex nervous systems utilize this information to help them survive. Their brains, usually larger than those of invertebrates, have a greater capacity for learning.

By studying fossils, scientists can trace the rise and spread of the backboned latecomers through most of their history. Where gaps exist in the fossil record, many details can be filled in by examining living animals, especially in their embryonic stages. But the origin of vertebrates will perhaps always remain a mystery, for their soft-bodied ancestors left few fossils in the rocks.

Most biologists believe that one present-day animal serves as a reasonably accurate "model" of the ancient, long-extinct invertebrate from which all backboned creatures arose. This animal is the lancelet, also known as amphioxus, found worldwide on shallow bottoms in temperate seas.

An adult lancelet looks like a translucent two-inch minnow. It spends most of its time buried in the sand with just its head protruding. When disturbed, it wriggles vigorously through the water for a short distance, then dives into the sand.

The lancelet feeds by pumping water into its mouth and out its gill slits. Bands of sticky mucus in its throat catch food particles, and cilia push them back into the intestine. The little creature has no bones or cartilage, no fins or limbs, no jaws, no brain, and, except for some light-sensitive spots, no sense organs.

The California sea lion, with its streamlined body and powerful swimming flippers, spends much of its life in the water, and comes ashore only to bask and to breed. But like all marine mammals, sea lions are descended from ancient ancestors that made their homes on dry land.

Lancelets are invertebrates and not fishes, despite their minnowlike appearance. Scientists believe, however, that lancelets are descended from some unknown, long-extinct ancestors that gave rise to all the vertebrates on Earth.

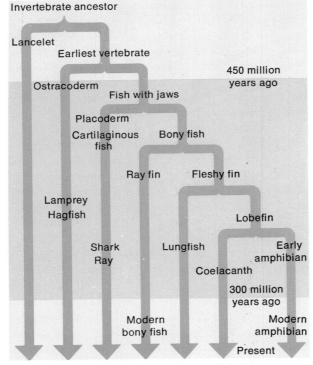

All fishes evolved—as this "family tree" indicates—from a primitive, lanceletlike ancestor. Most of the development occurred between 450 and 300 million years ago. By the latter date, modern types were well established.

The oldest known vertebrates were armored fishlike creatures that lived in shallow seas

The lowly lancelet seems an unlikely candidate for the progenitor of dinosaurs, birds, whales, and man himself. However, it combines characteristics not present in other invertebrates but found in most vertebrates. This combination makes it very probable that some ancient lanceletlike animal was the ancestor of the backboned animals.

Running the length of a lancelet's body is a stiff yet flexible rod called a notochord. A notochord is undoubtedly the evolutionary starting point for the sturdier, jointed backbone of all vertebrates. Also, a hollow nerve cord extends along a lancelet's back above the notochord. Just such a nerve bundle, its front end elaborated into a brain, is present in every vertebrate. Finally, there are the gill slits. In the lancelet these are feeding mechanisms, but with further evolution they could develop into internal respiratory organs similar to the gills of fishes.

Ancestors of Modern Fishes

Fossils of the oldest known vertebrates have been found in rocks laid down as sediments some 450 million years ago. These fishlike animals, called ostracoderms, were in several ways more advanced than the lancelets of today. Their name, which means "shell-skinned," refers to their external armor of bony plates, which may have protected them against water scorpions or other predators. Openings for eyes and a single nostril pierced the armor. Scientists believe that ostracoderms also possessed an internal skeleton of either bone or cartilage.

Less than a foot long, ostracoderms were far less agile than modern fishes. Like their living relatives, lampreys and hagfishes, ostracoderms lacked paired fins and jaws. They apparently swam along the bottom by wriggling their tails tadpole-fashion and got nourishment by filtering edible material from the mud.

Another group of armored fishes, the placoderms, appeared slightly later than ostracoderms in the fossil record. Placoderms did possess jaws and paired fins, adaptations that enabled them to pursue and catch prey. They usually grew longer than ostracoderms—up to thirty feet. Placoderms flourished for some fifty million years; they then

Caught in the act, a predator that may have choked on its meal, and the herring it gulped, are frozen in stone. Fifty million years ago, during Eocene times, these ray-finned fishes swam in ocean waters where Wyoming is today.

died out approximately 350 million years ago.

At some time during their existence, placoderms probably gave rise to a line of primitive fishes that eventually evolved into modern sharks and rays—fishes with skeletons of cartilage, or hard gristle. Because cartilage does not fossilize, the pedigree of sharks and their relatives is difficult to trace. The meager fossil evidence—mostly teeth—indicates that sharks became numerous about 350 million years ago; since then they have probably changed little in appearance.

From the same ancestral line that produced placoderms, another group of jawed, paired-fin fishes developed: the bony fishes. Scientists are not certain whether bony fishes arose in fresh water or salt water. The fossils that might provide details of their origin have either been destroyed by earth-forming processes or remain hidden in the ground.

Conditions on Earth 400 million years ago were different from those today. The climate was far more tropical. Periods of torrential rains were often followed by sustained droughts, when rivers and streams dwindled to chains of stagnant pools devoid of oxygen. Fishes that could only obtain oxygen by extracting it from water flowing over their gills died, but those that could use oxygen from the air survived. Gradually, fishes developed a throat pouch, richly supplied with blood vessels, that evolved into lungs. In all but a few kinds of bony fishes, these lungs are no longer used in respiration; they have become the swim bladder, a gas-filled organ that helps regulate buoyancy.

Early in their history, bony fishes divided into two groups: the ray-finned fishes, with paired fins of thin skin stretched between rigid spines; and the fleshy-finned fishes, with stumpy, "meatier" paired fins. The ray fins became outstandingly successful. By about 230 million years ago, they had spread from the rivers into all oceans. Of the 25,000 species of fishes now living in salt and fresh water, all but about 300 are ray fins.

The fleshy-finned fishes were clearly the losers among fishes in the conquest of water. They now include only six species of freshwater lungfishes and a single marine species, the "living-fossil" coelacanth. But the fleshy-finned fishes—or, rather, their descendants—have achieved lasting evolutionary success as the vertebrate invaders of the land.

Over millions of years, amphibians and reptiles evolved from aquatic to land creatures. Some reptiles returned to the sea

Life on land presented problems that the vertebrates had not encountered during their first 150 million years of existence. Prolonged exposure to air could result in a fatal loss of moisture. Out of water, animals were also subjected to the full effects of gravity. Moving by pushing against the surrounding medium with body and tail was far less efficient on land than in water.

With all the difficulties, the transition from life in water to life on land took millions of years. Some fleshy-finned fishes known as lobefins had long coped with the difficulties of life in stagnant swamp waters. They had lungs and breathed atmospheric oxygen when it was in short supply in the water. Never accomplished swimmers, the stout-bodied lobefins moved over shallow bottoms on muscular fins strengthened by bones.

The development of land-dwelling amphibians from water-dwelling lobefins involved the refinement of existing characteristics rather than the evolution of entirely new ones. The lungs became primary breathing organs rather than secondary ones. The sturdy bones of the skeleton were strengthened for movement on land. The lobed fins became walking legs, and the tail helped the animal keep its balance.

But amphibians never completely solved the problems of life on land. The earliest ones probably used their lungs and legs only when they moved from one pool to another. They spent most of their lives feeding and breeding in the water. Today their living descendants—frogs, toads, and salamanders—seldom venture far from ponds, streams, or moist places under rocks or forest litter. All but a specialized few return to water to lay their eggs, which quickly hatch into swimming, gill-breathing young. Some amphibians, such as mud puppies, never change to lung-breathing land dwellers. They spend their entire lives in fresh water, breathing with gills that can increase in size when the water is stagnant.

Amphibians might be viewed as "successful failures" in vertebrate history. Tied themselves to fresh water, they nevertheless opened up an evolutionary avenue for the development of more advanced backboned groups.

Rise of the Reptiles

The first reptiles severed their reproductive tie to water about 300 million years ago, after millions of years of evolution had produced a new, protected type of egg—the amniote egg. An amniote egg can hatch out of water in a completely dry place. Within its protective shell is a substitute for the moist or watery environment needed by developing amphibians. A liquid-filled sac, the amnion, surrounds the embryo and cushions it against shock. The embryo feeds on a large supply of yolk, breathes oxygen picked up from the air by blood vessels just under the shell, and deposits wastes in a membranous "bag" inside the shell.

The amniote egg gave reptiles a tremendous advantage. An egg laid on land and encased in a tough shell was less likely to be eaten by hungry predators than a fish or amphibian egg. Such an egg permitted a developing reptile to spend the

Ichthyosaurs and plesiosaurs evolved from land-dwelling, reptilian ancestors that took divergent paths in adapting to a marine environment. Porpoise-shaped ichthyosaurs (right) undulated swiftly through ocean waters; two types of plesiosaurs (left) used paddle-shaped limbs to propel themselves in water. All ichthyosaurs and plesiosaurs are extinct.

first, relatively helpless stages of its life protected against drying within a miniature fortress.

The first reptiles probably ventured on land only to seek new swamps and pools or to deposit their eggs. But as watertight skins and other water-retaining devices evolved, reptiles underwent an unparalleled explosion of varieties and numbers. For 170 million years, they ruled the land.

As some reptiles spread across the continents, where amphibians offered only the feeblest competition, others invaded the sea. All the marine reptiles remained air breathers, and most came ashore to lay their eggs. But a few became nearly as independent of land as fishes.

The most prominent ancient ocean reptiles were ichthyosaurs and plesiosaurs. Both apparently took to the sea soon after early reptiles developed from amphibians. Fast and agile swimmers, the streamlined ichthyosaurs bore a re-

markable resemblance both to sharks, which had developed earlier, and to porpoises, which were to come later. Well-preserved fossils, some containing embryos, reveal that ichthyosaurs did not have to come ashore to reproduce. The female retained eggs within her body until they hatched, and the young emerged live and swimming.

The plesiosaurs—less streamlined than ichthyosaurs, with turtlelike bodies and paddle-shaped limbs—were probably slow swimmers. Their long, serpentine necks may have compensated for their lack of speed by allowing the head to dart in various directions and snap up prey.

About sixty-five million years ago, the Age of Reptiles ended in a great wave of mass extinction. The nearly simultaneous disappearance of so many creatures has never been adequately explained. All that remains of this once dominant group are turtles, lizards, snakes, and crocodilians.

Many kinds of reptiles swam in the sea 100 million years ago; only about sixty species — mainly snakes and turtles — live there today

Of the reptiles that have survived to modern times, crocodilians face the most doubtful future. Their two dozen species are near extinction and are being hastened in that way by the activities of man, who kills them and destroys their habitat.

Only one species of crocodilian is fully adapted to life in the sea: the saltwater crocodile, still fairly common in coastal waters from India to Australia. It favors estuaries, but sometimes undertakes ocean journeys of several hundred miles or more.

Marine turtles have achieved much more success as invaders of the ocean than crocodilians. They remain air breathers, but their front legs have been elongated and flattened into powerful flippers for swimming. Their paddle-shaped hind feet are used for steering and for digging nests in the beach. Like open-sea fishes, some marine turtles bear the camouflaging coloration of dark above, light below. The bony shell of the "true" sea turtles—the green, hawksbill, ridley, and loggerhead—is reduced in size and weight as an adaptation for floating and swimming. The leatherback, whose weight of 1200 pounds or more makes it the world's largest turtle, retains only small, bony plates embedded in a tough, thick hide; it has no shell.

In one important respect, sea turtles are still tied to their terrestrial heritage. The females must come ashore to lay their eggs. At this time, these massive animals are the most vulnerable to the predations of man.

Snakes evolved relatively recently from the lizard line of reptilian development; the first snakes occur in the fossil record long after the heyday of the reptiles. In effect, snakes are lizards that have lost their limbs, perhaps in adapting to a now-abandoned burrowing way of life. Venomous fangs developed even more recently, appearing only within the last fifty million years.

Although most modern snakes dwell on land, some fifty kinds—each bearing venomous fangs—live in the sea. Less tied to land than marine turtles, only about half of these species come ashore

The saltwater crocodile reaches a length of nearly twenty-five feet. Highly aggressive, it is a dangerous maneater, attacking human beings without provocation. Hunting by man for its commercially valuable hide has reduced its numbers.

to lay their eggs. Like ancient ichthyosaurs, the other kinds produce eggs that hatch within the female's body. The young emerge able to swim and feed. All sea snakes breathe oxygen from the air, but they can remain underwater several hours at a time. Valves prevent water from flooding the sea snake's nostrils.

Most sea snakes stay close to shore, but the yellow-bellied sea snake has been sighted hundreds of miles from land. This snake has migrated east and west from the coast of Asia and is found off Africa and the Americas. Most other species confine themselves to warm coastal waters from the Persian Gulf to Japan and east to Samoa. Sea snakes sometimes congregate in enormous numbers. In 1932, a huge mass of writhing snakes "ten feet wide and fully sixty miles long" was reported near Indonesia.

Sea snakes lie quietly at the surface or on the sea floor waiting for prey—usually fishes—to come within striking distance. Then their movements are sudden and rapid. Like their terrestrial relatives, they can swallow meals more than twice their own diameter. When two sea snakes begin consuming the same prey at opposite ends, the smaller snake may disappear into the larger.

A black-banded sea snake slithers across a coral reef off the Loyalty Islands. Air-breathing sea snakes can slow down their metabolism to remain underwater for hours; some may even absorb oxygen from swallowed water.

A loggerhead turtle swims gracefully underwater. Huge, aggressive loggerheads are the least reduced in numbers of all sea turtles. But real estate projects on U.S. coasts, and poaching on Caribbean beaches, threaten nesting sites.

An early flying reptile (bottom) had a long, bony tail with a flattened end probably used for steering. Further evolution produced a pterosaur without a tail (center), closer to birds in form and with a twenty-five-foot wing span.

About 175 million years ago, the first vertebrate fliers, the pterosaurs, took to the air

The pterosaurs evolved during the period that dinosaurs ruled the Earth. They ranged from sparrow size to giants with wingspan of forty feet.

Pterosaurs never fully mastered the air. Their weakly supported wings could not lift them directly off the ground, so they must have launched themselves from trees and cliffs. Once aloft, these flying reptiles glided on winds and air currents, occasionally flapping their wings to gain altitude. Those that lived along the seashore swooped low over the ocean's surface to snatch fishes and invertebrates. Nearly all pterosaurs had elongated, beaklike jaws armed with pointed, grabbing teeth; some had throat pouches like those of pelicans in which to store their catch.

About the time the first pterosaurs were struggling into the air, another group of reptiles also began to fly. Unlike pterosaurs, which vanished with the dinosaurs sixty million years ago, these other fliers did not die out. They became the ancestors of birds. Birds are the most poorly repre-

sented vertebrates in the fossil record, but four specimens of a very early type, *Archaeopteryx*, have been discovered in a Bavarian limestone formation about 140 million years old. These crow-size creatures retain many reptilian characteristics, including teeth and a slender, bony tail. They are indisputably birds, however, for the limestone shows clear imprints of feathers.

Two other primitive birds have been discovered in west-central North American rocks about 100 million years old. Both are ocean species that exhibit evidence of much evolutionary progress. One resembles today's terns. The other, about five to six feet long, appears to have abandoned flight in favor of swimming and diving; it has small wings and powerful webbed feet.

Beyond these clues, little is known about the early history of birds. Bones and teeth provide important data in the story of vertebrate evolution, and birds are brittle-boned, toothless creatures. But despite the lack of fossil evidence, it is possible to speculate about how birds adapted to the demands of flight. Sustained flight requires quick responses and well-coordinated muscles. Such activity is beyond the small brain and sluggish metabolism of reptiles. In mastering flight, the birds evolved an array of adaptations that

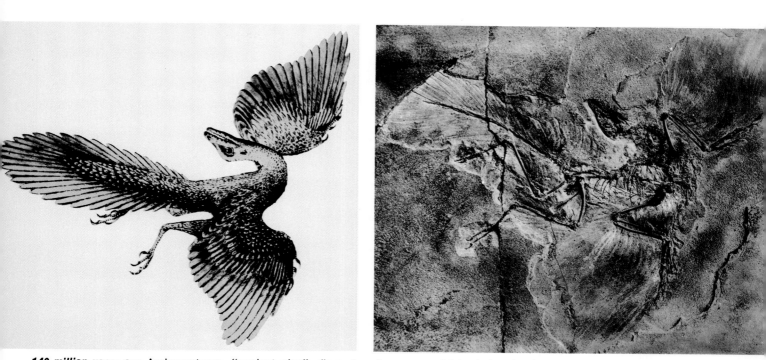

140 million years ago Archaeopteryx—"ancient wing"—flew clumsily over coral islands in what is now northern Europe. Some fossils, such as this one at the Berlin Museum, clearly show its feathers, wing claws, reptilian head, and long, bony tail.

speeded up the entire tempo of their lives.

Early in their history, birds became warm-blooded—that is, able to maintain a high, constant body temperature independent of the surrounding air's temperature. Cold-blooded animals —fishes, invertebrates, amphibians, and reptiles— slow down as temperatures drop, but birds remain alert and active. In becoming warm-blooded, birds acquired a large, efficient heart, which rapidly pumps large volumes of oxygen-rich blood to their strong muscles. They also acquired feathers, which insulate them and give them an aerodynamic shape.

Wheeling and diving rapidly through the air, birds need more information about their surroundings than can be supplied by "local" senses —taste, smell, and touch. It is not surprising, therefore, that they developed keener eyes than reptiles and that the lobes of their brain associated with vision are proportionately larger. In comparison with reptiles, birds' brains are also slightly larger in those parts associated with intelligence and much larger in those parts associated with movement. A modern bird comes equipped with an extensive repertoire of inherited responses to its environment, and with an ability to learn whatever else is needed for survival.

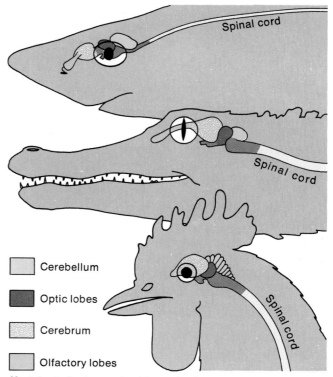

- Cerebellum
- Optic lobes
- Cerebrum
- Olfactory lobes

Vertebrate brains evolved from simple sense receptors into complex coordinators. From fish to reptile to bird the olfactory bulbs (smell) shrink compared to optic lobes (sight), cerebellum (orientation), and cerebrum (intelligence).

Albatrosses and petrels spend all their lives at sea, returning to land only briefly to breed

Only about 250 of the 8500 varieties of modern birds are adapted for life in and around the ocean. But if seabirds are less varied than land birds, they are nevertheless extremely numerous. Indeed, the most abundant bird in the world is probably a small marine species, Wilson's petrel.

Like most marine reptiles, seabirds lead a double life. They usually feed only in salt water, and many spend months out of sight of land. But they must return to shore for breeding.

The wandering albatross, largest of all flying seabirds, travels tens of thousands of miles without touching down on land. Found only in the violent wind-whipped oceans of the far southern latitudes, where it may circle Antarctica several times a year, this striking bird flies in gales that would drive most other creatures to shelter. It banks and wheels just above the crests of the waves, seldom rising more than fifty feet into the air. Now and then it settles onto the surface.

Aloft, the wandering albatross holds its long, narrow wings—almost twelve feet in span but only about ten inches wide—nearly motionless. It may soar for hours, making only slight adjustments to take advantage of the wind's constantly shifting gusts and eddies. In calm weather, an infrequent occurrence in the southern oceans, the bird waits on the surface for the return of the winds. To get aloft again, it must sometimes run clumsily along the waves, flapping its wings until it becomes airborne between two swells. Once in the air, any suggestion of clumsiness vanishes, for an albatross is a graceful and capable flier.

The wandering albatrosses are solitary travelers during their long journeys. Every year or two, however, they gather in breeding colonies on remote islands scattered between Antarctica and the southern coasts of Africa, Australia, and South America. After an elaborate courtship ceremony and mating, female albatrosses lay a single egg in a large grass nest. The incubation period is unusually long—about eleven weeks. After the young bird hatches, it spends nine months in or near the nest, then takes up the solitary life of an adult. Before returning to the colony, a young wandering albatross may spend eight or nine years at sea; when it is an adult, it returns to the colony to breed every other year.

Petrels are small relatives of albatrosses and, like them, come ashore only for reproduction. These agile fliers skim between the waves, snatching up shrimps and fishes with their hooked beaks. They range in size from the giant petrel, which is as large as a small albatross, to the storm petrel, which is as small as a starling.

Petrels may travel enormous distances to reach the breeding grounds that they sometimes share with albatrosses. Wilson's petrels breed on Antarctica and nearby islands in the southern summer, then fly as far north as California and Labrador during warm months in the Northern Hemisphere. These birds thus enjoy the most congenial seasons in both hemispheres, but commute as much as 20,000 miles a year to do so. Wilson's petrels are frequently seen on moonlit nights moving in large flocks close to the waves and uttering melancholy squeals. When feeding in calm weather, they stretch out their wings and hop or run across the water on their webbed feet.

Becalmed on the ocean's surface, a wandering albatross awaits the wind that will lift it into the air again. The birds breed on remote southern islands, each pair producing a single chick (right) every other year. It is believed that the young bird spends its first winter alone in its nest, probably sustained only by the fat that is stored in its body.

Wilson's petrel, the smallest seabird, characteristically skips and flutters across the waves, snapping up fish and invertebrates. Its yearly travels take it from the rim of Antarctica to the waters between Labrador and the British Isles.

Tobogganing down a snow bank, *penguins travel at surprising speed. The wings balance them and also act almost like forelegs; thrusts by their strong legs send them sliding forward. Penguins can even toboggan on flat ground.*

Penguins—Birds of the Southern Seas

Curiously, the far-flying albatrosses, petrels, and their relatives may share a common ancestor with the totally flightless penguins. Some evidence, at least, suggests that these two different groups are linked. One of the oldest fossil penguins has a skull and bill similar to that of the wandering albatross, and some young penguins develop tubular openings in their nostrils, a characteristic of petrels, albatrosses, and related birds. The two lines must have diverged long ago —fossils found in New Zealand indicate that penguins closely resembling modern species were alive seventy million years ago.

Although penguins are traditionally associated with Antarctica, only two modern species, the emperor and the Adélie, live there. Fourteen other species dwell on barren, rocky islands in the Antarctic Ocean and along the shores of the southern continents; one species, the Galápagos penguin, is found as far north as the Equator, where it can survive because of the cold, food-rich Humboldt current flowing up along the western coast of South America.

On land, penguins hop or waddle awkwardly on their stubby legs, or toboggan along on their bellies by pushing against the ice with flipperlike wings. In the sea, they display a degree of speed and agility surpassing that of many fishes. Penguins literally "fly" in the water with powerful strokes of their wings. They can swim fifteen miles an hour over long distances and can go twice as fast for short periods when pursuing prey or escaping from enemies. Their flat, webbed feet stretch out behind them and help steer their torpedo-shaped bodies. To breathe, penguins break the surface periodically, arch through the air like porpoises, and disappear again with

Plunging in and out of the sea, Adélie penguins breathe as they skim above the surface, then duck back a moment later with whirring flippers. Thus breathing does not impede their progress, which is about fifteen miles an hour.

scarcely a ripple. To come ashore, most species shoot vertically out of the water and land standing on their feet.

Penguins feed on fishes, squids, and krill abounding in the cold southern seas. In turn, leopard seals, and occasionally killer whales, eat them. On land, adult penguins are virtually without enemies, but skuas, gull-like hunters that breed on the outskirts of penguin colonies, take a heavy toll of the eggs and young chicks of their neighbors.

Adélie and emperor penguins breed on the Antarctic continent. The Adélies lay their eggs in summer when temperatures rise above freezing. But the three-foot emperors lay their eggs in the middle of the frigid Antarctic winter, when the temperature drops to −80° F. and blizzard winds blow 80 to 100 miles an hour.

Soon after a female emperor penguin has pro-

duced her single egg, she departs for feeding grounds in open water—a journey that may take her across vast stretches of ice. For two months, the male incubates the egg on his feet. A fold of skin on his lower abdomen covers the egg and warms the embryo inside. If the egg hatches before the female returns, the chick's first food is a secretion from the crop of the father, who has fasted throughout the incubation.

When the mother returns, her crop filled with several pounds of food, the parents reverse roles. The female takes charge of the chick, and the emaciated male sets forth on the long trek to open water.

After the growing chick is about six weeks old, it is fed by both parents. With the arrival of summer, young emperors are mature enough to reach the water, which is many miles closer because of the breakup of the sea ice.

Adélies catapult themselves several times their own height onto an iceberg. One penguin has just landed; others climb awkwardly, waving their flippers for balance.

From the top of an iceberg, Adélies plunge into the sea. Their buoyancy reduced by solid bones—unlike those of flying birds—Adélies can dive as deep as sixty feet.

The Agile Antarctic Adélies

Thirty-inch-tall Adélies are the best-known members of the flightless penguin family. Adélies spend the winter at sea, feeding on krill and small fishes. In October (the Antarctic spring), they waddle back to their breeding rookeries across as much as sixty miles of pack ice. Males arrive first, establish territories, then attract mates with ritual displays. After pairs form, both sexes gather stones for the nest, often stealing them from neighboring birds, and take turns incubating the eggs. At two-week intervals, one parent returns from feeding at sea and relieves the other, which then sets off to feed. The chicks hatch in about five weeks, then spend about a month in the nest and another month in a large group of youngsters, although parents continue to feed them. At the age of eight or nine weeks, the chicks molt and go off on their own, ready to face life in the sea.

Huge flocks of Adélie penguins gather near the edge of the Antarctic pack ice. As many as 100,000 gregarious Adélies may cluster in one rookery, perhaps finding safety in numbers from skuas and other birds that prey on eggs and chicks.

A predatory leopard seal seizes a luckless penguin head-first, preparing to gulp it down whole. The leopard seal is one of the few natural enemies of adult Adélies.

An Adélie penguin incubates its egg on a crude nest of stones, the only available nest-building material. Male and female take turns, freeing each other to feed at sea.

During the breeding season, the somber black-and-white plumage of the Atlantic puffin is relieved by multicolored horny shields on the bill and cheeks. When the birds molt after the breeding season, these bright ornaments are shed.

Incredible crowding is the rule at the nesting grounds of auks, puffins, and murres

Penguins live only in the Southern Hemisphere. In the north they have distant but strikingly similar relatives—the alcids, a family that includes auks, puffins, and murres. As awkward as penguins on land, the black and white alcids are remarkably agile in water. They, too, feed on fishes, squids, and shrimps, and "fly" underwater by means of stout swimming wings and webbed feet. These similarities are a striking example of parallel evolution—of two different groups independently evolving similar adaptations.

In one respect, however, all living alcids differ markedly from penguins: They can fly. The largest alcid, the thirty-inch-tall great auk, was the only flightless bird in the Northern Hemisphere during recent times. The great auk's flightlessness was its undoing; easy prey for hunters and feather collectors, the bird became extinct in the middle of the nineteenth century.

In spring, the islands and coastal cliffs of northern oceans bustle with crowded colonies of alcids. Auks and murres nest on ledges and among jumbled boulders, puffins crouch in crevices and burrows on the bluffs above. These precarious nesting sites have resulted in a curious adaptation: The eggs of the ledge dwellers are markedly pear-shaped, making them less likely to roll over the edge than round or oval eggs.

Common murres (also known as common guillemots) typify the ledge-nesting alcids. They spend the winter in offshore waters, then gather in dense, noisy colonies on cliffs along the northern Atlantic and Pacific coasts. By May, the murres have paired off and staked claim to a small bit of ledge space. On the bare rock, the female lays one egg, which is cared for by both parents. Egg and hatchling mortality is high. Jostling adults tumble many off the ledges; other eggs and hatchlings, momentarily unattended, fall prey to voracious, ever-present gulls.

In July, a young murre leaves its ledge and enters the ocean, although it has not yet developed its flight feathers. The bird literally "takes the plunge." Encouraged by its excited parents, it walks to the brink and, after much hesitation,

Great auk

Razorbill

Little auk

Crested auklet

The compact alcids stand erect on short legs set far back. With webbed feet and small wings, they are clumsy on land, but strong swimmers and divers. Unlike the penguins, whose evolution somewhat parallels the alcids, living Arctic-dwelling alcids can fly. Only the great auk was flightless—which probably hastened its extinction.

leaps into the sea. One or both parents join the newly launched young bird, and together they swim out to sea, their home for the winter months. The ledges remain quiet and deserted until the murres return the following spring.

The common puffins, easily recognized during the breeding season by the male's prominent red, yellow, and blue striped bill, nest in about the same localities as the Atlantic populations of murres. Puffins arrive at the cliffs and rocky islands in late March or April. After courting and mating, each pair finds a crevice or excavates a burrow several feet long. The female lays one egg, and both birds take turns keeping it warm. The parent on duty leans awkwardly against the egg, tucking it under one wing. In about forty days, the hatchling emerges—a black and white ball of fluffy down with an insatiable appetite. Both parents keep busy supplying the hungry offspring, sometimes carrying as many as eighteen fishes in one load. After six weeks, this parental care ends abruptly, and adult puffins depart for the open sea. The young puffin spends about another week alone in the burrow, then makes its way to the water. Here it learns to swim, dive, and fly without the guidance or protection of older birds.

No space is wasted in a crowded breeding colony of murres; here, adults and nestlings sit nearly shoulder to shoulder on a narrow Icelandic cliff ledge. Each pair of murres produces one pear-shaped egg. These eggs are less likely than rounder eggs to roll off the ledge when unattended. Even so, many eggs and chicks are by accident jostled off the cliffs when adults embark on or return from feeding trips, and many fall victim to gulls and other hungry predators.

Seabirds of the middle latitudes are resourceful and agile fishermen. Many dive; a few skim the surface; some rob others of their catch

South of the alcids and north of the penguins, temperate and tropical seas are populated by immense numbers of seabirds. Boobies, cormorants, pelicans, frigate birds, and skimmers live here, nesting on shore and feeding in coastal waters.

These middle-latitude birds use a wide variety of fishing techniques. Boobies plummet into the sea from heights of 60 to 100 feet and catch flying fishes just as they reenter the water. Cormorants swim along at the surface, periodically diving to chase fishes; the birds have been found tangled in fishermen's nets from depths of 70 to 100 feet.

Pelicans feed just under the surface, using their capacious throat pouches as effective seining nets. The brown pelican, the most fully marine of the pelicans, patrols about thirty feet above the water. When it sights a school of small fish, the bird noses over, folds back its wings, and crashes into the water like a falling rock. The impact stuns nearby fish long enough for the pelican to gather a sizable catch, along with two or three gallons of water, in its pouch. The bird cannot get into the air again until all water drains out of its pouch. Even then it flaps and flails a good deal before taking off.

In contrast to the diving birds, the frigate birds feed without wetting more than their bills. They skim along just above the waves, snapping up jellyfish, squids, fishes, young sea turtles, and bits of carrion. Particularly fond of flying fishes, the frigate birds sometimes catch them in midflight.

Frigate birds are nearly as capable in flight as albatrosses. With exceptionally light bodies and seven-foot wings, the birds can swoop and soar

The masked booby, with a wingspan up to sixty-eight inches, is the largest member of its family. The bird feeds mainly on flying fish; it can snap up a victim in mid-flight — or dive under the water and swim in pursuit of its prey.

on air currents for hours before returning to land to rest. But if a frigate bird is forced to settle onto the ocean's surface, it is unlikely to rise again; it has no oil-producing glands to waterproof its plumage. Unless a strong gust of wind quickly lifts it aloft, the bird will probably drown.

Frigate birds are accomplished pirates. A flying booby that has just swallowed a fish is no match for these swift, noisy marauders. The frigate birds pummel and jostle their unfortunate victim until it regurgitates its catch, then grab the morsel before it disappears into the ocean.

During the breeding season, frigate birds build loose, platform nests in trees and shrubs on isolated islands or mangrove tangles—locations somewhat protected from egg-eating mammals and reptiles. The birds gather feathers, bones, and other nesting materials from the ground, steal from other nesters, and break branches off trees and bushes. One parent always remains at the nest, for frigate birds regard the eggs and chicks of their neighbors as fair prey.

A scarlet throat sac identifies this magnificent frigate bird as a male. During the courtship and nesting season, the sac can be puffed up with air like a gaudy toy balloon.

The red-billed tropic bird, found in warm coastal seas around the world, is built for flying, swimming, and diving. The bird can neither walk nor stand on land, and to move about must rest on its belly and shove itself along with its feet.

A polar bear clambers onto a chunk of ice. A layer of fat protects it—like most marine mammals—from cold.

Polar bear

Brown bear

More streamlined *than the brown bears, slim long-necked polar bears are adapted for hunting on ice and in the water. Their claws are short and straight, and insulating hair protects their feet from the cold sea and ice.*

Basically a land animal, the polar bear is well adapted for a part-time life in the sea and on Arctic pack ice

The early history of mammals generally parallels that of birds. Like birds, mammals evolved from reptiles, became warm-blooded, and developed an insulating body cover (hair instead of feathers), keen senses, and a larger brain.

Unlike birds, however, nearly all mammals abandoned the shelled-egg method of reproduction. The earliest mammals, which may have resembled the modern platypus and spiny anteater, probably laid eggs. But most modern mammalian young develop within the mother's body and are linked by a placenta to her circulatory system. After birth, the young are nourished by the mother's milk and receive parental care for an extended period.

When many of the mammals' reptilian competitors became extinct between sixty and sixty-five million years ago, the pace of mammalian evolution accelerated tremendously. Their numbers, variety, and size rapidly increased, and they spread from dry land into rivers and seas.

The first mammals to enter the sea were probably the ancestors of the whales. Next came the ancestors of dugongs and manatees. Millions of years later came the ancestors of seals, sea lions, sea otters, walruses, and polar bears.

The gradual adaptation of mammals to life in the ocean is illustrated by the marine mammals alive today. From polar bears to whales, there are mammals in various stages of transition from a terrestrial to a marine way of life.

On the evolutionary time scale, the polar bear has only very recently become a part-time marine mammal; only a scant million years ago, its ancestors were land dwellers. The polar bear and the land-dwelling brown bear are so closely related that in captivity they can interbreed. But thousands of years of hunting on the pack ice and in the sea have changed the polar bear. Adapted for a life in which swimming plays an important role, it has a smaller head, a longer neck, and a more slender and streamlined torso than the brown bear. The polar bear also displays a "Roman nose" profile that cuts through the water with a minimum of resistance, while the brown bear's face is markedly dished in.

Nearly grown polar bear cubs (left and right) hunt with their mother. Born in the late fall, cubs stay with their mother almost two years. When seals—their preferred food—are scarce, polar bears eat seabirds, fish, lichens, and moss.

Polar bears venture hundreds of miles out to sea, but most commonly they frequent regions that offer a mixture of land, ice, and open water. They give birth to their young on land; they hunt for seals, the staple of their diet, out on the drifting floes of ice.

To catch a wary, fast-swimming seal, a polar bear relies upon stealth rather than speed. When it spots a seal dozing in the sun on an ice floe, the bear moves downwind and begins a slow, cautious approach. The seal may periodically wake up to make a quick check of its surroundings; the bear freezes motionless until the prey closes its eyes again. If the final approach must be made through water, the bear quietly eases itself in, hind feet first, and swims just beneath the surface. Occasionally it raises its head just above the water to breathe and to measure the remaining distance. Upon reaching the seal's patch of ice, the bear clambers out of the water and crushes the skull of its victim with a blow of its massive forepaw.

When seals are unavailable, polar bears consume anything edible: fishes, seabirds and their eggs, lemmings, plants, carrion. A dead whale washed ashore is a bonanza that attracts polar bears from many miles around.

During the brief midsummer breeding period, pairs may travel together; at other times, polar bears are solitary roamers. In fall, a pregnant female excavates a roomy den in a snowbank and slumbers until the birth of her twins in early winter. The den shelters the mother and cubs well; temperatures inside may be forty degrees higher than outside. The family leaves the den in April, and the cubs often remain with their mother until they are two years old. Under rather severe maternal supervision, they learn how to survive in a bleak world where starvation will be a lifelong threat.

Man is the polar bear's only enemy, but a formidable one. The bears have been badly overhunted, presently numbering less than 15,000. However, now that hunting is legally limited, hopefully the polar bear will not join the lengthening list of animals that have been wiped out by human greed or indifference.

A sea otter munches a starfish with powerful incisors and molars. Sea otters usually eat mollusks and other shellfish.

Sea Otters of the Pacific Kelp

The web-footed sea otters, members of the weasel family, are well adapted to ocean life and seldom come ashore except to give birth. They live in dense North Pacific kelp beds, where they swim or sleep among the algae's fronds. Unlike most marine mammals, sea otters are not insulated by a layer of blubber beneath the skin. Instead, they are kept warm by air trapped in their thick, heavy fur. These luxurious coats nearly doomed them; by the end of the 19th century fur trappers had almost exterminated the species. Through the efforts of conservationists, sea otters are now making a strong comeback.

An eighty-pound sea otter nibbles a mussel while floating on its back. To supply the energy needed to stay alive and active in the ocean, a sea otter must eat about twenty pounds of shellfish meat — one-fourth its body weight — every day.

One of the few animals to use tools, sea otters sometimes smash open abalones and other shellfish against flat stones balanced on their chests. Competing with man for the meat of abalones, sea otters are occasionally killed by fishermen.

Wrapping itself in seaweed to keep from drifting off, a sea otter rests, buoyed and warmed by the air pockets in its dense fur. Gregarious sea otters congregate among Pacific kelp beds in herds, or pods, of several dozen animals.

A manatee calf nuzzles its mother. Living on both sides of the Atlantic, manatees are closely related to elephants but have lost their hind limbs in adapting to aquatic life. They feed by everting their lip pads and sweeping in vegetation on the attached bristles. Bemused medieval sailors mistook manatee cows nursing their young in an upright position for mermaids.

Walruses are gregarious animals, and may congregate along northern shores and ice floes in herds of a hundred or more individuals. Bulls reach a weight of 3700 pounds—including 900 pounds of blubber.

Emerging from under the ice, *a Weddell seal surfaces near Scott Base, Antarctica. Weddell seals winter beneath the ice, cutting breathing holes with strong teeth. Scientists do not know as yet how seals locate the blowholes from underwater.*

Walruses and seals spend most of their lives in the sea and venture on land mainly to breed. Manatees never come ashore

Like sea otters, seals and their relatives still come ashore to bear their young. But in every other respect, these pinnipeds—"fin-footed ones" —are a more fully marine group of mammals. They travel far, swim fast, and dive deep in nearly all the oceans of the world. They are big animals: the smallest, the ringed seal, is 4½ feet long and weighs 190 pounds; the largest, the male southern elephant seal, reaches 20 feet and 8000 pounds.

The pinnipeds evolved at least fifty million years ago from four-legged land dwellers. The earless or "true" seals have progressed farthest toward a full-time oceanic life; their hind limbs have become almost tail-like and can no longer turn forward. As a result, an earless seal on land "humps" along somewhat in the manner of an outsized caterpillar. Eared seals—fur seals and sea lions—and walruses hobble slowly and awkwardly on all four legs.

The earless seals make astonishingly long and deep dives. The Weddell seal of the Antarctic Ocean can dive to nearly 2000 feet and remain submerged for more than an hour.

When it dives, a seal conserves oxygen with a number of extraordinary mechanisms. The animal's metabolic rate drops, so that its body consumes oxygen at a much slower rate. The heartbeat slows to one-tenth its normal pace. The pattern of blood circulation changes, and the heart and brain, the organs most quickly damaged by an oxygen shortage, receive a greater share of the blood flow. Also, because their blood carries more oxygen than that of most mammals, seals can take a larger supply of the life-sustaining gas down with them.

The ability of the seals to dive far beneath the surface of the sea demonstrates the versatility and adaptability of the basic mammalian design. But even the remarkable seals have not fully exploited the possibilities for ocean life. Among the mammals, the true conquerors of the marine environment are the whales.

Of Whales and Men

Whales range in size from 100-pound porpoises to 100-ton blues. Their ancestors once walked on land, but whales are as much at home in the water as fishes. Only one enemy—man—threatens their continued success

Whales are the mightiest creatures ever to live on Earth. A full-grown blue whale weighs as much as thirty elephants and could easily carry the largest dinosaur on its back.

Because whales are mammals, they must have evolved from land animals. But few fossils have been found to document their transition from a terrestrial to a marine way of life. Attempts at reconstructing their early history begin with the oldest known whale fossils, those of the extinct archaeocetes—"old whales." The archaeocetes had pegged-shaped front teeth similar to those of some modern whales, and triangular molars similar to those of certain primitive land-dwelling predators. The presence of molars, absent in modern whales, suggests that archaeocetes might have been descendants of small terrestrial meat eaters.

The first step in that long, mysterious evolution may have come as these land mammals began wading into the water along shores of lakes and shallow seas some seventy million years ago. During the next fifteen to twenty million years, their descendants ventured deeper and deeper and

Cruising underwater, a beluga whale can use echo-locating clicks to avoid obstacles. Belugas cluster in herds within the Arctic Circle, swimming south if the pack ice becomes too solid. Adult belugas weigh about 800 pounds, and feed mainly on cuttlefishes and crustaceans.

stayed longer and longer. Perhaps food was more plentiful, or enemies scarcer in the water. Whatever the reasons for leaving land, the ancestors of whales adapted to ocean life mainly in this period.

The fossil trail begins early in the great age of mammals, around fifty million years ago, with the appearance of the archaeocetes, which closely resembled modern whales. The skulls of these ancient whales were elongated; the nostrils had moved from the snout toward the top of the head —the ultimate location of the blowhole. During the twenty million years of whale evolution unrecorded in fossil history, the mammalian hind legs disappeared, except for internal remnants. Forelegs became flat flippers, used for steering and maintaining balance, while the tails assumed a dominant role in locomotion. The tail vertebrae increased in size to become the largest in the spinal column, permitting the attachment of powerful swimming muscles.

Archaeocetes reached their peak of development with a group of giants. The largest had slender, seventy-foot bodies and were proportioned more like fictitious sea serpents than like modern whales. Around twenty-five million years ago, the last of the archaeocetes vanished, but not before the appearance of ancestors of the two living whales—toothed whales and baleen whales. Toothed whales first show up in the fossil record about fifty million years ago, baleen types about thirty million years ago.

Tails aloft, two California gray whales head for the deep. By throwing their heavy flukes out of the water, the whales shift their center of gravity and point head down, ready to dive. These baleen whales can stay underwater over an hour.

Hitching a ride, dolphins speed in the bow wave of a ship and ride along like surfers. Adaptations such as friction-free, flexible skin and streamlined shapes help whales reach high speeds for short distances.

During millions of years of aquatic life, warm-blooded whales evolved fishlike shapes and an ability to dive deep

As whales evolved, they developed shapes strikingly similar to those of fishes. Indeed, fish and whale shapes differ in only one major respect: Fish tails are vertical, whale tails horizontal. Fishes swim by undulating their bodies and beating their tails from side to side; whales swim by fanning their broad tails up and down.

"In the tail," wrote Herman Melville in *Moby Dick*, "the confluent measureless force of the whole whale seems concentrated." With vertical sweeps of its great tail, a blue whale thrusts its ponderous bulk through the water at twenty-two miles an hour for short sprints. The sperm whale can match this swift pace when alarmed, or swim on long journeys at six to seven miles per hour. Even porpoises and dolphins, which are small whales, can outrun a ship steaming at sixteen knots (eighteen miles) an hour by flexing their tails three or four times each second. Sometimes

Two California gray whales spout *high geysers of stale air. Like all baleen whales, the gray whale has two breathing slits that lead directly to the lungs. Toothed whales have a single blowhole. Both types of nostrils close during a dive.*

these whales "hitch" rides in the bow waves of sizable ships. With a burst of speed, they swim into the waves and glide along effortlessly just beneath the surface.

Streamlining contributes to the whales' swimming ability. Shorn of the coat of hair that covered their land-dwelling ancestors, smooth-skinned whales slip through the water with little friction. The tender outer layer of skin covers a somewhat firmer but pliant inner layer. The layers wrinkle and flex together to keep water flowing smoothly past the body.

Whales do peculiar things with their tails. Just before diving, sperm, right, gray, and humpback whales often toss their enormous flukes—the fleshy tail lobes—into the air in what appears to be a magnificent salute. Since whales are buoyed up by their thick blubber, perhaps this gesture helps them to dive. Sometimes whales flip their tails out of the water and bring the heavy flukes down on the surface in a tremendous slap, creating a thunderous boom audible for miles. Whalers have dubbed this behavior "lobtailing," and it may be an act of sheer playfulness.

Like seals and walruses, whales are accomplished divers. Dolphins and porpoises dive to 650 feet. Baleen whales, such as fin whales, dive to at least 1500 feet when frightened. One harpooned fin whale was still sounding—diving straight down —when it broke its neck by striking bottom at 1600 feet. The deepest divers, sperm whales, are known to plunge to 3600 feet and stay underwater well over an hour.

When a whale submerges, its pulse rate drops. A dolphin's heart beats ninety times per minute at the surface, but only twenty-one times underwater. Blood circulation to skin and blubber diminishes as the whale sounds, conserving both body warmth and oxygen. As the animal plunges, blood retreats from limbs and muscle layers, and the life-sustaining oxygen supply is saved for the brain and heart. Additional oxygen in the blubber and muscles passes to the bloodstream.

When the whale finally surfaces, it exhales stale air from its lungs in great spouts. Geysers jet up from the puffing animal. In *Paradise Lost*, Milton compared the whale to "a moving land that draws in, and at his breath pours out a sea." Poets and whalers alike perpetuated the misconception that whales spout water. But the warm, fishy-smelling spout is actually exhaled air mixed with mucus and oils from the respiratory system and seawater from outside the blowhole, condensed into a visible cloud of water droplets.

The Largest Animals That Ever Lived on Earth

The most massive whales are the least formidable: Baleen whales, including the quarter-million-pound blue whale, feed on minute plankton. Rows of horny whalebone, or baleen, plates hanging in the whales' mouths strain tons of tiny organisms from the water. Baleen whales other than the 100-foot blue range from the fin (eighty feet), black (sixty feet), and humpback (fifty feet), to the—relatively—small thirty-foot minke whale. Several species migrate seasonally from polar feeding grounds—where nineteenth-century whalers nearly wiped them out—to breed in more temperate waters.

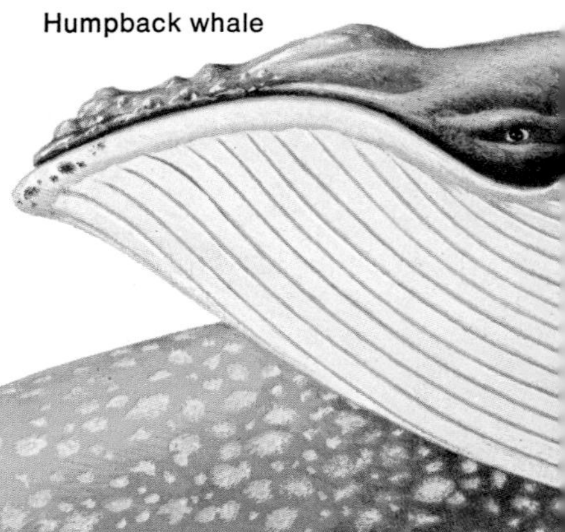

Humpback whale

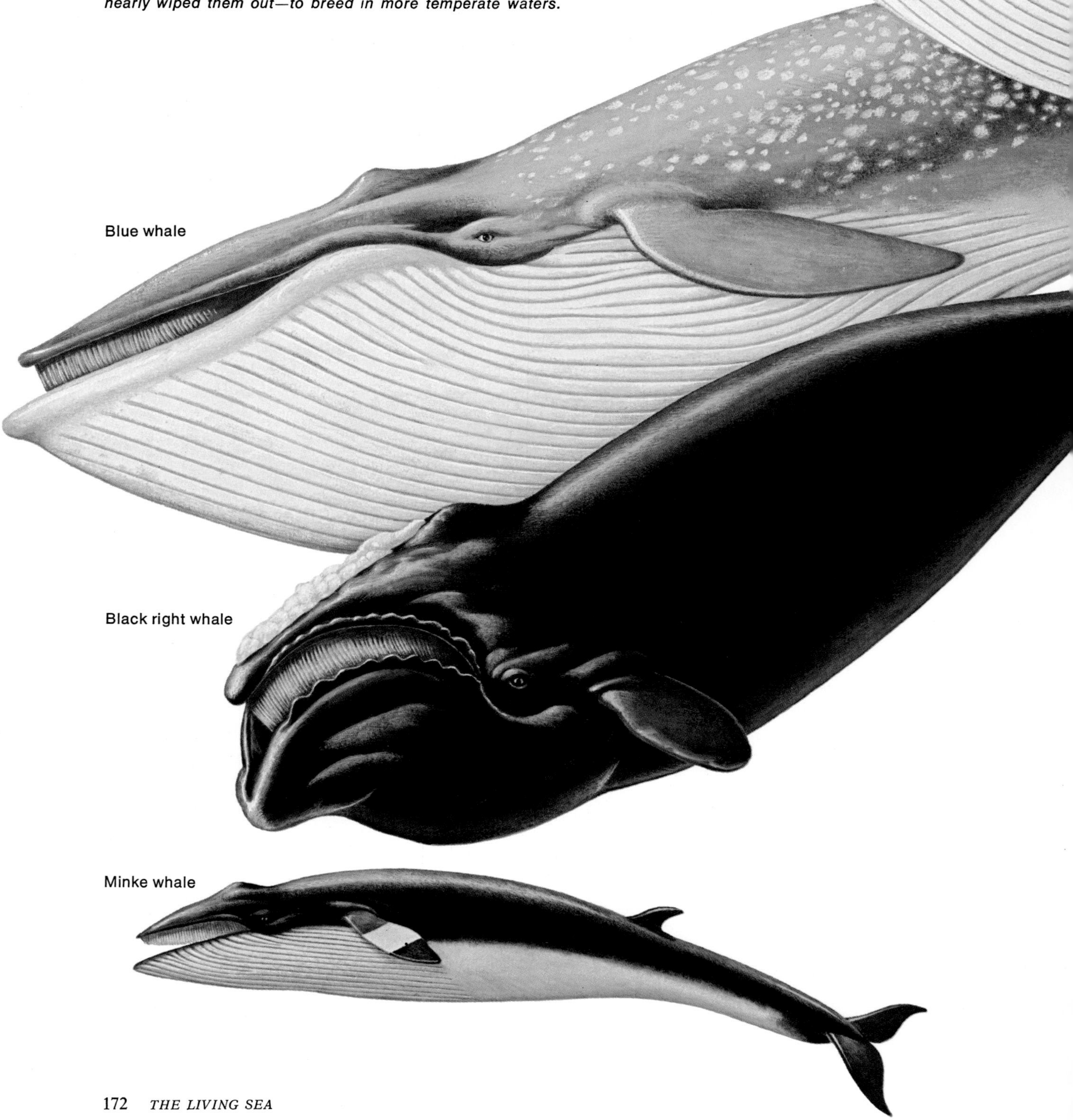

Blue whale

Black right whale

Minke whale

Baleen Whales

Baleen whales are named for the thin, triangular plates that hang from the roofs of their mouths. These tough, resilient baleen (or whalebone) plates are made of the same horny substance as fingernails and horses' hoofs. From the middle of the nineteenth century, baleen whales were hunted for these plates, which were used as corset stays, umbrella ribs, buggy whips, sled runners, and other items requiring both stiffness and flexibility.

A baleen whale's mouth contains 250 to 400 baleen plates hanging one behind another, less than half an inch apart. Long, hairy fringes on their inner edges strain food from seawater. To eat, a baleen whale lets seawater pour into its mouth. Then it closes its mouth and squeezes the water through the baleen and out the corners of its mouth by moving its tongue or contracting its throat muscles. Krill and other small organisms suspended in the seawater tangle in the baleen threads. The massive tongue, which may weigh as much as a full-grown elephant, licks off the food and pushes it down the throat. Thus the largest creatures in the ocean feed on some of the smallest, but in prodigious quantities. A full-grown blue whale consumes up to four tons of krill a day!

The largest baleen whale—and the largest creature that ever lived—is the blue whale. This species reaches a length of nearly 100 feet and weighs up to 135 tons. Named for its bluish back, it is also known as the "sulphur bottom" because a coating of yellowish diatoms lives on its flanks and belly when it feeds in polar waters.

For all its size, the blue whale is remarkably streamlined. Its body is relatively long and slender, its head fishlike and flat on top. The jutting lower jaw, together with the throat and chest, creates a bowl-shaped reservoir that holds a small lake of salt water and krill. The blue whale, like the fin, sei, and humpback, has grooves or pleats running along its undersurface. The function of these pleats is not known. They may expand and allow the tongue to move back, thereby increasing the mouth's capacity. They may function as stabilizers for swimming, or as brakes for quick stops.

Right whales, which grow as long as sixty feet, are less streamlined. Their rather thick, blunt shape makes them slow swimmers, and they rarely move faster than five miles an hour. Their backs are finless, their bellies pleatless. Their enormous arched heads contain up to a ton of ponderous baleen plates.

Before the days of fast boats and high-powered harpoon guns, these animals were the "right" whales to hunt. Their blubber contains so much oil that they float after being harpooned. Other large baleen whales sink unless they are inflated quickly with compressed air.

Courting gray whales frolic in the coastal waters off Baja California. Before mating, grays swim side by side and stroke and nuzzle each other for several hours of courtship play. The actual mating, performed as the whales face, may take only a few seconds.

Gray whales migrate yearly from rich polar feeding grounds to give birth, court, and breed in tropical waters

Baleen whales populate temperate and polar seas in both the Northern and Southern hemispheres. Blue whales and several other species are believed to feed only in the warm months, fasting and breeding in the winter. With their yearly life cycles out of phase by six months, herds from the Northern and Southern hemispheres do not mix.

Spring blooms of diatoms and krill attract blue, fin, sei, and humpback whales to the Antarctic, gray whales and other species to the Arctic. As sunlight wanes with the passing of summer, plant production dwindles and autumn ice begins to cover the feeding grounds. With the exception of Greenland right whales, baleen whale herds move out of polar seas and begin the annual migration to subtropical breeding areas.

In late fall, California gray whales set off on one of the longest migrations undertaken by any mammal—a 6000-mile journey from feeding grounds in the Bering Sea and the Arctic Ocean. By December or January, they reach the coast of southern California. First pregnant cows arrive, then other females and the males. This grand parade is always welcomed by crowds of whale watchers out in boats or perched on high vantage points near San Diego and Los Angeles.

The long voyage ends in shallow breeding lagoons on the coast of Baja California, Mexico. There, 1500-pound babies up to fourteen feet long are born. In March, April, and May, adults and young begin moving at a steady pace up the California coast on the return leg of their 12,000-mile round trip. Thousands of these barnacle-blotched creatures, some almost forty-five feet long, swim northward to their arctic summer home.

Scientists believe gray whales and other baleen species pair for life. They breed during winter in warm waters, returning there about a year later to give birth to their calves .

Courtship play, which sometimes lasts for hours before mating, takes a variety of forms. A pair of whales may rub one another with their flippers, bite, nuzzle, roll over and over in an embrace, or leap together from the water. Humpback whales are most demonstrative. Ugly in appearance, with unsightly lumps on their heads, chins, and jaws, they act like tender lovers. E. J. Slijper, a Dutch zoologist, reported that these forty-five–foot giants gently stroke their partners with their exceptionally long flippers before mating. They also use the flippers to give their partners slaps that can be heard for miles.

Female baleen whales usually produce a single calf every other year. In a lifetime of fifteen to thirty years, a female bears from six to fifteen young. The newborn baleen calf enters the world tail first, eyes wide open, and usually with enough stamina to swim past its mother to the surface for its first breath. If the calf cannot do so, the mother and other adults rush to shove the infant upward.

The calf is about one-third adult size at birth. A newborn blue whale may measure twenty-five feet and weigh 2½ tons. The calf wastes no time looking for food; it begins to nurse immediately after finding its mother's teats, concealed in two slits near the tail. On the fat-rich milk, a young blue whale gains up to 200 pounds a day. By seven months, it is fifty feet long and can be weaned.

Standing on its tail, a California gray whale shakes a mouthful of plankton off its baleen plates and into the first of four chambers in its enormous stomach. The whale can hold this vertical position for up to a minute without toppling over.

Gray whales hug the Pacific coast en route to Baja California. A migrating herd, or pod, may include as many as forty whales. On the trip north, the whales—no longer searching for their accustomed breeding lagoons—scatter more widely.

Sperm whale

Narwhal

Toothed Whales

None of the toothed whales are as big as the blue whale, but the biggest toothed animal is nevertheless a whale. Toothed whales use their teeth not for chewing but for grasping prey, which they swallow whole. Fishes use their teeth in the same way, but land animals do not.

In evolutionary terms, toothed whales are more successful than baleen whales. Seventy-five species of toothed whales survive, compared with ten baleen species. Among the toothed kinds are sperm whales, porpoises, dolphins, narwhals, belugas, killer whales, false killer whales, and pilot whales.

The giant of the toothed whales is the sperm whale. A sixty-foot bull sperm whale can weigh more than fifty tons. One-third of an adult's entire length is its formidable head, which gives the animal a majestic aspect. Herman Melville likened the flat front of a sperm whale's head to a battering ram. The eyes are low on the sides, just above and behind the lower jaw.

Compared with the rest of the head, the lower jaw seems absurdly small. It is a long, narrow boom, studded with thirty-six to sixty conical teeth, each weighing up to a pound. These the sperm whale uses to grab and hold giant squids and other large prey. Remains of a thirty-four–foot squid have been found in a sperm whale's stomach.

Behind the huge forehead is a large oil-filled reservoir. Whalers mistook the oil for the animal's semen—hence the name "sperm whale." Chilled sperm oil yields spermaceti, a waxy substance once in great demand for candles and now used chiefly in the manufacture of ointments. Refined sperm oil makes an excellent lubricant for watches and precision machinery. Scientists are not certain what use the whale makes of this reservoir. It may store oxygen for deep dives, or it may help regulate buoyancy, counteracting the natural tendency of the animal to rise when submerged.

The sperm whale also produces ambergris, a gray substance secreted by the intestine, possibly in response to constipation. Chunks of it are occasionally found floating at sea or washed up on shore, but more often whalers remove it from dead whales. Purified ambergris is an ingredient of expensive perfumes, although synthetics now frequently replace the whale product.

Most toothed whales do not migrate. Sperm whales, however, do make seasonal journeys between breeding and feeding grounds. During the mating season, a sperm bull lives in a harem, a group of about thirty cows and calves. In summer, some bulls leave their family groups in near-equatorial waters and swim as far as both polar seas. The migration may be connected with the movements of cuttlefishes and other prey. Remaining in warmer waters, cows carry their young for some sixteen months and produce a calf about once every four years.

Common dolphin

Mighty Hunters of the Seas

From a fierce fifty-ton sperm whale smashing a whaleboat to an eight-foot dolphin frolicking in a bow wave, toothed whales have intrigued and terrified man since Biblical times. These carnivores prey on fishes and mollusks. The thirty-five-foot bottle-nose and twenty-foot pilot are found mainly in northern waters, as is the distinctive narwhal, seventeen feet long—plus an eight-foot tusk. The voracious thirty-foot killer whale, easily identified by its dorsal fin, ranges the oceans, attacking fishes, seals, and even other whales.

Bottle-nose whale

Killer whale

Pilot whale

A female killer whale surveys her surroundings at Vancouver Aquarium. Females are only one-half as large as the thirty-foot males—an unusual difference in whales. In baleen species, the females are larger than the males.

At sea, killer whales prowl and attack in predatory packs; in captivity, they can be friendly and cooperative

Baleen and sperm whales have been decimated by centuries of whaling, but smaller toothed whales have generally escaped this fate. They make difficult targets and yield much less blubber than larger whales.

Killer whales are highly social creatures of considerable speed, power, and intelligence, with no natural enemies. They prey primarily on fishes and squids, but also devour seals, sea lions, young walruses, porpoises, and dolphins. They also attack large baleen whales. Reliable reports tell of gray whales so paralyzed with fear in the presence of killer whales that they roll over on their backs, as if helplessly awaiting the end. Not even the enormous blue whales are safe. When killers attack blues, rights, and other baleen whales, they tear away only the tongues, leaving the rest of the body.

Killers in packs of two to forty roam all oceans.

Easy to recognize, they have jet-black backs, white bellies and throats, and triangular dorsal fins as high as six feet on males. Females seldom grow longer than fifteen feet, about half the length of the biggest bulls. Both sexes have about fifty large, strong teeth.

For many years, killer whales were considered the most voracious predators in the sea. This impression was reinforced when a twenty-one–foot individual was found with thirteen porpoises and fourteen seals in its stomach. But in 1964, a killer was captured alive and studied closely for the first time. Named Moby Doll, it proved to be an intelligent, friendly, playful animal that allowed men to swim in its pen, liked to have its belly scratched, and ate fish out of a person's hand. Since then, several captive killers have been trained to perform in aquariums. Workers put their arms—and even their heads—into the whales' tooth-filled mouths, pull the animals around by the blowholes, and ride on their backs. The whales seem to enjoy leaping out of the water, and can be quickly trained to do so on command. Trainers and scientists agree that these once-maligned animals exhibit a gentleness and high intelligence matched only by dolphins and porpoises.

Watchful killer whales cruise off the coast of Mexico. Killers eat fishes and a variety of warm-blooded animals. They gang up to attack larger whales and sometimes tip over ice floes to dump penguins into the sea.

A dolphin streaks along at nearly thirty knots, powerful tail flukes driving its streamlined body through the water. Just before diving, a dolphin inhales a fifteen-minute supply of air through its blowhole, seen open here.

Dolphins and Porpoises

There are fifty species of dolphins and porpoises, and much confusion about which is which. Strictly speaking, porpoises are smaller than dolphins and have rounded snouts instead of beaks. But for most Americans and Europeans, "dolphin" or "porpoise" means the bottle-nose dolphin found in temperate waters of the Atlantic and Pacific. Named for its prominent beak, the bottle-nose can grow to twelve feet and 500 to 600 pounds.

In the wild, bottle-nose dolphins leap out of the water, frolic around ships, and shove floating objects about, sometimes tossing them into the air and catching them. Tales of dolphins and porpoises coming to the aid of drowning people date back to ancient times. These whales have undoubtedly pushed floundering swimmers ashore more than once, but there is no reason to believe that these animals deliberately try to save human lives. Rather, they seem to have an instinctive urge to push floating objects.

Extremely gregarious, dolphins live in groups of from six to several hundred individuals. Large groups usually consist of a number of smaller family units. The animals take excellent care of their young and are quick to help one another. A blast of dynamite once stunned one member of a dolphin school. Instead of immediately fleeing, the others took turns holding their injured companion at the surface until it revived. Then all sped away.

Playful common dolphins cavort off the coast of Mexico. Common dolphins range warm and temperate seas throughout the world, accompanying ships and leaping about the bows. They often gather in herds many hundreds strong.

A bottle-nose dolphin and her eight-day-old calf swim together at the Miami Seaquarium. Born underwater, dolphins surface immediately—often nudged by their mothers—to breathe. Dolphins nurse their young six to eighteen months.

In captivity, bottle-nose dolphins are playful and mischievous. They tease fishes by pulling their tails, take unwilling turtles for rides, throw objects out of their tanks, and squirt water at spectators. When rewarded with fish, dolphins can be trained to perform a variety of tricks. They jump through hoops, leap as high as thirty feet, toss rubber balls with their beaks, and dance on their tails. But captive dolphins are not all fun. They slap and bite one another in fights over females and food, and they attack humans when antagonized or handled roughly. Several scientists and trainers have been rammed or bitten during experiments and training sessions.

Some of the most fascinating stories about wild dolphins involve instances where humans have been given rides. The best known modern case refers to an eight-foot female bottle-nose named Opo. She regularly visited a beach near Opononi, New Zealand, and allowed children to ride on her back. All such rides, of which there are detailed and reasonably reliable accounts, took place after repeated meetings between animal and humans and some practice attempts.

Such behavior is by no means common among wild or even captive animals. Dolphin rides are evidently rare, special events involving exceptional animals. But rare or not, they show that dolphins can develop personal relationships with man — at least when no other dolphins are around.

Built-in sonar systems enable toothed whales to navigate and even locate food in the dark — but they sometimes fail

Relying primarily on echolocation—with a sense of hearing second only to that of bats—dolphins are superb underwater navigators. Dolphin vision is not particularly keen, but their eyes provide some depth perception in clear water.

For centuries, marine creatures were thought to be mute and the oceans silent. During World War II, naval technicians lowered microphones into the water to listen for submarines. To their amazement, they heard a bedlam of sounds produced by invertebrates, fishes, and whales.

Toothed whales most commonly produced staccato bursts of ultrasonic clicks. One of the first to discover the significance of these sounds was Arthur F. McBride, the first curator of Marineland in Florida. In 1947, he tried to capture dolphins for an exhibit. Every time he drove them toward nets, they would stop a good distance short. It made no difference whether he pursued the dolphins during the day or at night; they never even ventured close enough to glimpse the nets in the murky water. McBride rightly assumed that somehow the dol-

Whales Use Rebounding Sound Waves to Detect Objects Underwater

When a porpoise swims underwater, air under pressure circulates through its nasal passages, producing clicks or other echolocation sounds. These can be directed by bouncing off the fatty melon—a round mass of blubber between the blowhole and the end of the head. The sounds are focused on fishes and other objects in front of the whale, but not on objects below a line level with its jaws. (This

may be why whales cannot detect gently sloping bottoms and sometimes run aground.) Reflected sounds are probably picked up by sensitive areas in the lower jaw, which transmits sounds to the inner ear. Since lower-pitched sounds have longer wavelengths, whales probably use these for long-distance echolocation; higher-pitched clicks provide data about their immediate surroundings.

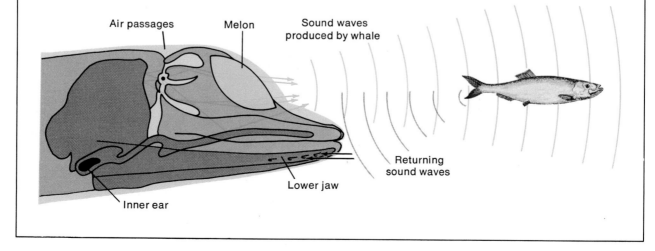

phins used sound to sense the obstruction.

In the early 1950s, Winthrop N. Kellogg of Florida State University showed that dolphins use their clicking sounds just as men use sonar devices. The clicking sounds travel through the water and bounce off anything solid. Dolphins determine the exact distance to an object by measuring the interval between an outgoing click and its echo. They can also tell a good deal about the size of an object. In tests, blindfolded dolphins have distinguished between 2½-inch and 2¼-inch ball bearings from as far away as ten feet. Therefore, avoiding rocks on a dark night or catching a four-inch herring in turbid water should not be the least bit difficult for any healthy dolphin.

The ability to echolocate is not confined to dolphins. All toothed whales produce high-pitched clicks. Baleen whales, on the other hand, apparently produce relatively low-pitched sounds, which bend around obstructions instead of bouncing back to the source. Gray whales, for example, moan and make bubbling noises but emit no clicks. One gray whale blundered into a barrier of sound-reflecting aluminum tubes stretched across a Mexican lagoon, became entangled, freed itself, and again swam into the barrier. During the same experiment, a group of bottle-nose dolphins detected the barrier from a considerable distance, inspected it, and retreated — all the while emitting clicks.

Despite their ability to echolocate, toothed whales periodically run aground and perish in shallow water. About 200 false killer whales — smaller than true killer whales and all black — beached themselves at Fort Pierce, Florida, in January 1970. Similar disasters have struck pilot whales, killer whales, sperm whales, dolphins, and porpoises.

The composition of the sea floor may be to blame. Some mud bottoms absorb sound instead of bouncing it back, and some gently inclined bottoms reflect sound waves away from the whales rather than back to them. Certain hard bottoms produce a confusion of echoes. Any of these situations can produce disorientation and panic, and whale strandings may be much like cattle stampedes. Whales have a strong instinct to stay with the herd, and if several run aground, the rest follow. Even whales pulled into deep water swim back to their stranded companions.

Stranded false killer whales lie helpless on the beach at Fort Pierce, Florida. Once beached, the whales may die; their massive bodies cannot support their own weight out of water. Dehydration and sunburn make the end come quickly.

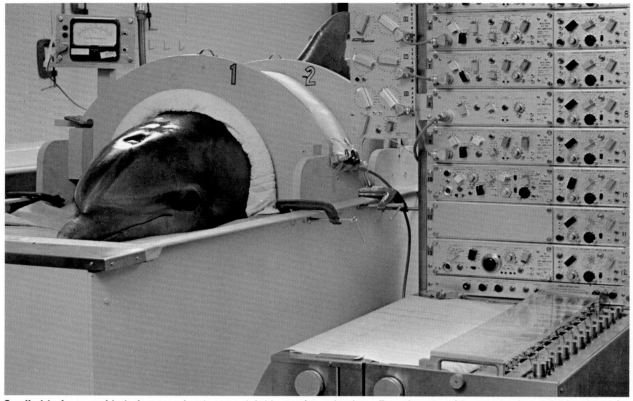

Cradled in foam-padded clamps, a bottle-nose dolphin awaits scientists. Experiments with cooperative dolphins have included research in echolocation and communication, as well as studies of various functions of the whale's body.

Whale Communication

Both baleen whales and toothed whales use low-pitched sounds for communication. Bottle-nose dolphins have thirty-two distinct whistling sounds. If each represents a complete expression, these whales are limited to thirty-two signals. Even this number is quite an accomplishment, but if each whistle pattern represents a symbol or "word," the sounds could be combined into what amounts to a language.

A bottle-nose dolphin in distress utters a short, sharp whistle over and over again. A captive female bottle-nose fell ill in her tank and could not rise to the surface to breathe. With the distress call, she summoned two companions; they held her for four days. The treatment then continued intermittently for two weeks until the sick dolphin recovered. Such rescues are always accompanied by frequent whistle exchanges.

Two male bottle-noses, separated and later reunited, often carry on dialogues that sound like old friends meeting. But vocalizations may be more than just calls of greeting or distress. Scientists studying sea noises in a Gulf of California lagoon observed a group of bottle-noses. When the dolphins found their way partially blocked by a line of buoys, they immediately huddled for a whistle conference. First one scout and then another left the group to examine the barrier. Each time a scout returned, another conference took place. Finally, the group moved off together and cautiously passed under the buoys.

Gregarious dolphins are among the most loquacious whales, but they are by no means the only ones known to "talk" frequently. Killer whales penned adjacent to open water carry on whistle exchanges with free killer whales outside the enclosures. Eskimos report that killer whales whistle to each other before launching group attacks. The false killer whales rescued from the 1970 stranding on the Florida coast communicated with those trapped on the beach.

Humpback whales sing during their northward spring migration, possibly to help keep the herd together. Roger Payne, of Rockefeller University in New York City, has recorded these calls of humpback whales, which he describes as haunting, warbling notes. Lower in pitch than those of

Singing Whales and Whistling Dolphins—What Are They Saying?

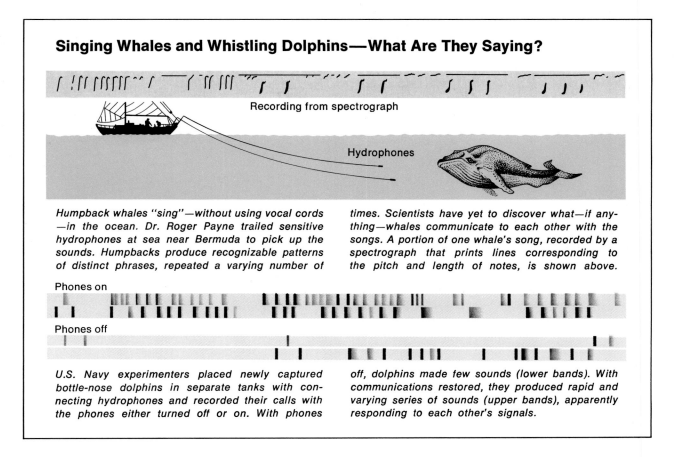

Recording from spectrograph

Hydrophones

Humpback whales "sing"—without using vocal cords—in the ocean. Dr. Roger Payne trailed sensitive hydrophones at sea near Bermuda to pick up the sounds. Humpbacks produce recognizable patterns of distinct phrases, repeated a varying number of times. Scientists have yet to discover what—if anything—whales communicate to each other with the songs. A portion of one whale's song, recorded by a spectrograph that prints lines corresponding to the pitch and length of notes, is shown above.

Phones on

Phones off

U.S. Navy experimenters placed newly captured bottle-nose dolphins in separate tanks with connecting hydrophones and recorded their calls with the phones either turned off or on. With phones off, dolphins made few sounds (lower bands). With communications restored, they produced rapid and varying series of sounds (upper bands), apparently responding to each other's signals.

birds, the calls are repeated from seven to as long as thirty minutes at a stretch.

No one understands exactly how whales make sounds, for they have no vocal cords. Evidently the sounds result from air forced past valves and tonguelike flaps in sacs below the blowholes. Differences in the way these structures vibrate probably account for the very noticeable variations in the "voices" of individual whales.

Even less is known about how whales "hear." Certainly their ear holes, seldom more than half an inch in diameter, are important. They channel sounds into the inner ears, linked by nerves to the brain. Bones are excellent conductors of sound, and some whales may use their skulls as sounding boards. Two narrow channels in the jaws of bottle-noses connect to the inner ear and may pick up echoes of the high-frequency clicks.

Scientists still question how much meaning whales convey by their vocalizations. Are their calls like the chirping and singing of birds and the barks and growls of dogs, or are they more like the human whistle languages of Mexico, Turkey, and the Canary Islands? Arguing for the latter idea, some scientists point out that a dolphin brain compares in size and complexity with that of a human adult.

Several attempts have been made to communicate with dolphins. One group of scientists tried to match recordings of dolphin sounds with movies of their actions. A computer was programmed to classify the sounds so people could learn their whistle "language," but the idea did not work out as planned.

John C. Lilly, who founded the Communications Research Institute in the Virgin Islands, tried to teach whales to talk English. He first succeeded in getting bottle-noses to make sounds in air instead of underwater, then to repeat a series of as many as twelve nonsense syllables. The dolphins accurately mimicked the number and duration of the sounds. Lilly taught a dolphin named Elvar to repeat such phrases as "More, Elvar," "Stop it," and "All right, let's go." But other scientists who listened to recordings of Elvar did not agree that the utterances sounded like human speech. Few scientists believe that men will ever "converse" with dolphins or with other whales.

A deadly harpoon hurtles toward a whale. Men once stood in small boats and flung harpoons at whales; now they fire cannons from swift "killer" ships. Most modern harpoons, fitted with grenades, explode and kill a whale within seconds.

Whaling Is a Brutal Business

Stone Age Scandinavians pursued whales; so did Eskimos 3500 years ago. For centuries men put out to sea in flimsy boats to challenge these giants. The opponents were not well-matched: both history and fiction tell of smashed boats and drowned sailors. Now the whales are losing; they are no match for grenade-tipped harpoons and diesel-powered whaleboats. Despite international agreements, more whales are caught each year than are born. At the present rate, both the whales and the whaling industry are doomed.

Inflated to prevent sinking, a fin whale carcass bobs alongside a catcher boat. Catcher boats harpoon whales within a 150-mile radius of the factory, then bring their catch back for processing of oil, meat, bone, and various chemicals.

Faeroe Island fishermen *still brave the North Atlantic to hunt whales from small boats. Here, two still-thrashing whales are impaled on hand-flung harpoons. Nineteenth-century whalers in similar boats faced sixty-foot sperm whales.*

Hide and blubber are quickly stripped *from a blue whale on a large factory ship. The strips of blubber are then boiled to yield valuable whale oil.*

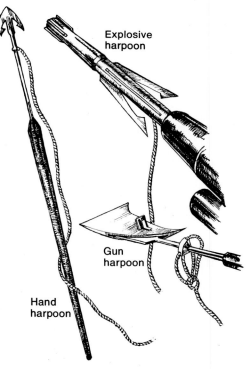

Explosive harpoon

Gun harpoon

Hand harpoon

Old-style harpoons *were hand-flung; gun harpoons widened the whalers' range. Cannons now fire harpoons with exploding heads.*

Man has hunted the great whales to the verge of extinction, but hope remains for rescuing some endangered species

The common enemy of all whales — baleen and toothed, large and small — is man. Records of whale hunts go back 4000 years. Drawings scratched on some Norwegian rocks by Stone Age men depict two porpoises, with a hunter in a boat close behind. Whale bones unearthed among the remains of Alaskan Eskimo settlements establish beyond doubt that Eskimos captured whales in 1500 B.C.

As early as the eleventh century, Basques and Spaniards sailed out to hunt black right whales in the deep waters of the Bay of Biscay, where these slow-moving creatures roamed in herds more than 100 strong. In the seventeenth and eighteenth centuries, large Dutch and English whaling fleets pursued right whales on a grand scale in arctic waters; in the nineteenth century, Americans extended the pursuit into the South

Concerned Canadians maintain a breathing hole for a herd of white beluga whales trapped in the Eskimo Lakes, fifty miles from the sea up the Mackenzie River, by an early freeze. One whale has come to the surface for air.

A gray whale, risking death, tries to aid her calf, harpooned in violation of conservation laws. Male grays rush to aid injured or threatened females, and females succor calves, but females swim away from male grays in distress.

Atlantic, Pacific, and Indian oceans. Right whales steadily disappeared from one area after another until they were given protection from commercial whalers by an international agreement in 1935. Some scientists think the ban may have come too late to save several species from extinction.

For hundreds of years, the sprinting speeds of large baleen whales protected them from capture. But fast steam-powered boats and the harpoon gun developed in the last part of the nineteenth century drastically changed the situation. In the peak year of antarctic whaling, 1930–31, about 30,000 blue whales were killed. From then on, the catch dropped steadily: less than 7000 in 1948, and only one in 1965. With just a few thousand of these great animals left, most whaling countries placed them under protection — again, not until the species was close to extinction.

As the blues disappeared, whalers first turned to fin whales — the second largest species — and then to the smaller sei whales. Blues could no longer be hunted, but blue whale units could. Under the system imposed by the International Whaling Commission, two fins or six seis equal a blue whale unit, since these whales yield an average of one-half and one-sixth as much oil, respec-

tively, as a blue whale. In 1970, the commission set a limit of 2700 units in the antarctic whaling grounds, where most large baleen whales are hunted. This meant that 5400 fin whales, 16,200 seis, or various combinations of the two could be killed that year. This was thought to be the maximum number of whales that could be taken without destroying the future productivity of antarctic whaling. But many conservationists believe quotas like these put too much pressure on individual species; they want limits defined in terms of numbers of each baleen species that can be caught, not in terms of the total oil yield.

The noble sperm whales, which escaped extinction in the heyday of American whaling, were threatened as stocks of baleen whales diminished. In 1970, biologists estimated that 9500 sperms could be harvested from the North Pacific without seriously depleting the stock. Under pressure from Russia and Japan, the only major whaling nations remaining, an upper limit of approximately 13,000 was set.

Attempts at international regulation probably will not save the great whales, but economic laws may. Large factory ships, with their retinues of smaller catcher boats and spotter planes, are expensive to maintain. At the same time, demand for whale products — for paints, soaps, cosmetics, pet food, and other items — declines as substitutes become readily available. The United States has banned the importation of whale products, thus eliminating about 20 per cent of the world market.

So long as any great whales remain, there is hope for their kind. Blue whales and others have a chance if proper protection is agreed upon and enforced. The story of the gray whale offers strong encouragement. In 1846, whalers began intensive harvest of gray whales. They tracked the animals to their shallow breeding lagoons, where hunting was easiest, and slaughtered them there. In the 1850s, an estimated 30,000 gray whales ranged the Pacific coast of North America; forty years later, the species was nearly extinct. Whalers turned their attentions elsewhere — but only temporarily. By the 1920s, the gray whale population had built up again, and a second great massacre almost exterminated the animals. Only 500 to 1000 survived. The remnant of the herd was saved by a 1938 international treaty. By 1943, the population had increased to near 3000; by 1970, to 6000.

Hopefully, other endangered whale species can make equally spectacular comebacks, and future generations may yet see right whales lobtailing and blue whales spouting.

Part two

Wonders of Island Life

Ranging in size from tiny atolls to continents, the
half-million islands of the world are intimately related
to the waters around them. They serve as breeding grounds
for birds and marine mammals, as homes for men who wrest
their livelihood from the sea, and as living laboratories
for some of nature's most fascinating experiments.
Islands are isolated worlds where evolution over thousands or
millions of years has produced many creatures startlingly
different from their cousins on the mainland

To Live Alone

Every island in the sea is an isolated miniature world. As plants
and animals colonize an island, it becomes an arena in
the struggle for survival, a testing ground of evolutionary change

An island! What images the word conjures up out of the experiences and dreams of men! It may be a coastal island dotted with weather-beaten summer cottages, a sun-bleached tropical atoll, a cold and barren rock off Scotland, or a volcano fuming itself into existence from the sea. Is it a vacationland overrun by hordes of tourists, a mountainous terrain inhabited by men still in the Stone Age, or a rock visited only by seabirds? Islands yet unborn are being formed today as seas gnaw at land projecting from continental coasts, as lava emerges from rifts in the ocean floor, as reefs of living coral build upward.

Islands are meeting places between sea and land. The land affords a home for plants and animals; the surrounding sea provides an equally important element: isolation. On each of Earth's 500,000 islands living things have evolved and may now be altogether different from their cousins on distant shores.

The five weeks the British naturalist Charles Darwin spent on the Galápagos Islands in 1835 gave rise to ideas that haunted his life until he expounded them in his book *On the Origin of Species* almost twenty-five years later. These ideas, born out of the study of island life, have changed man's view of the nature of all life.

But if islands have helped to explain the past, they are now the subject of study for lessons they can teach for the future—lessons on which man's survival may well depend. Every island has its own system of ecology: its balance of animals and plants, which have evolved in relationship to one another and to their environment. An understanding of these ecologies is vital for conserving the world's resources. For man now has the power to disrupt the balance of all living things and even to exterminate life on a massive scale.

Islands are natural laboratories. But some of the most beautiful and interesting of them are being disrupted and disfigured before naturalists have time to probe their secrets. Plants and animals are threatened with catastrophe when man brings in his domestic livestock or the rats and mice, weeds and weevils that travel with him.

Many islands have been ravaged beyond repair; some of the most fascinating of island creatures are lost beyond recall. But it is not too late to save something. The Earth itself is an island—well-stocked with an inconceivable variety of plants and animals, but extremely vulnerable and utterly isolated in the ocean of space that surrounds it, and there are signs that its people are awakening to their danger.

A red-footed booby surveys its nesting bushes on Wolf Island in the Galápagos. The bird's unusually flexible webbed feet are adapted for perching and for grasping sticks used in nest-building. The two other species of Galápagos boobies—the blue-faced and the blue-footed—are ground nesters.

Atlantic Ocean Floor

Europe

North America

Mid-Atlantic Ridge

Africa

Puerto Rico Trench

Two plates of the Earth's crust meet in the middle of the Atlantic, leaving a crack through which hot lava from the interior pours onto the sea floor.

Atlantic Ocean

The rocks on the north coast of South America match the rocks on the south coast of Africa's bulge.

East Pacific Rise

The Atlantic Ocean, born 150 million years ago, is still widening, about an inch a year, as the sea floor spreads out.

The Andes were pushed up where two sections of the Earth's crust collided.

Peru-Chile Trench

South America

Some peaks in the Mid-Atlantic Ridge are 10,000 feet high.

The rift that runs the length of the Mid-Atlantic Ridge is currently the most active volcanic segment of the worldwide rift system.

Antarctica

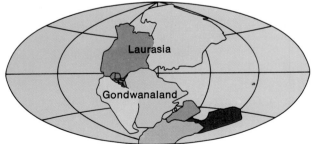

Laurasia

Gondwanaland

More than 200 million years ago, geologists believe, all land on Earth was joined in one great mass called Pangaea. Some twenty million years later the northern section, Laurasia, separated from the southern Gondwanaland. Over long ages the two supercontinents also broke apart. Today the continents are still riding on the Earth's crustal plates, divided from each other by a worldwide system of trenches and mid-ocean ridges on the sea floor.

This Unquiet Earth

Islands originate in two basic ways. *Continental* islands are fragments of land once part of a continental mainland. *Oceanic* islands emerged from the ocean floor without ever having been connected to another land mass. Some continental islands have been cut from the mainland through the erosion of a former land connection. Others owe their origins to geological forces that long ago led to major changes in the surface features of the Earth. The world has not always been as it now is; the continents have shifted about in a slow, ponderous movement that still continues.

Some 180 million years ago, scientists now believe, dry land was gathered together in two major

Pacific Ocean Floor

In the trenches (up to seven miles deep) hardened lava from the ridges is returned to the interior of the Earth.

Asia

Japan

Japan Trench

Mariana Trench

Hawaii

Indian Ocean

Pacific Ocean

Australia

Australia, India, and Antarctica were separated from Africa 150 million years ago, and then from each other.

The Pacific and Indian oceans, unlike the younger Atlantic, are shrinking, as the Americas are carried westward and Africa is carried eastward.

The 40,000-mile mid-ocean ridge girdles the Earth with a range of volcanic mountains, the Mid-Atlantic Ridge at one end and the East Pacific Rise at the other.

New Zealand

Antarctica

supercontinents: Gondwanaland, which gave rise to today's South America, Africa, India, Australia, and Antarctica; and Laurasia, consisting of North America, Greenland, Europe, and Asia all fused together. From the Earth's mantle—the layer of dense, plastic rock that extends 1800 miles down from the surface—fluid lava began rising through enormous cracks in the crust. Giant convection currents within the mantle are believed to have produced a slow rising and sinking of its material that caused some sections, or plates, of the crust to drift away from each other, perhaps a few inches in 100 years.

Riding on the crustal plates beneath, the land masses were eventually carried far from their original points of connection. Some of these points are evident where the contours and geological composition of continental shorelines match those of shores far across the sea. Along with the breaking up of the supercontinents came a separation of land into lesser fragments, which became islands at an early date. The slow drift of the great crustal plates continues today.

Oceanic islands are generally the product of volcanic activity. Where molten material emerges from a crack in the ocean floor, the slow piling up of lava flow upon lava flow over thousands of years builds a volcanic mountain. Eventually the mountain may grow to such a height that its summit breaks the ocean surface to become an island.

The life of every island is unique. Chance determines which species gain a foothold and become permanent settlers

From the moment of birth, volcanic islands are exposed to the relentless erosive action of wind, rain, and waves. In warm seas, however, the life-span of volcanic islands may be considerably extended by the growth of offshore coral reefs, which form a barrier against the crashing ocean waves. But even coral reefs carry no immunity against destruction. A change in environmental conditions may pose a threat to an island that depends on living reef builders to maintain its structure against the forces of erosion.

Throughout the history of the world, the state of the polar ice caps has played a significant role in the appearance and disappearance of both con-

Introduced by man to several of the West Indies and the Hawaiian Islands, the Indian gray mongoose has become a serious pest. Sugarcane plantation owners originally imported the mongoose from India to fight rats, but as the rodent population was brought under control, this agile, aggressive hunter turned to young pigs, goats, sheep, poultry, native birds, lizards, crabs, and even fruit.

tinental and oceanic islands. During the Ice Ages, when more of the water of the Earth was locked into massive glaciers, the seas were several hundred feet lower than they are now. Under such conditions, the number of islands must have been far greater, since many of today's underwater mountains and offshore slopes were exposed. Conversely, when the ice caps melted and the seas were higher than they are at present, many of today's islands were submerged.

It is impossible to determine how many islands have come into being on the face of the Earth, only to erode away or to be covered by rising seas. But during its transitory existence, almost every island is destined to be settled by organisms arriving from continents and from other islands. And as evolutionary mechanisms come into play, each island develops its own unique community of living things.

How do plant and animal inhabitants of an island come to be there? To almost every island that man has settled or visited, he has brought—sometimes intentionally, sometimes accidentally—ornamental and food plants, domestic pets, livestock, and even such pests as mice and rats. In the study of island life, however, these introduced forms are of secondary interest. The primary concern is rather with native forms, the species whose ancestors were the original colonizers. Species that evolved in their island environments and that live nowhere else are called endemic.

A continental island, of course, already supports a community of living things at the time it becomes separated from the mainland. At first, its populations may be similar to those of the mainland. But as colonizing species arrive from elsewhere, and as evolutionary processes give rise to endemic species, the composition of the island's life undergoes significant change. After long isolation, if the island is far removed from the life of its parent continent, its community of living things may come to be distinctly different from that of the mainland.

In contrast to continental islands, an oceanic island begins its existence devoid of surface life. A volcanic island is completely sterile when it emerges from the sea, and a coral island at first supports only the builders and marine inhabitants of its reef structure. The development of surface communities of plants and animals on oceanic islands thus depends entirely on the arrival of life from elsewhere.

The sea forms an impassable barrier to many forms of life. Prolonged contact with salty ocean water is fatal to most species of land plants and animals, and even to frogs, salamanders, and river fishes, which thrive in freshwater habitats. The plants and animals that reach an island in a condition to survive are those with special qualifications. Seabirds, sea turtles, and seals regularly breed on islands, where the scarcity of predatory mammals enables them to produce young in greater safety than on the mainland. But the true colonizers of an island are the organisms that become permanent settlers, sometimes changing in time into completely new species.

Plants and animals dwell on a mid-ocean island quite by chance. Since islands are generally small and scattered, the process of settlement is long-drawn-out and risky. Only a few species even arrive; of these, fewer still manage also to survive, to propagate, to become established. Those species that do gain a foothold may have a whole miniature world almost to themselves.

A native islander, the Japanese serow is smaller and has a woollier coat than its mainland relative. This sure-footed, forty-five-pound goat lives on forested hillsides and rugged mountain ridges. Only about 3000 now survive in the wild.

Island visitors, southern elephant seals come ashore on remote subantarctic islands only to breed and molt. Here a molting young male throws sand over himself, probably in an attempt to soothe the irritation caused by fur and skin sloughing off.

A log adrift at sea may carry a number of animal passengers, although not necessarily as many as shown here. If the log reaches land, and if a mated pair or a pregnant female survives the trip, the species may become established.

From every direction, by air and by sea, plants and animals come or are carried to islands

The land plant species that have the best chance of arriving are the simple forms that produce microscopic spores: algae, lichens, and fungi. Mosses, ferns, and their relatives—with somewhat bigger spores—are also good travelers.

Although seed plants are somewhat less promising candidates for long-distance dispersal, some island plants produce seeds with devices that catch the wind. Others grow small seeds that can be transported unharmed within the digestive tracts of birds. Some unusually successful plants produce seeds that adhere to the feet and feathers of birds. Birds that fly far out to sea may nest on heavily vegetated cliffs and in forests; others nest among ferns growing on the limbs of trees, or in dense plant growth on the ground. Such close associations almost inevitably result in the transportation of seeds and spores to distant islands.

Some twenty-odd plant species produce seeds that can float long distances without damage from seawater, and that readily take root when they reach a tropical island beach. Among the best

known of these species are the mangrove, the screw "pine" (or pandanus), several kinds of morning glory, and *Scaevola*, a low shrub that forms shoreline hedges on many Pacific islands. Conifers, on the other hand, have not done well in crossing wide stretches of ocean. Their seeds are neither well protected against salt water nor likely to be borne long distances by wind or by birds.

The animal champions in the long-distance sweepstakes across oceans include not only birds, turtles, and seals, but also bats, lizards, land snails, spiders, and insects. Young snails and insect eggs have been found encased in mud on the legs and plumage of wide-ranging birds. Larger animals travel on the foliage or among the roots of trees dislodged from shorelines by floods or storms and sent floating hundreds of miles out to sea. Rafts of vegetation are most often single trees or parts of trees, but sometimes they reach the proportions of small islets. Dense with grasses, and with trees rising twenty or thirty feet in the air, some rafts were even charted by early mariners, whose successors were puzzled when the "islands" could not be found later. When such a huge raft is beached on some island, it deposits a sizable cargo of living plants and animals.

Some spider and insect species on islands are derived from passengers on rafts of vegetation, but most have descended from strays caught in strong winds and carried into the sky and across wide expanses of ocean. Although spiders do not fly, it is common for their young to spin short strands of fine webs that catch the breeze and carry the tiny spiderlings far aloft. Sometimes the sky glistens with multitudes of these little parachutists transported in the air stream.

In the dispersal of insects, lightness and body-surface area are more important factors than the ability to fly. The wings of a flying insect add to its body surface and increase the chance of its being blown off course and carried long distances. But even a wingless insect, if its body surface is large in proportion to its weight, is easily borne aloft.

Throughout the world, at altitudes of 10,000 feet or more, there is a sparse but discernible aerial plankton composed of a variety of spiders and insects. Spitsbergen, 800 miles north of Europe, has been colonized repeatedly by insects carried by both birds and wind. On the barren St. Peter and St. Paul Rocks in the equatorial Atlantic, spiders are spinning webs in crevices. Atolls in the Pacific usually show a varied population of insects, most of them brought by winds.

The normal trade winds, although dependable and often quite brisk, account for only a few of the insect immigrants to tropical islands. Cyclonic storms have undoubtedly been of at least equal importance. When a tropical hurricane hits an island, it may uproot palm trees, and an insect or other small animal, whipped up with forest litter, may be transported a great distance. Newly arrived butterflies, locusts, flies, beetles, and other insects have been found on Pacific islands hundreds of miles from the nearest land, but almost always shortly after a storm. Birds and amphibians—even small fishes—have crossed salt water on storm winds.

Despite the hazards and improbabilities of transport, the single greatest challenge in colonizing an island is not getting there but becoming established. An animal or plant suddenly arriving on an island may have to make a rapid and difficult adjustment. The new environment may be too dry or wet, too cold or warm; it may lack the kind of soil, vegetation, or—most important—food to which an organism is accustomed. It is no wonder that many invaders, forms specialized for other environments, fail to survive. Success in becoming established is reserved for only those colonizing organisms able to become part of the island's living conditions.

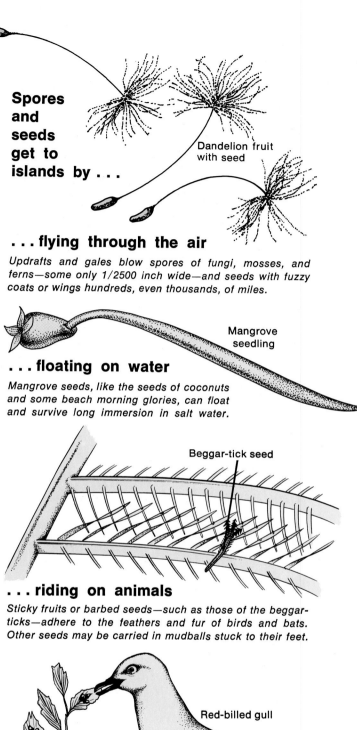

Spores and seeds get to islands by . . .

Dandelion fruit with seed

. . . flying through the air

Updrafts and gales blow spores of fungi, mosses, and ferns—some only 1/2500 inch wide—and seeds with fuzzy coats or wings hundreds, even thousands, of miles.

Mangrove seedling

. . . floating on water

Mangrove seeds, like the seeds of coconuts and some beach morning glories, can float and survive long immersion in salt water.

Beggar-tick seed

. . . riding on animals

Sticky fruits or barbed seeds—such as those of the beggar-ticks—adhere to the feathers and fur of birds and bats. Other seeds may be carried in mudballs stuck to their feet.

Red-billed gull

Phyllocladus seeds

. . . riding in animals

Birds and bats eat the fruit and leaves of plants; later, after flying perhaps many miles, they excrete the indigestible seeds.

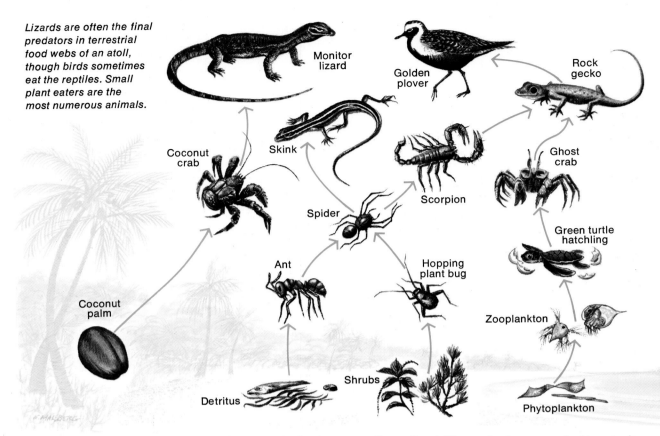

Lizards are often the final predators in terrestrial food webs of an atoll, though birds sometimes eat the reptiles. Small plant eaters are the most numerous animals.

Monitor lizard

Golden plover

Rock gecko

Coconut crab

Skink

Ghost crab

Spider

Scorpion

Ant

Hopping plant bug

Green turtle hatchling

Coconut palm

Zooplankton

Detritus

Shrubs

Phytoplankton

An atoll ecosystem is a complex web of life on the land and in the sea. Sunlight provides energy for plants, including drifters called phytoplankton, to make food from water, carbon dioxide, and basic nutrients. Plant eaters range from the drifting animals, or zooplankton, to insects, fishes, and large crustaceans such as coconut crabs. Some birds, turtles, and spiders eat plant eaters. Other predators, in turn, eat some of these carnivores or

Getting there is only half the battle; each species must make a place for itself

Isolated though it may be, an island is related to the world about it through tides and currents and through the winds that blow above. Yet each island is a separate entity, an ecosystem (ecological system) unduplicated anywhere else and embodying the relationships of all its plant and animal inhabitants to one another and to their physical environment. Time, geological change, biological opportunity, and the variations of living things mold the ecosystem into a distinctive bit of the thin zone of life enveloping the Earth.

Every plant and animal plays its own role in the functioning of its ecosystem and fills a specific niche. The ecological niche occupied by any organism is determined partly by the organism's physical makeup and partly by its specialized way of living: where it lives, how it secures nourishment, how it copes with competition from other organisms for food and living space, how it may supply other organisms with food or shelter, and how in life and death it affects the physical conditions of the environment.

The distinctions among ecological niches may be extremely subtle. Two or more species living in the same area and looking much alike may actually live quite differently from one another. For a long time, it was thought that all the grazing animals of the African plains ate the same food. But biologists have recently learned that each species has its individual plant preferences, and that when two species favor the same plant, for example, one may eat the top part and the other the lower portions after they are exposed.

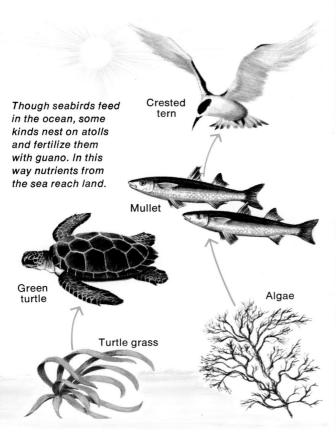

Though seabirds feed in the ocean, some kinds nest on atolls and fertilize them with guano. In this way nutrients from the sea reach land.

Crested tern

Mullet

Green turtle

Turtle grass

Algae

their young. Ants and other scavengers feed on decaying plants and animals. Some detritus is broken down by bacteria into its chemical components and returned to the sea and soil, to nourish a new generation of plants.

An ecological niche common to many parts of the world need not be occupied everywhere by precisely similar plants or animals. In Australia, which has no antelopes, the role of grazer has been filled by the large kangaroos. Similarly, in the absence of the evergreens and leafy trees common on continents, forests on some of the Galápagos Islands are composed of sunflowers and cactuses that have evolved into treelike forms.

With the passage of time, competition in an island environment increases. In the relatively limited space of an island, any competition may be short-lived, for there is no place to go. The less successful organism either takes on a new lifestyle or is eliminated. If large numbers of antelopes were introduced to Australia and competed with kangaroos for a specific kind of grass, and if neither could change its food preferences, eventual survival would be possible for only one —whichever proved more successful in foraging.

A Galápagos woodpecker finch digs a hole in a rotten tree trunk, probes with a cactus spine, and extracts a grub for a meal. True woodpeckers use their long tongues to reach insects; lacking such tongues, woodpecker finches became tool users and thus were able to occupy an ecological niche that had once been vacant.

A proboscis monkey troop leader rubs the exaggerated nose through which he makes a honking sound. Proboscis monkeys live only on Borneo, and only the large, mature males—weighing up to fifty pounds—have bulbous noses.

Galápagos prickly pear trees, giants in the cactus family, also have the largest seeds among cactuses. Pads at the top of the tree store water during the rainy season, and, when they fall, furnish moisture to giant tortoises.

Island Oddities: Products of Isolation

Isolated island dwellers have evolved some unusual adaptations to their physical environment and to each other. Giants or dwarfs may develop. Shape or habits startlingly different from those of the ancestral stock may appear—or a plant or animal may live unchanged for millions of years. The largest lizards on Earth, the only marine iguanas and the most primitive mammals live on islands.

Australian grass trees, up to twenty feet high, have thin three-foot leaves. When the leaves die, they droop and mat together with resin, thus forming the "trunk." Flowers are borne on a long stalk.

The ten-foot-long Komodo dragon is the world's largest lizard. Komodo, an Indonesian island, has monkeys, pigs, and deer; the dragon is the only animal large enough to prey on them. Thus the lizard fills an otherwise vacant ecological niche.

The unique upper tusks of Babirusa boars—native to a few Indonesian islands—grow through the muzzle, unlike those of other wild pigs. The inward-curving tusks function as sexual adornment.

Mouse lemurs, found only on Madagascar, are the tiniest primates. In addition, these four-inch-long insectivores are the only primates that estivate: after storing up fat in rump and tail, they spend the dry season in a torpid state.

Descendants of one species may evolve in different ways and eventually form many new species

A visitor to a tropical Pacific island relatively unchanged by man is often overwhelmed by the abundance of living things, such as the scuttling droves of land crabs, and by the variety of shapes, sizes, and colors. Since the original plant and animal colonizers were probably few in number and variety, and most islands have not had long ages in which to produce new forms, as continents have had, endemic species on islands must have changed in appearance and become specialized in a relatively short time. By what mechanisms do such changes occur?

All living things are forever on the move through time, most of them evolving into forms markedly different from their remote ancestors.

Every individual organism carries a unique combination of traits inherited from its ancestors, which make it different from all other individuals. The parts of living cells carrying these traits are called genes; all of an organism's genes together form the genetic makeup. Every organism with two parents has received half of its genes from each one, and its genetic makeup is different from that of either parent. Genes are reshuffled again and again in successive generations, with each individual offspring inheriting genes in unique combination from its parents and exhibiting traits that make it more or less adapted to survive.

The pool of genes available to an island species is likely to be severely restricted, for even a large island population has usually developed from a very few individuals that made a fortunate landfall in days long past. The first immigrants did not carry in their genetic makeup all the characteristics of their entire race. They were a chance sample, no more typical of the homeland population than any other group of a similar size. The newly

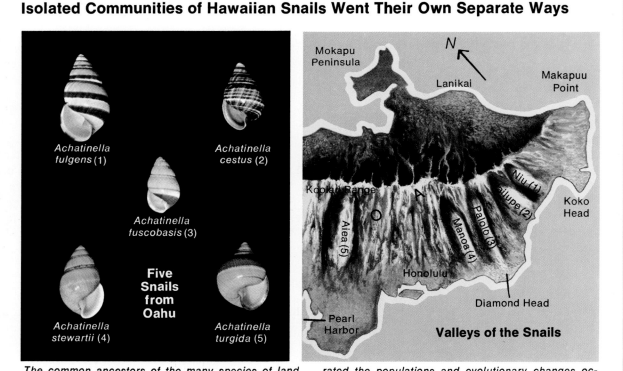

Isolated Communities of Hawaiian Snails Went Their Own Separate Ways

Achatinella fulgens (1)

Achatinella cestus (2)

Achatinella fuscobasis (3)

Five Snails from Oahu

Achatinella stewartii (4)

Achatinella turgida (5)

Mokapu Peninsula

Lanikai

Makapuu Point

Koolau Range

Niu (1)

Waialupe (2)

Koko Head

Aiea (5)

Manoa (4)

Palolo (3)

Honolulu

Pearl Harbor

Diamond Head

Valleys of the Snails

The common ancestors of the many species of land snails living on Oahu, one of the Hawaiian Islands, were brought to the island long ago by birds or natural rafts. As time passed, rivers and gorges sepa- *rated the populations and evolutionary changes occurred. Almost every valley came to harbor its own species, but now ranges overlap. Five snails, and the valleys where they were collected, are shown above.*

These five Madagascar vanga shrikes *share a common ancestor, whose descendants diversified to fill different ecological niches. Twelve species of vanga shrikes exist on Madagascar today; they vary widely in diet, beak shape, color, and size.*

Blue vanga

Helmet bird

Rufous vanga

Hook-billed vanga

Sicklebill vanga

established island population is therefore immediately somewhat different from the parent stock.

The kind of change called evolution begins when a random accident occurs to the molecules carrying the genetic makeup. Such accidental alterations, or mutations, of the genes are caused by a variety of environmental influences, including ultraviolet radiation from the sun and cosmic rays from far out in space. Heat, chemicals, and other physical factors may also alter a single molecule within a sperm or egg cell.

The vast majority of mutations are harmful and often fatal to the organisms in which they occur. The infinitesimally small percentage of mutations that are beneficial, however, improves the ability of the new organisms to adapt to environmental conditions. With enhanced powers of survival, such organisms are likely to pass on the mutant genes to their offspring.

Only a few members of a species are affected when a favorable mutation occurs and is inherited by the next generation. But if the change persists through successive generations, the species gradually comes to consist of two distinct and diverging groups of organisms: those with the mutant genes and those without.

As additional mutations reinforce earlier ones, the process of diversification is fostered within the mutant group. Natural selection becomes increasingly influential: The individuals that are most successful in a given set of conditions—plants with roots long enough to reach scarce water, birds with beaks strong enough to crush seeds, predator or prey with a good camouflage coloration—multiply and flourish. But organisms that are not so fit in one respect may, instead of dying off, become specialists in another direction and survive as another branch of the family tree. In time, both groups may take forms strikingly different from their pioneering ancestors, as well as from their neighboring cousins, and relationships may be nearly or quite impossible to trace.

A multitude of such specialized forms may come from just a few hardy colonizing species. The twelve kinds of vanga shrikes on Madagascar apparently evolved from a single species; the more than 3700 insect species on Hawaii radiated from only 250. Isolated from the competition of mainland life, islands have produced or preserved oddities such as the flightless kiwi of New Zealand and the two egg-laying mammals of Australia. Sometimes giants have developed: The Galápagos Islands harbor centipedes up to a foot in length, huge tortoises weighing as much as 600 pounds, and sunflower trees fifty feet tall.

The rate of mutations is not less on continents than it is on islands, but mutant individuals on a continent must face intense competition from an abundance of other well-entrenched individuals, and the new characteristic is more likely to be lost in the larger gene pool. In an island environment, many a mutant organism that would have met quick destruction on the mainland has become a successful experiment.

Nocturnal and omnivorous, foot-long Solenodon *of Hispaniola probes in the ground with a long snout or rips open logs. When pursued,* Solenodon *often trips and tumbles, but it has a formidable defense: toxic saliva that poisons its bite.*

On the oldest islands live a few species for which the ancestral form is good enough

As immigrants arrived, both they and the original inhabitants were usually forced to adapt or perish. Most of the island species of today are highly modified, some changed so radically that it is difficult to trace their origins. But occasionally some plant or animal was able to survive in its isolated environment without much change. Such a plant or animal is called a relict.

Among the more interesting animal relicts are those found on the ancient continental islands of New Zealand, Australia, the Philippine Islands, and Madagascar, and the Caribbean islands of Cuba and Hispaniola.

Possibly the most archaic of the larger land animals still living is the tuatara, a lizardlike reptile of New Zealand. Externally the tuatara super-ficially resembles some modern lizards, but its primitive skeleton identifies it as belonging to a family of reptiles widespread 200 million years ago. As dinosaurs came to rule the Earth, this group of small reptiles died out everywhere but in New Zealand; there, isolated from enemies, the tuatara managed to survive.

Three closely related kinds of New Zealand frogs are also very primitive, with muscular characteristics like those of their long-tailed salamander ancestors. In Australia, three freshwater fishes—the lungfish, barramundi, and blackfish—have persisted in isolation for millions of years, the only representatives of their kinds still in existence anywhere.

Small insect-eating mammals first appeared in large numbers over 100 million years ago, during the reign of the dinosaurs. They remained largely unspecialized and insignificant until most of the giant reptiles had vanished. Many of these furry little creatures lived inconspicuously in the thick undergrowth of forests, where their insect prey was plentiful, although some, as indicated by the grasping structure of their feet, evidently climbed trees. The only surviving descendants that strongly resemble them are the several species of insect-eating tenrecs found exclusively in Madagascar, and two species of another insectivore found only in Cuba and Hispaniola.

Cuba was once heavily forested and populated by a wide array of animals. Its coastline, over 2000 miles long, surrounds an essentially low country with few mountains. Its equable temperature and year-round, plentiful rainfall make it a semitropical paradise except when hurricanes roar over it. Today, most of the forests are gone, replaced by farms. A few native hardwoods, some pines, and many introduced trees still grow on the hills, and the shores remain heavily fringed by several types of mangroves. In the shallow bordering sea, life remains nearly constant.

Of Cuba's thirty-odd mammals, over two-thirds are bats, able to cross the interisland straits rather easily. Most of the others are several kinds of rodents. But it is the remaining two mammals that excite the greatest interest. They are insect eaters extinct elsewhere but related to the tenrecs of Madagascar. They belong to the genus *Solenodon*, and they resemble large, foot-long shrews. *Solenodon* is rare in both Cuba and Hispaniola (where it lives primarily in Haiti). It has scent glands, but the odor, though unpleasant, is not strong. Its many, rather unspecialized teeth are an archaic feature, although they are efficient in shredding insect prey. Its eyes are small, and its nostrils are directed sideward, possibly an adaptation to its snuffling, searching way of life.

Another interesting island relict is the tarsier, a curious little primate with a strange mixture of primitive and advanced traits. It survives today only in the Philippines and on other islands of the region such as Sumatra, Borneo, and Celebes. The tarsier is not easily observed: Small and nocturnal, it dwells high in trees.

The most startling feature of a tarsier's appearance is its pair of large, staring eyes, so huge that the rest of its face is pinched and reduced. Such eyes, of course, indicate a nocturnal habit of seeking food. A tarsier's sense of smell is poor, as is that of most primates, but its hearing is acute. Sound is channeled into its ear canals by big, almost batlike ears that move sensitively back and forth to identify the source of the slightest noise. The tarsier probably has the most mobile neck among present-day mammals: Without twisting or moving its body, the gnomelike little creature can turn its head nearly 180 degrees in either di-

A Philippine tarsier stares owlishly from its perch. Only six inches long, tarsiers are among the tiniest primates, and among the few that do not eat plants. Tarsiers, which possess primitive teeth, eat insects, lizards, and frogs.

rection to inspect an object directly behind it.

With its long, slender hind legs, the tarsier can make prodigious leaps from branch to branch. The tip of each finger and toe is a bulbous pad of flesh, with ridges and grooves that almost completely eliminate the chance of slipping. When a tarsier lands on a branch, it clings like a bit of iron to a magnet. There it rests, hunched up, ready for another springing leap.

The tarsier's place in the long sequence of primate evolution is somewhat ambiguous. Its brain, teeth, digestive tract, and fingers are essentially rather primitive, yet the tarsier displays a number of advanced, monkeylike characteristics: the structure of its retina; the rounded head, reduced face, and mobile lips; and certain features of its reproductive system.

All primates living today—the lemurs of Madagascar, tarsiers, monkeys, apes, and man—are of course modern creatures, and although all are more or less distant cousins, none is an ancestor of any other. Possibly some tarsierlike animal of the past was the ancestor of all the primates.

Mature scarlet ibises *mingle with brownish adolescents and related white ibises on Trinidad. Anhingas and a black-crowned night heron roost in the tree at right. These species, like most Trinidad birds, also breed in South America.*

The Colorful Life of Caribbean Islands

The 7000-odd lush islands and coral reefs of the Caribbean stretch from Florida to South America. A very few are continental in origin, but the great majority are the result of volcanic action long ago. Most of the volcanos that formed them are extinct, but in 1902 the eruption of Mt. Pelée on Martinique wiped out 30,000 inhabitants. Trade winds and ocean currents have carried spores and seeds from around the world to the islands; probably all land animals arrived on floating debris from the Americas. Populated by chance and by species introduced by man, each of the West Indies displays a unique array of plants and animals.

The West Indies, *with a total area of 91,000 square miles, dot the 971,400 square miles of the Caribbean.*

The red-necked parrot is the smaller of the two species endemic to Dominica, a heavily forested, mountainous island. Many of the larger West Indies have endemic species of parrots or parakeets.

A six-foot-long boa constrictor slithers up a tree in Trinidad. Boas, common in Central and South America, probably were carried to Trinidad and other West Indian islands on rafts of debris borne by the currents.

Towering agaves lend color to Puerto Rico's semi-arid rolling hills. Most species grow on the North and Central American mainland.

Jamaican todies, kingfisherlike birds, range island-wide. Tiny todies live only in the West Indies—Cuba, Puerto Rico, Hispaniola, Jamaica.

Wildlife of the Philippine Rain Forest

Rufous hornbill

Forest kingfisher

Marche's fruit dove

Hanging parakeet

Monkey-eating eagle

Palawan peacock pheasant

GILBERT

Some rare and exotic species live in the dwindling rain forests of the Philippine archipelago, such as the glittering peacock pheasants of Palawan and Marche's fruit doves on Luzon and Pollilo. Six-inch endemic falconets—among the smallest birds of prey—feed on insects. No more than fifty pairs of monkey-eating eagles still hunt monkeys and flying lemurs on Mindanao. Noisy flocks of rufous hornbills feed on fruit and small animals. Far from the sea, a forest

Life on a Tropical Archipelago

Most of the more than 7000 islands of the Philippine archipelago are small and without human settlement. Some of the larger islands are mountainous, and a few volcanos are still active. With an extraordinarily long shoreline of over 20,000 miles, and a breadth of climate extending from humid warmth at sea level to the chill of peaks over 9000 feet high, the Philippine Islands have presented a wide variety of habitats to colonizing plant and animal life.

The Philippine Islands were once joined to Asia, and this accounts for the many Malaysian species; the plants of the higher mountains appear related to Himalayan plants. Over half of the entire plant population seems to be native to the islands, and a great many species are found nowhere else.

Luzon is the largest island of the Philippines. Forests of lofty pines cover the slopes of its northern Mountain Province; dark, wet rain forests grow in the lowlands. On the sides of the mountains, extensive forest fires sometimes burn whole

Flying lemurs

Bushy-tailed
cloud rat

Trogon

Tarsier

Falconet

kingfisher is adapted to eat insects instead of fish. Trogons of the eastern islands perch motionless, awaiting insect prey. The curious endemic hanging parakeet sleeps upside down. Nocturnal mammals include a tarsier that leaps *among branches hunting insects, the bushy-tailed cloud rat of Luzon's mountains, and a flying lemur. Membranes between its legs enable this relative of bats—not a lemur at all—to glide from one tree to another.*

ranges. Even after the raging flames have subsided, fire may smolder for weeks in the resinous roots of the mountain pines, and then break out anew. Although some of the fires have been manmade, many are started during the frequent violent thunderstorms in the highlands. The full recovery of a fire-devastated forest may take a long time, but it begins almost immediately as cogon, a stiff, saw-toothed grass, sends up shoots in the opened areas. The prolific growth of this and other grasses makes rough going for animal or human travelers; the blades of the grasses are so sharp that heavy trousers are slashed and skin lacerated.

In the lowlands, fruit trees, broad-leafed timber trees, and flowering plants—especially orchids—grow in abundance. Monkeys, large fruit bats, and most of the carnivorous mammals live in the lowlands. Some monkeys are also found on the lower slopes, and birds, small mammals, lizards, snakes, and even freshwater crabs have invaded the higher elevations as well.

Among the great variety of spiders inhabiting the islands are large tarantulalike ground spiders that live in burrows, smaller tree-dwelling species, and mimics that live in populous ant colonies and are almost indistinguishable from ordinary worker ants. Some of the large tree-dwelling (and house-dwelling) huntress spiders spend the day hanging, completely relaxed, from the four legs on one side; three of the legs on the other side dangle, while the last leg forms a triangular brace to support the heavy abdomen.

Folklore everywhere in the world is full of myths that are really embellishments of natural phenomena. One tradition of Philippine folklore is the belief that small climbing lizards descend to the ground late every afternoon or early evening to kiss the earth, the implication being whatever human imagination wishes to make of it. Actually, the lizards do just that, but the reason is clear only to a careful observer. In the tropics, as the sun goes down after a hot and rather dry day, the air cools suddenly, and the moisture it held in the heat of the day quickly condenses on stones, soil, and leaf litter. The lizards descend to lap the surface moisture while there is still enough light for them to see.

In the northern part of Luzon, not far from the village of Bontoc, a mountain supports over a dozen species of rats found nowhere else. This forested elevation with thick undergrowth is an example of the environmental isolation that can occur within an island that has itself been separated from the mainland for millennia.

Mindanao, the other large island of the Philippines, has vast tracts of thick forest. The vegetation differs according to rainfall, which varies over the island from heavy to sporadic. In some of Mindanao's rivers are found sea-going crocodiles, which grow as long as twenty feet and belong to the same species as crocodiles in Borneo and other islands to the south.

A wandering albatross chick awaits its parents on snowy South Georgia Island, in the South Atlantic. Parents care for their young for such a long time that adults breed only every other year. But as the chick grows, it is fed less and less frequently; one adult, known to be still feeding its chick, was seen 2640 miles from the nest. When the young bird is about nine months old, after it has survived an antarctic winter, it flies for the first time.

Some island species are adapted to the blistering heat of the tropics; others, to perpetual cold on icy arctic and antarctic islands

By comparison with islands in tropical and temperate regions, polar islands are impoverished of life. Occasionally such islands support large populations of a few species, but inevitably they lack a wide variety of types. Cold in itself limits

the number of species, and an ice cover presents an even more serious handicap.

No matter how well adapted to the cold an animal may be, an ice cover almost assures starvation. Grazers cannot reach the few green things that are able to grow, and carnivores therefore have no animals on which they can prey.

The great ice sheet covering Greenland, one of the world's largest islands, is almost devoid of life. The ice-free fringes harbor only a few animals and stunted plants. There are no cold-blooded animals—freshwater fishes, amphibians, or reptiles. Fourteen different kinds of birds regularly fre-

quent the perimeter of Greenland, some of them only for breeding purposes; and there is a larger summer population of visiting water birds. Greenland has only eight mammals, ranging from the large caribou, musk ox, and polar bear to the tiny lemming, all of them originally from North America.

Antarctic islands, including Antarctica itself, support even fewer permanent residents: about fifteen species of birds—penguins, skuas, and snow petrels being the best known—and the year-round Weddell seal. Three other kinds of seals inhabit the pack-ice region all year.

Musk oxen huddle together, protecting their calves. Residents of the far north, primarily on the larger arctic islands, musk oxen have shorter legs than takins, their buffalolike relatives, which live in warmer regions in Asia.

A female Alaskan brown bear lumbers out of a Kodiak Island stream with a freshly-caught salmon in her mouth. Her five-month-old cubs are too young to catch fish but will share the feast. Waiting glaucous-winged gulls get leftovers.

Alaskan
brown
bear
9 ft. long
1700 lb.

Malayan
sun
bear
4 ft. long
140 lb.

Emperor
penguin

King
penguin

34 in. tall
40 lb.

46 in. tall
100 lb.

Colder climates favor larger animals, which have less heat-dissipating body surface in proportion to their bulk than have smaller animals. The largest bear, the Alaskan brown, lives in the subarctic; the smallest, the sun bear, lives in the tropics. The largest penguin, the emperor, nests only on the frigid antarctic continent; the emperor's smaller relative, the king, nests on the subantarctic islands.

A pair of macaroni penguins guards a single egg in a nest of mud and tussock grass. Females often lay as many as three eggs, but only one chick is usually reared. Macaronis are the largest of six species of crested penguins and breed the farthest south. They form rookeries on lonely antarctic islands in November; eggs hatch in December; chicks take to the water to fend for themselves by March.

In adapting to frigid polar islands, animals have evolved sizes and shapes that conserve body heat

There is evidence that Greenland and Antarctica have not always been as frigid as they are now, that both experienced completely different conditions in the remote past. Coal beds on Greenland indicate that it had a temperate or subtropical climate some 125 million years ago. Antarctica also has coal beds, as well as fossil skeletons of amphibians and reptiles. Neither coal-producing plants nor cold-blooded animals can live in a polar climate, with its long, dark, bitter winters.

Creatures of the far north and south tend to be large, a characteristic that allows them to conserve heat because their bodies possess a small surface in proportion to their bulk. The largest land carnivore in the world, the Alaskan brown bear, lives on the mainland and on Aleutian islands, while one of the smallest bears, the Ma-

layan sun bear, is tropical. Puffins—fish-eating birds found as far south as the Balearic Islands in the Mediterranean Sea—increase in size steadily northward through the British Isles, Iceland, and finally to the arctic island of Spitsbergen. The emperor penguin of the Antarctic is more than twice as tall as the little Galápagos species.

A related phenomenon is the reduced size of ears, legs, and tails of animals living in the polar latitudes. Small ears and short legs and tails lessen the amount of heat loss and the danger of freezing. The stocky musk ox and the short-eared arctic hare are quite different from their relatives far to the south; the lanky Arizona jack rabbit, for example, offers an extreme contrast to the arctic hare.

Island life around the world is characterized by its diversity. Each bit of land, after long isolation, shows its own unique set of plant and animal adaptations. It is this uniqueness—born of chance arrivals, nourished by isolation, and expressed through a multitude of bizarre and beautiful forms—that makes islands endlessly fascinating. Who knows what one will find next?

Island Pioneers and Their Descendants

On once-barren oceanic islands, the process of evolution gave rise to extraordinary life forms: the giant sunflowers, cactuses, and reptiles of the Galápagos; the versatile birds of the Hawaiian chain

The population of living things found on any island results not only from biological processes but also from a host of geological and geographical circumstances: the island's entire geological history, and its present size, terrain, location, and climate. The older an island is and the farther removed from sources of colonization, the more likely that endemic species—species that evolved there and exist nowhere else—will make up a significant percentage of its plant and animal inhabitants. Endemism, common on distant oceanic islands, is relatively rare on islands close to continental shores.

The British Isles, for example, are separated from the mainland of Europe by only twenty miles of shallow water. The islands were isolated so recently—about 7000 years ago—that most of their plant and animal life is indistinguishable from that of the continent. Ireland was cut off a little earlier than Great Britain, but since the separation of both occurred after the last Ice Age, when most of northern Europe was covered with glaciers, their plant and animal populations today are totally composed of modern European species.

When the ice began to retreat, the region stayed cool for some centuries longer, and sea levels were still so low that a land bridge to the continent remained. But for reptiles and amphibians—cold-blooded creatures unable to regulate their body temperatures—migration northward was difficult. When water from the melting ice caps flooded the English Channel, only a few of these animals had succeeded in penetrating the region.

The same holds true for freshwater fishes: Ireland has half as many native species as Britain, which in turn has only half as many as Belgium. The marked similarities between the freshwater fishes of the British Isles and those of the continent are due to the fact that the Thames and Rhine were once joined, before the North Sea flooded in and severed the connection. Since then the isolated populations have slowly diversified.

Warm-blooded mammals were somewhat more successful in their penetration of the colder lands. The appealing little European hedgehog is found on both Britain and Ireland, as is the red fox. Wolves, bears, and wild boars disappeared after the arrival of man. Today there are only half as many species of some major mammalian groups—rabbits, shrews, deer, rodents, and even bats—in Britain as on the continent, and half as many in Ireland as in Britain. This does not mean that the total animal population density is less—only the number of different kinds of animals.

A great gray heron, perched on a rock above a colony of sunbathing marine iguanas, surveys the waters surrounding the Galápagos Islands in the Pacific. The cool Humboldt Current from the Antarctic and the equatorial sun combine to provide a remarkably rich larder for fish-eating birds.

The highest peak in Japan, *Fujiyama (Mt. Fuji), has the most nearly perfect cone of all the world's large volcanos. The 12,388-foot top is nearly always snow-capped. Five lakes lie at the mountain's base, and its lower slopes are forested.*

Like the British Isles, the islands of Japan received most of their plants and animals from the adjacent mainland

A glance at a world map suggests that the islands of Japan occupy a position in the Pacific comparable to that of the British Isles in the Atlantic. Both groups are continental islands that not long ago were connected with their respective continents. Both also show evidence of considerable earlier volcanic activity. Britain's volcanos are long since extinct, but most of Japan's approximately forty volcanos are only dormant.

The most famous volcano of the archipelago—and certainly the most beautiful—is Mt. Fuji, which last erupted in 1707. A volcano on a small island in Kagoshima Bay off southern Kyushu erupted as recently as fifty years ago, and Mt. Asama, brooding over the international summer resort of Karuizawa in central Honshu, even today sends smoke and ash into the air.

Japan is a rugged land with great mountain ranges and isolated volcanic cones rising high above its coastal regions. Flatlands make up only a small portion of the terrain; central Honshu's plain, the single greatest agricultural area in the whole country, occupies only about 5000 square miles (about 3.5 per cent of Japan's total surface). The many mountains divide the islands into fairly distinct geographical areas; the differing species of adjacent areas reflect their partial isolation. Endemic forms are rare, however, because the nearby mainland has supplied numerous migrants over the millennia. For centuries, also, the Japanese have altered the natural landscape by cultivating some native plants and removing others, and by importing alien species.

In the same way that the climate of the British Isles is moderated by the warm Gulf Stream flowing eastward across the Atlantic, southeastern Japan is warmed by the Japan Current, or Kuroshio. But the coast of Japan facing Russia, especially northern Hokkaido, is chilled by cold water coming down from the north. Where the two currents meet off northeastern Japan, the warm air above the Kuroshio collides with the cold air above the Oyashio, and fog banks and unsettled weather frequently result. The upper side of Honshu, across the Sea of Japan from the Soviet Union, has heavy snows every winter.

Northern Japan harbors a few unusual plant species whose relatives on the mainland changed or disappeared. The katsura tree, which for long ages grew on all the northern continents, today survives only in Japan. The magnificent cryptomeria, which resembles the redwood and creates the mystical blue-shadowed atmosphere of deep Japanese forests, is nearly gone from the rest of Asia. In contrast, palms, cycads, banyans, and other semitropical trees of southern Japan are widely distributed on a host of more southerly Pacific islands, and the northern forests of Hokkaido could almost be mistaken for those of North America, northern Asia, or Europe.

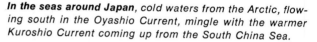

In the seas around Japan, cold waters from the Arctic, flowing south in the Oyashio Current, mingle with the warmer Kuroshio Current coming up from the South China Sea.

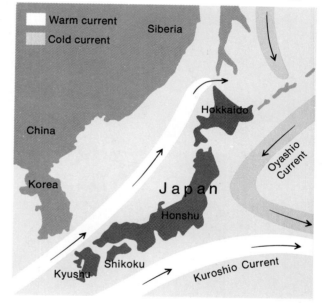

The British Isles have a mild climate, although they lie in northern latitudes, because of the warming effect of the North Atlantic Current, an offshoot of the Gulf Stream.

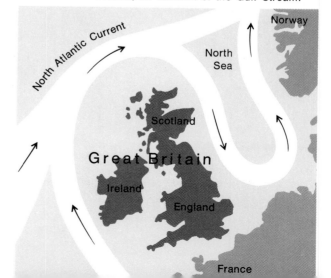

Japanese macaques, or snow monkeys, roam Shiga Plateau. When Japan's climate changed from tropical to temperate 35 million years ago, some monkeys managed to adapt to long winters and a diet of bark when leaves and fruit are unavailable.

Cavorting in a hot-springs pool, macaques evade the winter cold. Younger monkeys are more adventurous; they were the first to try these baths. Off the Japanese coast, young macaques frolic in the ocean; adults remain on shore.

Macaque mothers care for their infants for two years; daughters remain near their mothers much longer. Babies —occasionally twins—are born about six months after the early winter breeding season and are nursed for a year.

With the exception of man, no other primates live as far north as the snow monkeys of Japan

The animals of Japan are a little more specialized than those of Britain because the archipelago was not heavily glaciated and was separated from the mainland millions, rather than thousands, of years ago. The islands have received colonizers from all their neighbors: Siberia in the north, China in the south, and Korea in the west.

Japan's mammals, once abundant, today offer few surprises. The bears hunted and kept in captivity by the Ainus (the original human inhabitants of the archipelago) are much the same as those of Siberia. Wolves, foxes, badgers, otters, mink, and other carnivores scarcely differ from their Asian and American relatives. Large mammals are no longer common, but small species still live on forested slopes that have few human inhabitants.

Perhaps the most unexpected mammal in Japan is a light-colored monkey—a macaque—red-faced and cloaked in long fur that insulates it against the bitter cold of winter. Except for man, it is the only primate to inhabit such cold latitudes, and, like man, it must seek convenient local sources of warmth: In winter, the monkeys immerse themselves in hot springs. A few other colonies of the same species of monkey inhabit much warmer areas of Japan.

The birds of Japan, more than 400 species in all, are like those of the Asian mainland. Many of them —storks, herons, pheasants, ducks, and small songbirds—are frequently depicted in Japanese prints, paintings, and sculpture. Since no point on the islands is far from water, aquatic birds are especially numerous.

The archipelago possesses many species of freshwater fishes—sure proof of previous continental connections. Japan also has freshwater crayfishes and freshwater crabs similar to common Chinese species.

Amphibians, absent from distant oceanic islands, appear in variety on all the Japanese islands; some are large, but one minute green tree frog can easily sit on a child's fingertip. The giant among Japan's amphibians is the world's largest salamander, *Megalobatrachus*, a five-foot-long creature that lives in the cool mountain streams of southern Honshu and Kyushu. Like the New World axolotl, it matures without ever losing its external gills

and its ability to breathe under water. Because it has been a favorite delicacy for centuries, it is now rare.

Japan, like England, has very few venomous snakes. Much feared is the mamushi, with heat-sensitive pits beneath its eyes. Pit vipers are not common; most poisonous snakes, such as the cobra, have venoms that attack the nervous system. The venom of pit vipers, such as the Japanese species and North America's rattlesnakes and copperheads, destroys blood cells.

More common are Japan's non-venomous snakes, which include rat snakes up to five feet long. Among the other reptiles are lizards and two kinds of turtles, one of which is endemic to the islands. A turtle living in rivers in central and southern Japan is often represented in art; a long train of algae cascading down its shell lends grace and color to an otherwise rather solid and angular animal.

The Bivalve Snail

The Inland Sea, or Seto Nai Kai, is known around the world for its clear beauty, its multitude of picturesque islands, and the plentiful life of its waters. Among the marine animals found here, one green mollusk stands out. It is a snail, but the adult is difficult to recognize as a snail; encased in a pair of delicate shells hinged at the top, it is an almost perfect replica of a small bivalve clam. The snail grazes on green algal pastures in shallow water. If it is disturbed, it immediately withdraws, clapping its shells together.

When the larva hatches, it looks like any other snail larva about to grow a typical spiral shell. But the juvenile shell soon divides into two parts, which gradually become more symmetrical, and the spiral is all but lost. A hinged ligament holds the two valves together, and a single muscle closes them—two muscles close a clam's shell.

The little green snail is scientifically important because it suggests a possible explanation of how such highly specialized bivalve forms as the clam evolved in the distant past.

Even a casual survey of the animals and plants of the British Isles and Japan demonstrates that isolation on islands brings about changes in form and behavior as the few survivors settle into their new, more restricted environments. The animals of Japan have become more diverse and specialized than those of Britain, because they have had more time to do so. Far more complicated examples of the specializing effects of isolation appear on other islands, much farther from continents.

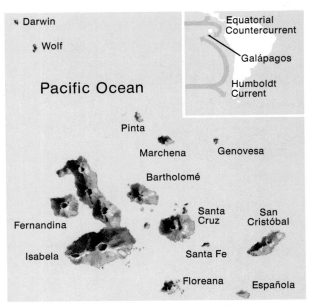

The Galápagos archipelago—sixteen major islands and numerous tiny ones—includes active volcanos; one erupted as recently as 1968. The cool northward-flowing Humboldt Current meets the warm Equatorial Countercurrent here.

Living laboratories of evolution, the Galápagos Islands inspired Darwin's monumental theories

Around the world, many long archipelagos consisting of hundreds of islands string out from their parent continents, or arise quite independently in the ocean. Or several islands may cluster far from any other land. The plants and animals living in such clusters or chains of islands reveal much about the slow sequence of colonization.

The earliest study of island specialties, and still one of the best, was made by Charles Darwin in 1835, during his trip around the world on HMS *Beagle*, a survey vessel. Darwin had already spent nearly four years studying the life of South America when the small ship arrived at a group of rocky islands 500 miles off Ecuador—the Galápagos Islands. Although the *Beagle* remained there only one month, the impression these islands left upon Darwin's receptive mind was out of all proportion to either their size or the diversity of living things.

For the first time, Darwin had a chance to see the effects of isolation on a number of familiar animals: birds, lizards, and tortoises. It is clear

A Galápagos penguin chick waddles across a lava shore. The only tropical penguin, the Galápagos species nests on two or three islands. Females lay eggs in holes in the rock, without other protection, a few feet above high water.

Galápagos sea lions, *related to species living on islands off California and Japan, share crowded rookeries with swallow-tailed gulls, which fly to Peru after breeding. Gulls and sea lions feed on the abundant fishes in the Humboldt Current.*

that at the time of his visit, he did not realize the importance of what he saw, but he made careful collections. Years later, as the germ of a great idea grew in his mind, Galápagos life provided his most important evidence.

In terms of geological time, the islands are of recent origin; the oldest fossils found there are perhaps no more than two or three million years old. Both the Hawaiian Islands and the Galápagos are the exposed tops of shield volcanos with huge bases, ten to twenty miles across, resting on the sea floor far beneath. Shores and flatlands are strewn with jumbled masses of lava blocks.

The communities of shallow-water marine creatures along the shores resemble those along the tropical and subtropical American mainland, or, to a lesser degree, those of distant Pacific islands. Because nutrient-laden waters from the deep sea are forced upward against the shores of the Galápagos, the shallow coastal seas are exceedingly rich in living things.

Other volcanic islands in the equatorial Pacific are densely covered with vegetation, but not the Galápagos. They lie in the path of the great Humboldt Current, which brings subantarctic waters up the west coast of South America. The current remains cool, and to some extent prevents rainfall on many parts of the islands. With little rain, the volcanic terrain does not easily erode to make soil in which plants can grow.

Because the Galápagos rose from the sea with no previous connection to the mainland, their life consists only of what was able to arrive by sea and air. There are now five large and eleven small islands, with a total area of slightly less than 3000 square miles. Geologists have worked out only part of their history; a larger amount of evidence comes from biology. The most dramatic evidence of change is the small lizards and snakes that cannot swim or fly across the channels but whose distribution, resemblances, and differences provide clues to the separation of the islands.

How did terrestrial life arrive? Opposite Ecuador, the cold Humboldt Current is deflected toward the Galápagos Islands and merges with the Equatorial Current. Thus it becomes a reliable conveyor belt from South America, and especially from more distant Central America.

Penguins from the far south and sea lions and fur seals from the north originally swam in on the currents. Other creatures, seeds, and living plants were carried from Central American jungles aboard natural rafts, on winds, or on the feet and feathers of seabirds. Of all the animals now inhabiting the Galápagos, only one—a land snail—is known to have come from the broad Pacific.

ISLAND PIONEERS AND THEIR DESCENDANTS 223

Distinct vegetation zones on a larger Galápagos island result from rainfall and temperature differences determined by elevation. Cactuses grow on arid lowlands; sunflower forests on uplands; shrubs and grasses on the heights.

On the Galápagos Islands prickly pear cactuses as high as fifteen feet provide food for 600-pound giant tortoises

The first successful settlers of the Galápagos were plants, since animals could not have survived without a resident plant population. Many of the plants are very ancient, some highly specialized. One of the living ferns is known elsewhere as a fossil over 150 million years old.

Each island differs from the others in area, in altitude, and in exposure to the rare rain-laden winds. The distinct zones of vegetation include mangrove stands along the shore; tough cactus and shrubs, leafless and flowerless except after the brief rainy season, in arid coastal lava fields; and trees, ferns, mosses, lichens, and other small plants on high slopes where moisture condenses from clouds and encourages their growth. At still higher elevations, 2000 feet or more, the constant cool winds evaporate moisture as it forms; here the dominant plants are grasses and low shrubs.

Several trees of the Galápagos are derived from small ancestors. The prickly pear cactus, common in the Northern Hemisphere, usually grows close to the ground or is only a few feet high. The flattened pads (actually modified stems) of this cactus are buoyant, and they can propagate new plants; it is likely such pads drifted to the Galápagos from Central America a long time ago. Prickly pears apparently became established in the Galápagos at least twice, for two basic kinds of specialization show up among the several major groups of their modern descendants. Some species that closely resemble their ancestors cling to rocky cliffs. Others produce exceptionally long pads that thicken into stout trunks more than three feet in diameter; dense clusters of more conventional spiny pads crown the tops, perhaps fifteen feet high.

Today this cactus and another treelike species —the candelabra cactus—play major roles in the biological economy of the islands. The cactuses propagate regularly and abundantly enough to sustain the islands' iguanas and tortoises, which eat some of the young plants as they appear above the ground. A significant percentage of cactuses, however, escape being eaten; once they produce massive trunks, the cactus trees are impervious to attack. Indeed, they seem to grow largest on the islands where tortoises live or have lived in the past, while prickly pear bushes, much lower in height, grow in areas never inhabited by tortoises.

When rainfall encourages the growth of less formidable plants, tortoises prefer food other than cactus, but in the dry season cactus pads are almost their only source of food and moisture. The pads, which have grown in profusion at the top of the tree during the beginning of the rainy season, become swollen with water, and are often so heavy that they fall to the ground. The tortoises then forage for the fallen pads, which have relatively small, soft spines.

A tortoise is not merely a consumer, however. The tough cactus seeds it swallows with the pads and fruits pass undamaged through its digestive system and are deposited, together with fertilizing waste matter, in other parts of the island, where many germinate and grow. In this way, the reptiles have widened the distribution of their essential food source.

The seeds or pollen of many Galápagos plants are scattered by other animals besides tortoises: Birds, flies, carpenter bees, and hawkmoths are among the most important. At the same time, these isolated islands also support many self-pollinating plant species, more than are usually found in continental environments, where numerous varieties of insects serve as pollinating agents.

Side by side with cactus trees, another tree, thirty to forty feet tall, has evolved from the weed-like sunflower family. On the Galápagos Islands the sunflower family has given rise to several species. "Sunflower" trees constitute the forests of the middle slopes, taking over where the cactus trees begin to die out. Farther up, guava and other smaller trees become dominant.

It is from the giant land tortoises that the islands take their name—galápago is the Spanish word for "tortoise." Darwin had been told that each island supported a different kind of tortoise and he was surprised to find it true. The fifteen different kinds that are or have been present are descended from one species that must have rafted from South America. Smaller relatives still live there and in the West Indies.

Long ago giant tortoises were abundant on at least ten of the islands. At mating time, the hoarse cries of the males, the most vocal of turtles, resounded over hundreds of yards. But early in the history of human exploration, the islands became ports of call for seagoing ships. Even a medium-sized vessel could stow away 300 tortoises in the hold, where they could be kept alive, without food or water, for as long as a year to provide meat and

A giant tortoise plods through a cactus forest on Isabela in the Galápagos. These tortoises weigh about three ounces when they hatch and take thirty years to reach 600 pounds. The immense reptiles may live for over 100 years.

fat for the crew. Later, during the early nineteenth century, whaling vessels were still removing thousands of the huge, completely fearless and defenseless reptiles.

Today there are self-sustaining colonies of tortoises on only three of the islands; the tortoises of the other islands are either gone or—because their reproductive rate does not make up for their declining numbers—in danger of extinction. The eggs and the young of the tortoises are often eaten by wild pigs, wild dogs, and rats, most of them brought in by man. The once-extensive plant food of the tortoises has been destroyed by the pigs and, even more, by goats, also imported.

Galápagos marine iguanas pile up on top of each other while sunbathing. Outside the breeding season, these lizards are gregarious; during the breeding season, they compete for territories, harems, and nesting sites.

The only marine iguanas in the world eat seaweed on Galápagos shores

The large and conspicuous marine iguanas of the Galápagos are descendants of green vegetarian iguanas similar to those that still inhabit mainland forests, where they feed on the abundant leaves. At some time in the distant past, a section of a Central American riverbank may have broken away, with the plants and animals living on it, and floated out to sea. There it was caught in an oceanic current and carried hundreds of miles to the islands. If, over many thousands of years, this happened repeatedly, it would have brought not only the iguanas but also smaller land animals.

Any forest iguanas that survived the trip clambered off the raft and sought food. Some wandered inland and ascended the slopes, where vegetation was already growing. There they could eat fruit and flowers part of the time and devour water-filled cactus pads, spines and all, the rest of the year. It was a great change from the lush tropical forests they had left, but there was enough food to keep them alive. When the day grew too hot, they retreated into burrows beneath the lava.

Greater difficulties confronted the iguanas that remained near the shore beside the barren lava flows. The only plant material they could reach was the thick mat of brown seaweed (mostly a kind of sargassum weed) exposed on the rocks at low tide. It was foreign but nutritious, and their food habits changed out of necessity. But more than diet changed.

As in all natural communities, individual differences favoring survival tended to persist, with each such feature emphasized in passing generations. Today the three-foot-long marine iguana is very different from its ancestral stock on the mainland. It is dark rather than green: Some races are black, others are a mottled red and black and show a trace of green only during breeding season. The dark color may make it possible for these cold-blooded reptiles to absorb heat. The rather long, leaf-gathering snout of the forest iguana has become a short, heavy, bulldog type, suited for browsing on the dense mats of seaweed hugging the rocks. Biting first with one side of its jaws and then the other, the big lizard tears at the tough plants, all the while clinging to the slippery rocks with powerful clawed toes.

Unlike the larger, land iguanas, which can obtain water from plant food, a marine iguana is obliged to swallow salt water when it feeds on seaweed at low tide. When it eats underwater—a feat made possible by the swallowing of small stones, which lessen its buoyancy and enable it to cling securely to coral heads—the iguana takes in even greater quantities of salt water. So much salt in its body would be fatal except for the specialized tear glands that secrete salt.

The marine iguana is a good swimmer; with legs folded to the side, it undulates its body and tail. It avoids heavy surf, and does not venture out more than a few dozen yards. Sharks are numerous in Galápagos waters and are known to prey on the lizards. An iguana rides in on a swell and crawls up the rough lava. If it does not find home immediately, it wanders about, touching the rocks with its tongue, which carries scent to a special sensory organ in the mouth. Once its own familiar scent is found, the iguana rests safely above high tide, almost motionless, even when bright red crabs scurry over its scaly body, stopping occasionally to pick off ticks.

Marine iguanas seldom travel more than ten yards inland. Lying in great swarms along the dark lava shore, they soak up the sun until the tide recedes and it is again time to eat. Each male occupies a small bit of territory, usually in the company of one or two females. If an intruder wanders by accidentally, it is attacked at once and bitten ferociously; it usually retreats in haste.

Most fights result from the deliberate challenge of an invader. Such contests begin with much threatening and bluffing: The males show their bright red mouths, rise high on their legs, and may squirt twin sprays of moisture from their nostrils. Each combatant, butting with its heavy, flattened head, tries to shove the other away. If the battle is decisive, the loser—often the challenger—lies down in a deflated attitude of submission, and the victor stands high and nods vigorously. Since no serious injury results from such a fight, the colony is not depleted, and the population on the rocks remains unaffected.

While females are excavating nests in the all-too-scarce volcanic sand, they too may come into conflict with one another. If the foot-deep burrows have not yet been covered when the fight begins, the pair of eggs exposed in each burrow may be destroyed by island mockingbirds, which dart in to feed on the nutritious yolks.

Lava lizards, which came from the same general stock, are slightly smaller than marine iguanas. All seven species of lava lizard retain much of the family's aggressive behavior; they threaten, chase, and fight one another. In the center of a lava lizard's head is a vestigial third eye, not totally functionless: It senses the amount of solar radiation received by the reptile, which accordingly regulates its body temperature by moving in and out of sunshine, or between hot rocks and cooler crevices. When light and heat are excessive, there is a marked reduction in the lizard's activity.

A male land iguana on his territory points his snout upward and jerks his head up and down to scare an intruder.

The five-foot-long males fight, each trying in vain to grab the skin on the other's flanks and force submission.

Wounded by his opponent, the intruder retreats. Iguanas rarely continue fighting after one has been injured.

A male frigate bird puffs up his bright scarlet throat sac in a courtship display, while his mate rests close beside him. The throat sac is conspicuous only in the breeding season.

Blue-footed boobies strut in an elaborate courtship dance. Males inflate their cheeks, cock their tails, and lift their webbed feet high. After prolonged courtship, pairs form for life. Galápagos boobies breed year round.

A Galápagos cormorant waddles past an iguana colony, clutching a greeting token of seaweed for its mate. With food plentiful and enemies scarce, the birds have no need to fly. Their atrophied wings are used to shade the young.

Native Galápagos birds share nesting sites with many visitors

The Galápagos are among the few islands in the world where large bird populations share their environment with large numbers of reptiles. Over 100 bird species, many of them migratory seabirds, nest on the islands. The land birds, probably blown in by storms, have become highly specialized. A few species of birds are almost extinct: There are only 200 Galápagos flamingos left. The flightless cormorants and the Galápagos penguins are abundant, principally because they can dive into the sea to feed on the inexhaustible supply of fish and octopus. There are hordes of boobies, too, and about 2000 pairs of Galápagos albatrosses.

The most famous birds of the islands are the finches that Darwin collected, described, and pondered for two decades. Forty years after their first mention by a Captain James Colnett, Darwin's more detailed account of them in his journal, *The Voyage of the Beagle*, gave no indication that they would become basic evidence in the development of a theory of evolution. Only gradually did he recognize that they, as well as the tortoises and iguanas, were descendants of immigrants from South and Central America, and that their ancestors, after reaching the islands, had found it difficult to survive according to their old habits.

The ancestor of the Galápagos finches is not known, but probably it was one of the common seed eaters of the mainland. Seeds are not plentiful on the islands, and those birds that found it possible to eat other things had an advantage. What Darwin finally realized, and scientists know today, is that different specialties may arise from a common ancestor. From the original finches arriving on the Galápagos thousands of years ago, there are now thirteen species of birds. All are still essentially finchlike, mostly brown, short-tailed birds that construct roofed nests in which they lay pink-spotted white eggs. But in size, beak structure, and habits they are widely divergent.

The shape of a finch's bill suggests its food preference. Some bills can tear at fruits, others are grain crushers; some are curved and can reach deep into flowers such as those of the coral tree; there are straight bills that bore into wood, a flycatcher type, and the usual finch shape. Once Darwin recognized that these different shapes were all

modifications of a single original bill design, the conclusion was inevitable: Given time and opportunity, species change. Undoubtedly the Galápagos finches are still in the process of specializing.

The Galápagos Islands have been studied repeatedly since Darwin's day, with new expeditions forming every few years. Despite the ravages of early visitors and of the once-domesticated animals they left behind, the natural life of the islands is still more nearly intact than that of many other islands. From this life scientists continue to learn the basic principles of the origins of modern plants and animals, and to gain insight into the effects of isolation on far more lush and densely populated islands around the world.

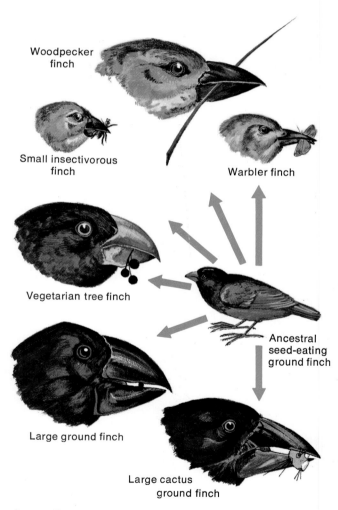

Woodpecker finch

Small insectivorous finch

Warbler finch

Vegetarian tree finch

Ancestral seed-eating ground finch

Large ground finch

Large cactus ground finch

One ordinary finch species, arriving by chance on the Galápagos, branched out over the ages to fill a variety of ecological niches. At present the thirteen distinct species include ground finches that live on the ancestral seed diet, others adapted for eating cactuses, leaves, or insects, and one that probes with twigs for grubs.

Isolated in the middle of the largest ocean, Hawaii has received settlers from all directions

Although the Hawaiian Islands have been tampered with by human invaders, both Polynesian and more recent settlers, they still offer some of the world's most dramatic examples of island life and of the changing of species from one island to the next. There are even clear gradations within a single island.

The area of the Pacific Ocean, the world's largest body of water, exceeds that of all continents and islands put together; it stretches nearly 9500 miles in one direction and 10,000 miles in the other. The Hawaiian Islands, in the middle of this vast expanse, are more isolated than most islands; the land nearest the archipelago is little Johnston Island, 600 miles to the southwest.

Yet animals and plants have succeeded in colonizing the Hawaiian group as they have most Pacific islands. There are no native amphibians; the freshwater fishes present evolved from marine species. The ancestors of the islands' geckos and skinks probably accompanied early Polynesian settlers rather than making the trip on their own. Except for one kind of bat, no mammals existed on the islands before the arrival of man.

Whereas Galápagos life is distinctly descended from that of South and Central America, the Hawaiian Islands are populated by species from all over the Pacific world, north and south, and from Asia and America. Oceanic and atmospheric currents have changed somewhat over the ages, and many stepping-stone islands have disappeared through erosion or submergence, and so the pathways taken by the first colonizers are now obscure. Only occasionally have scientists been able to dredge fossil evidence from the ancient sunken islands. Long periods of time have been involved: An average of one successful colonization every 20,000 years is in fact a triumph for islands that have been above water as long as the Hawaiian group.

The islands are of volcanic origin and have never been connected with any continent. Four of the major islands were formed by the union of smaller ones, and deep water now separates some of the small islands that were once joined. The islands at the northwest end of the chain are several million years old; today they are little more than slight protuberances above the sea. Sixteen hundred miles to the southeast, the great island of Hawaii, about one million years old, continues to grow through volcanic action.

The Hawaiian Islands offer many more examples of adaptive radiation from single ancestors than do the Galápagos; it is a pity that Darwin did not visit them or even know of their plant and animal variations, which have progressed much further along the evolutionary path than his examples on the comparatively barren islands off Ecuador. Most studies of the living things on Hawaii have been done in this century, and they deal with far more complex developments than those of the Galápagos.

The Green Pioneers

Colonization of the volcanic Hawaiian soil had to begin with hardy pioneer plants. Only after plants were well established could vegetarian animals survive, and of course neither predators nor parasites could live without an earlier resident animal population.

Before man arrived, the Hawaiian flora consisted of many grasses, tree-size lobelias, shrub violets, twelve-foot-high geraniums, and a host of other seed plants, ferns, and lesser forms. The more than 1700 kinds of seed plants were derived from perhaps 272 original colonizers, most of which came from the Indo-Pacific region. There were no mangroves or pines, and very few orchids

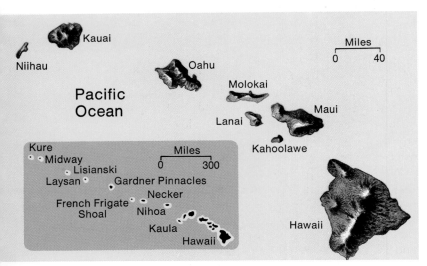

The volcanic Hawaiian Islands chain was formed along a crack in the ocean floor, beginning at the northwest end. The eastern islands are the youngest and largest; those at the other end, 1600 miles away, are greatly eroded.

Hardy silversword blooms in Haleakala Crater on Maui despite temperatures that may be as extreme as 90° F. by day and below freezing at night. A gelatinous substance in the leaves stores water; dense, silvery hairs reflect sunlight.

or palms; all of these are plentiful today. There were enormous hardwood forests forming an unbroken cloak of vegetation from shore to timberline. Man has changed all that—first the Polynesians, then settlers from modern Asia and America.

The original forests were composed of a wide variety of plants, but three trees peculiar to the islands are especially well known: the great koa, which grows on mountainsides; the widely distributed ohia lehua with its dense wood; and the fragrant Hawaiian sandalwood, a partial parasite that taps the roots of other forest trees.

Some of the rarest and strangest plants on any islands are those of the alpine zone on Maui and Hawaii, a region beginning at about 9000 feet and rising to almost 14,000 feet. Here are found thirteen species that exist nowhere else in the world,

while nearly two dozen equally rare species grow in the adjoining subalpine zone.

The spectacular silversword, a distant relative of the sunflower, is known as one of the oddest plants in the world. Its dense spherical cluster of pointed, silvery leaves is an adaptation to the severe dryness of volcanic cinders and the intense sunlight of high altitudes. After as much as twenty years of growth, it produces a towering complex of several hundred flowers, and then dies. The flowering stalk is thickly covered with sticky hairs that permit only flying insects to reach the pollen and nectar. The silversword has several relatives on the islands, including the greensword, but since nothing like it exists anywhere else in the world, its evolutionary history is obscure although it is related to the tarweeds of California and Chile.

Many Hawaiian birds closely resemble their mainland relatives; others have changed beyond recognition

Colonizers from North America were the ancestors of some of the bird species endemic to the archipelago: the Hawaiian crow, two ducks, a hawk, and the nene (Hawaiian goose). All have been on the islands long enough to differ perceptibly from their mainland cousins 2200 miles away.

The nene is obviously descended from the Canada goose, but so much changed that it has become a distinct species. No longer associated with water, it lives on the high, desolate mountainsides of Maui and Hawaii. Here it builds its nests and raises its young amid scrubby vegetation on the massive lava deposits. Although the nene flies, in historic times it apparently has inhabited only the high mountains of these two islands. It is rare today, but at times it can be seen walking slowly over the lava clinkers, its neck curved into a U-shape as it searches for food. The nene's feet have lost much of their webbing, its legs are extended, and its waddle is gone. On the ground the nene is rather quiet, making only short, creaking calls; its honk in flight has a higher pitch than that of mainland geese.

The Hawaiian duck, or koloa, apparently evolved from the American mallard, but the males fail to develop the resplendent and precisely delineated breeding plumage of the mallard. North America also furnished the ancestors of the Laysan duck, a coot, and a gallinule, none of which has changed much. A resident black-crowned night heron does not differ in the least from its North American relatives. The Hawaiian stilt belongs to the same species as the North American black-necked stilt. The honeyeaters seem to be descended from Australian forms that could have come by a series of stepping-stone islands. The Hawaiian owl has many close relatives in the Northern Hemisphere,

Nene geese hunt for berries near Haleakala Crater. The Hawaii Fish and Game Department, trying to save the state bird from extinction, raised these geese and released them to repopulate Maui. Identification bands circle their legs.

where such owls have been seen flying 1000 miles from land, but this owl is active by day. The ancestry of the Hawaiian and Laysan flightless rails is unclear.

The forebears of most of the endemic birds were accidentally deposited on the islands long ago, probably blown off course by cyclones. Such chance arrivals still occur. A few years ago, a pair of North American kingfishers appeared on the island of Hawaii; a Chinese cuckoo was sighted on Wake Island, about 3000 miles from home.

Unlike seabirds and regularly migrating species, none of the native birds leaves the islands voluntarily despite their migratory ancestry, although a Hawaiian hawk has been recorded flying over California. The birds no longer follow the old patterns of seasonal migrations, and breeding times may be prolonged or repeated within a year. Several strong-flying birds remain in restricted territories on only one or two islands of the chain: The hawk lives and nests on Hawaii and visits neighboring Maui, but is unknown on the other islands unless it is blown to them.

The Hawaiian hawk ranges in color from tawny to nearly black. Its principal food is mice, but it also eats eggs, insects, and spiders. It builds a circular nest in a high tree of open parklands on the island of Hawaii.

Treading lily pads on elongated toes, a Hawaiian gallinule searches for the mollusks and plants on which it feeds. A shy bird, the gallinule, also known as the moorhen, seldom ventures far from cover. It swims well but flies poorly.

One of the commonest honeycreepers, *an apapane perches on a cluster of endemic broussaisia flowers. The bird draws nectar from blossoms with a brush-tipped, tubular tongue and adds protein to its diet by eating caterpillars and pollen.*

The six-inch crested honeycreeper *is nearly extinct; it now lives only in remote forests on the northeast slopes of Mt. Haleakala on Maui. Its chief food is the nectar of the ohia lehua tree, but insects are also a part of its diet.*

Larger than other honeycreepers, *the seven-inch Laysan finch crushes tough seeds with a parrotlike beak. This species, found only on Laysan and Nihoa (it was introduced to Midway but later exterminated), is nearly extinct.*

The long bills of i'iwis reach nectar in deep-belled flowers or snap up insects. Inhabiting the five main islands, the i'iwis are rare except on Kauai and Hawaii. These honeycreepers nest in shallow cups of dry plant material placed in trees.

Hawaii's honeycreepers have found many ways to make a good living in a new world

The most interesting Hawaiian birds are the spectacular honeycreepers. These beautiful little birds greatly exceed the Galápagos finches in diversity; a wider variety of habitats has been available to them, and they have had more time in which to evolve. Their ancestors probably came from the New World tropics, but scientists cannot be certain because the birds have changed so dramatically.

Some species of honeycreepers are extinct, but the several surviving species inhabit the high forests of the larger islands. Two, the apapane and the i'iwi, are brilliant red; others are yellow, green, or olive. The apapane and i'iwi are often seen sipping nectar from the bright-red, brushlike flowers of the ohia lehua tree. Like the Galápagos finches, the various honeycreepers differ in their food pref-

erences, as indicated by their beak shapes, many of which parallel those of the far-away finches.

Some honeycreepers have large, powerful, parrotlike beaks well suited to crushing tough seeds, and short, thick tongues with which they efficiently manipulate hard seeds. Some have beaks specialized for tearing into fleshy fruits. Others have long, slender bills that fit the curve of native lobelia flowers, and long tongues that, when rolled into tubes, become organs for sucking up the sweet nectar. A woodpeckerlike honeycreeper opens crevices in trees with its short under-bill, then probes for grubs with its much longer upper-bill.

Although the first honeycreepers on the islands were probably nectar-feeding birds, some of their early descendants adopted the ways of seed-eating finches. They then branched out to fill the niches usually occupied, on continents, by other species of birds. The different kinds of honeycreepers, which evidently evolved from a single species, illustrate the tendency of island species to proliferate. Once a particular plant or animal has invaded an island, isolation and new opportunities usually evoke a rapid evolutionary response.

Islands from the Past

The creation of some islands dates back to the breaking up of the supercontinents. Isolated from mainland influences for tens of millions of years, life on such ancient islands developed in astonishing ways

Madagascar, lying in the Indian Ocean 250 miles off the east coast of Africa, is one of the world's most fascinating and puzzling islands. Popularly it is known as the land of the extinct elephant bird, the primitive lemur, and the curious traveler's "palm." It is a huge island—a thousand miles long and almost a quarter of a million square miles in area, with a varied topography.

On a map, Madagascar looks exactly like what it is—a broken-off piece of Africa. Evidence that dinosaurs once lived there shows that Madagascar was long ago part of the great supercontinent Gondwanaland. During the drifting movements and eventual fragmentation of the supercontinents, Gondwanaland broke up to form Africa, Antarctica, India, Australia, and South America. Among the many smaller fragments, which became what we call "continental islands," were New Zealand, New Caledonia, Cuba, Hispaniola, and Madagascar. Thus Madagascar's birth dates back at least seventy million years.

Madagascar has had time and opportunity to develop a richly varied flora and fauna of its own.

Madagascar's mongoose lemur, woolly furred and the size of a large cat, eats fruits and seeds. In a troop of five to twenty members, the lemurs communicate by means of grunts. They pause in their feeding for a midday siesta, and spend the night high in forest trees, but do not make nests.

Its long history as part of a continent, its relatively early isolation, and its prolonged exposure to invasion by outside forms of life have produced some truly extraordinary endemic species. Too little is known about them, and discoveries that are still occurring raise as many questions as they answer. Why, for instance, does Madagascar's plant and animal life differ so dramatically from that of the great continent to the west? Why does the island have some African plants and animals but not others? Why do some of its life forms occur elsewhere only in New Guinea, South America, or the Caribbean? Scientists have only partial answers to such questions.

Because of its size, its north-south orientation, and its central ridge of mountains, Madagascar offers a variety of environments: wet rain forests, dry upland forests, savannas, grasslands, near-deserts. Some of its plant adaptations parallel those of similarly specialized but unrelated plants of distant lands.

In the island's more arid regions grow many species of didiereas, plants unique to Madagascar. Tall, slender, and drooping, the didiereas have spines like those of cactuses, yet they evolved from small, herblike ancestors not even distantly related to the spiny plants of American deserts. The stems of the didiereas rise in clusters thirty or more feet in the air, each stem armored with spines and, in season, adorned with leaves and yellow, ivory, green, or bright-red flowers.

These bottle-shaped baobabs grow only in the arid regions of western Madagascar. Baobabs have so little solid wood and so much fibrous water-storing tissue that, when they fall and the water evaporates, they disappear completely. The last thing seen is a heap of pale, powdery fragments, which are blown away by the wind or eaten by termites.

Bloated baobabs and other fantastic plants store water in Madagascar's arid regions

Other plants growing in the dry areas of Madagascar are even more cactuslike. One species of kalanchoe has broad, fleshy, water-storing leaves two feet long. If these plants grew on the African mainland, they would be succulent fare for herbivores, but Madagascar has no large grazing animals to devour them or to threaten their survival. In contrast, the leaves of a vinelike species of kalanchoe are so narrow and curled that they resemble rings or hooks. Serving as tendrils, they curl around neighboring stems and leaves during the plant's upward growth.

Members of the sunflower family on Madagascar, as on many other islands in warm climates, have evolved into sizable trees, far exceeding the development of their continental counterparts. The island also supports many ancient forms of flowering plants that survive elsewhere only on islands nearby or—strangely—one-third of the way across the world, in New Guinea.

Two of these Madagascan oddities, the beautiful royal poinciana and the traveler's "palm," have become popular as ornamental plants throughout the tropical world. The traveler's "palm" is partly misnamed, since it is not a palm at all but a cousin of South Africa's spectacular bird-of-paradise flower. But the other part of the name is perhaps justified: The tubular base of each leaf forming the plant's fan-shaped crown traps rainwater with which, as legend goes, the parched traveler may conveniently slake his

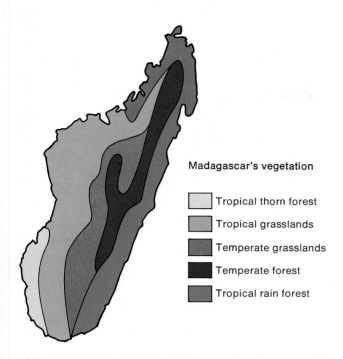

Madagascar has a remarkably diverse climate *and a wide range of habitats in spite of the fact that nearly all its 995-mile length is within the tropics. Just south of the Equator and some 250 miles off the east coast of Africa, Madagascar is in the belt of easterly trade winds and is also subject to Indian Ocean storms, with the result that its east coast receives heavy rainfall all year. The high interior of the island, with one peak of 9468 feet, effectively prevents much moisture from reaching the west coast, parts of which are semidesert. Lush tropical rain forest occurs on the east coast; tropical thorn forests and tropical grasslands are found on the arid west coast; in the cooler central highlands grows temperate-zone vegetation.*

Madagascar's vegetation

- ☐ Tropical thorn forest
- ☐ Tropical grasslands
- ☐ Temperate grasslands
- ☐ Temperate forest
- ☐ Tropical rain forest

thirst. The long, thin leaf stems also store water.

The baobab tree is certainly one of the world's most bizarre plants. Some kinds of baobab grow in Africa and Australia; one of Madagascar's varieties achieves a grotesqueness approaching the absurd. Fully grown, the base of the tree trunk is a great bloated cylinder thirty to forty feet in circumference, its naked bark stretched smooth by the spongy, water-filled tissues inside. The gross trunk rises tapering and branchless to a narrowed point, from which all the branches and foliage grow in a flattened and disorderly array. The whole effect is that of a child's drawing of a tree. Although the plant appears to be firmly based and sturdily built, its roots are shallow and the tree can be easily toppled to the ground. Once downed, it soon crumples up like a ripe fruit, rotting quickly and completely.

Many of Madagascar's animals are as unusual as its plants. Spiders in great variety populate deserts and forests alike. Termites inhabit the towering, rock-hard hills that dot the arid plains, each hill used century after century by successive generations of the light-shunning insects. Butterflies are abundant and dazzlingly conspicuous. They settle by the hundreds along shorelines of pools and streams, opening and closing their brilliant wings as they uncurl long tongues to probe for moisture.

Like their closest relatives, in South America, Madagascar's moths are mostly day fliers, so big and colorful that they have no equals in Africa. One moth in particular has a remarkable distinction: Its existence was predicted forty years before scientists found it. In 1862, Charles Darwin described the Christmas-tree orchid from Madagascar, with a spur ten or more inches long. No scientist had seen an insect that could reach the nectar in such a spur, but Darwin reasoned that the plant must be pollinated by a moth with a tongue more than ten inches long. When, finally, the moth was discovered, the scientists gave it the appropriate subspecies name *praedicta*.

Marine fishes, no matter how sluggish, theoretically can roam the wide oceans, so physical restrictions would not seem to be a problem for them. Yet even in the sea there are examples of geographical isolation. Living in pools along Madagascar's shoreline are some of the strangest fishes known, the mudskippers. Related species are found only in western Africa, Australia, Borneo, and a number of smaller Pacific islands.

Mudskippers spend much of their lives out of water, where they breathe partly through their skin like frogs or salamanders, and return only occasionally to the water to moisten their gills and bodies. Their blunt, froglike faces, complete with bulging eyes, and their habit of climbing up rocks and muddy beaches—even slanted tree trunks—make mudskippers droll and delightful little creatures. They scull up slopes by using jointed front fins, which are almost leglike in structure. To keep from slipping backward, they anchor themselves in position with other fins extending from their undersides and serving as suction disks. Pairs of mudskippers can sometimes be seen sunning themselves, raising and lowering their dorsal fins in a form of courtship display.

The ancestry of Madagascar's frogs is difficult to trace. It is supposed that one original frog species gave rise to nearly two dozen of the island's 150 species. Of the remainder, some are related to African frogs, others to Asian frogs.

Madagascar's reptiles include snakes, skinks, geckos, and that nemesis of insects, the amazing chameleon

The island's reptiles also present a panorama of mixed ancestries. Most of them are of African origin, with a few from the Orient. But the large snakes, unexpectedly, are boas, found elsewhere only in the Americas; there are no pythons as there are in Africa, or, indeed, any dangerously poisonous snakes, although one species reputedly has a mildly toxic bite.

Like other tropical islands, Madagascar has a population of skinks and geckos peculiarly its own. These creatures are often so camouflaged that they go unnoticed even by careful observers. One gecko not only mimics background color and texture, but also casts no shadow when it clings to a tree because folds of skin hang down like curtains from its jaws and body to touch the bark. Even its eyes are camouflaged by overhanging lappets of skin that obscure their margins.

Madagascar is the ancestral home of chameleons—gaudy, ornamented lizards with neatly coiled prehensile tails—and the island still harbors many more species than the few found in Africa, Ceylon, and southern India.

The chameleon's color, unlike a gecko's, does not always render it inconspicuous. At night the chameleon is white, but by day its colors seem to respond readily both to the brilliance of sunlight and to the animal's state of being. A frightened

*A **Madagascar chameleon**—a member of the largest and most aggressive species—clings to a twig. Its tail, here neatly coiled, can also form a tripod with the hind legs when the lizard stands erect, or extend straight back to aid in balance.*

or angry chameleon will puff out its throat; at the same time, its whole body blushes green or brown, perhaps with bluish stripes or bright yellow streaks, or it may even turn jet black. Color cells in the chameleon's skin enable it to put on this outlandish display. The cells contract in darkness, leaving the skin essentially colorless, but expand when the animal is excited or exposed to light. A chameleon sitting in shade-dappled sunlight shows distinct patterns of color on its scaly body where twigs or leaves have cast their shadows; this may help camouflage it.

Most chameleons have heads armored with long horns, ridges, shieldlike projections, flaps, and various other devices. A face-to-face encounter with one of the creatures is an unforgettable experience. The thirty-six species on Madagascar differ widely in size, ranging from two feet in length to fully grown adults not more than 1½ inches long from nose to stump of tail —possibly the world's smallest reptiles.

The chameleon's behavior is as bizarre as its appearance. On Y-shaped toes, it climbs trees slowly and deliberately, wobbling a little from side to side; its scaly, turreted eyes swivel independently, one watching where it is going, the other perhaps following the movement of a nearby fly or moth. In slow motion, the chameleon approaches its victim, then stops perhaps a foot away, its mouth slightly open. A sudden contraction of muscles, and out darts a tubular tongue faster than the eye can see. The blunt, sticky tip unerringly hits its target. Just as quickly, the tongue snaps back, and the insect prey is drawn into the chameleon's mouth, to be methodically chewed and swallowed.

Color changes in the pigment and reflecting cells of a chameleon's skin are triggered by light, temperature, or its emotions. A chameleon on an aloe shifts colors: Brown pigment, expanded above, contracts below; the yellow intensifies.

Its black bill identifies this four-inch Malachite kingfisher as a native of Madagascar. (*African kingfishers have red bills.*) Kingfishers nest in streambank burrows, and capture marine and freshwater fishes, forest insects, and frogs.

Madagascar's birds show typical island traits: giantism, flightlessness, and fearlessness

Nearly 200 different kinds of birds live on Madagascar; 118 species are found nowhere else on Earth. In addition to the endemic birds, there are many African ones, some of which fly back and forth in annual migrations. A smaller number of birds appears to be of fairly recent Asian origin. Strangely enough, despite the proximity of Africa, many African birds that could easily make

the flight have failed to emigrate to Madagascar, or have never succeeded in becoming established.

The most dramatic and colorful of the African visitors are flamingos. Huge flocks of two species feed in shallow lakes during morning hours, sifting out crustaceans and other tiny animals with their curious bent beaks held upside-down. Although the two species mingle, they apparently do not compete directly with one another for food, since the larger species reaches down farther into the water and the smaller feeds closer to the surface. After a busy morning of feeding and a period of inactivity at midday, they sweep into the air by the hundreds or thousands, their brilliant red-and-black wings flashing in the sunlight as they fly to a deeper portion of the lake. Here they group closely for the night, secure from danger because of the water's depth and their immense numbers.

Some other families of birds restricted to the island show typical island adaptations. Several rails do not use flight as a means of escape, although they can fly. They rely upon rapid and skillful running—surely a step toward the flightlessness characteristic of isolated rails. The eventual loss or weakening of their wings would hardly subject them to much of a handicap. Another group of birds, the mesites, have already lost the power of flight, although at times they may weakly and ineffectually flap their wings. The asitys, on the other hand, are able to fly but are relatively fearless, another result of long isolation in an environment with few predators. In the forests where they live they can be approached without difficulty.

Madagascar once possessed several species of elephant bird, the like of which the world had never seen before and will not see again. One species, the largest and heaviest of all birds, walked the island's countryside within the last thousand years, possibly as recently as three centuries ago. Ten feet tall and weighing up to 1000 pounds, the giant elephant bird was exceeded in height, but not in weight, only by the New Zealand moa. Although the elephant bird never flew, and its wings were mere vestiges, it apparently inspired the story in *The Arabian Nights* of Sindbad the Sailor's encounter with the giant flying roc. Earlier, Marco Polo had written that the bird could carry away an elephant. He reported seeing a feather of the bird, but his description suggests that what he had actually seen was just a dried palm branch!

Bones of the bird are still found today, not yet fossilized. Broken shells of eggs with a capacity of two gallons are often discovered in sandy soil, the thick pieces so preserved that a whole egg can be reassembled easily from the fragments.

Probably the elephant bird's extinction was caused partly by man and partly by a slow change in climate that altered much forest to near-desert. In any event, men once saw this enormous creature, ate its eggs, used the sturdy shells as water containers, and perhaps hunted the young chicks, only a few months old but as tall as a man.

Like the extinct moa, as well as today's cassowary and emu, the elephant bird illustrates the characteristics of flightlessness and giantism that can develop astonishingly in island birds.

Elephant bird   African ostrich

Now extinct, *Madagascan elephant birds were the heaviest ratites, a group of flightless birds including the also-extinct New Zealand moa, the emu and cassowary of Australia, the South American rhea, and the largest living bird—the African ostrich. Some species were as small as herons, but the biggest elephant bird, ten feet tall, weighed three times as much as an ostrich and laid fourteen-inch eggs, six times the size of ostrich eggs.*

Madagascar's lemurs and primitive tenrecs are the remnants of old and once widespread groups

Madagascar's largest carnivore, a fossa stalks its prey in a tree. During the breeding season, usually solitary fossas form aggressive bands, even attacking men. Annoyed fossas may release an unpleasant skunklike odor.

A bristly Setifer tenrec curls up in defense. Setifer lives in arid scrublands, fattening itself on grubs and other insects before hibernating —or being eaten by local farmers. An adult Setifer is six to seven inches long.

Madagascar has a limited and curious sprinkling of mammals. No large carnivores, antelopes, apes, monkeys, or elephants have ever lived there, although in prehistoric times there was a pygmy hippopotamus, clearly different from the one now living in Africa.

The largest carnivorous mammals on the island belong to the mongoose family. The fossa, which grows to a length of four feet including the tail, is a ferocious predator that somewhat resembles both a wolverine and a cat. Another predator is an endemic civet that feeds on lizards, frogs, and young birds.

Of course, a settled island the size of Madagascar has its share of rodents, and they, along with shrews and the African bush pig, were probably introduced by man long ago. Madagascar's bats, which arrived by themselves, present a mixture: Mostly African, they also include one species of the large "flying foxes" common throughout Malaysia and the islands of the Pacific.

Two groups of mammals especially interesting to scientists live on Madagascar: tenrecs and lemurs. Both were isolated there long before more advanced mammals evolved. Most tenrecs are insect eaters, whose rare foreign relatives include Africa's giant water shrews and the Caribbean *Solenodon* in the forests of Hispaniola and Cuba.

Among the most primitive of mammals, the twenty or more species of tenrec differ widely in appearance, but they have a similar internal structure. Nearly all are nocturnal and secretive.

With a shield of stout, sharp spines on their backs and flanks, two species of Madagascar tenrecs, five to seven inches long and nearly tailless, look like the European hedgehog (a more advanced insectivore). If they are disturbed, they hunch up into a partial ball; understandably, few predators will take such a prickly mouthful.

Some of the burrowing tenrecs are far better adapted to subterranean living than any other mammals except moles. The weak-eyed mole tenrec, with powerful front claws and fine, soft fur, is an efficient tunneler. Another burrower, about the size of a rabbit, has a number of distinctions. It is the largest of the burrowing group, the only tenrec to hibernate, and possibly the most pro-lific of all mammals (it averages twenty-five young per litter).

The smallest tenrec, whose tail may be longer than its head and body combined, weighs about one-third as much as a field mouse. It is a shy little creature inhabiting forest floors or mead-ows where the grass is long and tangled enough to give good cover.

Another tenrec has evolved especially far from its predatory ancestors, although it still eats some fish. Resembling a muskrat, it browses in streams and ponds, swimming powerfully by means of webbed feet and feeding primarily on aquatic plants.

Monkey Substitutes

Without question, the most famous of the Mad-agascan mammals are the lemurs. The name "le-mur" comes from the Latin word for ghosts—possibly because of the unearthly howls that ema-nate from some of these forest dwellers. Lemurs may have inspired the legends of dog-headed men, for one large species, the indris, is tailless and often stands erect.

The lemurs are primates and thus belong to the same group as monkeys, apes, and men. Since monkeys and apes had not yet developed when Madagascar broke away from Africa, the lemurs on the island proceeded to fill many of the same ecological niches there that monkeys have occu-pied elsewhere. No one could mistake a lemur for a monkey in appearance; its sharply pointed face is totally unlike that of its more advanced cous-ins. Both lemurs and monkeys have succeeded in the world (although not in the same places), but the lemur never developed a brain as large or as complex as a monkey's.

Lemurs range from mouse-size midgets to others the size of large dogs. Their specializations are as diverse as those of the tenrecs. Giant le-murs as big as a donkey, flying lemurs, and amphibious lemurs, all of which once lived on Madagascar, are now long extinct. So are the pre-historic lemurs of Europe and North America.

The so-called flying lemur of Malayan and Phil-ippine forests, the colugo, is not a lemur at all, but belongs to a different and separate group. The only lemur relatives outside Madagascar to-day are small and unobtrusive creatures of the deepest forests of Africa and Asia, such as the potto, loris, and galago. Most of them are slow and retiring animals, their ancestors having failed to compete with the more advanced monkeys.

The dwarf lemur's fat furry tail—half its total length of ten to twenty-one inches—can store food for the dry sea-son. Dwarf lemurs spend the daylight hours in globular nests of twigs, which they build in treetops or trunk holes.

On Madagascar, where there was no such com-petition, many of the twenty-one lemur species are highly energetic. They have diversified not only into monkeylike habits, but into ecological niches filled elsewhere by small apes, mice, squirrels, and other familiar mammals.

A lemur's hands and feet resemble those of monkeys and are well adapted to grasping limbs of trees and items of food. The eyes of most spe-cies are directed forward rather than to the sides, a necessity in arboreal life, where wide gaps must be jumped and distances accurately estimated.

Lemurs are divided into four groups: *typical lemurs, monkeylike lemurs, mouse* and *dwarf le-murs,* and the peculiar little *aye-ayes.*

Typical lemurs are busy animals, picking up food, grooming themselves and one another, leaping from tree to tree and using their long tails to maintain balance. At rest, a typical lemur wraps its tail around its body and up over one shoulder; several animals sitting together may drape their tails around one another. A baby clings to its mother's belly until it is three weeks old, and then begins riding on her back. After another week or so, it leaves its mother for short exploratory trips, returning to eat and sleep. Most typical lemurs are vocal when disturbed, screeching in alarm to warn others in the troop. When they descend to visit water holes, adults frequently stand erect on their long hind legs to survey the surroundings.

The typical lemur usually seen in captivity is the handsome, friendly ring-tail that, unlike other lemurs, lives mostly among rocks. A vegetarian, it can adapt to whatever plant food is available seasonally. The ruffed lemur, also a member of the typical group, is equally attractive, with dramatic black-and-white patterns on its woolly body and limbs, and a bright-eyed head surrounded by a thick collar of fur. It is the only species to build a nest, and is more nocturnal than other lemurs. As the sun rises over the forest, the ruffed lemur ascends to the treetops and stretches arms and legs to face the warmth, giving rise to the legend that it is a sun-worshiper.

Lemurs Big and Little

Monkeylike lemurs are considerably larger than the nocturnal typical lemurs and are active mostly in the daytime. With tails streaming behind them, they make prodigious thirty-foot leaps between trees, landing with audible thumps, their powerful hind legs acting as pincers to keep them in position. They climb upright hand-over-hand, and descend trees tail first. On the ground, they leap or hop upright, arms held to the front or up in the air.

The most remarkable of the monkeylike lemurs are the sifaka and the indris. The sifaka is a beautiful animal with golden eyes set in a black face, which in turn is surrounded by thick, silky, white fur. Its name is an imitation of the odd cry it utters when alarmed. Like the ruffed lemur, it raises its arms to the sun in the early morning. In the heat of midday it spends several hours lying horizontally on a lower branch, arms and legs dangling below. Or it may find a comfortable crotch in a tree and sit there, leaning back completely relaxed and comfortable.

Sifakas live in family groups but seem to lack the strong leaders that monkey tribes have. With no natural enemies, they spend their days in carefree eating, grooming, and resting. The inquisitive youngsters scamper about, investigating the forest surroundings or wrestling.

The tailless indris is probably the noisiest animal in Madagascar. At midmorning, an indris troop may "sing" in concert, rending the air with deafening howls. It is not always easy to pinpoint the source of the racket because the troop is frequently on the move, and even a stationary indris, by forming its lips into a funnel, has the powers of a ventriloquist. Lucky is the observer who gets more than a glimpse of these shy, handsome, black-and-white creatures. They can be seen only in the wild, for they do not survive even brief periods of captivity. The Malagasy government has wisely placed a ban upon the capture of these and nearly all other lemurs.

Very different from the big lemurs are the two other groups. The first of these, the little mouse and dwarf lemurs, are large-eyed, secretive, and mostly nocturnal, hiding during the day in foliage or in hollow trees. The mouse lemur, not much bigger than the rodent for which it is named, has a simple brain and is among the most primitive of all primates. It eats fruit, leaves, and possibly honey, but feeds primarily on insects; in turn, it is hunted by the island goshawk. The dwarf lemur, which estivates during the hot, dry season, has a more vegetarian diet, although it also consumes insects.

The aye-aye, with its big ears, is unlike any other lemur and is the sole member of its group. A strictly nocturnal forest dweller, it secures its insect food in an unusual manner. With the aid of acute senses of smell and hearing, it searches for wood-boring beetle larvae by tapping on tree trunks with its highly developed long middle finger. If a trunk sounds hollow, the aye-aye bites into it and the middle finger probes for the grub and extracts it. Fruits and bamboo shoots, chewed with powerful teeth, add variety to the aye-aye's diet.

Madagascar is a treasure house of unique plants and animals. No other island its size harbors so many examples of specialization among vertebrate animals and seed plants. Much remains to be learned about Madagascar's wildlife, much that will illuminate the pathways taken by living things in isolation. Unfortunately, man's activities are destroying many of the most interesting forms faster than they can be studied.

Lemurs of Madagascar

Mouse lemur

Verreaux's sifaka

Indris female with young

Red-ruffed lemur

Aye-aye

Ring-tailed lemur

GILBERT

Madagascar's only primates, the lemurs, rank high among the island's many wonders. The several species of lemur live in family groups, perhaps in troops of as many as twenty members. They are sociable animals and seem to enjoy contact with one another. The smaller kinds sit in little clumps; the larger ones may occupy a tree branch each behind the next, like children playing train. Grooming is a popular activity, any two members of the troop taking turns licking each other. Adult females are especially fond of grooming infants, and in some species even adult males join in. Quarreling may be frequent, but serious fighting is rare except at breeding season.

The granite rocks of the Seychelles especially interest geologists. The ninety-two Seychelles are the only granitic islands never connected to any continent.

The toq-toq weaverbird nests only on three Seychelles islands. Extinction threatens the toq-toq and other rare endemic birds such as the magpie robin and brush warbler.

Madagascar's Island Satellites

The warm waters of the Indian Ocean bathe Madagascar's satellite islands. Aldabra is dry and hot, while the Seychelles are visited part of every year by the heavy rains of the doldrums. The Mascarenes lie in the Indian Ocean storm belt and are subject to torrential rains and sometimes destructive typhoons.

The rugged terrain and rich vegetation of Réunion Island are characteristic of the Mascarenes, which are volcanic in origin. In spite of the tropical location, snowfall is frequent, especially on the 10,000-foot Piton des Neiges.

This small coral islet is in Aldabra Atoll. A poorly understood geological process raised the islands long after their formation under the sea, and erosion by waves has given them their unique appearance.

Indian Ocean giant tortoises survive in the wild only on Aldabra Atoll. The huge long-lived reptiles, weighing several hundred pounds each, were wiped out elsewhere by man and by introduced predators.

Cross section of seed

Stored food

Emerging root

Shell

Husk

Massive twin-lobed seeds of the coco-de-mer, a palm tree endemic to the Seychelles, weigh up to fifty pounds—the world's largest seed. The leaves, which may be sixteen feet long, are also record breakers.

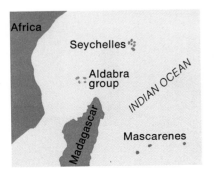

Africa

Seychelles

Aldabra group

INDIAN OCEAN

Madagascar

Mascarenes

New Zealand, one of the world's oldest island groups, harbors the tuatara — last survivor of a truly ancient family of reptiles

In the temperate South Pacific, nearly 7000 miles from Madagascar, lie two other large and much more ancient islands, those comprising New Zealand. New Zealand, including the small offshore islands, probably broke away very early from Australia, the island continent that was itself removed from the rest of the world before placental mammals became dominant. Except for an endemic short-tailed bat and another bat also found in Australia and nearby islands, New Zealand may never have had any native land mammals.

New Zealand's most famous reptile, the tuatara, is a true relict, the only survivor of the "beak-heads" that elsewhere vanished 135 million years ago. The ancient beak-heads—most of them larger than tuataras but like them in general structure—resembled the "stem" reptiles, from which evolved dinosaurs, big marine reptiles, flying reptiles, modern reptiles, birds, and mammals. The tuatara, then, is clearly similar to the ancestor of all the great land animals.

A tuatara requires less heat than any other modern reptile. Although it suns itself in its burrow entrance, its body temperature never rises very high because of New Zealand's cool climate. Under similar conditions, most reptiles would be sluggish; lizards, for example, typically need temperatures of at least 75° F. in order to be active. But the tuatara is fully active with a body temperature of just 52° F.; indeed, its highest recorded body temperature is only 56° F.

The tuatara's metabolic rate is the lowest known for any vertebrate animal. A perfectly healthy tuatara with a body temperature of only 48° F., observed for one hour, did not breathe once. Two results of such a low metabolic rate are slow growth and considerable longevity. An adult tuatara may grow no more than half an inch in eight years, and life-spans of close to a century have been thoroughly authenticated. New Zealand zoologists have been inclined to regard Maori records of 300-year spans as quite possible.

Maoris named this primitive reptile the tuatara ("spiny") because of the spines on its back. Fewer than 10,000 of these animals survive on some islands off the coast of New Zealand. Tuataras, which possess a tiny third eye covered by scales and apparently useless, become sexually mature only when they are about twenty years old. An entire year may elapse between mating and egg-laying, and another year after laying before the tuatara hatches.

Even a tuatara's start in life is unusual. In summer, the female tuatara excavates a shallow hole and lays yellowish, leathery eggs. The embryos begin to grow readily enough, but as winter approaches, their development almost ceases and they do not resume growth until the eggs are warmed by the spring sun. Eventually, thirteen or fourteen months after the eggs were laid, a little three-inch tuatara opens each shell with a horny "egg tooth," a temporary device that has grown at the end of its snout and will fall off within a week. Scrambling to the surface through the loose soil covering the nest, the hatchling hides under a nearby stone or in a crevice. In the next four months it will double its length—probably the most rapid rate of growth it will ever experience.

One of this reptile's remarkable physical characteristics is a third eye, called the pineal eye. Only one-fiftieth of an inch in diameter and covered by scales, it is not at all obvious in the adult tuatara. A few other animals have such an organ, although less well developed; among them are the anole lizards of the Caribbean islands and the primitive jawless fishes known as lampreys. Even frogs have a tiny brow spot. All higher creatures, man included, have deep within their heads a structure called the pineal body, which seems to have a glandular function. The tuatara's pineal eye is perhaps the remnant of a former pair of eyes that some distant ancestor had; it still retains a lens and a light-sensitive layer, but has no iris and only a degenerate connection to the brain. Although it does not work as an eye in the adult, it may be of some importance for very young tuataras, where the covering scales are transparent and not yet thickened and darkened by age.

Some of the structural features of a tuatara's skeleton are found in no other living reptiles. The presence in the skull of bony arches known only from fossils and crocodiles alerted zoologists to the tuatara's uniqueness. Its backbone is more like that of a fish than that of a lizard, and so are its teeth, which are enameled projections of the jaw instead of separate elements that fit into sockets. The front teeth are shaped into a beak like that of the tuatara's ancestors, the beak-heads. The tuatara further resembles some of the great reptiles of the past in having, besides ribs, a series of riblike bones in its abdomen.

The handsome, two-foot tuatara is dark gold in color, with beautiful gold-flecked eyes. The scaly, wrinkled skin often shows irregular red-

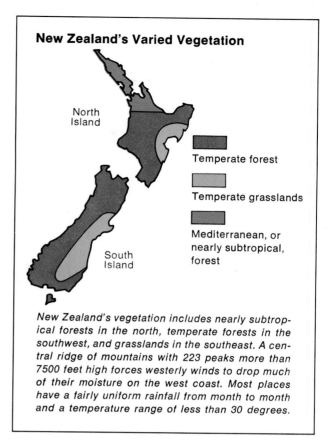

New Zealand's Varied Vegetation

North Island

South Island

Temperate forest

Temperate grasslands

Mediterranean, or nearly subtropical, forest

New Zealand's vegetation includes nearly subtropical forests in the north, temperate forests in the southwest, and grasslands in the southeast. A central ridge of mountains with 223 peaks more than 7500 feet high forces westerly winds to drop much of their moisture on the west coast. Most places have a fairly uniform rainfall from month to month and a temperature range of less than 30 degrees.

dish patches, which upon close inspection turn out to be masses of tiny orange mites. Large ticks lodged here and there on the skin also fatten on the reptile's blood, but apparently cause no real harm to their host.

The adult tuatara either excavates its own burrow or takes up residence in the burrow of a "muttonbird" (New Zealanders' name for shearwaters and petrels). It may also readily share its burrow with any muttonbird that chooses to use it during the few months the bird is raising its young. Although the reptile tolerates its burrow-mate and usually ignores the latter's eggs and chicks, it does prey on other birds, skinks and geckos, land snails, beetles, and large flightless crickets.

How has the tuatara managed to survive when all its relatives and a host of more highly evolved reptiles became extinct millions of years ago? Part of the answer probably lies in New Zealand's lack of mammals. If these quick competitors and predators had reached the islands, the small, cold, slow dragon could hardly have continued its way of life for 135 million years.

Just before dawn, sooty shearwaters leave their burrows and assemble on lofty seaside rocks. Unless strong winds are blowing, the heavy-bodied birds must launch themselves from a height and glide to gain momentum. Both parents incubate the egg and brood the single chick. After the breeding season, sooty shearwaters migrate thousands of miles to the North Pacific.

Snares crested penguins wade ashore on tiny Snares Island, south of New Zealand, the only place they have breeding rookeries. Year after year, the twenty-nine-inch birds select the same mates and nesting sites. They lay two eggs in stick nests lined with leaves and grass. Snares crested penguins produce sounds ranging from soft whistles to harsh screams, and engage in a variety of courtship displays. Hooker's sea lions, which also breed on Snares Island, prey on the penguins.

Seabirds range far from their coastal breeding sites, but the flightless kiwi stays concealed deep in New Zealand's forests

Many birds dependent upon the sea inhabit New Zealand's shores. One of the commonest, the sooty shearwater, is among the most abundant bird species on Earth. The twenty million or more sooty shearwaters are found worldwide. The sooty shearwater is a great wanderer, sometimes flying 600 miles on fishing trips. The solitary chick it leaves behind can survive for nearly two weeks without food, but when meals do come, they are substantial. Normally fishing flights are only daylong, and as flocks of 100,000 or more return to their breeding grounds in the evening, their loud cries drown out the noise of the sea. Despite the darkness and the huge numbers of birds and nests, each bird manages to find its own burrow, perhaps aided by a keener sense of smell than is usual in birds.

Albatrosses, such as the royal albatross of New Zealand waters, breed only every other year. The fledgling period lasts nearly a year, however, so colonies are always occupied. A single colony on South Island accommodates only a few pairs; many more nest on small, remote islands far from the mainland. The royal albatross is ungainly on land, but the wingspread of nearly ten feet makes it one of the finest marine soaring birds. Riding the westerlies, it stays aloft for many hours at a time without ever beating its wings. An ability to produce water by metabolism increases the albatross's independence of the land.

At least four species of penguin breed on New Zealand's islands, and others visit there. These penguins are a noisy lot, particularly in the dark of night, when their courtship displays are especially raucous, accentuated with a great deal of trumpeting and braying. The penguins venture some hundreds of yards inland, not always choosing the shortest route, their trails wandering up and down rough and scrubby country. They scramble up steep coastal slopes, occasionally following little streams, where they slip and slide over water-worn stones.

The kiwi, New Zealand's national bird, is so shy and elusive that few observers see it in the wild. It looks anything but birdlike—hairlike feathers; no visible wings or tail; sensitive bristles at the base of the long, down-curved bill that serve the same function as a cat's whiskers. Three species are still found in New Zealand.

By day, the kiwi hides in dense vegetation, or perhaps in a burrow between tree roots or in a hollow log. At night, it emerges to feed along the forest floor. Nostrils are at the tip of the bill; the kiwi is thought to have a keen sense of smell and the ability, unusual among birds, to scent out prey, although actual proof of this awaits further study. It stalks through thick underbrush with quick, nervous movements, picking up fruit and insects in the leaf litter and probing the soil with its bill for earthworms.

At nesting time, the female kiwi produces one or occasionally two enormous eggs, glazed and ivory white or greenish, which may be a sizable fraction—even one-third—of her own weight. Apparently this is quite enough for her, for the male, smaller than his mate, spends the next seventy to eighty days on incubation duty.

A Mantell's kiwi probes for food in forest litter. Vestigial wings are hidden in its plumage, but it lacks even the trace of a tail. One of the larger kiwis, this North Island bird may be up to fourteen inches high.

A weka scurries across a New Zealand beach. Fast runners and good swimmers, adaptable wekas even live in towns, raiding garbage cans. During the six-month breeding season a pair may raise four broods of one or two chicks each.

Odd form or behavior has helped some New Zealand birds, but made others vulnerable

The weka, a large flightless rail, scurries about in a variety of environments, from dry scrub to wet forest and even open beaches, seeking insects, lizards, mice, rats, or young rabbits. Its shrill, penetrating whistles may become a chorus as more wekas join in. Flocks of another rail, the pukeko, sometimes fly at night, and apparently use their earsplitting screeches to keep in touch. The takahe is a flightless gallinule, brilliant blue and green with touches of red. For fifty years it was presumed extinct, but in 1948 it was rediscovered. It now survives only in the high valleys of a small part of South Island, mostly grasslands.

The kea is a species of parrot that in recent years has added to its fruit diet by picking over sheep carcasses in the hills to get at layers of fat under the skin. Another large, handsome parrot, the kakapo, can glide but cannot fly; the loss of flight suggests a reason for the fact that it is now one of the rarest of all birds on New Zealand.

The forests of New Zealand often resound with the liquid, bell-like notes of two honeyeaters, the bellbird and the larger tui. The tui apparently is able to produce notes of high frequency, for it is sometimes seen to be singing vigorously although the human ear can detect only a few faint, squeaky sounds; its alarm note is high-pitched.

Not many years ago, clear chuckling calls of the huia were heard in the forests, but huias are now believed extinct. These birds had developed woodpeckerlike habits, as some of the Galápagos finches, Hawaiian honeycreepers, and Madagascan vanga shrikes have done. Rather than each individual's acquisition of a similar specialty, however, each pair of huias may have formed a dependent partnership: The male, with a short, nearly straight bill, excavated holes in soft, dead wood, while the female used her longer, scimitar-shaped bill to probe harder wood. Unfortunately, observations of the huia were inconclusive; since a male was seen alone only once, some biologists have assumed that the male depended on the long reach of the female's bill for the succulent grubs of longhorn beetles, the birds' favorite food. But there is little direct evidence of such cooperation.

A hardy kea parrot soars through New Zealand skies. Keas breed all year, but mainly in the summer, raising broods of two to four chicks. Female fledglings are fed by their father for several weeks after young males become independent.

The iridescent takahe survives in remote marshes. With its massive beak the bird strips seeds from snow grass, its only food, or chops off the tender lower stems. The takahe runs well, but cannot fly. Two introduced species threaten it: the stoat preys on the five-pound bird, and deer compete for grass. Efforts are being made to save the takahe by breeding it in captivity.

Moa   Maori chief

Most moas were killed off by early Polynesian settlers before the Maoris reached New Zealand in 1350. According to Maori accounts, the 500-pound birds were quite sluggish; this trait probably hastened their extinction.

As Madagascar had its great elephant birds, so New Zealand produced enormous flightless moas. One moa was about the size of a turkey, but the largest of the nineteen species reached a height of over eleven feet. These vegetarian giants perhaps knew no predators of any kind until Polynesians arrived 1000 years ago. From that day on, the moas were hunted for food and for bones used in personal adornment. Although accounts are confused, it is certain that not more than a few individuals, if any, of one species were left by the time Captain Cook arrived in 1769. The whole family is now believed extinct.

There are three species of chubby, nearly tailless "wren," three to four inches in length. A fourth lived on Stephen Island, a tiny spot of land between New Zealand's two main islands. The only European who ever saw it alive was the lighthouse keeper, who observed it twice. He reported that it ran rapidly but "did not fly at all." The last remaining individual was killed by the lighthouse keeper's pet cat.

New Zealand's ancient relics — tuatara, primitive frogs, and plants — open a window on the evolutionary past

Stephen Island is still the home of one of the most primitive species of frog on Earth. This frog has played an important role in establishing New Zealand's antiquity. It is restricted to an area of not more than 500 square yards of rock-strewn slope toward the top of the island; similar frogs are found high in the mountains of the larger islands. All are exceedingly rare and are protected by appropriately strict laws.

All the endemic New Zealand frogs are very small, less than two inches in length. Their various upland habitats have one thing in common: an absence of open water. This lack has led to a peculiar adaptation. The frogs lay eggs in damp crevices under boulders and rotting logs, where they can remain moist, each egg enclosed in a fluid-filled gelatinous capsule. The embryo becomes a froglet directly, not a tadpole. The young simply hatch out as miniature replicas of their parents.

Despite their specialized individual development, these frogs have several primitive features.

Hochstetter's frog, a primitive species found only on a few New Zealand islands, guards a hidden cluster of eggs until they hatch. Using long tails that disappear after birth, the froglets flail open the tough egg capsules that enclose them.

Their backbones, like a tuatara's, resemble those of fishes, and they retain tail-wagging muscles although they absorb their tails at about a month. They lack external eardrums, and the vocal apparatus is so undeveloped that the best they can do is to chirp slightly. They have little or no webbing between the toes. They swim, but they kick their hind legs alternately rather than together as most frogs do. Clearly, these New Zealand frogs are similar to the ancestors of all frogs.

Some of New Zealand's plants are as ancient as the tuatara, having come down almost unchanged from the distant past, millions of years ago. There are the circular, filmy fronds of kidney ferns, and the primitive Y-branching runners and stems of *Psilotum* and *Tmesipteris*, plants that evolved before distinctions between stem and root were developed in land plants. *Tmesipteris* grows only in New Zealand, Australia, and a few Pacific islands, while *Psilotum*, which is pictured in almost every botany textbook as a relict from

the earliest days of the invasion of land by plants, grows throughout the tropics, including Florida.

The cool climate of New Zealand—at times genuinely cold during storms sweeping up from Antarctica—has had an important modifying effect upon much of the life of the islands. The tuatara has survived because it can be active at low temperatures. Skink and gecko eggs elsewhere incubate in sun-warmed soil; the eggs of New Zealand's species hatch within the mother's body. Cold-tolerant conifers, rare in the South Pacific, are found in New Zealand.

When A. Conan Doyle and Edgar Rice Burroughs wrote of "lost worlds" and "lands that time forgot," they could conceive only of places that still sheltered great dinosaurs—adventures of pure fiction. They could not imagine the variety of surviving relicts—large plants and small animals —that in present-day New Zealand continue to provide insight into some of the life from the enormous span of time that is the past.

Gum Trees, Geckos, and Goannas

*For more than a million centuries Australian plants and animals
developed apart from the rest of the world, with results that are sometimes
bizarre, sometimes beautiful, sometimes just unexpected*

Australia is the Earth's second largest island continent—only ice-covered Antarctica is larger. With an area of 2,967,909 square miles, Australia is more than twelve times the size of Madagascar. The Australia-Antarctica section of Gondwanaland may have been the first major land fragment to drift into isolation, together with a variety of ancient forms of life. In Australia's present-day environments lives an astonishing array of the strange and beautiful: primitive palmlike plants and forests of tall eucalypts; earthworms the size of snakes and lizards without legs; brightly colored parrots, parakeets, and cockatoos; giant flightless emus and cassowaries; and a primitive lungfish thought to resemble the ancestors of all backboned land animals.

Perhaps most interesting of Australia's animals are the remarkable mammals: its two egg-laying mammals, the echidna (or spiny anteater) and the duckbilled platypus; plus a large group of marsupials, including the popular koalas and kangaroos, which carry their young in pouches. The key to Australia's special fascination lies in a

single historical fact: Its isolation occurred when mammals, extremely adaptable animals, first began spreading across the Earth.

The two early supercontinents, Laurasia and Gondwanaland, seem to have remained more or less intact during the long ages while dwellers of the seas and fresh water were evolving into land creatures. Separation of the continents did not occur until the Age of Reptiles was well along. As mammals began to fill the ecological niches being vacated by the disappearing dinosaurs and other reptiles, the supercontinents were breaking up. Between 100 and 150 million years ago, most of the rifts had become so wide that they were no longer passable by land animals, and isolation began to have its effects. The birth of modern continents had commenced.

Eventually, three of Gondwanaland's great slabs—South America, Africa, and India—pushed against and joined the North American and Eurasian pieces of Laurasia. Mutual exchange of animals and plants between the connected land masses gradually took place. Gondwanaland's two other large fragments—Antarctica and Australia—drifted into distant isolation, where they pursued independent patterns of development. Today, all of Antarctica's original life, including amphibians and reptiles, is long dead from cold, for that major fragment drifted into the frigid latitudes of the South Pole. But the outcome of Australia's isolation proved strikingly different.

Standing erect and alert, an Australian sand goanna balances on its long, muscular tail. The three- to four-foot monitor lizard preys on live food, including large venomous snakes. Sand goannas sometimes lay their eggs in termite mounds, which offer protection and good incubating conditions.

259

This weird, desolate landscape in Western Australia—known locally as "The Tombstones"—was carved from limestone bedrock by millions of years of erosion. The stark formations average ten feet in height but vary enormously in form.

Three groups of mammals were present on the unfragmented continents: the *monotremes*, which lay eggs; the *marsupials*, whose tiny, naked young are born so undeveloped that for months they must stay constantly attached to a nipple within the mother's pouch; and the *placentals*, whose young are born at a relatively advanced stage and are nursed only periodically. Outside Australia and New Guinea, all the marsupials except the opossums of North and South America and a small group of South American mammals called caenolestids became extinct.

When Australia broke away from the great land masses, the dominant mammals of the world were marsupials. The separation of Australia thus carried these primitive creatures far out of the reach of the rising placentals. In isolation, a great variety of pouched animals developed. Also, many of the continent's plants, snakes, birds, insects, and other living things are products of the same long history. Australia therefore can be viewed as a kind of living museum.

Several times submerged by ancient seas, Australia's western plateau is now an arid desert subject to sudden floods

Along the curved east coast of Australia run the mountains of the Great Dividing Range. Except for this range and a few lower ones scattered through the interior, Australia is generally flat, most of it less than 2000 feet above sea level.

The arid plateau occupying the western half of Australia is largely an expanse of hardened sand dunes. The only part of Western Australia that is humid enough for forests is the southwestern corner. Large parts of the interior receive no more than five inches of rain per year; the coasts get ten to twenty inches. The desert regions have varied in size over the ages, but apparently have never completely vanished.

Tropical rain forests of northeast Queensland flourish along the Great Dividing Range. This is the only region in Australia that has all the requirements of a tropical rain forest: high rainfall, good soil, and year-round warmth.

In the central eastern lowlands, salty remains of enormous lakes were left by several ancient invasions of the sea. Many of the lakes appear and disappear according to the rare and scanty rainfall; the erratic streams that feed them are dry most of the year. Even when the lakes are filled with water, they are too salty for most life. Dinosaurs once lived here, but neither their numbers nor the nature of their environment can be deduced from the few fossils that have been discovered thus far.

The eastern highlands encompass the Great Dividing Range and the mountainous island of Tasmania, off the southeastern tip of the mainland. Most of the mountain slopes are fertile and well watered, in some places receiving as much as 100 inches of rain annually. The highest parts of the range are in the Australian Alps in the southeast, especially in Kosciusko State Park, where Mt. Kosciusko, Australia's highest peak, rises to 7316 feet above sea level. The Great Dividing Range prevents easterly trade winds from reaching the interior and is thus largely responsible for the desert conditions existing there.

Off Australia's northeast coast lies the Great Barrier Reef, a product of corals and the largest single modification of the Earth's surface accomplished by living things. It parallels the coast of Queensland for 1250 miles, enclosing a sea area of about 80,000 square miles. For millions of years, the reef has served as a moderating, protective shield for the coast, absorbing ocean swells and preventing heavy surf from crashing on the continental shore.

The northern third of Australia is in the tropics; the remaining portion experiences mid-winter cooling in June and July, although not enough to have resulted in extensive plant and animal adaptations to a cold climate. Only in the mountains do alpine and cold-modified forms appear.

The major fact in Australia's climate is dryness. Especially in the interior, wherever and whenever rain does fall, it does so unreliably. Thus long droughts and sudden floods are common.

Ancient cycads rear their feathery crowns. Every plant bears either large female cones or smaller male cones. Each male cone produces up to five billion pollen grains.

Acacia blossoms derive their color from clusters of stamens, the male reproductive part of a flower. Valuable commercially, acacias range from bushes to lofty trees.

A Down-Under Plant World

Australia was not always so dry. Sixty or seventy million years ago, a profusion of vegetation grew across the southern half of the continent, and primitive conifers and cycads were widespread. Rain forests occupied vast stretches, and giant marsupial herbivores lived on the lush foliage—preyed upon by marsupial carnivores.

After the last Ice Age, a marked change of climate occurred: a far-reaching drying up, with the vegetation changing appropriately. As the deserts advanced southward, the ancient rainforest trees of earlier times gave way to a remarkable proliferation of that most Australian of trees, the eucalypt. With forests and grasslands disappearing over much of the island continent, the large marsupial grazers and beasts of prey also vanished.

Most Australian vegetation is composed of plants able to survive in exceptionally poor soil. At its harshest, the interior desert consists mostly of gravel and stone. Gradually it shades into desert country dotted with sparse tussocks of hardy grass. As the desert becomes steppe, scattered shrubs and wide tracts of mulga and other acacias appear. Mallee scrub, dwarf eucalypts growing on open grasslands, develops where rainfall is a little greater. Then, as high country and some parts of the coastline are approached, open woodland gives way to dense forests; wherever coastal areas are moist enough, there are rain forests.

Australia's three major zones of vegetation are the result of quite distinct climatic influences. Northern vegetation, much of which arrived long ago from the Indo-Malayan region, is tropical; mangroves, for example, commonly line the northern coastal shores and bays. The cooler southern zone is influenced by the Antarctic, and its vegetation is somewhat like that found in South America and South Africa, both also once parts of Gondwanaland. Nearly all the plants in this region are specialized as a result of long isolation. The third zone, in the center of the continent and extending toward the west, has many plants found nowhere else, most of them highly adapted to resist drought and fire, which often ravages the tinder-dry scrub. A small fourth zone includes the high mountains of the southeast.

The simply structured plants of Australia and the nearby islands are not nearly so unfamiliar as the more highly developed kinds, for fungi, mosses, and ferns propagate by means of microscopic spores easily carried by wind to all parts

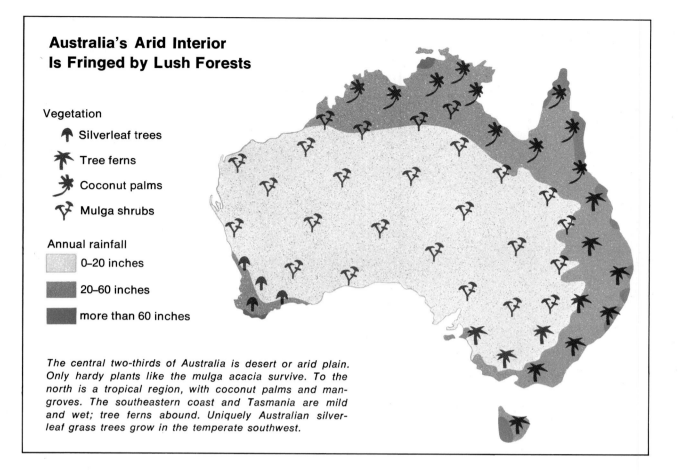

Australia's Arid Interior Is Fringed by Lush Forests

Vegetation

🡡 Silverleaf trees

🌴 Tree ferns

🌴 Coconut palms

🌿 Mulga shrubs

Annual rainfall

0–20 inches

20–60 inches

more than 60 inches

The central two-thirds of Australia is desert or arid plain. Only hardy plants like the mulga acacia survive. To the north is a tropical region, with coconut palms and mangroves. The southeastern coast and Tasmania are mild and wet; tree ferns abound. Uniquely Australian silverleaf grass trees grow in the temperate southwest.

of the globe, settling and growing wherever they can. Seed plants, on the other hand, achieve long-distance dispersal with much greater difficulty.

Australia has been a storehouse for the preservation of cycads, plants apparently derived from ancient seed-bearing ferns abundant when dinosaurs trod the Earth. Cycads are squat plants, palmlike in appearance (although unrelated to palms) and little changed through millions of years; the first ones were established in Australia long before the separation from Gondwanaland. They are able to survive in environmental zones ranging from desert to rain forest. Because of this wide tolerance, they have changed little in form or function. Of the 100 species of cycad scattered throughout the Southern Hemisphere and the tropics, one-fourth grow only in Australia, mainly in the southwest, which is their last major home. Usually cycads are not impressive in size—most are no more than ten feet tall, although one kind grows to sixty feet. Many are believed to live an exceedingly long time; one is estimated to be about 3000 years old.

Australia has only three dozen kinds of native conifers, including the ancient, primitive araucarias. One of the most curious endemic conifers, the kerosene bush—so named because of its combustible foliage—is found at high altitudes as in Kosciusko State Park, where, gnarled and twisted, it sprawls flat on rocky ledges. This small mountain plant, which lives for several hundred years, grows at maturity no more than an inch in diameter in a century.

One of the great tree groups especially identified with Australia is that of the acacias, or wattles. Of the 700 species in the world, 600 grow in Australia and its related islands. Acacias can withstand arid conditions, even far into the desert, where their yellow flowers give color to a sere landscape. They play an important role in providing food, shelter, and organic material for the sparse animal communities occupying much of the continent. In the past twenty-five million years, acacias have spread into different ecological niches elsewhere in the world, but Australia is the greatest showcase of their achievements.

Australia's Ancient Partnership

Some of Australia's flowering plants have evolved in unique partnership with birds and mammals that live partly or wholly on their nectar. The plants also benefit from their association with the visitors, which help them reproduce by transferring pollen from an anther of a flower, where it develops, to the stigma, where pollination occurs. Many flowers have specialized structures for picking up and depositing pollen as the visitors feed. Some lure insects, which attract birds and mammals, as does the showy red or yellow coloration.

A yellow-faced honeyeater thrusts its bill into a Christmas bell. To reach the nectar, the bird must plunge its entire head into the flower, and thus its head brushes against both stigmas and anthers at the flower's lip.

Two rare dibblers—speckled marsupial mice—cling to a massive banksia cluster. Dibblers, long believed extinct, visit banksias to drink nectar and to eat insects also attracted by the nectar. Their bushy fur picks up pollen.

A tiny honey possum grasps a banksia stem. The honey possum depends completely on banksia flowers for food. With mouth and snout evolved into a sucking tube, it eats only nectar and insects lapped up as its long tongue probes the flowers.

Remarkable tongue orchids, which are shaped and colored like certain female wasps, are such realistic imitations that some male wasps prefer the flowers to genuine females. When a male wasp attempts to mate with a tongue orchid, pollen is deposited on his abdomen. Further attempts to mate with other orchids will deliver pollen to the stigmas.

As a spinebill honeyeater sucks nectar from a grevillea blossom, anthers press pollen on the bird's head. Later in this flower's development, the stigma on the style will become sticky and pick up pollen from honeyeaters.

Karri gums up to 250 feet high grow in southwest Australia. Their rapid growth—as much as thirty-five feet in ten years—makes them valuable timber trees. Like other eucalyptus, karri gums shed their outer bark in patches.

Forest fires may not destroy these hardy eucalyptus trees. They grow in an extremely dry climate and are adapted to droughts and even to fires. Their tinder-dry outer bark can explode into flame, yet the trees generally recover.

Australia's aromatic eucalypts range from majestic giants in Victoria to small shrubs in deserts and on mountains

The most famous of Australia's plants are the eucalypts, in all their several hundred varieties —from huge gum trees and wizened scrub brush to the alpine snow gums that grow at the 6000-foot level in Kosciusko State Park. Like acacias, eucalypts have radiated widely in the past twenty-five million years, but in the south their growth rhythm coincides poorly with Australia's annual climatic cycle, suggesting that these trees originated in a different world of the past. Absent from the completely arid deserts as well as from the dripping rain forest of the east coast, they flourish in all kinds of intermediate conditions. Botanists believe eucalypts were much more diversified in ancient times, and that many were destroyed when the central region of the continent dried up.

Australian eucalypts—or "gums," as Australians call them—have never crossed Wallace's Line (between Bali and Lombok in the Malay Archipelago) by natural means. Despite noteworthy differences in size and form, all are aromatic evergreens sharing several basic similarities of leaf shape and flower structure. The diversity of species is great enough, however, so that several kinds of gum may exist side by side, each specialized to succeed in its own way, without challenging the survival of the others.

Probably the most impressive eucalypts are the huge gums in Tasmania and in the states of Western Australia and Victoria. In Western Australia's Valley of the Giants, their great, shining, silvery trunks rise to heights of over 200 feet. The gums of Victoria are among the world's tallest trees. One record reliably describes a Victorian specimen 374 feet tall; less reliable records claim heights of more than 400, and even 500, feet.

Many eucalypts have long, pointed leaves that

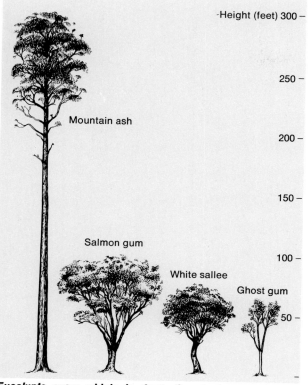

Eucalypts grow widely in Australia: *ghost gums in the tropical north, hardy white sallee in the mountains, drought-resistant salmon gum in the southwest, the 300-foot mountain ash in the temperate southeast.*

droop downward away from the sun and form hundreds of thousands of drip points during a rain. Other members of the family have different leaf structures, the oddest leaf being that of the spinning gum. An inhabitant of the cold, high altitudes of Victoria and Tasmania, the spinning gum has circular leaves growing at intervals around its twigs, each twig serving as an axle for the leaves. When the leaves die they remain in place, pierced instead of falling to the ground. There they stay, transfixed disks, spinning like pinwheels in the wind and producing a loud whistling sound audible all over the mountain slopes.

Because eucalypts do well in poor soil, a large area of Australia is dominated by the many-stemmed mallee scrub, only ten to twenty feet tall. Its scant foliage provides only moderate cover, but enough to secure the existence of the remarkable mallee fowl. The mallee scrub, like most eucalypts, grows from an underground root-stock and is thus able to withstand the brush fires that may destroy the exposed part of the plant but

not its buried portions, which respond to the destruction by sending up new shoots.

In such dry country, fires are a constant hazard. The oily leaves seem to explode, and glowing strips of bark caught in the updraft spread the flames. Forest fires in Australia are spectacular events.

At least half the plant species in the limited alpine areas of Kosciusko State Park are endemic to Australia, so this region is one of the most specialized within a specialized continent. The snow gum and kerosene bush are only two of 350 native seed plants found here. At times, whole mountain slopes are decorated with purple, yellow, red, pink, gold, and white as various alpine flowers, found nowhere else, come into bloom.

Of Giant Worms

Australian forest soils harbor several impressive relatives of worms that go almost unnoticed in other parts of the world. Here the lowly flatworm—represented elsewhere by tiny and insignificant planarians—takes a number of striking forms. One flatworm, three inches long, is a deep Prussian blue with a white stripe running down its back. Another, much longer, with a shovel-shaped head and dark brown stripes on its yellow body, attacks and eats a wide variety of insects, earthworms, and land snails.

Some of the earthworms in northeastern Australia are the bulkiest worms in the world, and among the longest. Several species are an inch or more in diameter, and eleven or twelve *feet* long; when one of these giants contracts, it swells to the diameter of a man's wrist. Some species are dark; others are salmon pink or banded with alternate cream and black stripes. Most of these big worms live amid tangled tree roots, emerging into the open when the forest litter is wet with rain. Their progress through the soil is often marked by loud gurgling and sucking noises. One species, the "barking" worm, emits a weird moan from within the soil when a man walks overhead.

Even when they are not making audible sounds, worms may sometimes be detected by a strong, sickly odor, a little like creosote, possibly derived from plant oils in their diet of fallen leaves. If a squirter worm, which inhabits the brush forest near Sydney, is uncovered and disturbed, it shoots jets of sticky fluid four feet into the air from pores along the top of its body. Normally serving to lubricate the burrow, the fluid may also discourage predators, for it is obnoxious in both taste and odor.

An Australian giant king cricket male "sings" by rubbing his wings together; rasps and resonators produce the sound. It is a mating call to attract a female, but she cannot answer since she lacks the sound-producing apparatus.

Two million termites—including a queen up to fifteen years old—may inhabit each of these sun-oriented mounds. Intestinal protozoans help the termites to digest vegetation as well as dead termites and other debris.

Insects and Spiders

Australia is an insect-fancier's paradise. Among its 50,000 insect species are many endemic to this island continent. One grasshopper changes from blue-green to blue-black according to the temperature—the only known insect in the world that can change color. Both males and females of one species of cicada sing busily at a pitch inaudible to the human ear. In Western Australia, a small gray-green grasshopper so perfectly mimics the woolly, rounded leaves of certain desert plants that, although it is not microscopic, it is difficult to see even under a magnifying glass. In eastern Australia lives the giant king cricket, a four-inch grasshopper with truly formidable jaws borne on a head one-third of the insect's total length. The world's largest moths and some of its largest butterflies also live here, as does a stick insect, ten inches long, with ridiculously tiny wings that serve only as glide planes when it swoops down from a tree to a lower level.

Termite hills are found elsewhere, but those of Australia's "outback" are constructed by the most primitive termites known. Still, their hill cities are marvels of construction and engineering. Each is built of particles of earth cemented by saliva and hardened to a concretelike mixture. A large hill may measure a dozen feet in circumference and rise more than twenty feet.

Other hills, up to ten feet high and eight feet wide but only three inches thick, are called "mag-

How Three Australian Spiders Catch Prey

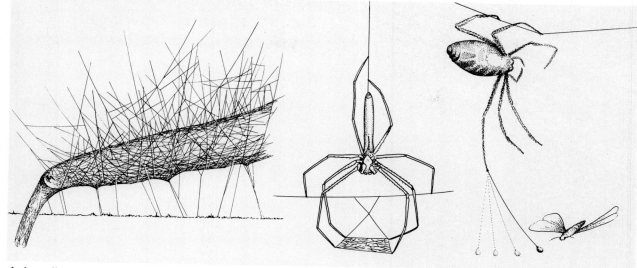

A funneling net channels prey toward the burrow of a platform spider.

Watchful ogre-faced spiders fling nets over insects venturing nearby.

Hairy imperial spiders swing threads ending in sticky drops to trap prey.

netic" because their narrow edges point north and south, and their broad faces catch both the rising and setting sun. Inside the hill, a maze of rooms, tunnels, and living galleries surrounds a central chamber packed with grass cut during the wet season for food. In early morning, the sun's rays warm the insects within, sending them into a frenzy of communal activity. By noon, with the sun overhead, the narrow top of the mound receives few hot rays, but the workday is prolonged by the heat of the setting sun.

Australia's spiders must be seen to be believed —but some should be seen from a safe distance: The bite of the Sydney funnel web spider has caused a number of human deaths. The large, hairy barking spider can reputedly kill newborn chicks. It produces a barking sound by rubbing a stiff-bristled comb on its leglike pedipalps against a similar comb at the base of its fangs.

Several spiders are remarkable hunters. Hanging head-down, the ogre-faced spider stretches between its front legs a small, thickly woven silk net, which it throws over a passing insect, hopelessly enmeshing the victim. Both the hairy imperial spider and the magnificent spider are aerial anglers, catching their prey somewhat like Argentine gauchos with their weighted bolas. The spider dangles a single long line with a sticky droplet at the end. As a moth is lured to the glistening droplet, the spider swings the line directly at it, seldom missing.

Australian giant stick insects mimic the eucalyptus twigs they live on. Their eggs resemble the seeds of certain shrubs. These cousins of American walking-stick insects often spread their wings in display when threatened.

Australian lakes and streams harbor some of the world's most ancient species of mollusks, crustaceans, and freshwater fishes

During droughts, many Australian rivers dry up, except for isolated pools—or billabongs—at what were the rivers' deepest parts. Life flourishes in billabongs, which may remain as stagnant water basins for months or even years.

Ghost nippers dig burrows in the muddy bottoms of Australian estuaries. These pale shrimps prefer to stay in their burrows, sifting through the sand and mud for food. The enlarged claw is used for both defense and attack.

Although Australia is remarkably dry, its sparse and unreliable inland waters support their own forms of life. Some of the rivers and billabongs (deeper parts of rivers that retain water in the dry season) contain ancient and zoologically important animals. Highland lakes common elsewhere in the world are almost absent from Australia except in the central plateau of Tasmania, where they cool perceptibly in winter but do not freeze over.

The major river system in the continent is the Murray and Darling in the southeast, totaling over 2000 miles in length but with a low run-off considering the area it drains. The wide annual fluctuation from torrent to trickle is characteristic of many Australian rivers. Native aquatic animals are adapted to contend with either prolonged drought or massive flooding, which for a brief time may cover vast flatland areas. Such floods are important to the distribution of all forms of aquatic life.

Like their counterparts elsewhere, Australia's freshwater clams and snails live on river bottoms. In times of drought, the mollusks are able to burrow four or five feet down into the mud, where they have been known to survive in a state of torpor for as long as three years before returning to active life in the water. Their anatomies show strong relationships to the mollusks of South America and Africa, and lesser affinities to those on the ancient islands of Madagascar and Ceylon—all former parts of Gondwanaland. Distinguishable from these old endemic species are newer forms of mollusks that arrived more recently from Asia by rafting or attaching themselves to visiting birds.

The smallest crustaceans living in the Australian rivers and lakes differ little from others around the world, for durable eggs of such creatures are often carried great distances by wind or birds. There are a few notable exceptions, however. In the cold mountain waters of Tasmania and southern Victoria live some of the most primitive crustaceans on Earth, the syncarid shrimps. These elongated little animals have few modern modifications. Their many legs are all of the same type, unspecialized for different functions; since there are no appendages for carrying eggs, a female must deposit her eggs immediately after fertilization—a rare necessity in the crustacean world. Syncarids closely resemble fossils of crustaceans that lived nearly 300 million years ago in the waters of Europe and North America.

Lake Surprise in Tasmania harbors a pair of relicts: a parasitizing crustacean and its host fish. Small parasitic crustaceans of this sort were known previously only from Africa and South America. But this relict was found on a host fish that could not possibly have migrated from either of those locations. The only explanation is that the ancestors of both host and parasite accompanied Australia when it was separated from Gondwanaland.

Although Australia has several other kinds of crustacean relicts from ancient times, most of its larger freshwater species, while themselves endemic to the continent, have cousins now distributed worldwide. Australia has both the largest and the smallest crayfishes: the Murray River "lobster" reaches six pounds, and a similar Tasmanian form may reach eight; at the other extreme, a tiny Queensland crayfish is scarcely an inch long at maturity. In abundance and diversity of crayfishes, Australia is exceeded only by North America.

Several Australian crustaceans have taken to life in damp-land habitats. Amphipods or scuds, isopods or slaters, and crayfishes can be found under fallen leaves and branches in the forest litter. Closer to the sea, in salt marshes and estuaries, more recent marine invaders live in abundance. Some beaches glisten with thousands of pink-and-blue soldier crabs, which disappear in a twinkling beneath the sand when anyone approaches.

Fewer than 200 species of freshwater fishes inhabit Australia's rivers—a meager fauna compared with that of other continents. Because of prolonged conditions of extreme drought and flood, not only must the freshwater fishes be extraordinarily tolerant, but their populations must be able to recover quickly after suffering a devastatingly high mortality. These fishes include some of the most interesting ancient kinds in the modern world. The three-foot barramundi is an Australian relict fish that resembles its ancestors of sixty million years ago; a few relatives still survive in the Americas and in India.

The Australian lungfish is considerably more ancient then the barramundi, dating back at least 325 million years. It is much more primitive than the lungfishes of South America and Africa (to which it has no direct relationship) and far more interesting to scientists. Australia's lungfish, covered with enormous scales—a primitive characteristic—may reach a length of six feet, weigh 100 pounds, and live for a century. In the muddy rivers in Queensland, it grubs slowly across the bottom, its small mouth searching for soft foods, mostly aquatic plants and fallen leaves, together with small crustaceans and mollusks.

The greenish eggs of the lungfish are quite unlike other fish eggs, somewhat resembling those of modern amphibians. They are deposited in large clusters, each egg surrounded by a thick envelope of gelatinous substance. The young hatch out in the form of "tadpoles," to develop gradually into adults.

The lungfish has a dual breathing apparatus: gills and a capacious airbladder-lung. When gills alone cannot take enough oxygen from the muddy water it often inhabits, the fish rises to the surface to breathe through its lung. In this feature, and in its flipperlike fins, the lungfish strongly resembles the distant ancestors of all terrestrial vertebrates that first emerged from water to take up an amphibian existence. Without a knowledge of such an archaic, relatively unchanged animal, it would be hard to conceive of the first slow invasion of the land.

The Australian lungfish can breathe air to survive in stagnant water. The lungfish resembles an ancient intermediate stage in development from fish to land-living vertebrate, but is not in the direct line of evolution.

Isolation and dry conditions led to unusual adaptations among Australia's frogs and lizards

Australia cannot boast of frogs as primitive as those of New Zealand, but some of its amphibian residents are remarkably well adapted to life in the desert, where streams run only occasionally. The frogs living in the center of the continent are likely to be almost spherical during wet periods: They have absorbed enough water to tide them over the long months of the dry season, when they remain dormant twelve to eighteen inches underground.

Many ground-dwelling frogs live in swamps and dig burrows in which to lay eggs. When the rains come and the water rises, the eggs are washed out and hatch into tadpoles, which soon turn into miniature frogs. Other ground frogs whip up masses of a sticky froth with which they are able to surround their eggs. The froth keeps the eggs moist and protected.

Tree frogs are small in most parts of the world, but one of the largest frogs in Australia is a tree frog. Its green body, not including the legs, is more than six inches long.

The history of reptiles in Australia is obscure. Fossils from dinosaur times are scarce—the most impressive remains are a few claw marks, some giant marine reptiles found far inland, giant lizards, and a few bones. Nearly 400 modern species inhabit the continent, with relatively few on Tasmania because of its cool climate. In the deserts, reptiles may be as numerous as birds.

One of the commonest reptilian groups is that of the skinks, those quick, slender, often brightly colored lizards. The more than 100 species of Australian skinks have diversified greatly in form and habit during their isolation. When the blue-tongued lizard, a heavily built skink, is frightened or irritated, it inflates its body with air, hisses slightly, and, head held high, faces the attacker with its mouth wide open, displaying a broad, bright blue tongue. If it manages to bite an opponent, it clamps down like a bulldog and is difficult to dislodge. Despite its seeming aggressiveness, it feeds only on insects, snails, and plants.

A bloated Holy Cross frog—named for its back pattern—stores water from desert rainstorms. When menaced, it exudes a distasteful fluid.

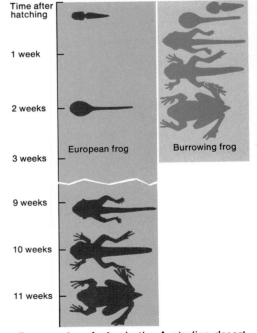

Frogs mature faster in the Australian desert than in milder climates. Burrowing frogs breed in pools created by floods or storms. Eggs hatch quickly; tadpoles become frogs in less than two weeks, compared with eleven weeks for common frogs elsewhere.

This desert skink can shed its tail—as many other lizards do—if it is attacked by a predator. In some skink species, the shed tail appears to have a life of its own: it thrashes about violently, confusing the attacker while the skink flees.

A western blue-tongued lizard sticks out its bright tongue in a threat gesture. It will bite an attacker that comes too close. These large, widely distributed skinks bear live young, after nourishing the embryos through a primitive placenta.

Sure-footed geckos store food in their tails, while the moloch sips moisture from its skin

Geckos, nocturnal lizards common around the Pacific and Indian oceans, are highly diversified in Australia; one, with a bizarre bony head, is regarded as the most primitive member of the group. There are more than forty Australian geckos, some a foot long but most considerably smaller. In several species, the broad tail serves as a reservoir of fatty food; the ultimate in this respect is the large leaf-tailed gecko of Queensland rain forests. Geckos can go without food (but not water) for as long as a year.

Most geckos are rather flabby lizards with fine, bumpy scales that do not overlap. The skin on their undersides is often so thin and translucent that internal organs may be seen as they climb across a windowpane. A gecko's feet enable it to climb any surface at all, no matter how slick. On the bottom of the splayed toes are ad-

The pupil of some geckos contracts to four pinholes. The faint images produced by the openings merge on the retina.

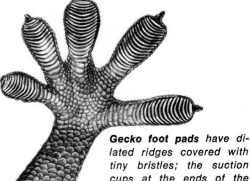

Gecko foot pads have dilated ridges covered with tiny bristles; the suction cups at the ends of the bristles hold even on glass. To release its grip, a gecko curls up its toes. To adhere, the palm touches and toes curl back down.

This southern leaf-tailed gecko is headed down, not up. The resemblance between its flat spade-shaped tail and its diamond-shaped head probably confuses predators, especially since the gecko discards its tail if attacked.

hesive pads, consisting of parallel vanes in the skin that can be raised or lowered, creating many microscopic vacuums. Its small claws help in running over wood or stone. When a gecko stalks prey (insects, spiders, centipedes), it rushes to within a short distance, then slowly creeps closer, lifting one foot at a time. With a sudden final lunge, it seizes the victim in its jaws, and swallows it whole without chewing.

The gecko's large, protruding eyes lack lids; like the eyes of snakes, they are covered by transparent scales, shed periodically with the skin. The gecko keeps its eyes clean by frequently wiping them with its long, flattened tongue.

Geckos are among the most vocal reptiles; the name suggests the kind of cry made by a few of the smaller ones. Others emit sharp clicks, barking sounds, or shrill, almost human wails. Their defense behavior is impressive: They puff up, open their mouths, rise high on their legs, and leap forward—but they are harmless to man.

Other kinds of lizards abound, some of which Australians call "dragons," despite their small size. Dragons come in many shapes. The strangest and most horrendous is a creature known as the mountain devil or moloch. Superficially resembling the horned toad of the southwestern United States, the mountain devil actually has no close relatives anywhere. A thorny armor of stout spines covers its body and head, and a spiked hump stands on its neck. If it is alarmed, the lizard pulls its head toward the hump, possibly for protection, although the true function of the hump has not yet been discovered. This grotesque, slow-moving animal waddles along in search of its only food, black ants, which it eats without haste, one at a time, 2000 making a meal.

The mountain devil, which lives in arid, rocky areas where rainfall is scarce, has a most remarkable skin that helps it acquire water. If the moloch merely settles one foot in a tiny puddle, its entire skin is wet within seconds. A network of microscopic canals running between the scales provides a capillary, blotting-paper action that instantly soaks up moisture and channels it to the mouth. When this happens, the lizard works its jaws slowly—it is drinking! The skin also changes color according to temperature, helping the animal absorb or reflect heat; the many long spines throw a certain amount of shade.

A prickly mountain devil—only about six inches long—slowly searches for black ants. Mountain devils mate in spring, and two months later the females produce as many as ten inch-long eggs, enormous compared with the lizard's size.

Threatening an intruder, *a frilled lizard displays its wide neck ruff. The color of the lizard and its frill varies from place to place in Australia: It is tan in Queensland; pinkish, with black chest and throat, in the Northern Territory.*

Another spectacular dragon is the frilled lizard, which, as it walks on all fours through the underbrush after insect food, does not look unusual except for its length of two feet or more. A membrane extends back from the head, covering the neck. Usually this membrane remains neatly folded, but when a snake or man approaches and escape is impossible, dramatic events follow.

First, rising high on its legs, the lizard opens its mouth wide to display a bright yellow lining. As the jaws open, a bony apparatus at the base of the tongue automatically erects a wide, umbrella-like frill around the head. This stands out at almost right angles to the body, making the creature suddenly appear many times its former size. It puts on such a show that no predator or uninformed person would want to get closer. At the first chance for escape, however, it runs off, soon attaining sufficient speed to rise on its hind legs, dashing and staggering along at a furious pace, body almost erect, mouth still open. Few sights in the world can equal this bizarre exhibition.

Some biologists believe the umbrella frill may serve another use besides that of bluff, for it is plentifully supplied with blood vessels. This wide, thin membrane may function as a radiator, allowing the escape of excess heat built up through the absorption of sunlight. Such an adaptation would not be unique; erect membranes on the backs of several dinosaurs very likely served the same purpose. The frilled lizard does spend some time trying to regulate body temperature. It lies facing the sun at noon, and at right angles to the sun in early morning and in the evening to catch the weakened rays; it searches for shade when the day becomes too hot.

Even at rest, the frilled lizard behaves oddly. Now and then its head bobs up and down; no one knows why, but perhaps a frequent change of head position provides some measure of depth perception. Or the dragon may wave its arms about, slowly if it has been resting for a time but more actively after one of its mad dashes. Again, the significance of this is not known.

Australia teems with small and medium-size lizards, many found nowhere else. Even better than the frilled lizard at running on its hind legs is the bicycle lizard, which seems to be forever hurrying about in a frenzy of activity.

A group of burrowing lizards found only in Australia varies oddly from the lizard body plan: They are entirely legless. Unlike snakes, they have external ears, which are simply holes leading into the hearing organ. The small, scaly flaps that replaced the hind legs can be held at right angles to the body to give better traction in a burrow.

Legless lizards apparently evolved from legged forms, as has occurred elsewhere. Since some lizards normally live under stones and wriggle through tight places, muscular thrusts of the body may be more important than the efforts of feeble legs. Thus deterioration of lizard legs seems to be an instance, like flightlessness in birds, of losing an organ through chance mutation without penalty to security or food-gathering.

The Largest Lizards

The most impressive lizards of the continent are the monitors, or, as Australians call them, goannas (probably a corruption of "iguanas," although there is no relationship). These are usually larger than the dragons. The largest lives not in Australia but in Indonesia on the small island of Komodo. It is twelve to thirteen feet long and preys on pigs, deer, monkeys, and even young buffaloes, in addition to eating carrion. Other monitors are found as far away as Africa, but Australia contains the greatest variety. Australia was also the habitat of the largest monitor the world has known. About three million years ago, long after the dinosaurs, a dinosaur-size monitor about thirty feet long roamed the plains. Even today, the perentie goanna, at seven or eight feet, and a larger goanna from New Guinea are among the giants.

Australian monitors come in all sizes and occupy a wide range of habitats. The sand goanna lives far out in the desert. Others, such as the lace monitor, live high in the trees of dense forests. The perentie, despite its size, is primarily a burrower. Another monitor wedges itself into rock crevices by means of a spiny tail. There is even an aquatic monitor swimming in some of the continent's rivers and lakes.

Monitors attack their prey with speed and agility, sometimes using their powerful muscular tails to knock over and stun a victim. They may swallow their food whole, or first shred it with long, curved claws. A monitor's teeth, like those of most snakes, curve backward; food bitten, therefore, is not easily dislodged and must be swallowed. The lizards give the impression of being nervous as they walk along, flicking a long, forked tongue in and out; chemical particles picked up from the soil convey information about food to a special head organ. At times, a monitor may stand erect to look around, or even run short distances on its hind legs.

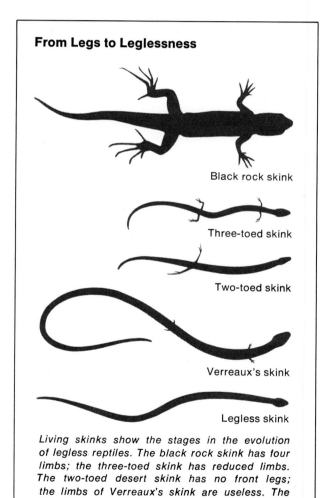

From Legs to Leglessness

Black rock skink

Three-toed skink

Two-toed skink

Verreaux's skink

Legless skink

Living skinks show the stages in the evolution of legless reptiles. The black rock skink has four limbs; the three-toed skink has reduced limbs. The two-toed desert skink has no front legs; the limbs of Verreaux's skink are useless. The final step is a completely legless skink.

Blind snakes are well equipped for burrowing for termites and ants. They have strong skulls, smooth non-catching scales, and tail spines that dig in and push them along.

Well-adapted to a marine environment, sea snakes have a flattened tail paddle, a flattened body, and valves that seal the nostrils underwater. All sea snakes are tropical.

Many of Australia's snakes, although not aggressive, are dangerously venomous

Sharing the underground habitat of legless lizards are more than twenty species of blind, non-venomous snakes. Blind snakes use their projecting snouts as scoops or wedges to take advantage of the least crevice or soft spot in the soil.

The other snakes of Australia fall into peculiar pattern types. Some of the pythons arrived well after the last Ice Age, probably from Malaysia. Some Australian species reach considerable size, one attaining a length of twenty feet or more —the largest snake on the continent.

Everywhere in the world except in Australia the most numerous snakes belong to a group called colubrids—either non-venomous or with venom harmful only to small animals. In Australia, the colubrids are outnumbered by the dangerously venomous elapids: 60 per cent of the 130 species of snakes. Elapids living elsewhere include African and Asian cobras, African mambas,

Asian kraits, and American coral snakes. Fortunately, the Australian species are not especially aggressive.

The taipan, ten or eleven feet long, is a contender for the title of the world's most dangerous snake. The venom from a single taipan could kill 200 sheep; Asia's king cobra could kill only 34.

The amount of venom injected by many Australian elapids is harmless to man, but quickly kills small animals—birds, frogs, lizards, or other snakes. Although Australia has the highest proportion of venomous snakes of all countries, the non-urban human population is so sparse that snakebite fatalities are much less common than in Asian countries.

Sea snakes related to the elapids inhabit Australia's shores. Although venomous, they are shy and escape-minded creatures; only fishermen handling crowded nets need fear their bite. Nostrils, located high on the head, are equipped with valves that close during submergence, and the tails are flattened vertically into efficient sculling paddles. Some sea snakes spend much time on coral reefs or in mangroves along the tropical northern shore; a smaller number are found in the temperate southern regions.

A Murray River turtle plods across a dried-up streambed. *The necks of these turtles account for half their total length of ten to fifteen inches, but they can retract neck* and head under the shell. Instead of pulling its neck straight back, a long-necked turtle tucks its neck and head sideways under the edge of the upper shell.

Only a few freshwater turtles live in the area. Close relatives of one freshwater species, the pitted-shell turtle of New Guinea, lived in Eurasia and North America over sixty million years ago. Australia's mainland once harbored giant tortoises.

The present distribution of freshwater turtles on the continent is at first puzzling, for a few live in the most arid regions where river flow is undependable and the rate of evaporation high. Their range of habitats is thus reduced to certain spots, seemingly unconnected. But the explanation is clear. During times of flood, the turtles literally swim over the desert. When the waters disappear, many turtles undoubtedly die, but some are near enough to the remaining streams to survive. The Murray River and its tributaries are well stocked with turtles.

From the standpoint of geological time, these freshwater turtles—long-necked and short-necked—are apparently newcomers. They may have arrived from Asia, but many are related to South American turtles. Certainly they have no close connections with the ancient land tortoises that lived in Australia when it was a wetter, more heavily forested land. Sea turtles come ashore here to lay eggs as they do on other islands throughout the tropical Pacific and Indian oceans.

The largest Australian reptiles are two species of crocodiles. The estuarine or sea-going crocodile, a monster reported to grow to thirty feet in length (but averaging only fifteen), is known throughout Malaysia. It frequents north coastal river mouths, but in times of flood may swim upriver fifty miles or more. It sometimes ventures out to sea as far as forty miles. Although the estuarine crocodile feeds mostly on fish, it is also a predator of other reptiles, water birds, and mammals. Like other crocodiles, it seizes its terrestrial victims—including man—at the water's edge, dragging them below the surface to drown before being devoured. Johnston's crocodile is an eight-foot freshwater crocodile found only in the rivers and billabongs of northern Australia, where it eats waterfowl and shoreline animals.

Australia's living things never lose their fascination; no other island can boast so many unique species. Superlatives become commonplace—the tallest trees in the world, the largest coral reef in the world, the biggest worms in the world, the most kinds of poisonous snakes in the world. But even these hardly prepare a visitor for the bowerbirds and egg-laying mammals.

From Emus
to Kangaroos

Australia's birds are unequaled in their diversity of form, color, and behavior. Its curious mammals — monotremes and marsupials — provide clues to the island continent's geological and evolutionary past

Australia has over 650 species of birds—more than most other islands. Parrots and cockatoos flashing brilliant colors, tailorbirds stitching leaves together to form nests, crested bellbirds with their ringing cries, brolga cranes in group courtship dances, magnificent black swans with crimson beaks, muttonbirds taking flight by the thousands for the yearly journey to the northern Pacific—all these birds are exciting enough, but Australia harbors still others ranked among the most remarkable in the world.

The Australian emu is the world's second largest bird, ranking just behind the African ostrich, with which it is often confused. An emu may weigh as much as 120 pounds and stand six feet tall. Like some kangaroos, this flightless bird is a grazer, and thus occupies an ecological niche filled elsewhere by deer, antelope, and wild cattle. The emu, camouflaged by its shaggy brown plumage, inhabits Australia's plains and forests, where it dashes along as swiftly as a galloping horse, swaying from side to side, and swims across creeks and rivers. Scarcely discriminating

Approaching its nest in a hollow tree, a mulga parrot extends wings and feet to slow down. Foot-long mulgas thrive in the dry scrublands of central Australia. They spend much time on the ground, in pairs or small flocks, foraging for the seeds of grasses and shrubs.

about what it eats, it picks up grass, flowers, berries, other fruits, leaves, and insects. One emu's stomach was found to contain 3000 caterpillars destructive to farm crops.

A characteristic of all running animals is a reduced number of toes, with a consequent lessening of frictional contact with the ground. Horses, for example, run on only one toe; deer and ostriches have two toes on each foot. The three-toed emu runs with great bursts of speed, although not quite so swiftly as the ostrich with its longer legs and only two toes.

At mating time, the male emu calls out in deep, guttural tones as he approaches a female, driving off rival males with powerful forward kicks. The female replies in low-pitched booming sounds that resonate in an air sac in her neck. After courtship and mating, she builds a nest of grass, bark, and dry leaves, in which she lays nine to fifteen dark green eggs weighing up to two pounds each. The eggs are tough enough to withstand the attacks of most predators, but black-breasted buzzards shatter them by dropping stones onto the nests from above.

Egg-laying is the female emu's sole task, and she then leaves with no further maternal concern. The male broods the clutch for two months until the downy, yellow-and-brown striped chicks hatch out. But his responsibility has not ended. The chicks follow him everywhere, running back and forth between his legs, keeping in touch by

The cassowary's horny crest butts aside thorny shrubs as it runs swiftly through dense underbrush. Although large and adorned with spots of bright colors, the birds are nearly hidden by the vegetation of their habitat.

means of intermittent piping calls. At night, when the male settles down, the chicks cluster beneath his plumage, there to sleep hidden and protected. The paternal guardianship and guidance go on for at least a year as the chicks slowly learn to get along by themselves. In the meantime, the female has mated again with another male, and has laid a new clutch of eggs. Males, on the other hand, are free to breed only every other year, spending nearly all their time bringing up their chicks.

In tropical northern Australia and New Guinea lives another large, flightless bird, the cassowary. Five feet tall, it stalks alone through dense tropical brush, a tough horned helmet keeping branches and leaves from its face. Although primarily a vegetarian, the cassowary catches crabs and fishes by wading up to its neck in streams. It is a pugnacious creature capable of delivering furious kicks with its powerful, heavily clawed feet. Despite its great weight—sometimes well over 100 pounds—the cassowary is a prodigious jumper, able to clear seven or eight feet in one bound. In contrast to the drab emu, it has glossy black feathers, a blue neck, and red wattles, yet the two birds belong to related families. The eggs are similar and, like its emu counterpart, the male cassowary has full responsibility for brooding the young and shepherding them about until they can care for themselves.

A male emu guards his clutch of eggs. During the incubation period he rarely leaves the nest, living mainly on stored-up fat. Emus form pairs in December—the Australian summer—and eggs are laid in May and June.

The great island continent of Australia harbors some of the most unusual birds on Earth

The perfectly camouflaged tawny frogmouth, a member of the nocturnal whippoorwill (or nightjar) family, often spends hours perched on a branch stub. If it is disturbed, it may fly away or it may present a horrifying spectacle of great opened beak and staring golden eyes—pure bluff. It hunts nothing more than insects, centipedes, scorpions, or possibly an occasional small mouse, frog, or lizard.

Apparently the first Australian bird seen by European explorers was a black swan, which confirmed their impression of the southern hemisphere as an upside-down place. In most regions of Australia, flocks of black swans are seen at dusk or occasionally on moonlit nights, flying in V-formation from one feeding ground to another.

Two groups of songbirds, mostly five to six inches long, with several species each, bear names belonging to unrelated European birds, obviously because they reminded English settlers of their homeland. The robins have crimson, flame-colored, pink, or yellow breasts; some of the robins use cobwebs to bind together their carefully constructed nests. The fairy wrens have long, erect tails, and most of them have at least some blue in their plumage. Their nests are usually domed.

One of the best known bird attractions in Australia is the nightly parade, during nesting season, of the little fairy penguins on Phillip Island southeast of Melbourne. Each evening, just before dark, the sea suddenly reveals amid its breaking waves hordes of small penguins skimming in toward shore. As each wave breaks and recedes, hundreds of the little birds pop upright and walk up the beach, flapping their finlike wings and conversing loudly.

Determinedly they march uphill to their burrows, where vociferous exchanges occur between the returning bird and the mate that stayed behind to incubate their two or three eggs during the day. Duties are exchanged the following day, and the other goes forth, after noisy farewells, to fish in the sea. This procedure continues for three months while the eggs hatch and the chicks grow, until finally the young are left on their own—first to live on their fat for a week or so, and then to take their first plunge into the sea.

A tawny frogmouth gapes, showing its pale mouth lining to scare off an intruder. Owl-like, the frogmouth flies silently on downy feathers, but does not hunt on the wing. It preys on insects and large spiders on the ground.

An adult black swan's plumage contrasts strongly with the cygnets' fluffy gray down. The black swan builds a nest of plant material on a hummock in a swamp, or it builds a tiny islet. Each brood consists of five or six young.

Vivid parrots and lorikeets enliven Australia's forests with shrill cries and gay colors

Australia harbors about sixty species of parrots and their cousins—lorikeets, parakeets, cockatoos, and budgerigars. The colorful little budgerigars, popular as lovebirds in pet shops all over the world, darken the inland Australian sky with their enormous numbers and create a sound like thunder with their fluttering wings. A flock looks like a dazzling, wheeling storm until suddenly it settles in open forest, decorating every tree with brilliant, living ornaments.

Few birds anywhere can excel the bold colors of Western Australia's red-capped parrot. Below the red crown of its head are yellow cheeks; its body is purple, with green wings and a yellow rump; the leg plumage and underside of its tail are red, while the upper tail surface is blue with a green overlay. The parrot looks like a child's attempt to produce the most colorful bird possible with an elementary paint set containing only the gaudiest pigments.

Of the several species of cockatoos in the world, nearly all are native to Australia. They range in form and color from the sulfur-crested cockatoo to the huge black palm cockatoo, which is able to crack large, hard nuts that no other bird can break. Cockatoos feed in flocks; when any bird becomes alarmed it screeches, and the whole flock explodes into the air with earsplitting shrieks that would confuse any predator.

Rainbow lorikeets perch in a thicket. With brushlike tongues, these raucous birds take nectar from the blossoms of eucalypts and banksias. Flocks of rainbow lorikeets follow the seasonal flowering of trees and shrubs in eastern Australia.

An acrobatic sulfur-crested cockatoo dangles from a branch. Huge flocks of these handsome cockatoos range across the plains of northern and eastern Australia, eating beetle larvae and seeds—unfortunately, they especially like wheat.

A red-capped parrot of southwest Australia bursts into flight. Its unique hooked upper beak can pry eucalyptus seeds from their capsules. The parrot also raids orchards —and is becoming scarce since angry farmers shoot it.

A pink cockatoo displays its gorgeous crest. With a strong bill, it digs insect eggs and roots from the hard ground of sparse grasslands in the semi-arid interior. Pink cockatoos often nest in the same tree hollows year after year.

A male mallee fowl (right) *busily tends the nesting mound while his mate prepares to lay an egg. Mounds are built in April; the winter rains will begin fermentation of the plant material, creating heat to incubate the half-pound eggs.*

Mound-building mallee fowl tirelessly regulate the temperature of their nests

The most extraordinary Australian birds are the mound builders, bowerbirds, and lyrebirds. Many mound builders (or megapodes) shape heaps of forest litter into incubating chambers for their eggs; some mounds measure thirty feet in diameter and fifteen feet in height, although most mounds are smaller.

The mallee fowl of the hot, dry, inland regions is probably the best known megapode, famous for regulating the environment of its eggs with an ability and energy that defy explanation. The male constructs a massive, intricate nest while the female stays nearby, doing little to help. He first excavates a hole two or three feet deep in the soil. Then he scratches up leaves and twigs over a fifty-yard radius to fill the hole and raise the

mound a foot or more above ground level. Finally, he digs a chamber in the mound, fills it with sand and more vegetable debris, and smooths over the surface.

When the rotting of the vegetation has raised the mound's internal temperature to 92° F., the male exposes the egg chamber, and the female, now allowed to enter the nest, digs a niche in the side wall of the chamber and lays a single egg. She retires, and the male spends the next two hours building the mound back to its original height. At intervals of several days, the female lays five to thirty-five more eggs in the mound. The male attends the nest daily, probing into the mound with his bill and determining the temperature by his tongue—with a degree of sensitivity not yet satisfactorily explained.

At first, there is danger that the mound's temperature may rise excessively; later on, as the rate of decay diminishes, it may fall below the optimum. Also, since egg-laying and nest-caring activities may go on for six or eight months, changing seasonal temperatures can further com-

Just hatched, a scrub turkey chick emerges from the nesting mound. These chicks develop to an advanced stage in the egg. After hatching, they dig their way to the surface unassisted, fend for themselves, and often fly within a day.

plicate the problem of environmental control. But it is the male's responsibility to maintain the mound at 92° F., and he does so by a variety of corrective activities. If internal heat raises the temperature too high, he uncovers the egg chamber enough to allow cooling; if the internal temperature falls, he adds more vegetable debris, which accelerates the rate of decay and increases the amount of insulation. In summer, he digs up the egg chamber material very early in the morning, spreading it on the ground and allowing it to cool before returning it to serve as insulation against the heat of midday. In autumn, he waits until the sun is overhead before digging up the chamber; the leaves and debris are then warmed in the noon sun before being returned in early afternoon. Each one of these corrective adjustments takes him several hours to perform, making him surely one of the busiest animals and most solicitous fathers alive.

Because egg-laying extends over several months, the first chicks begin hatching before the last egg is laid. After seven weeks of incubation, they emerge from their shells as much as three feet below the surface of the mound and struggle upward, at about a foot an hour, purely by their own efforts. With all that the parents have had to do, it is perhaps understandable that they now take no interest in the chicks. But no matter: The offspring are at once independent and go about their solitary business. In due course they too will mate and become slaves to an inherited ritual that provides for the survival of the species.

Other mound builders have different behavior patterns, more or less intricate. The jungle fowl, found in Queensland and on several Pacific islands, frequently has an easier time of it, for this bird often makes its nests in warm sand on the slopes of dormant volcanos. There the nests can be left unattended, for the heat source is constant; all the bird has to do is determine where the proper temperature prevails. In Australia there are no volcanos, and there the jungle fowl builds huge but conventional mounds of organic debris. No other megapode is so adaptable in the measures it can take to incubate its eggs.

The accomplished bowerbirds are builders, painters, collectors, and superb mimics

Another feathered wonder of both Australia and New Guinea is the male bowerbird. With much artistry, it builds a structure with the sole function of attracting a female. Bowerbirds are a bit drab, and the behavior of the male has suggested to some observers that the bower, decorated and even painted, may serve as a substitute for male finery. Bowers built by different species fall into several major categories, ranging from a simple platform decorated with leaves and stones to an elaborate structure that early European explorers assumed were the work of native people.

The arbor of avenue builders, such as the satin bowerbirds, consists of a small platform surmounted by two walls of fine sticks about eighteen inches high, and decorated with blue feathers,

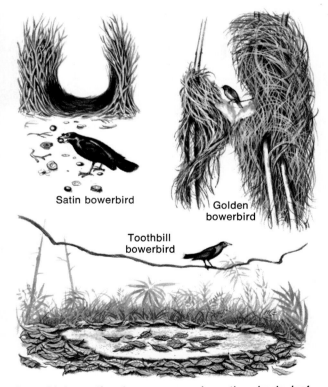

Satin bowerbird

Golden bowerbird

Toothbill bowerbird

A fawn-breasted bowerbird daily paints his walled avenue with a wad of chewed-up plants. The dark-green juice oozing down the wall from his bill dries a red-brown hue. Spare "paint" sources lie just in front of the bowerbird.

Bowerbird courting bowers range from the simple leaf-decorated clearing of the toothbill, to the walled avenue built and painted by the satin bowerbird, to the golden bowerbird's maypole mound—sometimes nine feet high.

flowers, scraps of paper, shells, and cicada cases. The bower of the golden bowerbird, one of the maypole builders, is constructed around two thin tree trunks spanned by a vine, upon which flowers and lichens are placed as decorations. The walls of this bower may be as much as nine feet high.

Even after erecting a bower, the male spends nearly all of his time improving and rearranging his collection of ornaments. Dried berries and withered flowers are discarded and replaced with fresh ones. Hundreds of shiny pebbles, animal vertebrae and knucklebones, snail shells, colorful feathers, iridescent beetle wing-covers—the kind of collection depending on the species—are constantly cleaned and arranged. Some species of bowerbird are even more artistic: The male chews colorful berries, mixes them with saliva, strips off a piece of frayed bark to use as a brush, and actually paints the walls of his bower.

When a female begins to show a little interest, the male hops up and down in increasing excitement, displaying his beautiful neck feathers. When mating is completed, the female flies into a tree to build a conventional, purely functional nest. In some species, the male helps to feed the female while he continues his elegant housekeeping activities, decorating and redecorating, hoarding and arranging his treasures, putting things in readiness until the next female passes by.

Other mounds, used only for display, are built by lyrebirds, which exhibit the most magnificent feathered tails imaginable, and possess a gift of mimicry equaled by no other creatures on Earth. A species known as the superb lyrebird is one of the largest perching birds in the world; it spends much time on the ground, however, where it appears pheasantlike when its tail is unopened. As a male embarks upon his courtship display, the curved bronze side feathers of the great tail swing far out to each side, and the finest filigree of shining white feathers spreads over the wide space between. Each morning the lyrebird stands upon his display mound and sings his own natural song, as sweet and rich as that of any bird known.

But this is only the beginning, for he then embarks on a vocal performance of truly astonishing virtuosity. He utters a fantastic variety of sounds, often with baffling ventriloquism. In his repertoire is the song of every bird in the forest, as well as a composite of these sounds. A single lyrebird can imitate the noisy flight of a flock of parrots, complete with dozens of simultaneous calls and the rush of wind through their feathers or the rustle of leaves. It sings, shrieks, trills, squawks, warbles, and caws in a continuous and dizzying exhibition of versatility. One of its favorite squeaking calls is that of the pilot bird, a creature usually nearby when the lyrebird ceases its morning song and begins scratching about for copepods, insects, and worms. Dancer, architect, singer, mimic—the lyrebird in many ways is the most remarkable of Australia's birds.

But the favorite of many Australians is another, more common bird, not remarkable except for its raucous, hilarious, infectious laughter—the kookaburra. Its cries are among the best known in the world, for hardly a jungle movie has been made, no matter what the scene, without the dubbing in of the kookaburra's rollicking laughter. This large kingfisher does not feed on fishes, preferring instead to hunt snakes, lizards, and rodents. The Australians have so much regard for the prowess of kookaburras as snake-killers that they have introduced the birds into new regions. Kookaburras often hunt in pairs or in groups, and by cooperating they can attack prey much larger than themselves, such as thirty-inch snakes.

Aborigines named the kookaburra for its harsh call. Crow-sized kookaburras steal eggs and nestlings from many birds; their own nests are in hollows high in trees, chambers dug in termite nests, or, rarely, tunnels in earth.

A male Raggiana's bird of paradise arches his body forward and spreads his wings to display. During the breeding season he performs to an audience of females perched in nearby trees, until one joins him on his branch and the pair mates.

Sprucing himself up, a magnificent bird of paradise sits on a branch near the edge of his territory in the New Guinea mountains. He eventually announces his readiness to mate with a loud call that sounds like lip-smacking.

The Spectacular Birds of Paradise

The birds of paradise live in the tropical rain forests of New Guinea and Australia. Males perform courtship displays to attract mates. Unlike their plainer bowerbird relatives, which construct artificial lures, they merely spread their gorgeous plumage. After mating, the drab female rears her single chick alone. The lovely feathers attract men as well as mates; for hundreds of years New Guineans have made headdresses from the plumes. In the nineteenth century European fashion "discovered" the bird of paradise and so many were killed that their numbers were seriously reduced. Export was banned, but smuggling is practiced.

The glowing six-inch king bird of paradise is the smallest member of its family, and the only one known to nest in tree holes. It inhabits the lowland rain forests of western New Guinea and some of the nearby islands.

At tribal festivals in New Guinea, men and unmarried women wear headdresses and nose ornaments of bird of paradise plumes. These may be taken from birds killed for the purpose, or from birds captured and released.

Iridescent plumage—including an unusual neck ruff—marks the Princess Stephanie's bird of paradise. The tail feathers, several times the body length, are especially valued by New Guineans for headdresses.

Propelled by broad, webbed forelegs, a platypus swims underwater, leaving a bubble trail (it surfaces every minute or so for air). The platypus is well suited for an aquatic and burrowing life. It swims insulated by thick fur and body fat. Skin folds protect eyes and ears while its leathery bill probes for prey. The flat tail is a swimming rudder and also tamps down the earth around burrows. The hind legs of males bear venom spurs.

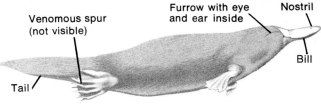

Venomous spur (not visible)

Furrow with eye and ear inside

Nostril

Bill

Tail

A female platypus sprawls at the opening of her burrow, guarding her light-colored baby. Blind for eleven weeks, a young platypus takes its first brief swim at about four months and is independent after another month.

Primitive features of Australia's monotremes — the platypus and the echidna — suggest the probable nature of early mammals

Looking on as more or less insignificant spectators during the age of the giant reptiles were the first mammals. Although their remains are rare, enough fossils have been found to indicate they were delicate, rat-size creatures that fed upon insects. Details of the anatomy and habits of these ancient mammals may never be known, but scientists believe that the monotremes of Australia and New Guinea, the world's only egg-laying mammals, provide some clues.

The most revealing features of the two monotremes—the duckbilled platypus and two species of spiny anteaters (echidnas)—are certain skeletal and other anatomical parts and their means of reproduction. All else, although fascinating, is of much less significance.

Both the platypus and the echidna have chest bones that support forelimbs, as well as bones jutting out from the pelvic girdle that are clearly of reptilian origin. The brains of these monotremes, although not much inferior to those of marsupials, have certain primitive features that have been greatly improved upon by placentals. A monotreme's abdominal organs terminate in a single opening through which the excretory, digestive, and reproductive systems empty; such a single orifice is characteristic of amphibians, reptiles, and birds, but not of most of the modern mammals.

Other primitive features are the relatively poor regulation of body temperatures (which are often quite low) and milk glands that exude their fluid not through nipples but through pores in two areas of the abdomen.

Of course, the single most important characteristic of both animals is the laying of small, rubbery, compressible eggs. The platypus usually produces two light-colored eggs, the echidna only a single egg.

The platypus is a highly efficient aquatic animal that grubs along the bottom of cool, upland streams, eyes and ear apertures tightly closed by skin folds. It gobbles up worms, mollusks, crayfish, aquatic insects, and anything else that comes in contact with its soft, sensitive bill. The food is packed into expandable cheek pouches, along with pebbles, which assist in crushing whole organisms to a manageable size. The platypus swims with its forelimbs, sculling along vigorously. Since the fan-shaped webbing on its front feet spreads under and well past the stout, sharp claws, the animal folds the webbing under its palms out of the way, when it walks on dry ground.

A platypus burrow extends deep into the bank of a stream, perhaps fifty feet or so, with the entrance opening six to twelve inches above the waterline. The separate resting chambers of male and female give off a musky odor, the result of pungent secretions from throat glands.

At mating time, the female makes a more elaborate tunnel with a spacious chamber at the end, which she pads with moist leaves and reeds brought in tucked under her broad tail. She then plugs the tunnel to the nest at several places with thick, firmly tamped earthen barriers. Finally ready, she lays two small eggs, which usually adhere to each other, and incubates them for ten days by curling her body around them. After the young hatch, naked and sightless, they lap milk

A short-beaked echidna probes for insect prey with its birdlike bill. A threatened echidna digs rapidly straight down into the ground; its peculiar splayed hind claws actually point to the rear and thus dig more efficiently.

from her fur. The mother holds the tiny creatures in the curve of her body, where their feeble, spasmodic movements stimulate the milk flow, but she has to leave them periodically to feed herself, wash, and carry out waste. After each trip, she carefully plugs the tunnel again.

The short-beaked echidna is more widely distributed than the platypus; several varieties are found in Tasmania and New Guinea, as well as on the Australian continent. In deserts, savannas, and rain forests, it digs rapidly in search of ants and termites, capturing them with its darting tongue. Its thick covering of spines parallels the defensive coats of the tenrecs, hedgehogs, and porcupines found on other continents. Although toothless, the echidna uses horny structures on the roof of its mouth and back area of its tongue to crush insect prey; it also swallows dirt, which helps grind food in its stomach.

The female echidna incubates her single egg for about a week inside a temporary pouch; here the defenseless, squirming infant remains during its early growth, stimulating the flow of thick, yellowish milk.

Animals with Pouches

As the age of dinosaurs drew to a close and the supercontinents were beginning to fragment, placentals and marsupials coexisted on the larger land masses. But in the course of time, placentals or some natural phenomenon eliminated most of the marsupials except for the opossums and caenolestids of the Americas. In the absence of placentals, Australia developed its own mammals, the monotremes and the marsupials.

Finding themselves in ecological voids, Australia's marsupials evolved into innumerable forms and specialties, some of which no longer exist. Two or three million years ago the continent supported kangaroos that were ten feet tall, swamp-dwelling animals the size of rhinoceroses, and marsupial "lions" that were probably the largest pouched carnivores the world has ever known. Changes in climate and vegetation eliminated their respective habitats, however, and these creatures eventually disappeared. But modern-day Australian marsupials have surmounted environmental difficulties as successfully as the most specialized placentals.

The present marsupials that most resemble Australia's early inhabitants are all carnivorous, preying upon insects, lizards, and other small ground creatures. Their primitive traits include distinctly separated fingers and toes, a rudimentary pouch, and, usually, many small teeth with some specialization according to diet. Tiny marsupial "mice" feed on a steady diet of insects, snails, worms, and anything else they find on or beneath the soil. Silky-furred, blind marsupial "moles" tunnel a short distance under the surface and consume insects.

The alert and sprightly bandicoots are larger than the "mice" and "moles," resembling rats and even rabbits; but their diet, too, consists of insects, lizards, and other small animals. The numbat (or banded anteater) is an insectivore with fifty-two teeth—more than any other land animal. It licks up termites with a long, wormlike tongue; its hairy tail effectively keeps the disturbed insects from countering the intruder's attack. The female has four nipples but no pouch, and drags her young under her as she walks. Both bandicoots and numbats are busy creatures, constantly searching for food. The rearward-facing pouch of the female rabbit-eared bandicoot is especially convenient when the animal burrows in the sand. But this variation of pouch is shared by many other marsupials, including some that never go underground.

Marsupial Pegs in Ecological Holes

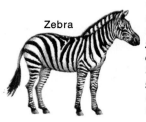

Zebra

Open grasslands offer food to large grazing animals like Australia's kangaroos and Africa's zebras. Grazers eat enormous quantities of grasses in order to make maximum use of the grasses' low nutritional value. Lack of concealment forces them to be wary and swift.

African hunting dog

Large carnivores hunt primarily large grazers. Like African hunting dogs, the Tasmanian thylacine (which may be extinct) relied on endurance rather than speed for running down its quarry, and on its strong jaws. The thylacine was able to prey on such a swift, large animal as the kangaroo.

Grasshopper mouse

Small plains predators such as marsupial mice feed voraciously on insects and other animals to satisfy their high metabolisms. Vulnerable to larger hunters, they live in hiding, making quick dashes at their prey. The marsupial mouse's flattened head can probe among roots and crevices.

Marten

Arboreal hunters are solitary, agile, and quick. They prey—mainly at night—on small animals and eggs. Both the Australian tiger cat and the marten of Europe and America have long bodies and short legs with tree-gripping feet. Adapted for tree climbing, they also hunt on the ground.

Anteater

Mammals feeding on ants and termites have long snouts and sticky tongues to thrust into crannies and lick up prey. Powerful clawed forelimbs rip open termite mounds and rotten logs. Teeth are weak and degenerate, as in the numbat, or have disappeared, as in some South American anteaters.

Mole

Burrowing mammals such as true moles and marsupial moles rarely appear on the surface. With strong forelegs and enlarged nails they dig underground in their unending search for worms and small insects. Their eyes have degenerated, but they have acutely sensitive organs of touch.

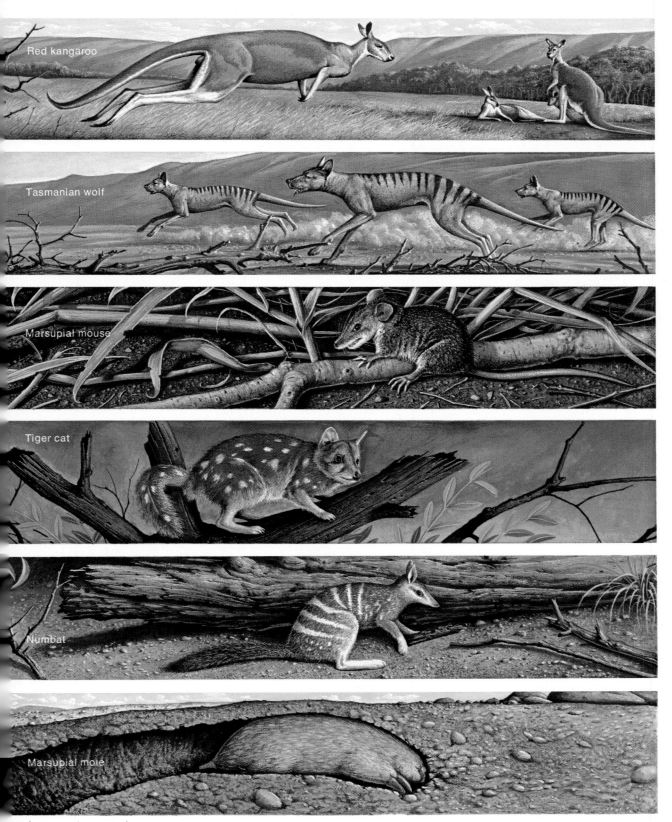

Each way of life, or ecological niche, has certain requirements. Adapting to similar niches often produces similar physique and behavior in different groups. Australian marsupials (below) occupy niches filled elsewhere by placental mammals (left).

Red kangaroo

Tasmanian wolf

Marsupial mouse

Tiger cat

Numbat

Marsupial mole

A numbat licks up termites from a nest that it has just torn open with its powerful claws. Fallen logs, hollowed out by termites, provide the unaggressive numbat with shelter from dangerous introduced predators such as dogs and foxes.

The pouched predators of Australia resemble weasels, dogs, or mice

The so-called native cats and tiger cats are another group of relatively primitive and unspecialized marsupials. They are usually nocturnal predators living principally on the ground. Tiger cats or quolls climb well in pursuit of reptiles, birds, and small mammals. The inaccurate "cat" designation probably derives from the way these creatures attack their prey. They approach stealthily, then with a springing charge land on a victim's back and quickly bite through the spinal cord.

Mystery surrounds the fate of the thylacine, or Tasmanian wolf, which is also called the Tasmanian tiger because of the narrow, dark stripes across its back. No thylacines have been seen in several decades, although paw prints are reportedly found from time to time. This largest marsupial predator, if it still exists, stands two to three feet high and measures about six feet long. At first glance, the thylacine appears very doglike until the proportions of its long hind legs and thick-based tail are seen. The rigid tail is unresponsive and does not wag. When a thylacine yawns, all dog illusions vanish, for its mouth opens at what seems an impossibly wide angle—among the greatest gapes in the mammal world.

A solitary hunter, the thylacine trots determinedly after its prey, putting on a burst of speed only at the end of the chase. Unfortunately the thylacine was not studied scientifically or even carefully observed in the wild and little is known of its habits. The Tasmanian wolf's overall effect upon sheep in the early part of this century is debatable, but since Tasmanian sheep raisers were convinced that the thylacine was harmful

Two Tasmanian devils feast on a large lizard. Devils eat practically any animal, dead or alive. Male and female devils share a den for two weeks before mating, six months later make beds for the babies when they emerge from the pouch.

and economically undesirable, it was ruthlessly hunted into near or total extinction. Its coughing barks are no longer heard in the forest, and the world has perhaps lost one of the most interesting archaic predators in the recent history of mammals. In any case, the forests have been so altered that the thylacine could hardly survive.

The Tasmanian devil, a stocky, barrel-shaped animal with a furless pink nose, is the second largest marsupial predator. Although in its wild habitat it appears to be an intractable bundle of fury, the devil can be tamed with good results. It is a clean animal that washes its face much as any house cat does. It likes water and swims and dives with ease, but hunts and scavenges mostly on land. Its heavily constructed head bears powerful jaws able to crunch through muscle and bone without difficulty. A fair number of devils still exist in Tasmania, but they are nocturnal and seldom seen, spending daylight hours hiding in rock crevices or hollow logs.

These Tasmanian wolves, photographed around 1900 in the Washington Zoo, were among the last of their species seen alive. Because of their secretive habits, no one knows whether or not they are extinct.

Some marsupials have taken to the air as gliders. Others have become burrowers

The marsupial plant eaters are much more evident than the secretive, nocturnal carnivores. Kangaroos, among the best known animals in the world and almost synonymous with Australia, are only one of the forms that the vegetarian marsupials have assumed.

Several species of possum (quite unlike the American marsupial opossum, except for their prehensile tails) live in Australia's forests, where they eat foliage and insects, sip nectar, and are important as flower pollinators. The brush-tailed possum well illustrates the typical marsupial means of reproduction. Only 17½ days after mating, the female gives birth to a single infant measuring but half an inch in length—so tiny that its mother outweighs it 10,000 times. (A human mother outweighs her baby by only 15 to 20 times.) Like other marsupial newborns, the baby brush-tail finds its own way into the mother's pouch, attaches to a nipple, and does not leave the pouch until it is four or five months old.

Some possums have taken up a way of life like that of flying squirrels and Malaysia's flying lemurs. One of them, the greater gliding possum, is over three feet long; floating downward from tree to tree or from a tree to the ground, it may span distances of 300 feet or more. Unlike a flying squirrel, it does not extend its front legs outward to stretch the membrane joining the front and rear limbs, but bends its arms at the elbows so that the forearms point inward and the paws

A feather-tail glider sails toward a eucalyptus twig, where another glider sips nectar. The four- to six-inch marsupials (*half this length is tail*) also eat eucalyptus buds and insects. In the air, their prehensile tails are used for steering.

meet beneath the head. This posture allows the membrane to billow up and form a concave surface—an airfoil much more efficient than a flat surface. Since smaller marsupial gliders extend all four legs when gliding, stretching the membrane surface into a flat plane, most of them are less likely to cover as much distance, although yellow-bellied gliders can float even farther.

Sugar gliders, among the most numerous of all eastern Australian mammals, are often seen climbing trees rapidly with nesting material clutched tightly in their coiled tails, or sailing down from the trees for 100 feet or more, using their tails for steering. Quite unlike these agile gliders but closely related are two species of cuscus, a beautifully furred tree dweller. Its moon face, with inconspicuous ears, has a perpetually wide-eyed expression, at once quizzical and placid. Australian cuscuses live only in Queensland.

Living on the ground are two kinds of wombat, tubby, almost tail-less creatures. Despite their size (three to four feet in length) they are remarkably fine burrowers.

A wombat's tunnel may have a diameter of two feet and run underground for dozens of feet. A powerful digger, a wombat, up to seventy pounds, uses the claws of all four feet to excavate vast quantities of earth in a short time. Even in its tunnel the animal defends itself effectively, lashing out violently and crushing an attacker's head or limbs between its body and the sides of the burrow. Wombats lead a solitary life and are very quiet creatures.

As might be expected from its tunneling habits, the wombat's well-developed pouch opens backward. Because the stump of a tail still retains vestigial muscles, scientists suspect that the wombat's ancestors lived in trees.

Coiling its prehensile tail around a branch, a cuscus clings to its perch. About 3½ feet long, including the tail, the sluggish cuscus forages in trees at night for fruits, leaves, insects, and occasionally birds and eggs.

The wombat munches grass and roots with continuously growing teeth. To excavate its burrow—up to forty feet long, ending in a bark-lined nest—a wombat digs with its front feet and removes dirt with the hind feet.

A highly specialized diet of tree leaves ties the koalas' survival to that of a few species of eucalypts

Unlikely as it seems, the wombat's closest relative is one of Australia's most beloved tree-dwelling animals, the koala. Zoologists believe the koala may have returned to arboreal life from a land-dwelling, wombatlike ancestor. Many basic koala characteristics resemble those of a wombat, including the absence of a tail and a rear-facing pouch that may seem a hazardous arrangement in an animal that sits and climbs upright. Actually, it is a good design that prevents snagging on branches, and the pouch muscles are strong enough so that the infant cannot fall out. When the young koala is sufficiently mature to leave the pouch, however, it climbs on its mother's back to ride around, hugging her tightly, for nearly a year before taking up life on its own.

The koala is an outstanding example of specialization carried to a dangerous degree. Although Australia has hundreds of species of eucalypt, the animal eats little but the leaves of about twelve of them, prefers five, and has one favorite among the five. Even then there are hazards. The koala likes tender leaves when they are available, but must select them with care: In the Australian winter, young gum leaves and shoots produce excessive quantities of hydrocyanic acid—a quarter pound of such leaves is enough to kill a sheep. Moreover, the older leaves in the koala's diet contain tough fibers and strong-smelling oils that impair their digestibility. Perhaps it is to cope with such fare that the koala has a large, coiled appendix—up to eight feet long—in which digestion takes place slowly. Swallowing such quantities of pungent oils does bring one distinct benefit: Koalas are entirely free of lice and other vermin. Some people think they smell like cough medicine!

The differing diets of northern and southern koalas reflect both temperature and the kinds of eucalypts available. In the warm north, the animals select trees with leaves containing substances that lower their blood pressure and body heat; the koalas of the cooler south seek trees producing chemicals that increase body heat.

The koalas' total dependence upon just a few species of eucalypts makes their extinction a constant possibility. If plant disease should attack their food trees, the koalas could quickly vanish from the face of the Earth.

Perhaps the specialized diet of koalas would be easier to understand if eucalyptus leaves were not so oily and tough. But even young koalas cannot go immediately from milk to an adult diet. They must subsist for a time upon a regurgitated vegetable mush predigested by the mother, probably in her appendix.

Once successfully on its own, a koala may live out a long and quiet life for up to twenty years. Sluggish much of the time, it can move quickly from limb to limb. If hurt, koalas cry like babies; if they are caught in one of the explosive fires that occasionally rage through the gum forests, they have been heard to scream piercingly. Despite the dangers and uncertainties of life, these gentle, appealing little creatures with their woolly ears and sleepy eyes are still to be seen in parklands in Queensland and Victoria, under the protection of the Australian government.

Range of eucalypts preferred by koala

Range of koala

Koalas can eat only mature leaves of certain eucalypts. They are thus restricted to eastern Australia, where their food trees grow. The range of these appealing marsupials, however, is even smaller than that of the eucalypts.

Grasping a eucalyptus branch with its paws, a koala devours a bunch of the pungent, fibrous leaves, its only food. An adult eats about two and a half pounds of leaves daily. Moisture in the leaves enables the koala to survive without water.

Sparring male kangaroos clutch with their paws or kick sideways in a stylized trial of strength. Unlike the powerful downward clawing kicks used for defense, these kicks are aimed to throw the opponent off balance and knock him down, rather than to kill or injure him.

A large joey peers from the haven of its mother's pouch. At birth, after a gestation period only about a month long, a kangaroo infant weighs less than 1/25th of an ounce.

Kangaroos of the Australian Outback

The largest living marsupials are the kangaroos of Australia. The graceful, long-tailed wallabies inhabit the brushlands; the grays, the open, grassy forests; the richly colored reds, the vast inland plains; the powerful walleroos, the coastal mountains and parched interior ranges. Mature male reds and grays are known to grow over eight feet tall and weigh well over 200 pounds. Able to disembowel almost any enemy with their huge hind legs, kangaroos are threatened more by hunger, drought, and man than by such natural predators as dingoes.

Springing on its powerful hind legs, a large gray or red kangaroo can leap as far as 27½ feet and as high as 10 feet.

Whiptail wallabies, like other kangaroos, travel in small troops led by a dominant male. They rest during the heat of the day and feed at night on various grasses. Intestinal bacteria aid in digesting the tough plant fibers.

Waterholes are vital to kangaroos in arid regions. The animals can dig these holes with their sharp claws. To conserve vital nitrates, kangaroos avoid overdrinking, which increases the use of nitrogen by the body.

A kangaroo can bound along at twenty-five miles an hour for some distance and, reportedly, reach fifty-five miles an hour in spurts. The height and length of leaps vary with the condition of the ground.

A rock wallaby shelters in a crevice by day. It will emerge at dusk to bound over rocky slopes and climb trees in its search for plant food. Rough footpads give this nimble marsupial a grip when jumping chasms as wide as thirteen feet.

Unchallenged by placental mammals, kangaroos became the dominant grazers of Australia's vast grasslands

Without antelope herds to graze on its dry grasslands, Australia had a vast, unoccupied habitat available for marsupial exploitation. When one considers the characteristics of antelope, deer, bison, and other hooved placental mammals, the marsupial response, although entirely successful, is unexpected. It is the creature that in the rest of the world *means* Australia: the kangaroo. When Europeans first discovered it, they had a hard time describing or even drawing it, so unfamiliar were the proportions. Yet a large kangaroo is a magnificent animal, admirably suited to its way of life. Few sights are more thrilling than a group of big kangaroos bounding across a plain at full speed, tails waving up and down and serving as counterbalances as they cover twenty to thirty feet with every graceful leap. Surely a kangaroo is one of the great achievements of evolutionary design.

The kangaroo pattern takes a variety of forms. There are arboreal kangaroos, wallaroos, wallabies, and little rat kangaroos, in addition to the impressively large red and great gray ones. Rat kangaroos are the least specialized of all, while the tree kangaroo is a reversion to the arboreal life that kangaroo ancestors probably led before becoming ground dwellers. Wallaroos and wallabies vary only slightly from the basic kangaroo design, differing in size more than anything else. The one significant departure from the design was the extinct marsupial "lion," about the size of a leopard and a kind of kangaroo turned carnivore.

The larger kangaroos, although not predators, are formidable and often cantankerous antagonists to animal or man. When a 150-pounder stands erect to a height of over seven feet, balanced back on a powerful tail, it is an imposing sight. Only the males fight; the females are much smaller and less muscular. In a fight, the animal tears furiously with its forearms—the biceps are considerably larger than those of a strong man. Its characteristic method of attack is lashing out and downward with its huge hind legs in one of the most powerful blows delivered by any mammal.

A newborn kangaroo is ridiculously small, yet very much on its own. Guided only by instinct, the one-inch creature must crawl from the birth orifice up the abdomen of its mother and into her pouch, a distance of a foot or more. Once inside, it descends to seek one of the nipples, which soon swells with milk inside the baby's mouth, making a secure anchoring seal between the almost embryonic infant and its mother. The tiny kangaroo has no real features yet: Its eyes and ears are unformed, as are its hind legs and tail. However, its stubby front legs have minute claws to help it climb, and since its nostrils and the olfactory portion of its brain are well developed, zoologists believe that it finds its way by scent. The mother, 30,000 times the weight of her baby, does nothing to help; there is no truth to the story that she licks a path in her fur to guide the young one. She does, however, lick whatever blood and mucus is left in the baby's wake, for at birth the infant is still connected to its rudimentary placenta by an umbilical cord. Only rarely are twins born, but if they are, the mother looks after both—a feat that seems incredible if one considers the cramped quarters of the pouch. Most of the young are born in winter; the breeding season of some kangaroos is tied to rain and the growth of plants.

The baby, known as a joey, spends much of its time in its mother's pouch for almost a year, until it weighs eight to ten pounds, or even more. At the end of the year, the mother has had enough and no longer lets her joey enter; from then on it lives outside the pouch, although she still feeds and defends it.

While a joey is developing, the female may mate again, but the five-week development of the fertilized egg is suspended by hormonal control until the pouch is finally vacated. With such assembly-line production, a female kangaroo is seldom without at least one joey in some stage of growth.

In the more arid regions of Australia, kangaroos have an important effect on the populations of other animals. With powerful limbs, they excavate water holes where no surface water is visible. These are then visited regularly by emus, native cats, and cockatoos, as well as many other creatures. The margins of the water holes may also support short-rooted plants unable to tap subsurface waters.

The swift-running dingo, about the size of a small German shepherd, is probably descended from India's plains wolf. Introduced by Aborigines about 30,000 B.C., dingoes are now wild and wolflike—they howl but do not bark.

The Latecomers

When Australia separated from the rest of Gondwanaland, the early placentals had not evolved enough to compete effectively with marsupials. Reliable evidence indicates that no placentals except bats and rafted rodents lived in Australia until early aboriginal settlers brought an Asian dog—the dingo—several thousand years ago. The wild dingo is now widely distributed over much of Australia, its habitats ranging from forest to arid country. Traveling in small packs, it prowls in search of kangaroos and other marsupials. It is also a predator of Australia's present huge population of rabbits, whose progenitors were brought in by Europeans.

Fruit bats (or flying foxes) have been in Australia since early times. In addition, two age-old species of seal come ashore regularly to bask or rear their young: the fur seal (once hunted nearly to extinction) and the hair seal. They are now protected by the government.

Despite the advent of Western man, the island continent of Australia remains the greatest living laboratory of evolution. No other island supports so many truly distinctive plants and animals.

Islands Born of Fire

Appearance, disappearance, and reappearance. Birth, death, and rebirth. Settlement, holocaust, and resettlement. The rhythm of change governs the destinies of volcanic sea islands

Shortly after 7:30 on the morning of November 14, 1963, the captain of a fishing vessel off the southern coast of Iceland trained his binoculars on a column of dark smoke rising from the sea about a mile to the southeast. As he studied the billowing black cloud, his questions gave way to suspicion, and finally to astonishment. He ordered his crew to sail closer and then called the nearest radio station. He wanted to report, he said, a volcanic eruption.

To scientists, the rising black eruption column —about 200 feet high at the time of the captain's report—clearly suggested that molten material from a fissure on the sea floor had built a volcanic mountain, and that the summit cone was already near the surface. Within three hours of the first report, scientists and journalists began arriving at the scene in ships and planes. By this time the column of smoke had attained a height of 12,000 feet. Explosions almost every half-minute were sending volcanic ash, dust, and rock bombs 500 feet into the air. Waves were breaking on something new just under the surface. All signs pointed to a single outcome: An island was about to be born.

That same night, the volcano's smoking cone pushed up through the waves, and by the following morning had grown to a height of thirty-three feet. As the explosions roared on, the flanks and summit continued to build. By the 19th, the island was 200 feet high and 2000 feet long.

The Icelandic government named the island Surtsey, after Surtur, a fire demon in Norse mythology. Surtur was a powerful giant, and Surtsey has proved a worthy heir to the reputation of its namesake. When the eruptions quieted down in August 1965, after almost two years of intermittent activity, the island was 550 feet high, 6900 feet long, and nearly one square mile in area, and it continued to grow for two more years.

Born of volcanism, Surtsey was the first new known island to appear in the North Atlantic in over 1000 years. The growing island greatly excited scientists, two of whom made a landing during a lull in the eruptions in December 1963. Now volcanologists could observe at close hand what the volcano was doing. Biologists saw the island as a totally new environment; there they could study in detail the arrival and development of life on isolated, barren land. For scientists, then, Surtsey was a laboratory. For the rest of the world, it was a dramatic reminder that the Earth is not a mass of dead rock, but a dynamic structure continuously undergoing change.

A towering column of steam and smoke heralds the dramatic birth of a volcanic island. Surtsey emerged from the North Atlantic off the coast of Iceland in November 1963. Within two years the island was a square mile in area, and the first hardy plants and animals had colonized it.

307

Clouds of steam hiss where red-hot lava from Surtsey volcano meets the chilling sea. Flows of lava solidify at the shore to form a "collar" around the island, protecting its cinders from erosion and binding the loose material together.

Molten rock and expanding gases trapped under pressure beneath the Earth's crust may spew out in a violent volcanic eruption

Most of the time the Earth as a whole gives the impression of unending stability. But all its various components—atmosphere, seas, land, and the molten masses of rock beneath the surface—are actually in a process of constant change. The dense core, composed largely of iron and nickel, is still close to the temperature that prevailed when the planet was formed—about 5400° F. The core, 4400 miles in diameter, is surrounded by a zone called the mantle, nearly 1800 miles thick; together they account for most of the Earth's volume.

Early in the history of the Earth, heat from the interior was radiated into space, until the final layer of lighter-weight rock, the crust, solidified as a crystalline skin floating on the mantle. The Earth is a sphere 8000 miles in diameter, and its crust is remarkably thin—thinner proportionately than an eggshell, since under the oceans it is only five miles thick and elsewhere about thirty miles. Stretched, wrinkled, torn, and shoved about ever since its formation, the crust has developed all kinds of irregularities and weaknesses.

Beneath the crust, mantle rock (or magma) is still hot and under great pressure; many geologists believe it is plastic enough for slow convection currents to pass through it, carrying superheated material up toward the surface, where it cools slightly and sinks again. In some places, the magma becomes trapped in a reservoir or magma chamber pressing up into the crust, where the weight of overlying rocks is less confining. As the magma rests in its chamber, some of the minerals in it crystallize, and the freed gases expand. When the pressure on the surrounding rock becomes intolerable, the crust above the chamber breaks to form a conduit or passage, and material from the chamber is ejected, usually violently, in a volcanic eruption.

Nearly every land mass has remnants of ancient volcanism. In historic times, about 500 volcanos around the world are known to have been active. Sixty or seventy million years ago, a stupendous amount of volcanic activity all through Europe covered thousands of square miles with lava and ash. There is no reason to doubt that volcanic eruptions will continue into the future, with the rate of activity fluctuating over time. The fires of the Earth burn on, and the molding of its crust is far from finished.

Mechanics of Volcanism

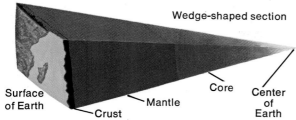

Wedge-shaped section

Surface of Earth

Crust Mantle Core

Center of Earth

The interior of the Earth consists of two principal regions: the central core, 4400 miles in diameter, and the 1800-mile-thick mantle just under the thin crust.

Birth and Death of a Volcanic Island

A volcano on the sea floor begins where liquid rock from the mantle rises through a weak spot in the crust.

A volcano that continues to build until it reaches the surface of the ocean becomes a volcanic island.

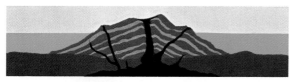

The life span of a high island with a peak thousands of feet above sea level may be millions of years.

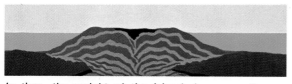

In time, the weight of the island depresses the sea floor, and winds and waves erode the island to a plain.

As the island disappears below the surface, it is called a guyot; it continues to support life above the abyss.

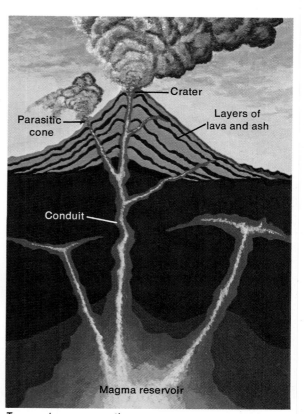

Crater

Parasitic cone

Layers of lava and ash

Conduit

Magma reservoir

Tremendous convection currents carry superheated plastic rock from near the core up through the mantle. As the rock rises up and pressures are slightly relieved, the rock becomes molten and gases are freed. When this rock is trapped in a magma chamber with a conduit to the surface, it bursts out in a volcanic eruption.

Varieties of Volcanic Eruptions

Hawaiian eruption

Strombolian eruption

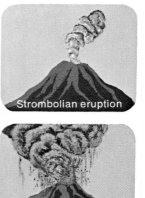

Pelean eruption

Vesuvian eruption

Volcanos differ widely in their eruptions—in the type of materials ejected, and in the height and direction of the explosive cloud. The most violent eruptions occur where mantle rock contains the most gas.

Lava seethes in a volcanic cone on Surtsey soon after the 1963 emergence of the island. Rivers of molten rock escape from fissures below the crater's rim and roll seaward. Lava flowed, with lulls, for over three years on Surtsey.

Carpeted a velvety black by the latest lava flow, a volcanic crater lies desolate in the mountainous terrain of Reunion Island in the Indian Ocean. Cinder cones and a fire pit near the rim interrupt the level, featureless floor.

The Life Cycle of a Volcanic Crater

A volcanic eruption leaves in its wake a bowl-shaped depression, the crater, at the top of the conduit. Later, other eruptions may form small cones in the old crater. But gradually all volcanic activity ceases. Enough rain may fall to make a crater lake. Vegetation, followed by an animal population, may fill the crater. The floor may collapse and become a caldera. In the end, erosion will destroy the crater.

Long dead, the crater of Rano-Raraku volcano on northeastern Easter Island holds a shallow lake of trapped rainwater. The lake, which has neither inlets nor outlets, is being invaded by vegetation moving in from the crater rim.

Lehua volcano, probably an offshoot of the nearby larger Hawaiian island of Niihau, has been worn away into a crescent shape by the action of the sea. Lehua is a tuff cone of ash and glassy fragments, which erode readily.

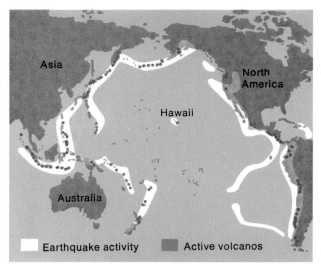

Earthquake activity   Active volcanos

A ring of volcanos—most dormant, some active—skirts the edge of the Pacific Ocean, along major fault lines in the Earth's surface. Called the "Circle of Fire," this zone is subject to earthquakes as well as to volcanic eruptions.

Thousands of active and dormant volcanos, above and below sea level, trace globe-girdling rifts in the ocean floor

The Pacific Ocean contains an enormous aggregation of islands. Most of the large islands along the western rim are probably continental rather than volcanic, although many contain volcanos. Nearly all the smaller islands farther from Asia are of volcanic origin. Some are exposed summits of volcanos; others are atolls, coral reefs built on the flanks of volcanos that long ago sank back into the sea or were eroded to below sea level. A ring of coral islets may surround a volcanic cone.

The small Pacific islands appear in greatest profusion to the south and west. Clustered in

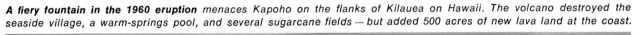

A fiery fountain in the 1960 eruption menaces Kapoho on the flanks of Kilauea on Hawaii. The volcano destroyed the seaside village, a warm-springs pool, and several sugarcane fields — but added 500 acres of new lava land at the coast.

groups, strung out like beads in gently curving chains, or aligned in straight rows, they form patterns that correspond to areas and lines of structural weakness in the sea floor.

Most of the 10,000 volcanos in the Pacific are hidden beneath the sea and no longer active. The undersea volcanos are distributed throughout the entire ocean; a considerable group lies under the Gulf of Alaska. One recently discovered submarine volcano known to be active today is 750 miles southeast of Tahiti in a straight line with Neilson Reef, Rapa, and Morotiri. Ten thousand feet above the sea floor, its summit still lies 1500 feet below the surface of the ocean, and it continues to build upward. Such volcanic seamounts—huge underwater mountains that have never broken the surface—are characteristic of this submarine world. Other undersea mountains of volcanic origin, with flat tops, are called guyots. Once visible islands, they were planed level by water erosion and later became submerged. In a sense, both seamounts and guyots are "islands": If their summits are close to the surface, they offer isolated, relatively shallow, dimly illuminated environments for marine life, and each one is the center for a small marine community.

Fires of the Earth

Since ancient times, man's terror and awe before the spectacle of an erupting volcano has been reflected in myths and folklore. Between the fifth and eighth centuries B.C., Mt. Etna in eastern Sicily figured prominently in Greek mythology as a site of the gods' activities. After an eruption in 1104 A.D., Icelanders believed their great volcano, Hekla, was the entrance to a hell populated by furious demons.

No two volcanos are alike. Each is an individual, differing from others in structure, eruptive activity, composition of ejected materials, and life cycle. Despite such variations, however, all volcanos obviously share one common feature: the passage and ejection of mantle material from the interior of the Earth through a conduit and out a vent.

When ash, rock, and gas spew forth from a vent, differences in volcanic activity become apparent. Some eruptions are quiet, massive, and long-lasting. Others are sudden and so cataclysmic that they dwarf all other known earthly events. Mauna Loa and Kilauea, active volcanos on the island of Hawaii, grow slowly and predictably, but Bandai-san, dormant in Japan for over 1000 years, gave only two minutes' warning before

it blew apart in 1888. Most eruptions fall somewhere between the two extremes, with days or weeks of ominous preparations, followed by dramatic ejections of clouds of incandescent gas and dark ash, showers of rock bombs, and great flows of lava. A series of eruptions may last for days, weeks, or months.

A few volcanic islands, such as Bogosloff Island north of the Aleutians and Ilha Nova in the Azores, do not always remain above water, but appear and disappear—then bafflingly appear again. If a cone composed of loose cinders is formed, the sea may erode it away before lava has had a chance to consolidate it. The permanence of Surtsey was much in doubt until a flow of lava began 4½ months after the island first appeared. Syrtlingur, a nearby islet that had emerged as Surtsey quieted down, failed to produce lava and disappeared after only a few months of existence.

Submarine volcanic material spouted hundreds of feet into the air in 1965, to form Syrtlingur Island. Less than a mile from Surtsey, Syrtlingur was thirty-seven acres in area when storms swept away the ash-and-cinder islet.

Hot springs, boiling mudholes, and geysers—like Pohutu, which spurts steam 60 to 100 feet high almost continuously—abound in New Zealand's Whakarewarewa Thermal Region. Maoris launder and cook in the hot springs.

A geothermal power plant near Wairakei taps underground supplies of volcanic steam to produce nearly 10 per cent of New Zealand's electric power. Its continued use, however, may affect the region's famed geysers.

Over the centuries, men have repeatedly risked death to exploit the beneficial effects of volcanic activity

Volcanic processes are often disastrous, but they may sometimes benefit life. For thousands of years, the magma reservoir beneath a volcano continues to heat ground water that seeps to the chamber zone. The mixture of steam and other gases with heated water may then issue at the surface as hot springs and steam fumaroles, and sometimes as geysers. In regions close to the poles, the warmth from such springs and fumaroles provides opportunities for plant and animal life to exist in otherwise unfavorable latitudes. In New Zealand, Iceland, and Italy, subterranean steam and hot water are major sources of heat and electrical power. Several other nations without fossil fuels are planning to tap the heat energy of the Earth. A small start has been made in California, where the relative lack of air and water pollution of this source, as well as decreased costs, is proving an attractive incentive.

Although volcanic soils look sterile and hostile to life, they are rich in basic plant nutrients that encourage the growth of vegetation soon after an eruption subsides. Unfortunately, the richness of volcanic soils is indirectly tied to an extensive loss of human life. From ancient times, men have cultivated the slopes of volcanos and the valleys below, since they are among the most fertile areas on Earth. Sizable populations on Stromboli and on Mt. Etna in the Mediterranean illustrate the willingness of men to settle close to active volcanos despite awareness of the ever-present danger of a new eruption.

The same kind of clustering has resulted in devastating human disasters throughout Indonesia and in the area around Mt. Taal in the Philippines. Taal, which has had at least eighteen major eruptions since 1572, has killed two of every three persons residing in nearby villages, yet its periphery is regularly recolonized after each eruption has run its course.

Volcanic eruptions can affect established life on islands in two fundamental ways. First, they may add to or subtract from an island's mass and land area. Second, they may destroy part or all of an island's plant and animal life. It is not only direct contact with volcanic material and gases

Stromboli volcano looms over a village *perched on its flank. For over 2500 years mild flows of ash and lava have been erupting from the volcano. Every few years the flows plug the vent, and internal pressures build to explosive levels.*

that causes destruction of life. Hurricane-force winds resulting from the violent explosion in 1815 of Tomboro, east of Java, pulled whole trees and large animals, even villages, straight up into the air. A huge sea wave (tsunami) produced by an eruption may be more destructive than the eruption itself.

Two of the most dramatic geological events of the last hundred years were the terrible eruption of Mt. Pelée on Martinique in the Antilles, and one of the greatest volcanic explosions known, that of Krakatau in a strait of the Malay Archipelago. When the side of Mt. Pelée burst in 1902, it set free an enormous, dense cloud of mud, ash,

and incandescent solid matter. The fiery cloud swept down a broad valley at estimated speeds of up to 180 miles per hour, within minutes destroying everything in its path, including the city of Saint-Pierre. Only sterile land was left in its wake. Of the 30,000 people in the city, two survived—one at the very edge of the catastrophe, the other in a completely enclosed dungeon where he was awaiting execution. Despite the vast destruction, plant and animal life from the margins of the area began to invade the barren soil in the months that followed, and in only a few years the whole region was again clothed in vegetation and populated by animals.

The Violent Death of Krakatau

The cataclysmic explosion of Krakatau volcano in 1883—modern scientists estimate it had the force of a million H-bombs—destroyed two-thirds of the island. Prehistoric Krakatau is believed to have been 6000 feet high until, after a great explosion similar to that of 1883, the central core collapsed, leaving several small islands. Cones developed on the islands and ultimately merged into a single island. Following the 1883 explosion on that island, the sound traveled 3000 miles in all directions; the seismic wave raised the sea level more than a foot 4550 miles away in South Africa, traveled around Africa, and was still noticeable as a two-inch surge in the English Channel. Airborne dust particles, reported to reach a height of 17 miles, gradually spread to cover more than 135 million square miles; two months later unusual sky glows caused by the fine dust were seen in the United States, halfway around the world. In 1927, intermittent volcanic activity began to build a new island—Anak Krakatau, or "Child of Krakatau"—in the center of the old crater.

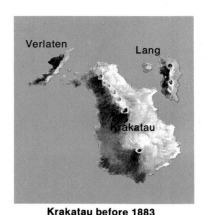

Krakatau before 1883

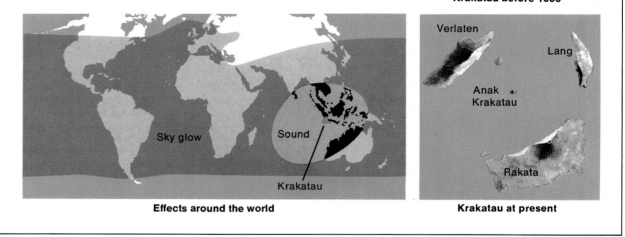

Effects around the world

Krakatau at present

A devastating eruption shook the world and wiped out all life on Krakatau and nearby islands

The world has seldom experienced so terrifying an explosion as the one that destroyed Krakatau in 1883. Possibly the most tremendous eruption in recorded history, it occurred in a region where a great rift in the ocean floor crosses the curve of the Malay Archipelago at the Sunda Strait, between the two large islands of Sumatra and Java. Here, truly, *X* marked the spot. In the strait lie a number of volcanic islands, one of which, Krakatau, had been formed by the slow coalescence of several smaller islands and craters.

In May 1883, the residents of the large islands in the chain heard explosions and saw seven-mile-high columns of pumice and ash coming from Krakatau. The eruptions continued all summer, growing increasingly violent. By late August they had become a series of continuous roars, audible hundreds of miles away.

Finally, on the morning of August 27, came four explosions that no one nearby lived to tell about. In the third, most of an island 1000 feet high vanished, leaving a thousand-foot hole beneath the surface of the sea. As the summit cone collapsed, the sea engulfed two cubic miles of rock. Giant tsunami waves—one reaching points on coastal hills as high as 135 feet above sea level—thundered out across the strait, destroying all seaside villages on neighboring islands and carrying ships with their dead crews miles inland. The waves traveled far enough to raise the water level in the English Channel.

Ash and gases rose fifty miles into the sky,

spreading total darkness for 150 miles in every direction. Nearly 4½ cubic miles of volcanic material had been hurled into the air. Sounds of the explosion were heard clearly over one-seventh of the Earth's surface; as far away as Rodriguez Island, 3000 miles distant in the Indian Ocean, residents thought great naval guns were firing nearby. For two years, dust in high-altitude jet streams created the most brilliant sunsets, sunrises, and twilight glows ever seen.

The disaster brought death to more than 37,000 human beings on islands throughout the region, some of them hundreds of miles away. The loss of plant and animal life was incalculable, but certainly, that morning, every living thing on the fragments of Krakatau and on the small neighboring islands, including worms and roots deep in the soil, ceased to exist. For a while Krakatau, or what was left of it—the islands of Rakata (also called Krakatau), Verlaten, and Lang, as we know them today—was as lifeless as the Earth had been four billion years before.

New Colonizers

A cataclysm of such magnitude attracted scientists from all over the world. Botanists and zoologists went to the islands to look for life as soon as conditions were thought safe. Making their investigations nearly a century ago, when the science of microbiology was just getting started, they apparently did not search for microorganisms in the 200-foot drifts of cinder and ash. If they had done so, it is unlikely they would have found them any sooner after the eruption than did modern Icelandic scientists on Surtsey—almost six months after eruptions ceased.

The first scientific visitor to Krakatau after the eruption was a botanist who carefully went over the island in the autumn of 1883 but was unable to find a single living thing. A few months later, another investigator found the first recorded animal: a tiny red spiderling just arrived on its silken-thread balloon. Instinct had already led it to spin a web on the barren ground, despite the absence of prey.

The first summer after the eruption, a few little shoots of grass appeared. In 1886, botanists found thirty-four species of plants, ranging from blue-green algae, lichens, and fungi, through ferns, to fifteen different seed plants. After this, colonization by plants progressed steadily. In 1897, the total number of species had risen to 61, and in 1906 to 108. By 1928, some 276 species of plants of all kinds were present on the islands.

Nearly a century after the devastating Krakatau explosion, Rakata, the largest fragment (center), has made the best plant recovery. Anak Krakatau, which emerged in 1927 in the center of the old crater, is still nearly barren.

All the plants found by the first collectors belonged to varieties dispersed by winds or ocean currents. None, of course, could have grown from the rootstocks that existed before the holocaust and were now all dead—buried as deep as 260 feet beneath the new surface. The early plants were grasses, herbs, and flowering shrubs; low-growing forest plants could not get a footing until trees had taken hold and established the necessary dense thickets. Not until fourteen years after the eruption did plants grow from seeds carried by bats or birds, for until then the island had not attracted animals.

Eventually, complex communities began to develop. Sparse grasses gave way to steppe, then to dense, tangled stands of grass with a few ferns. Shrubs became established slowly, but as they increased, trees began to grow in the shelter they provided, creating shade for other plants.

As wind and sea carried plants and animals to its shores, Krakatau was slowly resettled

Some of the plants that arrived soon after the eruption flourished in surprising ways. *Cyrtandra*, normally a little ground-hugging herb, grew into large bushes with heavy, stout, erect stems. As this occurred, various epiphytes (air plants), including ferns and orchids, began growing abundantly in their branches. Then trees invaded and took over, reducing later generations of *Cyrtandra* to its usual subordinate role of small shrub. As a result, the epiphytes were again limited to their normal, rather sparse populations.

Well established today, less than a century after the great eruption, the plant communities of Verlaten, Lang, and especially Rakata show signs of becoming the climax forests that grow throughout the Malay Archipelago. These communities are permanent, of course, only while the powerful geological forces beneath them lie dormant.

Like the pioneering plants, the first animals to resettle Krakatau were those carried by wind and sea. Hordes of butterflies, as well as the first spider, starved to death. But fourteen years after the eruption, 132 species of birds and insects were found on the island. Fifty years after the event, the total number of animal inhabitants was still only about two-thirds of that normal for islands in the region.

Two weeks after the new island of Surtsey rose in 1963 from the sea south of Iceland, seabirds and seals came to rest on its still-warm shores. Undoubtedly, many kinds of birds stopped also at Krakatau within days after its eruptions subsided; unless they found food in the surrounding waters, they must have departed soon for the vegetated islands on either side of the Sunda Strait. Although their brief visits may have brought occasional seeds and spores, the birds probably contributed little to establishing an animal population, for any parasites they carried could not have survived without hosts. Eggs—of snails, insects, or fish—adhering to the feet of birds could not have developed on the barren land. Someday, long after the plants have achieved a normal equilibrium, the animals of the Krakatau islands may again be those of the archipelago.

The sequence of animal colonization of Krakatau is not well recorded. There was the spiderling found among the cinders, and scientists soon afterward observed the arrival of flying insects, which left or died. In 1908, no earthworms were found; twenty years later, a population of earthworms had become well established on Rakata, their forebears probably having been rafted on vegetative debris floating across the straits.

Land snails had been numerous on Krakatau before the eruption, but six years later the only snails were marine species living along the shore. Today, land snails of many types again flourish on Rakata, as do many species of ground insects, not all of them strong fliers.

The first land vertebrates to resettle Krakatau seem to have been a monitor lizard and a gecko. Monitors swim well, and the distances through the straits are short enough to be negotiated without difficulty. Gecko eggs, which are small, could have come on driftwood from nearby islands.

Forty years after the extinction of all life on Krakatau, almost 600 animal species had become established, including a python (also a good swimmer), a crocodile, lizards, more than two dozen resident species of birds, three bats, and a rat. Eighty per cent of the animal inhabitants on the fragmented island had wings, and 90 per cent were of species that had arrived by air, wings or no wings. Those animals that reached one of the islands and survived usually increased prolifically before settling down as part of a more balanced community. A species of lizard that arrived in the early 1920s was extraordinarily abundant by 1924; in 1928, one species of rat swarmed on Lang Island, where earlier there had been none.

Whether an immigrant animal took hold or not depended largely on the availability of food. Scavengers able to survive on dead plant and animal material, scarce as it may have been, probably were the first to become established. Second were the grazers, which fed on the increasing vegetation. Last came predators and parasites, subsisting directly on established animal life.

Krakatau illustrates how an island denuded of life is repopulated by a succession of accidental arrivals. Pioneers establish themselves and set the stage for more and more complex communities, until a stable climax is reached. The earliest arrivals may be unseen or scarcely noticeable: bacteria, tiny spiders, insects, fungi, lichens. But the pace of development soon quickens, and new life becomes more visible. Within eighteen months after the appearance of Surtsey in the far North Atlantic, seedlings of sea rocket were growing— one was sighted and a week later dozens more.

Life on Krakatau—1910

Twenty-seven years after an eruption erased all life on Krakatau, plants and animals were thriving once again. But since only chance decides which species will reach an island, and when, the variety of living things present was unique to that time and place. Spore-dispersed ferns dominated the plant life, small lizards and passing birds the animal population.

Life on Krakatau—1930

Twenty years later, seed plants whose seeds were inadvertently brought by birds, winds, or currents, had come into prominence, especially fig trees. Many larger animals, including such mammals as rats and bats, had arrived. The increased plant population supported a greater variety of birds and insects. Since 1930 many more species have settled on Krakatau.

The glowing walls of a Hawaiian lava tube indicate fierce heat—about 1500° F. Lava tubes form when the surface of a lava flow solidifies and the liquid lava drains off. Lava caves, open at one end, have the same origin.

Rough lava, with crevices, is more hospitable to new life than lava with a smooth surface

Despite shortcomings of early investigations, the pattern of Krakatau's resettlement is fairly clear. Far greater mystery surrounds the original arrival of life on the Hawaiian archipelago. This great chain of volcanic islands is thousands of miles from the nearest continent and hundreds of miles from other islands. Because the older islands of Hawaii appeared over ten million years ago, no accurate reconstruction of the sequence of plant and animal colonization is possible today. Fossils of land forms are extremely rare, and since men did not settle on the islands until 1000 years ago, not even an oral history of the early years is available.

Nevertheless, by observing what occurs on a new lava flow at high and low altitudes, and under water, scientists have learned much about the way colonization takes place. Such new flows are continually available on the large island of Hawaii, which is less than one million years old and still growing to the southeast. The 1960 eruption near the shore at Kapoho, a seaside village on the flanks of Kilauea, added 500 acres to Hawaii's land mass.

Most magma—the mantle substance lying deep within the Earth, composed of plastic rock and gases under great pressure—emerges as lava, which may flow in either of two distinct forms. The forms have been given Hawaiian names: *aa* lava is rough, chunky, and very dense; *pahoehoe* lava is smooth, billowing, or ropy. The kind of lava depends on the quantity and condition of gases in the rock as it begins to cool. Aa, with its multitude of crevices, encourages the relatively early establishment of life; pahoehoe, until it weakens and cracks, provides few places where roots can penetrate or insects hide.

The 1960 Kapoho eruption produced both kinds of lava, but especially vast fields of aa rubble. When the river of crumbling aa reached the sea, it spread out into a fan and poured down the submerged slope over old rocky shores and coral reefs. The lava fan created a new shoreline of rough and lifeless rocks and low cliffs that cooled quickly in the water.

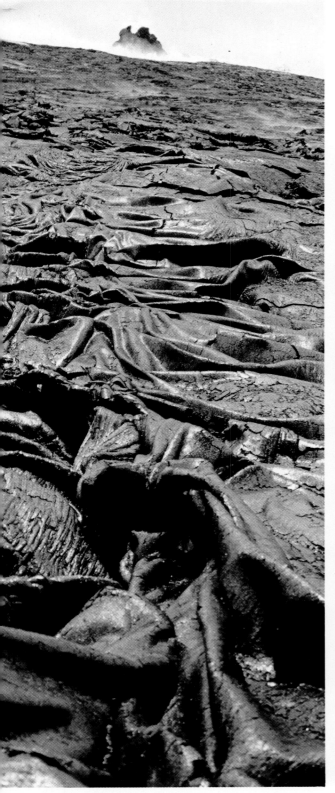

A field of pahoehoe lava stretches down the flank of a Hawaiian volcano. Pahoehoe is formed by fluid, fast-moving lava that cools with an unbroken surface. Liquid lava flowing beneath the plastic crust distorts it into folds.

Weathered and dun-colored, blocks of aa lava contrast with the billowy black surface of a more recent pahoehoe flow. Chunky aa is formed from slow-moving lava with a thick, brittle crust that crumbles as the mass moves.

Lush, Dramatic Beauty—Hawaii's Volcanic Heritage

Haleakala "crater" on Maui *was formed by erosion, not volcanic activity. Later, eruptions of Haleakala—active until 1790—formed lava and cinder cones.*

Millions of years ago, awesome forces along a Pacific floor rift began shaping the Hawaiian Islands, the chain that extends sixteen hundred miles from Midway to Hawaii. Powerful eruptions—like those that created Surtsey—spewed out billions of tons of lava and ash. Volcanic activity ran from west to east: Midway and its neighbors, their volcanos long extinct, have been eroded by the sea; Hawaii—the easternmost, newest, and biggest island—still has active volcanos. Over the ages living things have colonized the islands, and once-barren volcanic rock often supports dense vegetation. Erosion by wind and rain has worn deep ridges in the rock; rivers have cut channels.

Scarlet gingerlilies bloom near Rainbow Falls *on Hawaii. The rich volcanic soil of the Hawaiian Islands supports a profusion of plants, and the heavy rainfall feeds rivers, which leap a large number of waterfalls in their downward course.*

Rain-gouged grooves *scar the steep sides of Kauai's Napali Valley. On the gentler slopes such plants as the red-blossomed ohia lehua hold the soil in place.*

Surf and wind pounded black lava *to sand-size particles to create the beach at Kalapana, Hawaii.*

The steep cliffs and rugged depths *of Waimea Canyon on Kauai were created by several weathering forces: rainfall, streams diverted by cliffs, water seeping into rocks.*

Cascades of liquid fire in the 1959 Kilauea Iki eruption set a 1900-foot record for Hawaiian lava fountains. Varying in height, the eruption lasted for about five weeks and poured out nearly 160 million cubic yards of lava.

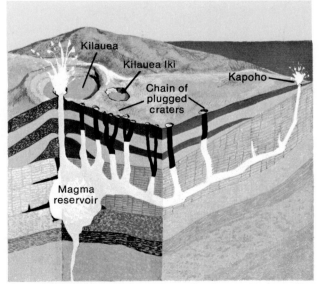

Kilauea

Kilauea Iki

Chain of plugged craters

Kapoho

Magma reservoir

Currently the most active volcano in the world, Hawaii's Kilauea has erupted frequently over the past several years. Its complicated structure includes a main crater and a chain of craters, connected by underground conduits.

At Kilauea Iki, biologists study the process of colonization in a living laboratory

The mountain above Kapoho is one of the most active volcanic zones in the world. Near the center of the island of Hawaii, Mauna Loa rises from a base 18,000 feet below sea level to a peak more than 13,000 feet above the surface. The large oval caldera (crater) at its summit is three miles long. Some 10,000 feet down from the summit, on the southeast slope, is Kilauea, currently more active than Mauna Loa itself, with a caldera 2½ miles long. Its magma chamber supplies not only Kilauea but also several smaller vents, including that of Kapoho. Most lava flows from this reservoir originate at or near Kilauea rather than near the shore as at Kapoho.

In 1959, a few months before the Kapoho eruption, volcanologists, who had detected a swelling of Kilauea, were expecting an eruption from its fire pit, Halemaumau. Instead, Kilauea Iki, a smaller adjacent crater, began one of the most dramatic displays in Hawaiian history. Incandescent fountains of spatter, ash, and cinders rose nearly 2000 feet into the air, where trade winds caught and blew them as far as two miles away. When the eruption subsided, the floor of Kilauea Iki hardened into a crust of massive pahoehoe.

Immediately thereafter, scientists began studying the lava, the enormous cinder cone just downwind of the crater, and all the regions of diminished fallout within a two-square-mile area, which ended where ash was only an inch deep. These investigations, mostly by Dr. Garrett Smathers of the National Park Service, are among the most thorough ever undertaken. They concentrated on the development of soils in which life gradually appears, and on the nature and interaction of that life, both plant and animal.

On bare continental granite, schist, and other ancient surfaces, hardy lichens are the first pioneers. This is not necessarily the case on ejected volcanic materials, which may contain many basic plant nutrients and thus be able to support less tolerant plants. The first plants to become established on the floor of Kilauea Iki crater were certain algae (mostly blue-green algae). Mosses followed, then a native fern, and, finally, hardy native Hawaiian seed plants. Although lichens did appear in the early stages, they did not seem to

The pahoehoe lava floor of Kilauea Iki crater appears lifeless ten years after an eruption, contrasting with the lushly
vegetated rim. Since pahoehoe resists weathering, it is
slow to become soil in which plants can grow.

A closeup view of Kilauea Iki's floor shows tiny ferns
growing in a crack in the mineral-rich lava. As the pioneer
plants die, their remains add to the organic debris collected in cracks, and help other plants take root.

play a substantial role in helping other plants to
get started. The ferns, especially sword fern and
two or three others, were able to begin growing
soon after lava or cinders cooled; in one spot,
tiny forms of some of these ferns appeared only
six weeks after the eruption.

A visitor to Kilauea Iki today sees light yellow
and white lines and spots on the massive pahoehoe lava crust where hot steam rising from cracks
has altered the basic composition of the basalt,
principally through oxidation. Here new plant life
is most prolific, and blue-green algae are able to
invade such fumaroles. As the crater cools, many
kinds of more highly developed pioneer plants
appear. The invasion of vegetation from the margins is slow, for the surface at the center—at
170° F.—is still too warm for any but the simplest
life. Not only does the black lava absorb the sun's
heat, but temperatures only eighty feet beneath
the crust still run around 2000° F.

The same succession of pioneer plants occurs
on the cinder cone. Steam escapes through the

cone's structure of loose material, especially
from the great cracks caused by settling. As the
emerging gas becomes mostly hot water, chemical
alteration of the loose rocks and cinders proceeds
more rapidly, permitting the growth of ferns,
mosses, and lichens. They grow out of new and
temporary crevices, especially where the cinders
are compacted into almost solid rock walls. A little farther away, well down the slope of the cinder cone, seed plants have begun to take hold.

Other craters nearby that have not erupted for
a century or more show small trees spaced out
across their floors, almost as in a well-planned
orchard. In cooling, the floor surfaces cracked in
a network of polygons, each crevice becoming a
place for lava to alter into more usable soils and
for organic matter to collect. With the trees
spaced out as they are, competition between individual plants is practically absent. Indeed, in
the dry lava and cinder deposits of the Kilauea
region, there seems to be little or no competition
among the uncrowded plant and animal species.

An ohia lehua tree burned by a lava flow often manages to survive. Even a dead tree may play a role in life's renewal

Because the Hawaiian Islands have been volcanic from their very beginning, many of the first plants to invade new surfaces are hardy native species already adapted to volcanic soils. Nonnative plants often follow soon after and may flourish for a while, but in the long run some of them seem to lose their vigor and are replaced by native forms.

The trees endemic to the Hawaiian Islands are extremely durable. After an eruption, the ohia lehua tree, unless it was completely buried by a shower of burning cinders, usually makes a remarkable recovery. If a tree's conducting tissues on the side toward the volcano were destroyed, new shoots often appear on the sheltered side and take over the production of food for the entire tree. Another whole root system grows just beneath the new surface, which may be several feet above the old, and often this is enough to ensure survival. The injured tree grows at a phenomenal rate, soon covering over the burned side and sometimes in as little as six years nearly doubling its circumference. Those trees or shrubs that remain stunted invariably produce heavy crops of fruits and seeds. Plant hormones undoubtedly induce both the active growth and the seed production as a reply to the holocaust just experienced.

Trees killed in an eruption may contribute in several ways to the renewal of life. New lava and cinders contain nearly all basic plant nutrients, but they lack one nutrient necessary for life: nitrates, which normally take some time to accumulate from dead organic material and bird wastes. Where lava has streamed over a forest, however, the burning of trees may have intro-

An ohia lehua tree catches fire as hot lava flows past it. The ohia lehua, native to Hawaii, has remarkable powers of recovery; if it is burned on one side only, shoots on the other side soon cover over the burned area.

duced an appreciable amount of nitrogen into the volcanic materials, enabling plants to invade such an area more quickly than would otherwise be possible.

If a burned tree remains standing, it serves as a waterspout for rain and condensed fog, and invading plants cluster thickly at the foot of the stark skeleton. Ferns, mosses, and other plants may grow under the length of a fallen tree, especially at points where water drips on rainy or damp days. If a tree is completely incinerated, a tubular lava mold may be left standing, the inner cavity—with its shade, moisture, and collected nutrients—often sprouting a luxuriant growth of ferns and other plants.

In the short time that has elapsed since the 1959 eruption, only small forms of animal life have recolonized Kilauea Iki. Among the earliest settlers were ciliated one-celled protozoans, which appeared in the water-holding vesicles of porous lava and cinders along with their food plants, bacteria and blue-green algae. As at Krakatau (and Surtsey), the first visible terrestrial animals were tiny spiders of the orb-web group. Ballooned to the region as airborne spiderlings, they immediately constructed webs, which caught newly arrived flies and organic matter blown across the wasteland by trade winds.

Land snails from unaffected neighboring terrain are now found on the lava around the periphery of Kilauea Iki. Large wolf spiders live in the loose cinder deposits, where they hunt on the surface at night. During the day, they seek moisture and protection inches down in the loose material. Here they may come across food in the form of mites, isopod crustaceans, small insects such as springtails, and other creatures. Many of these smaller animals feed upon the algae and fungi that grow an inch or two beneath the rough cinders.

The rewards of observing plant and animal recolonization of volcanic terrain exceed those of simply seeing what appears first. The emergence of materials from deep within the Earth, their slow chemical alteration into soils capable of supporting life, and the appearance of bacteria and blue-green algae are events that resemble those of the primordial Earth. To study the ways highly developed plants and animals invade and settle a totally new and barren environment is to be struck anew by the awesome persistence of life.

Scientists have only inexact estimates of the number of volcanic islands that have existed in

A scarlet-flowered ohia lehua seedling sprouts at the base of a dead ohia lehua. Water seeps from a ''reservoir'' in the hollow trunk, which also gives shade, and the burned tree's ashes supply nutrients for plant growth.

the past, and an incomplete understanding of how they were populated and used as stepping-stones for the dispersal of life to other islands. As man's knowledge is limited, so is his sense of history and time. Man tends to think of himself as at the end of a series of events, when more likely he is somewhere in the middle.

It seems evident that the Earth is far from finished. The continents continue to drift and to create new stresses and weaknesses. Volcanologists see persisting signs of opening rifts, submarine volcanism, and vast alterations of the sea floor. Stretching into the future are millennia of continuing volcanic events that will bring new islands rising from the oceans. As they emerge and cool, these islands of the future will be populated by plants and animals according to the same means of dispersal, colonization, and succession that have existed through past ages.

Standing at this moment of time, man may look in either direction, wondering what lived on ancient guyots now drowned a thousand feet under the sea, and what will take hold and grow on some garden island a million, or ten million, years from now. He may wonder, too, whether men will still be here to see the dramatic events of the future. Will they watch in awe as new islands thunder up from the deeps, and as other organisms find new homes in which to settle and evolve?

The Builders of Islands

Not all tropical islands are the direct products of geological forces.
Billions of tiny sea organisms build islands of coral, and a single seedling in
shallow waters may mark the beginnings of a mangrove islet

Some islands separate from continents, some roar up out of the depths as volcanos, and others are created slowly and quietly by living island builders: corals, coralline algae, and mangroves. Thousands of years ago in the western Pacific, Micronesian and Polynesian voyagers, possibly impelled both by population pressures and by their questing spirit of exploration, sought out such islands. In recent centuries, island folklore, British Admiralty reports, literary narratives, and Hollywood films have intrigued Western man, luring him to the South Pacific with images of high, cloud-wreathed volcanic islands and coral atolls lying low in the dark-blue tropical ocean.

Dissimilar as they are, volcanic islands and coral atolls owe their origin to the same violent forces arising from the Earth's interior. Lying beneath nearly every atoll, serving as its foundation, is an ancient, hidden volcano. An atoll remains above the surface of the sea, however, only through the growth over thousands of years of the most complex assemblage of organisms known: a living coral reef.

Cup coral polyps extend food-gathering tentacles. With cups about a third of an inch across, these are among the largest of the reef-building corals. Over thousands of years the limestone skeletons of countless tiny polyps accumulate to form mighty coral reefs and islands in tropical waters.

An atoll is a coral island, or a chain of coral islets, partly or wholly encircling a shallow lagoon. Each islet is the raised part of a ring-shaped reef formed primarily by the skeletons of innumerable tiny animals living and dead, called stony corals. Dozens or even hundreds of species of such corals may participate in building the reef through long ages.

The fertilized eggs of reef-building corals grow into free-swimming, pear-shaped larvae, the largest about one–twenty-fifth of an inch long. A larva settles onto a solid surface, broad mouth end up, and cements its narrow base in place. It secretes a limestone cup around itself, and spends the rest of its life in this external skeleton. The soft part of the animal within the skeleton, called a polyp, seldom reaches more than one-third of an inch in size. Surrounding the mouth are delicate food-gathering tentacles that collect plankton from the water.

Like many other simple animals, corals reproduce in more than one way. New coral colonies are started by sexual reproduction, but old colonies extend themselves both upward and outward through a completely different method.

The polyp sends out little branchlike buds, and these grow into other polyps that remain attached to the parent. As time goes on, each new polyp buds in turn, and a closely knit community of corals develops. The shape of the community depends upon the particular species.

As a volcanic island sinks into the sea, its reef of living coral grows upward to form an atoll

Corals are not the only reef builders. In some parts of the reef, coralline algae—simple marine plants—may contribute at least as much to the structure by depositing calcium compounds in dense fronds or heavy, encrusting mats. Elsewhere on a reef, the tiny skeletons of one-celled animals called foraminiferans may make up most of its bulk. Tube worms, moss animals, and mollusks also contribute substantially to reef structure since they too have hard skeletons.

The creation of an atoll begins soon after a volcanic island rises above warm tropical seas. Coral larvae swimming in the plankton settle on the flanks of the island, where the polyps form colonies. Upon the limestone skeletons of old corals, a fringing reef is built over the years. Hugging the island closely, the reef grows outward from the shoreline, its leading edge harboring the densest and most varied populations of coral, as sand and silt fill the old reef area left behind. By making waves break far out from shore, the developing reef helps to preserve the island from erosion. Since the reef also grows upward, rising near enough to the surface to be exposed at low tide, it effectively increases the area of the island. It makes a direct contribution to the shore when storm waves tear off chunks of coral and cast them upon the beach, or when the sea level lowers over long periods of time and wide limestone benches become exposed.

If the sea floor on which the huge conical mountain rests begins to subside, the peak that forms the island, together with all the living things on it, sinks also. This process continues for hundreds of thousands of years, and if the

How a Coral Atoll Develops

Living coral grows in warm, shallow waters, forming reefs on the fringes of land masses. According to Darwin's generally accepted hypothesis, atolls begin to form after coral encircles the slopes of a sinking volcanic island.

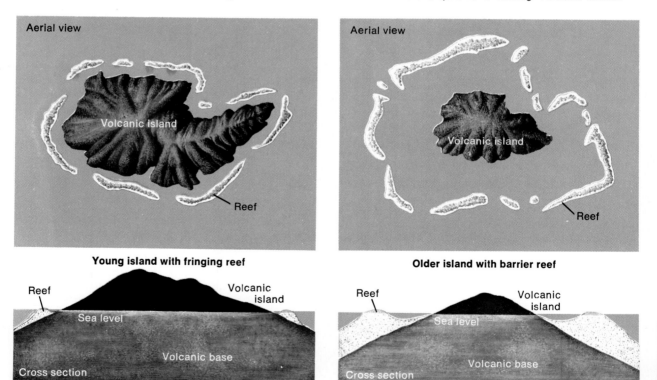

Young island with fringing reef

A fringing reef, hugging the shoreline of a volcanic island, is the first step in the slow formation of any coral atoll.

Older island with barrier reef

If the sea floor drops, the island sinks. Whenever this takes place slowly, the near-surface coral can continue growing.

descent is gradual enough, coral growing upward about an inch a year can keep pace. The distance between the shore and the reef slowly widens. Meanwhile, weather and waves work their destruction upon the sinking peak of the basaltic mountain. Finally, its last vestiges disappear from the center of the ring-shaped reef, and coral and coralline algae soon grow in the vacated area. The reef has now become an atoll, and the water-filled basin inside it is called a lagoon.

Under favorable circumstances, as the mountain continues to sink, the coral colonies grow ever upward to maintain the atoll. That circumstances have not always been favorable is shown by the numerous flat-topped guyots with coral crowns: They obviously sank faster than the corals could grow to the surface.

Hawaii's volcanic island of Oahu, on which Honolulu is situated, demonstrates the disparities between an island and the level of its associated reef. An ancient drowned reef, now many miles southwest of Honolulu, once grew on the flanks of the island. In the last several million years, however, Oahu has sunk over 1500 feet, carrying with it the reef, which was unable to grow fast enough to remain at the surface. Measurements taken at Honolulu's pleasure beach, Waikiki, show that the region is still sinking, but some attribute this to the crowded forest of huge hotels growing unabated!

Volcanos are rarely perfectly conical. Since those that rise from the sea are often irregular, the fringing reefs, which follow the outline of the shores, do not form perfect circles in the sea. As an island sinks and the reef grows on, becoming a barrier reef far out from shore, the developing atoll may take on any shape from roughly circular to elongate. It may be crescent-shaped if the reef did not completely surround the island. Because of differences in winds and waves, an atoll rarely has above-surface islets all around it; a submerged reef usually completes the ring.

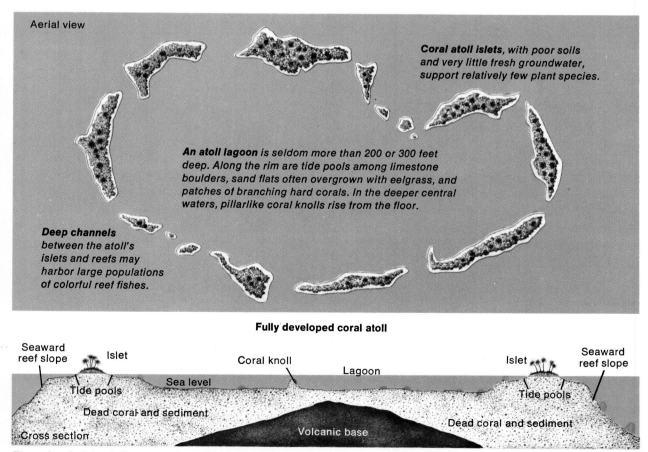

Aerial view

Coral atoll islets, with poor soils and very little fresh groundwater, support relatively few plant species.

An atoll lagoon is seldom more than 200 or 300 feet deep. Along the rim are tide pools among limestone boulders, sand flats often overgrown with eelgrass, and patches of branching hard corals. In the deeper central waters, pillarlike coral knolls rise from the floor.

Deep channels between the atoll's islets and reefs may harbor large populations of colorful reef fishes.

Fully developed coral atoll

Seaward reef slope — Islet — Tide pools — Sea level — Coral knoll — Lagoon — Dead coral and sediment — Cross section — Volcanic base — Dead coral and sediment — Islet — Tide pools — Seaward reef slope

The volcanic island disappears beneath the surface. The reef, now an atoll, continues to grow; waves and wind change it further, bringing debris to fill the lagoon, or eroding the coral. And if the sea floor drops, the atoll may be drowned.

Fishes of the Coral Atoll Reef

The seaward side of an atoll presents a host of environments for fishes, from shallow tide pools to intermediate zones to the sea floor where rays and burrowing fishes lurk. Fish habits and defenses differ: Surgeonfishes and butterfly fishes are active during the day; moray eels and soldierfishes hunt at night. In coral crevices, blennies and damselfishes hide from predators such as groupers; triggerfishes lock dorsal spines to wedge themselves in holes. Pufferfishes inflate themselves to avoid being eaten; scorpion fishes blend with the background of coral and other immobile invertebrates to elude hunters. Some fishes flaunt bright colors, advertising formidable defenses such as the sharp blades of a surgeonfish or the distasteful flesh of a Picasso fish. The dark-above, light-below camouflage of such larger predators as the barracudas helps them to avoid alerting their wary prey.

Key to Fishes Shown on Reef

1. Blenny	10. Unicorn fish	19. Pufferfish	28. Grouper
2. Damselfish	11. Imperial angelfish	20. Moorish idol	29. Garden eel
3. Barred surgeonfish	12. Undulate triggerfish	21. Scorpion fish	30. Barracuda
4. Sergeant major	13. Butterfly fish	22. Blue-and-yellow snapper	31. Manta ray
5. Young mullet	14. Parrotfish	23. Lionfish	32. *Anthias*
6. White-breasted surgeonfish	15. Royal angelfish	24. Soldierfish	33. Blue triggerfish
7. Moray eel	16. Coral cod	25. Nurse shark	34. Silverside
8. Picasso fish	17. Boxfish	26. Stingray	35. Horse mackerel
9. Wrasse	18. Pennant coral fish	27. Jawfish	36. White-tipped shark

The steep seaward slope of an atoll reef is an eerie world of beauty and danger

A coral atoll has several major zones both above and below the water surface, and each zone has its own association of plants and animals. At the same time, every atoll and reef in the world is different from all others.

The outer seaward slope of an atoll is often precipitous, plunging steeply toward the supporting mountain far below. Treelike branching soft corals, called gorgonians, grow far down the slope, but they are not involved in building the reef. A small base anchors each gorgonian to the limestone slope; the rest of the coral extends far out into the dim water in a pattern of thin, branching whips that sway in the gentle currents. As live reef-forming corals approach their limit in the dim waters 200 feet down, their numbers are greatly diminished.

The seaward slope is where the great predators lurk. Tuna, sharks, jacks, and barracudas constantly patrol the shadowed rise, and huge sea basses peer out from dark caverns in the coral wall. Closer to the surface, tangs, or surgeon-fishes, triggerfishes, and unicorn fishes swim in the clear blue water; within the confines of coral formations, smaller fishes abound. Wrasses, blennies, and gobies dart over the entire face of the slope in the brighter water.

The slope of an atoll is cut in many places by numerous deep, narrow canyons, leaving spurs of coral extending outward between them. The grooves, which go all the way up into the shallow tide pool zone, shelter a wide variety of life. Rock-hugging coralline algae may be abundant enough to color the slopes and ridges pink and violet. The channel walls abound with sponges, cowries, chitons, embedded clams, and a multitude of active rock crabs, hermit crabs, and shrimps. Large purple slate urchins, each with its own associated species of purple shrimp living among its heavy spines, conspicuously occupy indented ledges.

Toward the upper end of a groove, the surge of waves is strong, and the environment is good for hawkfishes, tangs, parrotfishes, and many others, which move in toward the shoreline when the tide rises. Nocturnal squirrelfishes hide deep in the most shadowed recesses.

Scuba divers explore the precipitous seaward face of a Palauan atoll in the south Pacific. Sprouting from the reef's craggy surface are gorgonians, fan-shaped corals. Their flexible bodies contribute little to the reef.

Blue freckles on a coral cod's scarlet skin may camouflage the fish against a coral background. Coral cod, also known as coral trout, frequent reefs north of the Tropic of Capricorn, from the Pacific Ocean to the Red Sea. These brightly colored fish grow to a length of eighteen inches.

Cardinal fish shelter among the spines of a sea urchin. The sea urchin can move its ball-and-socket spines into a clump; the fish then move in and remove parasites from exposed skin. In turn, the urchin's spines, needle-sharp and highly venomous, protect the fish from predators.

Green and pink sea squirts encrust a yellow sponge under a ledge in a reef channel of a southwest Pacific island. Currents that ebb and flow through the channel carry ample nutrients for a richly varied community of fixed feeders.

Pale blue sea squirts flourish in the warm waters of the Great Barrier Reef. Growing among them are light green sponges. Both the sea squirts and the far more primitive sponges filter food particles from the water.

Every nook and cranny of the seaward atoll reef wall teems with life

The ridges between the deep grooves are thickly capped with coralline algae building upon a coral foundation, the whole mass cemented together by the algae and by the fused skeletons of one-celled foraminiferans. Live corals look as though they had burst up through the clutter of organisms, adding greater height and width to the entire reef. Colorful sponges and sea squirts live here in profusion, as do many non-stony algae. Vast numbers of worms, snails, crustaceans, and small fishes seek out and occupy the narrower cavities in the coralline growth. The larger apertures in the stony corals are occupied by proportionately larger forms. Spiny lobsters, slipper lobsters, and crabs walk slowly over the surface, picking up live food or organic matter.

To a diver, this is a noisy place because of the huge populations of pistol or snapping shrimp.

A pair of cuttlefish—mollusks related to octopuses—mates in shallow reef waters. During the breeding season the colors of both sexes become brighter, and one of the male's arms becomes specially modified to transfer sperm to the female.

Each shrimp has one claw consisting of a hinged, movable finger with a peg and immovable palm containing a socket; as the peg snaps into the water-filled socket, there is a sharp cracking sound, which can stun small fishes. Whether or not the shrimp actually uses this method to catch prey biologists have by no means settled. These thousands of little shrimps hidden away in the reef produce an endless series of tiny firecracker-like explosions, a din greatly amplified whenever their home is disturbed.

In cavities between limestone chunks, where soft corals grow from a common rootlike mass, fragile, colorful flatworms move across the surface like brilliant leaves. Many other kinds of less conspicuous worms are here also. Ribbon worms lie twisted together in narrow cracks; stout peanut worms remain out of sight beneath loose chunks of coral or under sand accumulated in depressions. Segmented parchment worms live in U-shaped burrows within the sand, while other segmented worms lie secure in limy tubes of their own construction. Barnacles and tiny, branching, varicolored moss animals grow wherever they can secure a footing on the crowded floor.

A two-inch banded coral shrimp emerges from its crevice in a New Hebrides reef, near a clinging starfish. These shrimps eat parasites that they pick from the bodies of fishes, which do not attack them when they approach.

Concealment and camouflage help small, slow-moving tide pool dwellers to survive

Where a reef rises close to the surface and is exposed at low tide, the pools formed in depressions harbor large concentrations of small plants and animals. Each time the tide floods in, the depressions become part of the sea, well flushed by wave action. As the water level falls again, they are isolated and become a little more difficult to live in; a pool less than twelve feet across is too hot to support much. High water temperature is not in itself very dangerous to heat-tolerant reef life, but warm water contains less oxygen than cool water. If a pool cannot produce enough of this vital gas through the activity of its algae, the animal population diminishes.

The walls of a tide pool may be honeycombed by black or brown sea urchins that generation after generation excavate deep, round holes in the limestone. Sometimes they are so deeply ensconced in old holes that their outermost spines barely extend past the mouth of the cavity; no matter how violent a storm wave, they remain

Covered with bright, ruffled breathing organs and lacking a shell, this reef sea slug would appear to be highly vulnerable. Its flesh has an unpleasant taste, however, and its conspicuous coloration may actually warn off predators.

secure unless a whole section of coral is torn loose. Vacated holes may be occupied anew by other urchins, cowries, blennies, and additional small animals seeking relief from waves.

Chunks of coral lying loose on the bottom of a pool hide long-limbed brittle stars, burrowing snails, worms, and many other creatures. Under a rock are hordes of fast and slow animals, as well as those that are fixed in place and cannot move at all. Sausagelike objects that resemble rocks are actually large sea cucumbers slowly creeping across the pool floor. In the anal portion of the body of such a sea cucumber may live an elongated pearlfish that emerges only to feed, after which it dashes back to the security of its living cave.

Small sea anemones may decorate the sides and crevices of a tide pool, their delicate tentacles contrasting with the hard, enameled encrustations of purplish coralline algae. Feathery hydroids stand out like tiny bushes.

A tide pool, like a reef, has zones, each preferred by its various inhabitants. Coralline algae and small sea anemones are close to the surface, where crabs, colored exactly like the coralline patina, are also found. Red-eyed rock crabs run over the upper levels of the walls of the pool.

Below this zone, round, short-spined sea urchins cover themselves with algae and bits of shell debris, successfully disguising their forms. Toward the bottom, along the pitted walls, black long-spined sea urchins wave their venomous needles, pointing as many as possible at any intruder; instead of conventional eyes, they possess light-sensitive cells that respond to shadows and movement. Peacock worms encrust lower sections of the walls, and small clumps of living coral protrude where there is room.

Part way down the side of the tide pool, small knobs stud the limestone, each covered by coralline algae except for the wavy line running through the center, which indicates the knob is an almost perfectly disguised rock clam. Where bushy, non-stony seaweeds hang down into the quiet pool, sea slugs may be found in quantity, the leaflike respiratory projections along their backs wonderfully mimicking the fronds of seaweed. Small crustaceans and browsing snails of many kinds also gather here. Under the projecting ledges of coral, brilliantly colored sea squirts and sponges cluster tightly, leaving no area of limestone uncovered. Often such a stony ceiling holds mirror-bright bubbles of air trapped when waves surged and broke overhead.

Finger and staghorn corals carpet the floor of this tide pool. A giant clam's fleshy mantle, colored blue-green by algae tenants, is just visible. Only hardy coral species can survive in the brightly-lighted, turbulent environment of a tide pool.

Protected from more active predators, colorful communities of encrusting animals and plants live beneath seemingly dead coral fragments in tidepools. This fragment shelters a yellow sea squirt, a red starfish, algae, and bryozoans.

On the sunlit sandy bottom of a South Pacific lagoon, colorful fishes swim among outcroppings of staghorn cora

In the calm, clear waters of a coral atoll's central lagoon, reef life is abundant

On the lagoon side of an atoll islet, the shore slopes down through several successive zones to the floor of the enclosed basin. The distribution of plants and animals in each zone differs somewhat from that on the seaward side, primarily because there is no strong wave action. The lagoon waterline, which rises and falls with the tides, harbors swarms of rock crabs, hermit crabs, and snails. The slow-moving snails escape the greater heat of this sheltered shore by burying themselves deep beneath the coral rubble. Where the limestone has become finely pulverized coral sand, it offers a favorable habitat for burrowing bivalve mollusks, worms, shrimps, and other creatures. Certain kinds of long, delicate sea cucumbers lie in profusion upon the sandy bottom. Their translucent red or orange bodies, perhaps two or three feet long, terminate in finely branched tentacles that sweep the floor for food particles lying in the sand.

Tide pools in the lagoon reef may be even more heavily populated than those on the sea side, but usually with a smaller and different variety of animals because of the quieter, warmer water. Representatives of the world's only marine insects, water striders, which range far out to sea, are often found here, skating across the still water in search of living and dead animal food trapped in the surface film, exactly as their freshwater relatives do on ponds.

Where sand stretches out into shallow portions of the lagoon, conditions permit the establishment of turtle grass, one of the marine seed plants found not only in the Pacific but in extensive beds off the Florida Keys. The detritus-laden sand in which it grows, as well as the blades of the grass itself, provides a habitat for a unique community of animals and microscopic attaching plants.

On the downward slope of the lagoon bottom, corals become abundant, often assuming more elaborate forms in the absence of heavy wave action. As on the seaward side of the atoll, no one coral species dominates. Many branching corals in weird and beautiful shapes grow on the sloping floor—some slender, tapering, and often intertwined, others heavy and massive. Lower down are the solid, rounded corals that occupy a great

e fishes include a gaily striped royal angelfish, two plainer Gaimard's rainbowfish, and two kinds of wrasses.

deal of space but do not rise high into the water. Some corals look like thin sheets; others curve outward as shelves. The variety seems endless. Lying loose in depressions are the mushroomlike, notched disks of giant solitary polyps that produce ridge skeletons several inches in diameter.

Amid the corals are all the various members of a reef community: giant clams, black-spined sea urchins, beautiful but dangerous cone shells with hidden, venomous, harpoonlike teeth, worms that form the staple food of the cones, handsome cowries, a miscellany of sedentary clams, and, of course, crabs, shrimps, tube worms, and a multitude of less conspicuous creatures. A pair of small *Trapezia* crabs living deep within each coral head is quite invisible unless the head is cracked open.

A lagoon may be up to 300 feet deep, the water a clear luminous blue-green except when wind stirs the fine sand. Usually studding the lagoon floor are many pillarlike knolls or patch reefs, which rise nearly to the surface. These are constructed mostly of corals; but close to the surface, where sunlight is intense, coralline algae make a contribution. Eniwetok has over 2000 such knolls; even a much smaller atoll may produce hundreds.

A knoll is a great towering city of marine life, ecologically isolated from others rising mistily

through the water 50 or 100 feet away. The walls, often almost vertical, support an enormous assemblage of living things. The corals are of many kinds, including massive brackets of *Porites* extending outward and intermixing with long arms of fragile staghorn. Each knoll has its own population of brightly colored reef fishes that hover nearby, ready to dive into the protective crevices of the coral formations or to defend their own small territories on the face of the wall. At times, the large shapes of open-sea predators appear in the lagoon: a shark, manta ray, eagle ray, or barracuda.

With so much growth and deposition in a lagoon, the enclosed body of water in many atolls becomes increasingly shallow, even to the extent of disappearing altogether. Jarvis and Baker islands are examples of a "pancake" atoll—a perfectly flat, dry, saucerlike island, with a slightly raised rim of sand and rubble heaped up by wave action. There are also, of course, many intermediate atolls with greatly reduced lagoons that have lost all connection with the sea. In such lagoons, the water may be excessively salty because of evaporation, or nearly fresh as a result of recent rainfall; in either instance, typical lagoon life is absent or severely reduced.

Coconut palms

Casuarina

Barringtonia

Messerschmidia

Guettarda

Scaevola

Lepturus

Blue-tailed skink

Lovegrass

Ocean

Beach morning glories

The female green turtle lumbers onto the atoll, lays her eggs, and returns to the sea. Males never come ashore.

Hermit crabs are residen of the sea during the earliest stages of their liv

Only hardy plants can establish a firm hold on the seaward shore of an atoll, splashed with salt spray and buffeted by win

Coral atolls harbor far fewer plant and animal species than tropical volcanic islands

Above sea level, the living things of little coral islets are highly variable. In the composition of their plant and animal communities, these low sandy and rocky islands have been affected by the same vagaries of dispersal as all other islands.

The soil of newly emerged volcanic islands is rich in a variety of inorganic nutrients for plant growth, but the basic limestone of a coral islet limits atoll vegetation to a comparatively few species. Since the phosphates and nitrates important to plant growth are in low supply and are slow to accumulate, an islet must be colonized by hardy pioneer plants such as those able to extract nitrogen from the air through the help of specialized bacteria inhabiting their tissues.

Coral sand and rubble, moreover, cannot support surface water. In a rainstorm, water immediately filters downward, coming to rest at a level only a little above that of the sea. A plant must have long roots to reach this water, which remains fresh only if the islet is broad enough to prevent contamination by salt water.

Since fresh water dissolves limestone, rainwater sometimes changes an atoll's structure. Over a period of time, the islet may develop a central depression as limestone is dissolved. Here, the lower surface of the ground is closer to the water table, and breadfruit and food plants of the taro family are able to flourish.

Because of few nutrients, dryness, or salinity—temporary or chronic—vegetation on atolls may at times show signs of food deficiencies: lessened fruit production, stunted growth, pale leaves. Handicapped by an unstable environment, atolls are generally incapable of supporting a wide variety of vegetation. Depending on their size and the amount of annual rainfall, islets in the South Pacific may harbor from 2 or 3 to 100 plant species, a far cry from the thousands found on typical volcanic islands.

Plants are carried to an atoll, as to any island, by prevailing winds, cyclones and typhoons, ocean currents, birds, or man. Some of the plants that float in by sea—especially the low-lying strand plants that carpet the upper beach of an atoll—have seeds so remarkably resistant to salt water that they can drift along in a current for four or

Coconut palms

Pisonia

Pandanus

Breadfruit

Lagoon

Morinda

e fern Nephrolepis *may*
w directly on the ground,
on tree trunks and stumps.

Brought to coral atolls as
stowaways, destructive black
rats often nest in palms.

The coconut crab, which can
climb trees and open cracked
nuts, weighs up to six pounds.

A shrub of the drier
atolls, Suriana grows just
outside the reach of high tide.

re varied and abundant vegetation grows in the relatively protected island interior and sometimes extends to the lagoon shore.

five months without very significant damage.

The most famous of all floating seeds, the coconut, may owe its wide distribution to man, since it is probably unable to survive long sea journeys. If it is introduced to one of a group of coral islets, however, it will eventually spread to the others by floating. Most atolls today show a silhouette of coconut palms growing wild or cultivated purposely for copra, from which coconut oil is extracted for commercial use.

Plants usually first touch land on the windward side of an islet, but this is the most difficult place for them to become established. Only those able to withstand continuous salt spray can live here, such as *Morinda* (a member of the coffee family), *Scaevola*, tree heliotropes, beach morning glory, and climbing *Wedelia* shrubs.

It is not known what the vegetation of atolls was like before the arrival of man on these islets 1000 to 2000 years ago. Because atolls promised little in the way of food, migrating Polynesians and Micronesians brought with them not only coconuts but breadfruit, taros, bananas, sweet potatoes, and other useful plants. After the Pacific was opened to the Western world, Europeans, Orientals, and returning islanders brought with them all kinds of ornamental and food plants.

On only a few of the very small uninhabited atolls do original scrub forests still exist nearly unchanged. Often these are dominated by some of the most ubiquitous and successful atoll trees: *Pisonia*, tree heliotropes, screw "pines" (or pandanus), and others. Most of these plants are distributed throughout the South Pacific. *Pisonia*, whose sticky, elongated fruits have been carried great distances by boobies and other seabirds, ranges from the Indian Ocean to the volcanic island of Pitcairn, and often grows 100 feet tall.

Tree heliotropes characteristically fringe atolls with giant plants occasionally up to sixty feet tall, sometimes in a forest, sometimes individually. On low, dry islets, *Cordia*, only twenty feet high, can form an extraordinarily dense forest thicket, successfully preventing the growth of other plants. At one time, *Ochrosia* forests may have been dominant on many atolls in moist climates; today, few of these slender trees with their spoke-like branches grow on the islets that man has cleared and settled.

Of course, many atolls lack these large trees. Their vegetation consists of small plants such as mallow scrub, which produces attractive yellow flowers that temporarily decorate the arid islets with bright patches of color.

Clusters of fruit bats hang by their feet from roosting trees during the day. At dusk they fly to fruit trees, where they squeeze juice from the fruit and discard seeds and pulp. While they digest their meals they rest at the feeding trees. Flying foxes, as these little mammals are also called, often eat flowers as well as fruits.

A limited variety of animals inhabits atolls, but each species present may produce large populations

Because of their ancient, mid-oceanic origins, most atolls are far from continental sources of supply for animals as well as for plants. They harbor bats, especially the fruit bats, introduced land mammals, and possibly introduced amphibians. The variety of all animals is severely restricted. Insects, scorpions, centipedes, and crabs are usually present, as are a few kinds of skinks and geckos—all animals with relatively impervious skins that withstand the effects of salt spray during voyages on rafts of vegetation. Great marine turtles—green, loggerhead, or hawksbill— may surface offshore, the females lumbering onto coral beaches to lay eggs during breeding season in the summer.

The parent volcanic island of an atoll may once have been heavily populated, but as the island sank and the surrounding reef grew upward from its crown, few if any of its animals could have made even a slow transition; most of them must have starved or been unable to breed. Early volcanic islands probably supported skinks and geckos, but most species of these lizards now present on atolls no doubt arrived much later on natural rafts or aboard the canoes of early voyagers. That they are almost identical over vast reaches of the Pacific suggests a recent arrival.

The same supposition may be true for many kinds of insects, for rarely is an insect species peculiar to one atoll; rather, it is usually distributed widely over a number of atolls. Insects, despite their large number of species—more than those of the rest of the world's animals combined —may be represented on Pacific atolls by fewer than 2000 species altogether, and by only a fraction of that number on any one atoll. Because the small variety of insects meant fewer competitors, the species that did establish themselves often multiplied prodigiously. Similar circumstances explain the small number of varieties, but large populations, of land snails, lizards, and other forms of native atoll animal life.

Other than birds, the most conspicuous animals on atolls are crabs. On many atolls, the dominant crustaceans are hermit crabs and land crabs, with far fewer of the large coconut crabs. Along temperate shores, hermit crabs live in the water and cannot stand exposure, but in the tropics some of them spend much of their time either on the beach or far inland in scrub or forest. The abandoned snail shells that hermit crabs inhabit protect them against both predators and the searing heat of midday, when they often rest quietly in the shade of shrubs or limestone rocks. In the evening, they migrate to the lagoon, where they immerse themselves briefly to renew the small supply of seawater held in their shells. As the water bathes their gills during the day, oxygen from the air diffuses through it into the bloodstream. A female hermit crab seeks the lagoon for another reason. She must release her eggs in the water, where the young can pass through their normal larval stages as members of the plankton.

Hermit crabs are not finicky about their diet, devouring any organic substance available. They may eat drying seaweed or a dead bird on the beach, or climb trees to eat flowers, fruits, bark, and twigs.

Stoutly constructed land crabs, often almost as plentiful as hermit crabs, burrow into the coral sand and rubble. These crabs are so numerous that their excavations have a major effect on the surface structure of an atoll. They are also omnivorous feeders and scavengers, but cannot climb trees.

The least numerous but most interesting of atoll crustaceans is the big, colorful coconut crab. Not only does it attain great size—reaching a length of up to a foot and a leg span of nearly 1½ to 2 feet—but its powerful claws are truly formidable. Except for periodic trips to the sea to moisten its gills or to release eggs, it is completely divorced from its marine origins. It eats the fruit of screw pines and other atoll plants, as well as animal carcasses. It readily climbs coconut palms, but some biologists doubt that it can break off the tough nuts or even open an intact one that has fallen to the ground. In any case, its claws can force open a nut that is already cracked and scoop out the nutritious meat.

Through the dispersal of their planktonic larvae, coconut crabs are widely distributed in the tropical Pacific, although apparently they do not become established on arid atolls where there is little food. Nor have they reached the remote Hawaiian Islands. Since a crab of this size provides a good meal for several people, the species has suffered extensive hunting by island residents. Coconut crabs are probably far less numerous today than in the past, and they have vanished

A coconut crab wedges open the already-cracked fibrous husk of a coconut to reach the succulent meat. This large land crab conserves moisture by resting in a cool, damp burrow during the day and feeding at night.

completely from many of the smaller islands.

Giantism is often a characteristic of island life, especially of large islands, as exemplified by the giant sunflower trees and iguanas of the Galápagos and the emus and cassowaries of Australia. But on small, arid islets, some animal inhabitants exhibit precisely the opposite condition: dwarfism. Tiny lizards live on small islands near Madagascar, related to larger lizards on the larger island. Other minute lizards live on small islands in the Gulf of California, and uncommonly small snakes occur on islands in the Gulf of California, in the Mediterranean, and in the Florida Keys. Even domestic mammals such as pigs and introduced pests such as rats are smaller on many atolls than their relatives on continents and large volcanic islands. The reasons for dwarfism are not clear, but an insufficiency of food may be one of the important causes.

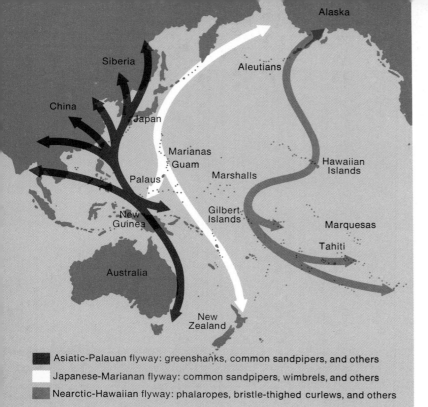

Asiatic-Palauan flyway: greenshanks, common sandpipers, and others
Japanese-Marianan flyway: common sandpipers, wimbrels, and others
Nearctic-Hawaiian flyway: phalaropes, bristle-thighed curlews, and others

Birds migrate over the Pacific on three main routes. Most spend April to August in the Northern Hemisphere, then fly south for six months in the Southern Hemisphere summer. Some breed in the north; others, in the south.

For some birds, an atoll is a place to nest and feed; for others, it is a temporary way station along the migratory route

Many birds that frequent atolls are small: the Micronesian pigeon, the Micronesian starling, a reed warbler, among others. The many shorebirds and seabirds that visit the atolls only to nest or feed naturally interbreed with their relatives ranging over the wide Pacific, and so their genetic heritage is kept open.

With the coming of autumn in the Northern Hemisphere, thousands of birds leave Canada, Alaska, Siberia, and other North Pacific lands to fly to milder climates. One of the migratory birds commonly seen on atolls is the Pacific golden plover; but other plovers, curlews, sandpipers, and phalaropes also visit to rest briefly on their way to more luxuriant islands or to remain until it is time to return north. Even the familiar North American pintail and mallard ducks sometimes land on the lagoons of Kwajalein and other atolls in the Marshall Islands.

The seabirds of coral islets range from the smallest terns, such as the white-capped noddy, to the three large boobies of the Pacific: red-footed, blue-faced, and brown. Frigate birds and tropic birds are also present, although white-tailed tropic birds prefer to nest on the cliffs of mountainous islands. Besides a variety of noddies, several other terns frequent atolls, including the crested tern and the beautifully distinctive fairy tern. Most of the seabirds nest on the sand amid scrub vegetation, which offers a little shade, but the fairy tern precariously balances its single egg on a tree limb or on top of a rock; the chick's claws cling securely to the perch from the moment it hatches.

The water birds that nest on atolls are among the most important animals in an islet's ecology. Since they consume both plant and animal life—especially fishes, crabs, and mollusks—their waste products are sometimes abundant enough to alter the chemistry of the limestone soil, which in turn determines the kinds of plants that can live here. Bird wastes dropped in lagoons and pools enrich the waters and encourage the growth of algae.

If large numbers of shorebirds live on an islet, the high mortality rate ensures potent enrichment; the carcass of a dead bird on land or in shallow water provides an intense concentration of fertilizing organic matter. It is principally through fish-eating birds that the nutrients of the ocean cross the barriers of the shore to be deposited upon the islets of an atoll; accumulations of phosphate-rich guano are especially noticeable on drier atolls such as Baker and Howland islands. Terns, noddies, and boobies are the principal producers of guano, although shearwaters, petrels, frigate birds, and tropic birds also contribute to its accumulation. Guano deposits have led to the exploitation and ruin of many small islands as men have arrived to mine the valuable substance. Nauru, an elevated "pancake" atoll, has been mined for its phosphates since the late 19th century.

Like birds everywhere, atoll birds show distinct preferences in feeding and nesting grounds as well as different ranges in flight. The terns, for example, may be divided into those species that habitually feed close to shore and those that fish several miles out to sea. Birds of the open sea, such as tropic birds and albatrosses, are sighted hundreds of miles from the nearest land.

Just as birds living on the major continents use

Sooty terns nest among the sparse grasses of Johnston Atoll in the Pacific. Each pair of "wide-awakes"—they scream day and night during the breeding season—raises one chick, as do most of the other tropical terns.

regular flyways during their annual migrations, the birds of the Pacific follow established routes, using groups of islands as way stations. One flyway is far west in the ocean and includes the Palaus and parts of Asia; another connects Japan with the Marianas; a third passes through the Hawaiian chain to the northern breeding grounds of Alaska and the Aleutians. On all the flyways, small islands play an important role as resting and feeding bases.

At nesting season, many atolls are alive with bird activity. Noddies and other terns, especially, fuss and cry constantly night and day. These little birds fly busily back and forth across the shoreline, hovering and repeatedly diving after the multitudes of small fishes in the shallow water. With their white bodies and black caps and backs, most island terns resemble their counterparts along the American shoreline. The white-capped noddy is the image reversed. A noddy often feeds only a few feet from shore, in enclosed pools or in shallow parts of the lagoon. It hovers skillfully, at times remaining for minutes above a huge school of minnows before selecting an individual, plunging down, and with surgical precision plucking it from the horde of nearly identical fishes.

Far above may loom the ominous, dark shape of a frigate bird patrolling the air currents with unmoving wings. Those sharply raked wings and forked tail suggest both speed and predation. And indeed, these large birds are robbers. They sometimes fish for themselves, but more often hover high in the air, on the watch for a booby fishing down below. When the frigate bird sights a successful fisher, it plunges in a hawklike and often accurate dive. It pummels the booby, perhaps even turning it upside down, until the booby releases or disgorges its catch. The frigate bird then dives after the prize, snatching it in mid-air. On land, the frigate bird is still a predator, eating eggs and young birds of any kind that it finds unguarded.

The extraordinarily high mortality rate among birds nesting on atolls approaches or even exceeds 50 per cent in some species. Storm waves and winds can devastate a nesting colony, and if a small island is swept by tsunami waves, its entire bird population may be almost obliterated. If rats, dogs, cats, or pigs are allowed to invade an islet, nearly all nesting birds are doomed.

A brown booby huddles over her three-week-old chick in a crowded nesting colony on Johnston Atoll. Chicks are naked when hatched but soon become covered with white down. In five months, they are fully feathered and can fly.

On Takutea Atoll in the South Pacific, a red-tailed tropic bird broods its egg. Many birds nesting in isolated spots have no fear of man; islanders can even pull out their tail feathers to use for ornaments.

Birds That Nest on Pacific Coral Atolls

From birds that do not venture far beyond sight of land—some boobies and frigate birds and others—to strong fliers ranging half the world, many bird species nest on atolls. Led by instinct, navigating, perhaps, by sun and stars, world travelers such as albatrosses locate tiny nesting islands hundreds of miles from other land. Most nesting islands are near surface currents, which supply nutrients for plankton growth. Fishes feed on the abundant plankton, and birds eat the fishes. The birds get water from the fishes they eat; thus they can survive even on atolls without a freshwater supply. Birds swallow seawater while feeding, but secrete super-salty fluids and thus prevent dangerous levels of salt in their bodies.

Four young great frigate birds *await their food-gathering parents on Johnston Atoll. Frigate birds prey on the young of other birds nesting nearby, as well as on each other's unguarded eggs and newly hatched chicks.*

Foam-flecked after a storm, *a black-footed albatross sits on its grass-and-mud nest on Midway Island. After hatching, the young bird may have to withstand intense sunlight until it can fly away.*

A fairy tern guards its single egg, *balanced without benefit of a nest on a tree limb. The chick will automatically cling to its perch when it hatches. Fairy terns never build nests, and may lay eggs on bare rock.*

Hundreds of arching prop roots on mature mangrove trees trap sediment and create islets in shallow water. Barnacles, oysters, and other animals settle on the roots.

Hundreds of arching prop roots on mature mangrove trees trap sediment and create islets in shallow water. Barnacles, oysters, and other animals settle on the roots.

White egrets speckle the foliage of an Indonesian mangrove

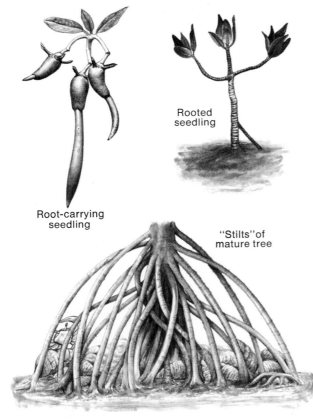

Red mangrove fruits still on the tree send down seedlings. When a seedling reaches six inches, it drops and roots in shallow water. Prop roots arching from the seedling trap mud and debris, and an islet slowly forms.

Root-carrying seedling

Rooted seedling

"Stilts" of mature tree

As leaves, sediment, and rubble pile up about its tangled prop roots, a mangrove thicket becomes a tiny island

Mangroves are the familiar trees fringing many continental and island shorelines in the tropics. Less well known is the ability of the mangrove itself to establish small islands. Near the Florida Keys, where underground springs dilute the seawater and limestone rises close to the surface, dense stands of mangroves grow. Their seeds probably germinate best in brackish water, but the trees also thrive in pure seawater.

In the area of the Keys and in the rest of the Caribbean, the comparatively small red mangrove is the first of the family to appear in shallow water. Its fruit, still on the trees, grows a dart-like root; on falling, the fruit may stick upright in the soft mud at low tide, establishing a new plant within the protective radius of the parent. Other seedlings float away and take root elsewhere when they wash ashore, perhaps some distance from dry land if the water is shallow enough to expose the bottom at low tide. Before long, a thicket of trees is growing from the sea. Leaf litter and sediment collect in the tangle of the prop

land where they nest. Small animals in the swamp, and fishes in nearby coastal waters, assure a bountiful supply of food.

roots, and with continuing accumulations, eventually rise above the surface to form a soft, swampy island. In a few years, the little island is so dense and strong that it can withstand even violent storm waves.

As new generations of red mangroves move outward from the collected sediment, widening the island, another species, the black mangrove, begins to take hold in the vacated center, by now perhaps elevated a foot or more above sea level. The process continues, and other plants, such as sea grape, appear and add to the structure of the island and to its diversity of plants. Flotsam and sediment, shell and coral rubble continue to wash in, and are retained in ever-increasing quantities.

Early in the island's growth animals arrive. As soon as the first young mangroves are securely rooted, oysters, barnacles, sponges, and many other sedentary marine creatures adhere to stems and prop roots. The accumulated silt attracts the larvae of burrowing worms, clams, and shrimps, which soon begin to establish large populations. Mobile mud crabs and small fishes throng in the warm, turbid water, while fiddler crabs, land crabs, snails, and insects swarm in the swamp and on the jungle of woody prop roots. Land hermit crabs climb to the tops of the mangroves, where they devour both fruit and foliage. Seabirds and shorebirds and even inland water birds visit mangrove islets.

A mangrove island is not easy to explore, for what appears in the distance to be a pleasantly forested shoreline turns out to be an incredibly tangled mass of woody stems and roots. If the supporting structures arch high enough, a small boat can pass under them; otherwise, the explorer must clamber over the rigid but often slippery stems and roots. In the interior of the islet, the soft, wet soil does not provide secure footing. Over a very long period, however, the soil packs, and mangrove islands may become firm and large enough to coalesce, or even join and extend the mainland shore. Such islands occur not only in the Caribbean but also in the Pacific and Indian oceans, especially in the vicinity of river mouths.

Long before man, corals, coralline algae, and mangroves were adding to the land mass of the Earth, and they will probably continue to do so long after he vanishes. The efforts of these animals and plants seem minute compared with the vast geological forces that have shaped our world, and the islands created by living things are almost ephemeral in the course of time. But such reef and island constructions have established whole new environments for the development of plant and animal specialties, and important way stations in the migration of terrestrial and shoreline life across the sea. Their effect has been profound, and both marine and mid-ocean island life would be poorer today had they failed to develop.

Islands and Men

With few navigational aids, but with great daring, man long ago began making his way to islands. Now his growing populations and technology threaten their devastation. Has he the wisdom — and the will — to save them?

Profound impulses seem to attract men to islands. For the human spirit an island is a refuge as well as a mettle-testing challenge. The crabbers of Smith Island in Chesapeake Bay, the whalers of Nantucket, the lobstermen of Monhegan were recognized breeds of men: tough, self-sufficient, courageous, and very much in tune with the surrounding sea. The same sort of men inhabit the Orkneys northeast of Scotland and the islands of the Sea of Japan, of the Aegean, or of any other waters in the world. To be an islander is to belong to a special class, a proud fraternity envied by city dwellers and midlanders alike.

Anthropologists know little about how soon early man was able to reach islands. Java man, *Homo erectus*, who lived more than one million years ago, was limited in intelligence and technical skill; he was probably unable to cross straits of open water, although he may have ridden logs, at least, on rivers and lakes. Much later, modern man, *Homo sapiens*, built rafts and canoes with which he successfully journeyed across seawater to offshore islands. He may have been seeking

food, avoiding enemies, or simply responding to that irresistible urge common to all men, curiosity. The distances traversed were not great at first, but the barrier had been broken.

The Western world usually associates the "discovery" of islands with the ancient Greeks and Phoenicians, the Vikings, and the Portuguese, Spanish, Dutch, and British mariners of the last few centuries. Most histories of European explorations scarcely mention that many of the Asian and Pacific islands visited, even those far removed from continents, already had human inhabitants. The references are usually disparaging comments about "savages." Such history underestimates or ignores previous explorative ventures that — in the opinion of a growing number of anthropologists and historians — were the greatest of all time, trips to the moon notwithstanding.

Early European mariners were beset by doubts and fears; they saw the world as essentially hostile. Nearly 2000 years of maritime history had to elapse — as myths and superstitions were dispelled, navigating instruments developed, and records accumulated — before Western man would venture away from continental shores to strike out boldly into uncharted seas. When the Portuguese finally began sailing the Atlantic and Indian oceans, they were equipped with the astrolabe, a forerunner of the sextant. They were provisioned for a return trip as well; there was always concern for getting back home and no thought of settling elsewhere.

Samoan fishermen survey the water from harbor rocks near the town of Pago-Pago. The Polynesians are superb fishermen and navigators, whose ancestors undertook long and strenuous voyages into the unknown. Over hundreds of years they settled thousands of far-flung islands from New Zealand to Hawaii.

While early western mariners hugged the coasts, Pacific peoples braved the open ocean

The Phoenicians and Vikings, two of the most adventurous Western peoples, covered great cumulative distances by hugging coasts or by sailing relatively short passages from island to island. The Phoenicians reached both the British Isles and the Indian Ocean by following continental margins. The Vikings apparently arrived in North America by sailing to the Orkneys or Shetlands and from there to Iceland, Greenland, and the mainland. Arabian and Indian explorers were also coastal sailors, as were the Chinese, who arrived in Taiwan to find it already populated by a Malay people, and who landed in Japan to find it occupied by the Ainus.

Islands in the Atlantic, some only a few hundred miles from a continent, were not discovered by Europeans until about the fifteenth century, when the Portuguese and others came upon Madeira, the Azores, and the Cape Verde Islands, and later, Bermuda, Ascension, St. Helena, Tristan da Cunha, and the Falklands. In the Indian Ocean, only Madagascar was found to be inhabited—not predominantly by Africans, however, but by people of Asian derivation.

While Western mariners imagined falling off the edge of the world (provided the fearsome monsters of the deep allowed them to get so far), other men were sailing across one-third of the Earth's surface, exploring and settling thousands of Pacific islands. Southeast Asia seems to have been the starting point for the migrations of peoples through the largest ocean.

The story of the settlement of the Pacific is known today in only small fragments, pieced together from legends of the people, comparisons of widely scattered cultures, and archaeology. Reasons for migrating included exile or defeat in war and a desire to escape population pressures or to improve one's economic position. But the commonest cause may have been sheer accident: an unexpected and unfamiliar ocean current, an unfavorable wind, a faulty memory. Modern records are full of tales of fishing boats blown off course, even well-stocked boats heading for one island and arriving at another hundreds of miles away. This apparently happened again and again.

The earliest people to set sail may have ridden rafts. But as time went on, both the coastal mainland people and those who were already islanders learned by experience to build more seaworthy craft, and they became incredibly skillful sailors. The migrations, especially those over great distances, almost certainly involved single canoes (including double-hulled ones), since keeping track of another canoe on a dark night would have been extremely difficult, if not impossible.

The earliest Australian ancestors of the present-day Aborigines had arrived on the island continent by twenty-five or thirty thousand years ago.

Major Exploration Routes of Pre-Columbian Mariners

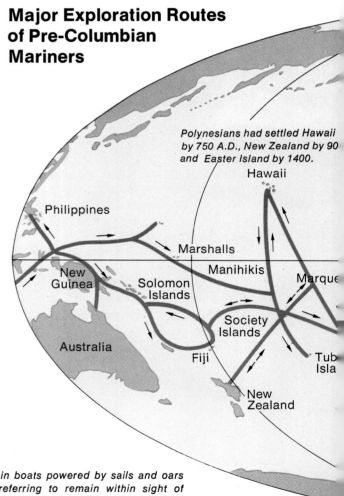

Polynesians had settled Hawaii by 750 A.D., New Zealand by 90_ and Easter Island by 1400.

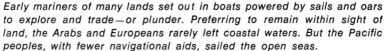

Early mariners of many lands set out in boats powered by sails and oars to explore and trade—or plunder. Preferring to remain within sight of land, the Arabs and Europeans rarely left coastal waters. But the Pacific peoples, with fewer navigational aids, sailed the open seas.

Other peoples, coming later, mingled with the first settlers.

The Philippine Islands and New Guinea were also settled by food gatherers, who carried their few possessions about with them; they built no houses, domesticated no animals, and cultivated no plants until taught to do so by subsequent cultures. Later, more experienced seamen with better boats populated the islands of Melanesia, probably beginning with New Caledonia and the New Hebrides, and eventually getting as far as the Solomon Islands and Fiji.

Anthropologists are hesitant to describe the racial characteristics of any of the original settlers of the Pacific, for too little is known about their places of origin, and too much mingling of stocks has taken place in the intervening millennia. Nevertheless, the people who sailed west to become the dominant inhabitants of Madagascar near Africa, and east to populate the islands of Micronesia, apparently were enough like the present-day people of Indonesia to be called Indonesians, or Proto-Malays.

Their culture was more sophisticated than any established previously in the Pacific. For many centuries, this culture, or its variants, stretched from Madagascar to the central Pacific and influenced all the islands in the area. Research has so far yielded few reliable dates of their history, but it is fairly certain that these people were in the Philippine Islands as early as 6000 B.C. Few scientists take seriously the suggestion that the Indonesians or the Polynesians who followed them came from Central or South America; nearly everything about them links them to Asia rather than to America.

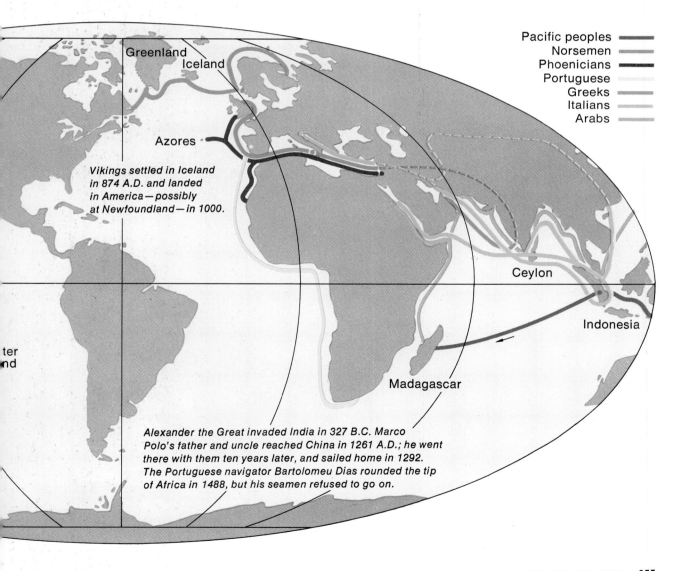

Pacific peoples
Norsemen
Phoenicians
Portuguese
Greeks
Italians
Arabs

Greenland
Iceland
Azores

Vikings settled in Iceland in 874 A.D. and landed in America—possibly at Newfoundland—in 1000.

Ceylon

Indonesia

Madagascar

Alexander the Great invaded India in 327 B.C. Marco Polo's father and uncle reached China in 1261 A.D.; he went there with them ten years later, and sailed home in 1292. The Portuguese navigator Bartolomeu Dias rounded the tip of Africa in 1488, but his seamen refused to go on.

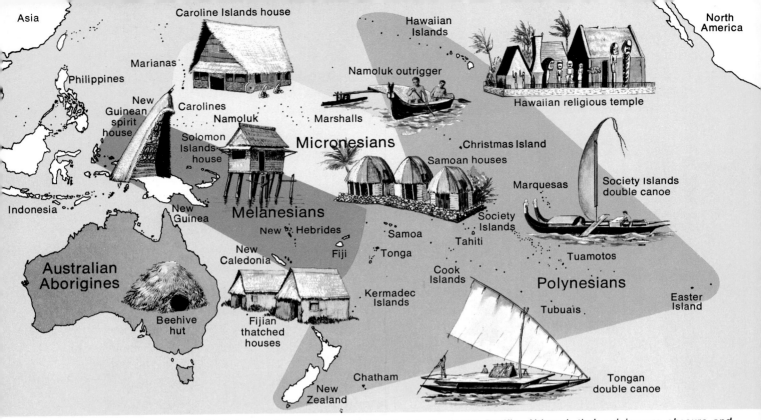

Several different prehistoric peoples settled the habitable islands of the Pacific. Although their origins are obscure and races intermingled during the course of their migrations, anthropologists divide the islanders into four major groups.

Stone heads up to twenty feet high dot the lower slopes of Rano-Raraku on Easter Island. Carved from volcanic rock more than 300 years ago, the busts were connected with burial rites; many wore hats of red volcanic tuff.

The Polynesian triangle includes more than 7 million square miles in the central Pacific

Finally came the Polynesians, whose origins, like those of their predecessors, are almost totally obscure. Their culture cannot be traced back to the Asian continent; the thread to their identity seems to be lost well out at sea on certain islands east of the New Hebrides. They were definitely not South American.

The Polynesians began their voyages several thousand years ago. They depended on tools of stone and shell (there is no metal on volcanic or coral islands), and they had no navigational instruments. Although winds, currents, and stars changed so much en route as to make it appear that the Polynesians were in a different world, their sensitivity to the sea, unequaled by that of any other people in history, enabled them to go on. They gradually populated almost every island in the tropical Pacific.

The travels of the Polynesians form a record of

Skilled Polynesians fashion a canoe almost as their ancestors did, but they use modern tools and nails. Ancient craftsmen working wood with rock adzes and chisels made dugouts of logs or hulls of planks sewn with coconut fibers.

almost incredible achievement. Nearly 3000 years ago, they passed through Fiji in Melanesia, settled in Tonga, and gradually moved into Samoa. They sailed on to the Marquesas, where they were living 2000 years ago. This island group seems to have been the point of departure for their final and greatest voyages into the unknown. They went on to settle distant and lonely Easter Island in the east, the Hawaiian Islands in the north, and New Zealand in the south—their farthest adventure into temperate regions. The huge triangular area they populated stretches 3000 miles from Hawaii to New Zealand, with Easter Island in the southeast forming the third apex.

There were later repetitions of some of these journeys. Several centuries after the original voyages and settlements, other boatloads of Polynesians, primarily from Tahiti, reached Hawaii and New Zealand, establishing or possibly adding to the modern Hawaiian and Maori cultures, each of whose folk histories mentions prior settlement. The Polynesian culture—traditions, language, and artifacts—spread with remarkable rapidity. A modern Maori visiting Hawaii can understand much of the language, and many geographical names of Polynesian origin occur, with only slight variation, all over the Pacific.

Sailing a model canoe is fun for a Society Islands boy, and good practice for a nautical life. Polynesian canoes have rowing and steering paddles, as many as three masts, and an outrigger or second canoe for stability.

Topped with a sail made of coconut fibers, this double-hulled canoe was typical of early Polynesian vessels. The hulls—sometimes as long as eighty feet—were lashed together, with a deckhouse for living quarters between them.

The Polynesians ventured forth in mighty canoes with their families, plants, and animals

The story of the Polynesians is only partly known today. Without a written language, their history had to be transmitted in long and complex chants, which few people now understand or have even heard. Some of the chanted histories were recorded by early Western explorers such as Captain James Cook, but of course they heard and comprehended only a few of them. Modern archaeology, carbon-14 dating, linguistic comparisons, and anthropology help to link groups of these great seafarers, but knowledge of them will always remain fragmentary and raise more questions than can be answered.

Polynesian transoceanic vessels, with or without sails, were huge, consisting usually of two canoes up to eighty feet long lashed together side by side with a deckhouse between them and held together by fiber ropes and wooden pegs.

The boats sailed before the wind beautifully. They could travel upwind reasonably well, their deep, round hulls resisting drift, although the pounding they must have taken in sailing into the wind weakened the lashings and was probably hazardous if prolonged. In the thousand or more years of trans-Pacific voyaging, some of the vessels must certainly have broken up. Others must have been carried out of control by storms, especially if the trip lasted beyond the summer months.

Populations can grow explosively in the restricted area of an island, and there is evidence that this may have been one factor behind intended migrations. When the Polynesians undertook such trips, women, children, plants, and domestic animals went with the men. When landfall was successfully made, the colonizers were immediately ready to begin a productive new life.

But it was not always easy. Pacific islands vary widely in form and climate. Some are low atolls, others are high and mountainous; some have heavy rainfall, others are almost desert. After an exceptionally long voyage, the plants and animals brought by the colonizers, upon which they depended for food, might be too weak to survive. Even if they were healthy, the plants might not be able to grow in the soil (especially on coral islands), and the animals might not find the right food. Only rarely did an island offer the settlers a satisfactory staple food already growing wild.

Even a successful start might not assure the future. Islands in dry regions might suffer severe droughts. Plants would then wither, and lagoon fishes, which are heavily dependent on the land, would die or leave. The human islanders would be left without provisions and possibly without enough strength to migrate. Only the more recent tragedies are reliably documented, but archaeological evidence suggests that, earlier, whole island populations of human beings perished.

European explorers reported traces of former populations on a number of uninhabited islands. Fanning Island is a small coral island north of the Equator, between Tahiti and Hawaii. There Captain Cook found the remains of a rectangular building made of coral blocks, a few basaltic adzes, some fishhooks, ornaments, and several graves. On Malden Island, dippers still lying in water-collecting hollows spoke eloquently of the hardships of drought.

Some groups of colonizers must indeed have been confronted with a serious shortage of drinkable water. In a few Pacific islands, the "lens" of fresh water usually present under atolls and low islands is either absent or contaminated by salt water. Many present-day inhabitants of the Gilbert Islands have become accustomed to drinking brackish water that other people, even neighboring islanders, find almost impossible to swallow or keep down.

The farther the Polynesians migrated across the ocean, the fewer familiar reef fishes they found. Although reef fish populations throughout the Pacific are fairly similar to one another, the diversity of species decreases toward the east. In addition, a number of ordinarily harmless reef fishes can become toxic, their toxicity varying from region to region according to the algae they eat. Polynesians therefore could not always rely on the same reef fishes for sustenance.

Their many hardships did not deter the Poly-

South Sea islanders carried seedlings, fruits, and animals, including stowaways, in their canoes during long voyages. En route, some of the cargo was used for food; some of it helped to stock the island where the voyagers landed.

nesians. An adaptable people, they found ways to conserve their limited resources. Manihiki and Rakahanga atolls are twenty-five miles apart. The Polynesians dwelt on only one island at a time, periodically moving back and forth. Thus each atoll could recover part of its original vegetation and fish populations from previous exploitation.

There is considerable evidence that the Polynesian settlers of the Hawaiian Islands, possibly for several centuries after their first arrival, made repeated voyages to Tahiti and back. In time, however, for unknown causes, the great double-hulled canoes were scrapped, the art of making them was lost, and all communication ceased. The Hawaiians continued to sail about their own archipelago, at times using canoes made from Oregon firs or California redwoods that had drifted across from North America. Except for these short voyages, the isolation of the Hawaiians was complete until the arrival of Europeans in the latter part of the eighteenth century.

New Guinean men, *resplendent as the birds of paradise whose feathers they pluck for their headdresses, mimic the movements*

Peoples of the Pacific Islands

On the Pacific islands, which range in size from tiny atolls to the Australian continent, live four peoples. Polynesians share a heritage of organized community life and craftsmanship. Rank and lineage are important to the superb sailors of Micronesia (the Marshalls, Carolines, and Marianas). Culturally diversified Melanesians, on the islands strung from New Guinea to Fiji, engage in ritual bartering. Aborigines from Asia settled Australia thousands of years ago; some of their descendants still live in isolated tribes.

Australian Aborigines imitate the display dance of brolga cranes during a corroboree (song and dance gathering). Their bodies are painted to represent the feathers of the brolga. Each Aborigine tribe—sometimes only a single family—has a mythology, dialect, and culture of its own.

Stone money symbolizes a village's wealth on Yap Island, but is not used in trading. These Micronesians bring stones from other islands by canoe.

...f courting male birds in their dances. At a singing festival, tribesmen vie to display vivid costumes and makeup.

Fijian fire walkers tread red-hot stones in a rite of faith (preceded by prayer and purification) that Western scientists cannot explain except by a theory of self-hypnosis. Burning logs heat the stones in the fire pit for ten hours or more; ashes are removed before the walkers enter.

A Society Islands sailor balances his canoe by standing on the outrigger. Polynesians and Micronesians voyage hundreds of miles in such small craft.

Pacific mariners sailed hundreds of miles by reading birds, clouds, and waves instead of maps and sextants

Gulls and terns fly no farther than about twenty miles from their home islands to fish, and always return at night. Mariners watching a flock of birds at dawn or dusk can deduce the direction of the island on which they roost.

For Westerners, the science of navigation requires a high degree of technical skill and sophisticated instruments that keep track of position and course. The astrolabe, derived from an ancient Greek invention and used until it was superseded by the sextant in the middle of the eighteenth century, enabled a mariner to deduce time and latitude with remarkable precision. The Polynesians had nothing of the sort; they had no maps, written records, or even the crudest instruments. They estimated distance only by the passage of time; the longer the voyage, of course, the greater the chance of error. They relied primarily upon their sense organs.

Western man, in attempting to comprehend the feats of the Polynesians, has on occasion incorrectly described a calabash with holes drilled in it (actually a vessel for carrying fluids) and stick "maps" (teaching aids) as navigational aids. He can only partly appreciate what these sailors were able to sense and understand. Even the instruments of the last century were not always able to locate an island. In 1837, a British ship set sail for Raratonga from an island less than 150 miles away. Despite knowledge of Raratonga's location and possession of compass, telescope, and high crow's nest from which to keep watch, the captain gave up after a week of fruitless searching.

The Polynesians were well aware that the visible signs of a tropical island appear long before the island itself comes into view. Birds and floating vegetative debris (flotsam) indicate land, and often the direction in which it lies. The high islands of the Pacific are nearly always wreathed in clouds formed by the elevation and cooling of moisture-carrying trade winds. Such a stationary cloud formation on the horizon is a sure sign of an island's existence, although if the winds and ocean currents are adverse, a day or two may be required to sail close enough to see the mountains themselves. Thermal updrafts from an atoll may also cause characteristic clouds to develop and hang almost motionless. The undersides of these clouds often reflect the pale azure of lagoon waters, very different from the deep blue-black of the open sea. An atoll's presence may thus be discerned before its vegetation sketches the barest outline on the horizon.

Maps of familiar individual islands and groups of islands were, of course, made for local use. Islands were shown on such maps by shells or pieces of coral fastened to sticks, and the best route of navigation might also be indicated.

One of the most remarkable techniques by which Polynesian mariners sensed the presence of islands was instilled in childhood into those trained to command the canoes. The famous *mattangs* that can be found in museums, or are now made in non-authentic form for tourists, were not maps at all, but Micronesian-invented devices for instructing boys in the principles of wave motion. Such a stick chart could very well be used today as a visual aid in a physics laboratory, for it represents nearly every possible configuration of wave reflection and refraction.

Waves streaming across the ocean from a distant storm move in a regular pattern until they are steepened by a shoal or beach, or are bent out of their parallel array by a bit of land. When waves hit an island, some are reflected back in the direction from which they came, while others are deflected at angles and warped around the island to continue in altered form on the other side. A stick chart indicates all the basic patterns of such wave action.

Each basic wave pattern had its own name and could be pointed out on a chart to others, no matter which way the chart was oriented. In this way, an experienced navigator could transmit his knowledge to youngsters, who then went to sea with him to practice and develop their uncanny sensitivity to the great ocean surrounding them.

From an airplane or a high cliff, wave effects are readily observed. But how can they be recognized at the surface, especially in a small boat that rises and falls not only with these waves but also with ocean swells of a different frequency? It is quite possible that three or more different sets of waves may affect a boat simultaneously.

The Polynesian navigator went to the bow of his canoe, crouched down in the hull, and literally *felt* every motion of the craft. Within minutes he was able to determine the position of the nearest island, of intervening reefs, and of other islands nearby. So accurate was the technique that he might not even need visual confirmation. No one knows precisely how effective the feeling for waves was for ancient navigators; they may have been able to locate the position of islands and reefs as far away as 100 miles.

Telltale Signs Reveal the Presence of Islands

Polynesians followed signs in the sea and the sky to locate new islands. Navigating between known islands, they observed the rising of specific stars, or lined up with landmarks on the island they were leaving to head the right way.

Towering cloud banks often hang motionless over islands.

Birds in the sky and flotsam at sea mean land is nearby.

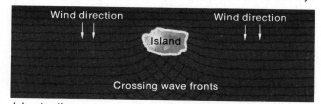

Islands disrupt wave patterns, making wave fronts cross.

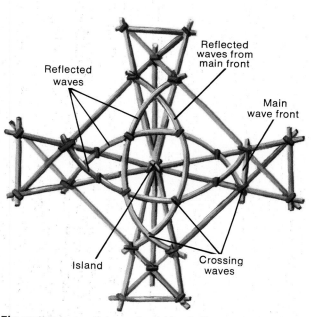

The mattangs *or stick charts of Marshallese navigators are made with pandanus roots tied with coconut fibers. Mattangs show the wave patterns a canoe encounters in approaching an island. By following the line where certain wave fronts cross, a navigator can reach shore. Mattangs are teaching charts; they do not show specific islands.*

On long voyages across the Pacific, the Polynesians used celestial navigation

Interpreting wave patterns was only a secondary navigational technique for the Polynesians. Like the later Westerners, they are primarily celestial mariners, using stars as fixed points, especially when they sail to known destinations.

At the time of the earliest Polynesian voyages, Polaris, the North Star, did not lie due north, but described a small circle in the northern sky.

The navigators therefore used two other major stars, Sirius and Arcturus, as their main guides. Sirius, the brightest star in the sky, passed directly over Tahiti. The red star Arcturus traveled over the island of Kauai in the Hawaiian chain (it now passes over Oahu). Since relying on only two stars would have been dangerous, a good navigator knew, by name, from 150 to 300 stars. With such knowledge, he could take rear sights if the stars ahead were hidden by clouds. But Pacific islanders generally sailed during the most favorable season, when storms were rare and summer westerlies were more or less constant, and so there was little likelihood of a complete and long-lasting overcast.

As a night of sailing wore on, each of the main guide stars appeared to dip into its own "pocket" on the horizon. In other words, it set in the same place each night so long as the observer remained at the same latitude. To reach another latitude, a canoe sailed north or south until a given star dipped into the ocean in its known spot every night. Thus the passage of zenith stars over various parts of Polynesia and the setting locations of others were of immense importance to inter-island navigation.

When a voyage began, the great canoes set sail at dusk, using island reference points to head in the proper direction, which, especially for the Hawaii-Tahiti trips, was often known from previous expeditions. An immediate fix was made on a star nearing the horizon; when it dipped below, the next descending star became the new guide star, and so on.

The Pacific sky was as familiar to the Polynesians as a hometown road map to a motorist. During the day, a mariner navigated chiefly by following the fairly dependable trade winds, but because these changed from time to time, he had to take corrective action at night. His only means of determining longitude was to estimate elapsed time. When he arrived at the proper latitude, he simply turned and sailed due east or west, estimating his longitudinal progress until the destination was reached.

At least one Westerner has demonstrated that the Polynesian method of navigation by stars was workable. To do so, he sailed from Tahiti to New Zealand. Lacking the confidence of the old Polynesians, however, he took along a skilled scientific navigator whose readings were to be kept secret—but available in case of emergency!

Modern islanders in the more remote parts of the Pacific even today think nothing of sailing off to another island cluster a few hundred miles away; they now use compasses, of course, if nothing else. A generation or two ago, they did not consider voyages of 1500 miles extraordinary.

For more than 1000 years, the Polynesians remained seafarers par excellence, even though their voyages, according to available accounts, could be of incredible hardship and danger. They spanned the whole Pacific island world long before Western man ventured away from his continents. They knew well their world's northern and southern limits, which coincided with the edges of that region in which the sun's rays seem to shine directly down to Earth during the course of a year and which correspond closely to the boundaries of the tropics, the Tropic of Cancer and the Tropic of Capricorn.

It is possible, too, that they journeyed far enough east to reach South or Central America. The sweet potato, which the first European explorers found to be an important part of Polynesian diet, is believed to have originated in the New World. Could it have been carried west by Polynesian mariners returning home?

Flashing torches to lure fish, Tahitians circle a placid lagoon. Adept fishermen and sailors, Polynesians frequently undertake night journeys, navigating by stars and keeping in touch with the other boats by torches.

Man's crops and livestock have done incalculable damage to island plants and animals

Undoubtedly the Polynesians and their predecessors altered the ecological system of every island they landed on, no matter how brief their stay. One large double-hulled canoe could transport not only several dozen human beings, but perhaps twenty tons of provisions—breadfruit, bananas, coconuts, taros, sweet potatoes, sugarcane, various seeds, pigs, dogs, and fowl—as well as stowaway rats. Once an island was reached, the pigs, and possibly the fowl, were set free to forage for themselves, and were allowed to go wild to be hunted later. The destruction of vegetation by such grazing and rooting land animals was incalculable.

In more recent times, European mariners released goats on islands in various parts of the world to assure themselves a source of fresh food on their return or in case of shipwreck. Close-cropping goats are even more destructive than wild Asian pigs. The barrenness of several of the Antilles in the southern Caribbean is in part

Introduced species such as these goats on St. Barthélemy, one of the smaller Leeward Islands in the Caribbean, can quickly overrun endemic plants and animals. Serious erosion results when goats uproot the ground cover.

Sixty million sheep, raised on huge farms such as this one in Makarora Valley, graze New Zealand's pastures. Early Polynesians, hunting moas, burned forests; European settlers, clearing forests for pasture, caused serious erosion.

accounted for by the large herds of semiwild goats that roam the hillsides.

Since the Polynesians were not great hunters, they often employed fire to drive animals toward traps or confined areas, there to be killed. In New Zealand, the first human inhabitants were Polynesians, whose whole economy centered on the hunting of that huge flightless bird, the moa. These Moa hunters used fire to concentrate their prey, and in only a little over 500 years it disappeared forever.

Later New Zealanders, the Maoris, found the starchy root of the bracken fern to be a useful staple food. Unfortunately, they also discovered that bracken fern flourishes best after fire. The burning had a major impact on the land. The forests of endemic trees that blanketed New Zealand from coast to high mountains all but disappeared, and with them the rich, varied bird life the islands had supported.

On many smaller islands across the Pacific, forests were destroyed, and grasses grew in their stead. If an adequate grass cover was too slow in developing, whole regions became eroded, revealing the many-hued volcanic soils beneath. Scrub forests burned on atolls were replaced by cultivated groves of coconut palms and by other planted crops. Cultivation of food plants was especially important on the smaller islands where burgeoning human populations required an increasing supply of staples. The Polynesians often excavated, terraced, and enriched the soil, and by their farming increased the diversity of plant species present.

Among the few visible works of ancient Pacific islanders still extant are the famous rice terraces of the Ifugao in the Philippine Mountain Province north of Baguio. The terraces, which are so arranged that water can spill from each paddy to the one below, are among the greatest works of man. The Ifugao, sturdy mountain people, are descendants of a wave of Proto-Malays long preceding both the Philippine lowlanders and the Micronesians elsewhere. They are highly efficient hydraulic engineers and have established a harmony with nature seldom achieved by other cultures.

The isolation of an island is shattered when the first human being sets foot on its shores. As the previously uninhabited Atlantic islands of Madeira, St. Helena, and the Canaries were subjected to deforestation and grazing, their appearance and whole basic ecosystems changed markedly. Charles Darwin commented on the barren and devastated island of Ascension when he visited it in 1836.

Built over a period of 2000 years, incidible rice terraces 6000 feet up in the Luzon mountains are the most extensive on Earth, providing 100,000 acres of level ground. Philippine farmers work constantly to keep paddies in repair.

A water-filled crater is a grim reminder of the atomic and hydrogen bombs that devastated Eniwetok Atoll during tests in the 1950s. As radioactivity faded, plants and animals began recolonizing Eniwetok and nearby Bikini.

Sugarcane plantations and refineries have permanently changed the Hawaiian environment, even though the yearly crop of more than one million tons is raised on only 221,300 acres—an area about the size of New York City.

Island life that has survived man's agriculture is now threatened by his technology

In the Pacific, the changes brought about by the arrival of the Polynesians actually had a more profound effect on endemic island life than did the advent, much later, of Western agriculture, which wreaked such final devastation. When the first Western explorers entered the ocean, it is doubtful that a single island still retained its original association of plants and animals.

Even though the Polynesians had brought foreign species to long-isolated spots, their islands were still comparative paradises of indigenous life when Western man arrived in the Pacific. But in the two centuries since, the story has been an increasingly gloomy one of agricultural, industrial, and urban alterations. Forests have been razed and obliterated; seals, turtles, and other large marine animals have been hunted into extinction; reef fishes and mollusks, when not poisoned by pollution, have been collected to near-oblivion. A vast array of plants—weeds as well as ornamental and food species—have been introduced to all islands, as have insects, European rats, mongooses, South American toads, Malayan birds, and a multitude of other creatures. Sizable repositories of endemic life exist today only in inaccessible mountain valleys on some of the higher islands. Unless such regions are soon declared preserves, they are in jeopardy.

The Hawaiian Islands have lost to extinction more endemic species than any other place known, and possibly have received more introduced species as well. Since 1860, three billion sheep have grazed New Zealand pastures—composed of imported grasses—ruining the soil and contouring the land as they pass from one spot to the next. On all too many islands, erosion proceeds unchecked. Eniwetok still bears the scars of atom-bomb testing. And who can recognize in Waikiki, with its crowded high-rise hotels, the former fishing grounds of chiefs?

These are only a few examples of man's alteration of fragile island ecosystems. Phosphate mining has almost obliterated the vegetation of some islands where once great numbers of seabirds nested. On Midway Island, heavily populated by albatrosses, attempts have been made to remove or exterminate the birds because the island is

Strip mines scar the flanks of New Caledonia's mountains, rich in nickel—the island is third in world production—and other minerals. Strip mining destroys topsoil; when mines are abandoned, plants and animals return very slowly.

also used as a naval base. Copra plantations on many atolls cover vast tracts where native vegetation once grew. On Hawaii, a road was cut through endemic trees on a high mountain to enable tourists to see an untouched tropical island forest. It is untouched no longer: Every car brings seeds, and the new, foreign plants are spreading like a disease through the older vegetation, which is unable to compete.

Above all, there is the presence of man and his new age of technology. Even small islands in any ocean may have towns with inadequate sanitation, muddy streets filled with ancient jalopies, and shoreline refuse dumps piled high with indestructible bottles and aluminum cans. Oil from faulty outboards floats over lagoons; effluent from

sugarcane processing plants poisons the shore; some of the high islands, their coastal towns and cities sheltered from the passing trade winds, are in the grip of serious air pollution. An island is a precious bit of the Earth, a fragile jewel in the ocean; its natural luster is easily dimmed by thoughtless intruders.

Probably nowhere are the unsightly and destructive effects of civilization more evident than on the little islands of the South Seas that continue to be romantically presented in travel brochures. Their distant guardian nations are largely unaware of the devastation of the land, and of the poverty and frustration of the local human populations, or, if they are aware of the problems, they have been unable to solve them.

Man and introduced species have profoundly affected the life of nearly every island on Earth

Evolving on predator-free Mauritius, the dodo became large and fat and lost the power of flight. Sailors killed many of these heavy ground-nesting pigeons, and then the pigs and monkeys introduced by man finished them off.

In the past, isolation allowed—and indeed encouraged—the emergence of strong nations: Great Britain, Japan, the Philippines, Australia, New Zealand, and others. But centralized government in the mid-Pacific, for example, is difficult to achieve or administer, so great are the distances between islands. In recent years, only a few island groups (none in the mid-Pacific) have been able to band together into nations with unified voices in the world, most notably the West Indian Federation, Trinidad-Tobago, Indonesia, and Malaysia. Western dominion over many other islands has lacked true concern for the permanent inhabitants, who have lost their old

Forty per cent of the island of Mauritius in the Indian Ocean is occupied by sugarcane fields. Before European colonization in the seventeenth century, forests of ebony covered the mountains, and palm savannas the lowlands.

Turquoise waters washing over a fringing coral reef lap Mooréa's white sand beaches. Like nearly all the world's islands, Mooréa has been altered by man, but it is still one of the most beautiful of all the South Pacific islands.

ways but often are unable to assume the ways of the present.

Many islands are seriously overpopulated. Heavy concentrations of people alter the land that should support them. The destruction of forests results in decreased river flow—island rivers are seldom large or vigorous anyway—in turn making agriculture more difficult and less fruitful. When cover vegetation is gone, erosion quickly delivers topsoil to the nearby sea, where it may suffocate formerly productive reefs and fishing grounds.

The governments of the larger islands are now actively engaged in their own programs of conservation. In New Zealand naturalists are determined that the takahe, the bird that for fifty years was believed to be extinct, must not vanish a second time into oblivion. Efforts are being made to guard the country's symbol, the kiwi, and other flightless birds. The offshore islands that have become the last refuge of the tuatara are closed to all except naturalists with special passes. In Madagascar, forest wildlife parks are being established in an eleventh-hour attempt to save the hard-pressed families of lemurs.

But the small remote islands present problems that can be solved only by concerted international efforts. On the Galápagos Islands and on Aldabra (saved a few years ago from a military airfield) scientific research stations are trying to ensure that the giant tortoises do not follow the dodo into extinction. A plan to protect all the unspoiled islands of the Pacific has been developed under the International Biological Program, and agreements on island conservation are of vital importance to the common effort.

Islands are especially vulnerable to changes that on a continent would be insignificant. But if these programs for conservation can prevail against short-term greed, there is still hope for preserving the wonders of island life—evolved over many millions of years—for the future.

Bibliography

and recommended reading

The publishers wish to acknowledge their indebtedness to the following books and periodicals, which were consulted for reference or as sources of illustration. The fields of marine and of island biology are fast-moving. We hope that reading *Secrets of the Seas* will encourage you to delve into the recommended books and periodicals. Publications of particular interest to the general reader are marked with an asterisk (*).

GENERAL

* BERRILL, N. J., *The Life of the Ocean.* McGraw-Hill, 1966
* BERRILL, N. J., *The Living Tide.* Fawcett, 1951
* BERRILL, N. J., and MICHAEL BERRILL, *The Life of Sea Islands.* McGraw-Hill, 1969
* CARLQUIST, SHERWIN, *Island Life.* Natural History Press, 1965
* CARSON, RACHEL, *The Sea Around Us.* Oxford University Press, 1961
* CROMIE, WILLIAM J., *Exploring the Secrets of the Sea.* Prentice-Hall, 1962
CROMIE, WILLIAM J., *The Living World of the Sea.* Prentice-Hall, 1962
DARLINGTON, P. J., JR., *Zoogeography.* Wiley, 1957
* ENGEL, LEONARD, *The Sea.* Time Inc., 1961
HALSTEAD, BRUCE W., *Dangerous Marine Animals.* Cornell Maritime Press, 1959
HARDY, SIR ALISTER, *The Open Sea: Its Natural History.* Houghton Mifflin, 1959
KLINGEL, GILBERT C., *The Ocean Island.* Doubleday, 1961
MAC GINITIE, GEORGE E., and NETTIE MAC GINITIE, *Natural History of Marine Animals.* McGraw-Hill, 1968
MAYR, ERNST, *Animal Species and Evolution.* Harvard University Press, 1963
* ORR, ROBERT T., *Animals in Migration.* Macmillan, 1970
RAY, CARLETON, and ELGIN CIAMPI, *The Underwater Guide to Marine Life.* A. S. Barnes, 1956
* READER'S DIGEST, *Fascinating World of Animals.* 1971
ROMER, ALFRED S., *The Vertebrate Story.* University of Chicago Press, 1959
RUSSELL, FRANKLIN, *The Secret Islands.* Norton, 1966
WALLACE, ALFRED RUSSELL, *Island Life.* Macmillan, 1880

ECOLOGY

ALLEE, W. C., and K. P. SCHMIDT, *Ecological Animal Geography.* John Wiley, 1951
ELTON, CHARLES S., *The Ecology of Invasions by Animals and Plants.* Wiley, 1958
* FARB, PETER, and the Editors of LIFE, *Ecol-* ogy. Time Inc., 1963
FOSBERG, F. R., *Man's Place in the Island Ecosystem.* Bishop Museum Press, Honolulu, 1965
GOTTO, R. V., *Marine Animals: Partnerships and Other Associations.* American Elsevier, 1969
ODUM, EUGENE P., *Fundamentals of Ecology,* W. B. Saunders, 1971
SMITH, ROBERT L., *Ecology and Field Biology.* Harper & Row, 1966

SEASHORES

* ABBOTT, R. TUCKER, *Seashells of North America.* Golden Press, 1968
* AMOS, WILLIAM H., *The Life of the Seashore.* McGraw-Hill, 1966
* CARSON, RACHEL, *The Edge of the Sea.* Houghton Mifflin, 1955
DAKIN, WILLIAM J., and others, *Australian Seashores.* Angus & Robertson, Sydney, 1952
* HAY, JOHN, and PETER FARB, *The Atlantic Shore.* Harper & Row, 1966
MINER, ROY WALDO, *Field Book of Seashore Life.* Putnam, 1950
MORTON, J., and M. MILLER, *The New Zealand Seashore.* Collins, London, 1968
RICKETTS, EDWARD F., and JACK CALVIN, revised by JOEL W. HEDGPETH, *Between Pacific Tides.* Stanford University Press, 1968
SOUTHWARD, A. J., *Life on the Sea-Shore.* Harvard University Press, 1965
TINKER, SPENCER W., *Pacific Seashells.* Charles Tuttle, 1968
YONGE, C. M., *The Sea Shore.* Collins, London, 1949

CORAL REEFS

BATES, MARSTON, and DONALD ABBOTT, *Coral Island.* Scribners, 1958
EIBL-EIBESFELDT, IRENAUS, *Land of a Thousand Atolls.* MacGibbon & Kee, London, 1965
* FAULKNER, DOUGLAS, and C. LAVETT SMITH, *The Hidden Sea.* Viking Press, 1970
GILLETT, KEITH, *The Australian Great Barrier Reef.* A. H. & A. W. Reed, Sydney, 1968
SMITH, F. G. W., *Atlantic Coral Reefs.* University of Miami Press, 1948
WIENS, HEROLD J., *Atoll Environment and Ecology.* Yale University Press, 1962

DEEP-SEA BIOLOGY

* IDYLL, C. P., *Abyss.* Crowell, 1964
MARSHALL, N. B., *Aspects of Deep Sea Biology.* Hutchinson, London, 1954
SOULE, GARDNER, *Undersea Frontiers.* Rand McNally, 1968

OCEANOGRAPHY

* BARDACH, JOHN, *Harvest of the Sea.* Harper & Row, 1968

COKER, R. E., *This Great and Wide Sea.* University of North Carolina Press, 1947
COWEN, ROBERT C., *Frontiers of the Sea.* Bantam Books, 1960
* DUGAN, JAMES, and others, *World Beneath the Sea.* National Geographic Society, 1967
* GASKELL, T. F., *World Beneath the Oceans.* Natural History Press, 1964
MARX, WESLEY, *The Frail Ocean.* Coward-McCann, 1967
MENARD, H. W., *Marine Geology of the Pacific,* McGraw-Hill, 1964
MILLER, ROBERT C., *The Sea.* Random House, 1966
RUSSELL, FREDERICK S. and C. M. YONGE, *The Seas.* Warne, London, 1963
* SCIENTIFIC AMERICAN, *The Ocean.* W. H. Freeman, 1969
SHEPHARD, FRANCIS P., *The Earth Beneath the Sea.* Johns Hopkins, 1967
SVERDRUP, H. U., and others, *The Oceans.* Prentice-Hall, 1942
WEYL, PETER K., *Oceanography.* John Wiley & Sons, 1970

EXPLORATION

ATTENBOROUGH, DAVID, *Bridge to the Past.* Harpers, 1961
BARRAU, JACQUES, *Plants and the Migrations of Pacific Peoples.* Bishop Museum Press, 1963
BEEBE, WILLIAM, *Half Mile Down.* Duell, Sloan & Pearce, 1934
BRUUN, ANTON F., *The Galathea Deep Sea Expedition.* Allen & Unwin, London, 1958
BRYAN, E. H., JR., *Life in Micronesia.* Hourglass, Marshall Islands, 1965–66
* BUCK, PETER H., *Vikings of the Pacific.* University of Chicago Press, 1959
HIGHLAND, GENEVIEVE A., and others, editors, *Polynesian Culture History.* Bishop Museum Press, Honolulu, 1967
IDYLL, C. P., *Exploring the Ocean World.* Crowell, 1969
SHARP, ANDREW, *Ancient Voyagers in Polynesia.* University of California Press, 1964

VOLCANOS

OLLIER, CLIFF, *Volcanoes.* The MIT Press, 1969
* THORARINSSON, SIGURDUR, *Surtsey, The New Island in the North Atlantic.* Viking, 1967
* WILCOXSON, KENT H., *Chains of Fire: The Story of Volcanoes.* Chilton, 1966

INVERTEBRATES

BUCHSBAUM, RALPH, *Animals Without Backbones.* University of Chicago Press, 1948
* BUCHSBAUM, RALPH, and LORUS J. MILNE, *The Lower Animals.* Doubleday, 1961
* LANE, FRANK W., *Kingdom of the Octopus.* Sheridan, 1962
WIMPENNY, R. S., *The Plankton of the Sea.* American Elsevier, 1966

FISHES

* COUSTEAU, JACQUES-YVES, and PHILIPPE COUSTEAU, *The Shark: Splendid Savage of the Sea.* Doubleday, 1970

HELM, THOMAS, *Shark! Unpredictable Killer of the Sea.* Dodd, Mead, 1961

* HERALD, EARL S., *Living Fishes of the World.* Doubleday, 1961

LINEAWEAVER, THOMAS H., III, and RICHARD H. BACKUS, *The Natural History of Sharks.* J. B. Lippincott, 1969

MARSHALL, N. B., *The Life of Fishes.* World, 1966

NATIONAL GEOGRAPHIC SOCIETY, *Wondrous World of Fishes.* 1965

NORMAN, J. R., *A History of Fishes.* Hill & Wang, 1931

OMMANNEY, FRANCIS DOWNES, *The Fishes.* Time Inc., 1963

PERLMUTTER, ALFRED, *Guide to Marine Fishes.* New York University, 1961

RANDALL, JOHN E., *Caribbean Reef Fishes.* T. F. H. Publications, 1968

REPTILES AND AMPHIBIANS

* CARR, ARCHIE, *So Excellent a Fishe.* Natural History Press, 1967

COGGER, HAROLD, *Australian Reptiles in Colour.* East-West Center Press, Honolulu, 1967

GOODE, JOHN, *Freshwater Tortoises of Australia and New Guinea.* Lansdowne Press, Melbourne, 1967

SHARELL, RICHARD, *The Tuatara, Lizards, and Frogs of New Zealand.* Collins, London, 1966

BIRDS

ALEXANDER, W. B., *Birds of the Ocean.* Putnam, 1928

AUSTIN, OLIVER L., JR., *Birds of the World.* Golden Press, 1961

* CHISHOLM, ALEC H., *Bird Wonders of Australia.* Angus & Robertson, Sydney, 1965

FALLA, R. A., R. B. SIBSON, and E. G. TURBOTT, *A Field Guide to the Birds of New Zealand.* Houghton Mifflin, 1967

FISHER, JAMES, and R. M. LOCKLEY, *Seabirds.* Houghton Mifflin, 1954

FISHER, JAMES, and ROGER TORY PETERSON, *The World of Birds.* Doubleday, 1964

HARRISON, P. P. O., *Sea Birds of the South Pacific Ocean.* Princeton University Press, 1967

HILL, ROBIN, *Australian Birds.* Funk & Wagnalls, 1967

HINDWOOD, KEITH, *Australian Birds in Colour.* East-West Center Press, Honolulu, 1966

LACK, DAVID, *Darwin's Finches.* Peter Smith, 1968

* MATTHIESSEN, PETER, edited by GARDNER D. STOUT, *The Shorebirds of North America.* Viking, 1967

MAYR, ERNST, *Birds of the Southwest Pacific.* Macmillan, 1945

MUNRO, GEORGE C., *Birds of Hawaii.* Ridgeway Press, 1960

* NELSON, BRYAN, *Galápagos: Islands of Birds.* Longmans, London, 1968

PALMER, RALPH S., editor, *Handbook of North American Birds,* Vol. I, Yale University Press, 1962

* SPARKS, JOHN, and TONY SOPER, *Penguins,* Taplinger, 1967

STOKES, TED, *Birds of the Atlantic Ocean.* Macmillan, 1968

THOMSON, S. LANDSBOROUGH, editor, *A New Dictionary of Birds.* McGraw-Hill, 1964

MAMMALS

ANDERSEN, HARALD T., *The Biology of Marine Mammals.* Academic Press, 1968

* GRZIMEK, BERNHARD, *Four-Legged Australians.* Hill & Wang, 1967

JOLLY, ALISON, *Lemur Behavior: A Madagascar Field Study.* University of Chicago Press, 1966

KING, JUDITH E., *Seals of the World.* British Museum (Natural History), London, 1964

LILLY, JOHN C., *Man and Dolphin.* Doubleday, 1961

MAC KINTOSH, N. A., *The Stocks of Whales.* Fishing News (Books) Ltd., London, 1965

* MATTHEWS, LEONARD HARRISON, and others, *The Whale,* Simon & Schuster, 1968

* MEDWAY, LORD, *The Wild Mammals of Malaya.* Oxford University Press, London, 1969

NORRIS, KENNETH S., editor, *Whales, Dolphins, and Porpoises.* University of California Press, 1966

* PERRY, RICHARD, *The World of the Polar Bear.* University of Washington Press, 1966

* PERRY, RICHARD, *The World of the Walrus.* Taplinger, 1968

SCHEFFER, VICTOR B., *Seals, Sea Lions and Walruses.* Stanford University Press, 1958

* SCHEFFER, VICTOR B., *The Year of the Seal.* Scribners, 1970

* SCHEFFER, VICTOR B., *The Year of the Whale.* Scribners, 1969

SLIJPER, E. J., *Whales.* Basic Books, 1962

SMALL, GEORGE L., *The Blue Whale.* Columbia University Press, 1971

TOMICH, P. QUENTIN, *Mammals in Hawaii.* Bishop Museum Press, Honolulu, 1969

* TROUGHTON, ELLIS, *Furred Animals of Australia.* Livingston Publishing, 1966

WALKER, ERNEST P., *Mammals of the World.* Johns Hopkins Press, 1968

REGIONAL BIOLOGY

* AUSTRALIAN NEWS AND INFORMATION SERVICE, *Bush Dwellers of Australia.* Rigby, Adelaide, 1964

BEEBE, WILLIAM, *Galápagos, World's End.* Putnam, 1924

* BREEDEN, STANLEY and KAY, *Tropical Queensland.* Collins, London, 1970

* CARLQUIST, SHERWIN, *Hawaii: A Natural History.* Natural History Press, 1970

EIBL-EIBESFELDT, IRENAUS, *The Galápagos, Noah's Ark of the Pacific.* Doubleday, 1961

* GRESSITT, J. LINSLEY, *Pacific Basin Biogeography: A Symposium.* Bishop Museum Press, Honolulu, 1963

* FEHER, JOSEPH, *Hawaii: A Pictorial History.* Bishop Museum Press, Honolulu, 1969

HARRIS, N. V., *The Tropical Pacific.* University of London Press, 1966

* KEAST, ALLEN, *Australia and the Pacific Islands: A Natural History.* Random House, 1966

LIVINGSTON, JOHN, and LISTER SINCLAIR, *Darwin and the Galápagos,* Canadian Broadcasting Corp., Toronto, 1966

MC MICHAEL, D. F., editor, *A Treasury of Australian Wildlife.* Ure Smith, Sydney, 1968

* MITCHELL, CARLETON, *Isles of the Caribbees.* National Geographic Society, 1966

* MORCOMBE, MICHAEL K., *Wild Australia.* Lansdowne Press, Melbourne, 1966

POIGNANT, A., *Animals of Australia.* Dodd, Mead, 1967

* PORTER, ELIOT, *Galápagos: The Flow of Wildness.* Sierra Club, 1968

READER'S DIGEST, *The Reader's Digest Complete Atlas of Australia.* Sydney, 1968

* ROEDELBERGER, F. A., VERA I. GROSCHOFF, and PETER J. WHITEHEAD, *Wildlife of the South Seas.* Viking, 1967

* SHADBOLT, MAURICE, and OLAF RUHEN, *Isles of the South Pacific.* National Geographic Society, 1968

SLATER, PETER, and ERIC LINDGREN, *Wildlife of Western Australia.* West Australian Newspapers, Ltd., Perth, 1966

STRATTON, ARTHUR, *The Great Red Island.* Scribners, 1964

Periodicals

* *Animal Kingdom,* New York
* *Audubon,* New York
  BioScience, Washington, D.C.
  Birds of the World, London
* *International Wildlife,* Milwaukee, Wisconsin
* *National Geographic,* Washington, D.C.
* *Natural History,* New York
  Nature, London
  Oceanology International, Houston, Texas
* *Oceans,* San Diego, California
  Oceanus, Woods Hole, Massachusetts
* *Purnell's Encyclopedia of Animal Life,* London
  Science, Washington, D.C.
* *Scientific American,* New York
  Sea Frontiers, Miami, Florida
* *Smithsonian,* Washington, D.C.

Index

Page numbers in bold type refer to illustrations

Index

Page numbers in bold type refer to illustrations

Index

Page numbers in bold type refer to illustrations

Index

Page numbers in bold type refer to illustrations

Index

Page numbers in bold type refer to illustrations

Index

Index

Page numbers in bold type refer to illustrations

Picture Credits

Picture Credits

Associates. **163** Fred Bruemmer. **164** William F. Bryan. **165** (top) Herbert Clarke; (bottom) William F. Bryan. **166** (top) Russ Kinne / Photo Researchers; (bottom) Steve & Dolores McCutcheon. **167** Thase Daniel. **168** Gerald Ferguson. **170** (top) Alfred L. Pentis; (bottom) Ron Church. **171** Bucky Reeves / National Audubon Society. **172–173** Harry McNaught. **174–175** Theodore Walker. **176–177** Harry McNaught. **178** Douglas Faulkner. **179** Jen & Des Bartlett / Bruce Coleman Inc. **180** (left) John G. Ross / Photo Researchers. **180–181** (top) Jen & Des Bartlett / Bruce Coleman Inc. **181** (bottom) James W. LaTourrette / Miami Seaquarium. **182** (top) Jack McKenney; (bottom) Kellner Associates. **183** Peter L. Vila. **184** George Musil. **185** Kellner Associates. **186** (top) Bob Brooks; (bottom) N. Merritt / Photo Aquatics. **187** (top) Adam Woolfitt / Susan Griggs; (bottom left) N. Merritt / Photo Aquatics; (bottom right) Ralph Pinto. **188** (top) Chuck Diven. **188–189** (bottom) Sven Gillsäter. **190–191** Robert I. Bowman. **192** Alan Root. **194–195** H. C. Berann, based on material by Prof. Bruce Heezen (Lamont Geological Observatory) and Marie Tharpe (U.S. Oceanographic Office) / © Verlag DAS BESTE GmbH. Stuttgart. **194** (bottom left) George Kelvin. **196** Russ Kinne / Photo Researchers. **197** (top) T. Iwago / Photo Trends; (bottom) Sven Gillsäter. **198** Raul Mina Mora. **199** George Kelvin. **200–201** Edward Malsberg. **201** (right) Sven Gillsäter. **202** (top left) James A. Kern; (top right) Edward F. Anderson; (bottom) Photographic Library of Australia. **203** (top) James A. Kern; (bottom left) E. S. Ross; (bottom right) Edward Malsberg. **204** (top) Sherwin Carlquist; (bottom) George Kelvin. **205** Eva Cellini. **206** N. Smythe. **207** Tom McHugh / Photo Researchers / Courtesy of the Chicago Zoological Park. **208** (top) Karl Weidmann / National Audubon Society; (bottom) George Kelvin. **209** (top left) Fred Ward / Black Star; (top right) Roy Woodbury; (bottom left) Thase Daniel; (bottom right) William J. Bolte. **210–211** Albert E. Gilbert. **212–213** Lancelot Tickell. **214** (top) Leonard Lee Rue III; (bottom) Tee Balog. **215** (left) Raul Mina Mora; (right) Lancelot Tickell. **216** Alan Root. **218** Orion Press / FPG. **219** George Kelvin. **220** Eiji Miyazawa / Black Star. **222** (left) George Laycock; (right) Mary Kellner. **223** Grant Haist. **224** Charles Fracé. **225** David Cavagnaro. **226** Alan Root. **227** (top; bottom) Alan Root; (middle) Okapia. **228** (top) Grant Haist; (bottom) Thase Daniel. **229** Mary Kellner. **230** George Kelvin. **231–232** William H. Sager. **233** (top) Thase Daniel; (bottom) Werner Stoy / Camera Hawaii. **234** (top; bottom left) Richard E. Warner; (bottom right) George Laycock / Photo Researchers. **235** R. E. Warner. **236** Quentin Keynes. **238** Roland C. Clement. **239** Mary Kellner. **240** Howard Uible. **241** Peter Johnson. **242** Howard Uible. **243** Eva Cellini. **244** (top) Quentin Keynes; (bottom) Edwin Gould. **245** Howard Uible. **247** Albert E. Gilbert. **248** (top left) Anthony Bannister; (top right) Tony Beamish / Bruce Coleman Ltd.; (bottom) Quentin Keynes. **249** (top) Peter Johnson; (middle left) Mary Kellner; (bottom left) Evelyn Bauer; (bottom right) George Holton / Photo Researchers. **250** New Zealand Information Service. **251** Mary Kellner. **252** John Warham. **253** Kenneth W. Fink. **254** M. F. Soper. **255** (top) Michael C. T. Smith; (bottom) G. R. Roberts. **256** Eva Cellini. **257** M. F. Soper. **258** Stan & Kay Breeden. **260–261** M. K. Morcombe. **262** (top) Douglass Baglin; (bottom) Harold J. Pollock. **263** George Kelvin. **264–265** M. K. Morcombe. **265** (top right) Eva Cellini. **266** (left) M. K. Morcombe; (right) Okapia. **267** George Kelvin. **268** (top) Stan & Kay Breeden; (bottom) Douglass Baglin. **269** (top) George Kelvin; (bottom) Stan & Kay Breeden. **270** (top) Steve Pearson; (bottom) Anthony Healy. **271** Harry McNaught. **272** (left) Stan & Kay Breeden; (right) George Kelvin. **273** (top) Anthony Healy; (bottom) Stan & Kay Breeden. **274** (left) Alan Root / Okapia; (right) Eva Cellini. **275** Stan & Kay Breeden. **276** Okapia. **277** George Kelvin. **278** (left) Anthony Healy; (right) Eva Cellini. **279** Len Robinson. **280** M. K. Morcombe. **282** (left) Alan Root; (right) John Carnemolla. **283** (top) John Markham; (bottom) Harold J. Pollock. **284** Len Robinson. **285** (top) Alan Root; (bottom left) M. K. Morcombe; (bottom right) Douglass Baglin. **286** David Corke. **287** (middle) Alan Root. **288** (left) William S. Peckover; (right) Edward Malsberg. **289** Alan Root. **290** (top) Photographic Library of Australia; (bottom) Len Robinson. **291** (top left) Len Robinson; (bottom left) Harold McNaught; (right) Alan Root. **292** (top) Alan Root; (middle) Edward Malsberg; (bottom) Warren Garst / Van Cleve Photography. **293** Okapia. **294–295** Harold McNaught. **296** M. K. Morcombe. **297** (top) Okapia; (bottom) National Zoological Park. **298** M. K. Morcombe. **299** (left) Jack Fields; (right) Okapia. **300** Edward Malsberg. **301** M. K.

Morcombe. **302** (top left) Harold J. Pollock / FPG; (top right) John Carnemolla; (bottom) Eva Cellini. **303** (top) John Kaufmann; (bottom left) M. T. Tanton; (bottom right) Alan Root. **304** Stan & Kay Breeden. **305** Russ Kinne / Photo Researchers. **306** Wallace A. Cole. **308** Aevar Johannesson. **309** Richard Frohs. **310** (top) Aevar Johannesson; (bottom) Quentin Keynes. **311** (top) John E. Randall; (bottom) T. Stell Newman. **312** (top) George Kelvin; (bottom) Camera Hawaii. **313** Aevar Johannesson. **314** (top) Harrison Forman; (bottom) G. R. Roberts. **315** G. Tomsich / M. Grimoldi. **316** Mary Kellner. **317** Ivan Polunin. **319** Edward Malsberg. **320** Peter Sanchez. **321** (left) P. Sanchez; (right) W. H. Amos. **322** (top) Werner Stoy / Camera Hawaii; (bottom) David Muench. **323** (top left; right) D. Muench; (bottom) Werner Stoy / Camera Hawaii. **324** (top) Hawaii Volcanoes National Park; (bottom) Mary Kellner. **325** W. H. Amos. **326** P. Sanchez. **327** W. H. Amos. **328** Keith Gillett. **330–331** Harold McNaught. **332–333** Charles Fracé, after Eibl-Eibesfeldt. **334** David Doubilet. **335** Allan Power / National Audubon Society. **336** (top) Douglas Faulkner; (bottom) Walter Deas. **337** (top) Douglas Faulkner; (bottom) Allan Power. **338** Anthony Bannister. **339** Keith Gillett. **340–341** Wayne & Karen Lukas / Group IV / National Audubon Society. **342–343** Harriet Pertchik. **344** (top) Morton Beebe / Photo Researchers; (bottom) Photographic Library of Australia. **345** S. Arthur Reed. **346** George Kelvin. **347** Cameron B. Kepler. **348** (top) Cameron B. Kepler; (bottom) Douglass Baglin. **349** (top; bottom right) Cameron B. Kepler; (bottom left) George Holton / Photo Researchers. **350** (top) G. R. Roberts; (bottom) Eva Cellini. **350–351** (top) M. Philip Kahl. **352** David Moore / Black Star. **354–355** George Kelvin. **356** (top) Mary Kellner; (bottom) John E. Randall. **357** David Moore / Black Star. **358** Paul Rockwood / National Park Service. **359** Eva Cellini. **360–361** (top) Jack Fields. **360** (bottom left) Jack Fields / Photo Researchers; (bottom right) Harold J. Pollock. **361** (bottom left) Jack Fields / Photo Researchers; (bottom right) David Moore / Black Star. **362** John Carnemolla. **363** Mary Kellner. **364–365** Robert Lebeck / Black Star. **366** (top) Bill Atkinson; (bottom) G. R. Roberts. **367** International Foto File. **368** (top) S. Arthur Reed; (bottom) Van Bucher / Photo Researchers. **369** Jack Fields. **370** (top) Eva Cellini; (bottom left) Frederick Ayer / Photo Researchers. **370–371** Jack Fields.

Photo Editor: Robert J. Woodward

Acknowledgments

The editors of Reader's Digest and the contributors are indebted to the following authorities for their generous assistance and advice: Andrew Berger, University of Hawaii, Honolulu; Alec Chisholm, Cremorne Point, New South Wales, Australia; Harold Cogger, Australian Museum, Sydney; Maxwell S. Doty, University of Hawaii, Honolulu; R. Hamond, Division of Marine Biology, Commonwealth Scientific and Industrial Research Organization, Cronulla, New South Wales, Australia; Allan Keith, New York City; Gordon A. Macdonald, University of Hawaii, Honolulu; Basil Marlow, Australian Museum, Sydney; Michael Morcombe, Armadale, Western Australia; Dieter Mueller-Dombois, University of Hawaii, Honolulu; Sidney Townsley, University of Hawaii, Honolulu; and most especially Joseph P. Branham, University of Hawaii, Honolulu; and Arthur Reed, University of Hawaii, Honolulu.